Arthur Bennett Allen

SHAKESPEARE
ON THE STAGE

*"Clay and clay differs in dignity,
Whose dust is both alike."*

CYMBELINE.

MACKLIN   GARRICK

                    KEMBLE

                KEAN   MACREADY

    BOOTH   IRVING

            FORREST   BARRETT

                    MANSFIELD

    MANTELL   SOTHERN

SHAKESPEARE
ON
THE STAGE

BY

WILLIAM WINTER

———

"I have told you what I have seen and heard."
—Shakespeare.

———

New York
MOFFAT, YARD AND COMPANY
1911

To the Memory of

AUGUSTIN DALY

Honoring the Wisdom Devotion Courage
And Industry Which Made Him the Greatest
Of American Theatrical Managers
And Honoring His Signal and Brilliant Services
To the Cause of Shakespearean Drama in America

I DEDICATE

These Studies of Shakespeare on the Stage

His lot was cast where giant forces met;
He battled bravely, and he gained his crown:
Detraction cannot stain nor time forget
The living splendor of his just renown.

BRIEF INDEX

9

ILLUSTRATIONS

PREFACE.

This volume attempts accomplishment of a work which I have had in contemplation for many years,—a work designed to tell the story of the manner in which, from the time of their origin till the present day, Shakespeare's Plays have been represented, and to name and briefly describe the principal actors who have been eminent in the representation of them. In my youth I became deeply interested in the Stage and during more than fifty years I have been continuously writing about it, celebrating its worthy votaries and advocating its advancement. In my study of that institution I early learned that sound judgment as to Acting in the Present imperatively requires to be informed and aided by precise knowledge of Acting in the Past, and for the acquirement of that knowledge I read many books, biographical and critical, about the actors of old. Those books were more or less interesting, but I found that, in general, they furnished little specific information as to the methods of those performers,—the expedients of their stage business, the countless details which, dexterously and suitably combined, constitute works of dramatic art. Some knowledge of such things could, indeed, be gleaned by industrious investigation of authorities scattered far and wide, but a compendium of instruction relative to those methods was not to be found. I therefore determined to accumulate knowledge of stage traditions and to observe with care the methods of contemporary actors, particularly in the plays of Shakespeare,—which afford the widest arena for the display of the actor's art,—and I entertained the project, should opportunity ever occur, of contributing to the chronicles of the Theatre such a record as might, in some degree, repair the deficiency which I had observed and furnish to other students and enthusiasts of the Stage the readily accessible summary of which I had felt the want.

Opportunity has been slow in coming, and many obstacles have intervened to compel postponement of the work. One step toward the fulfilment of my plan was made more than thirty years ago, in the publication of THE EDWIN BOOTH PROMPT BOOK. *In 1877, in conversation with Booth, I mentioned this subject, adverting to the difficulty that even the most diligent student of Acting encounters when trying to ascertain the exact method and spirit in which Hamlet and other Shakespearean parts were performed by great representatives of dramatic art, from age to age, and upon that conversation the project of publishing his* PROMPT BOOK *eventually ensued. Booth's customary repertory, in the maturity of his powers, comprised eleven Shakespearean parts and five miscellaneous ones: Hamlet, Macbeth, King Lear, Othello, Iago, Shylock, Wolsey, Brutus, Richard the Third, Benedick, Petruchio, Richelieu, Lucius Brutus, Bertuccio, Ruy Blas, and Don Cæsar de Bazan. Each of his* PROMPT BOOKS *contains the text as preferred and used by him, together with a Preface and Notes by me. Those books, of which the publication was first accomplished in 1878-79, are now issued by the Penn Publishing Company, of Philadelphia. They contain many of Booth's stage directions and, in particular,—fulfilling to* some extent the object sought in my editorial work on them, —they prescribe some of the stage business that he invented or employed. They might have contained more of it, and they would have done so but that Booth thought a more extensive and minute specification of such details would prove wearisome, and also, though he was willing that other actors should use his acting arrangements of the plays, because he was averse to providing them with written specification of all his business. The work that I wished to accomplish, however, was in that way begun.

An exhaustive exposition of the manner in which Shakespeare's Plays have been acted is impracticable. There is no one of them which, if its stage business were fully set down, would not require a volume of about 200,000 words, while in each of several cases three or four such volumes would be required to contain all the materials of narrative, commentary, and stage direction that might be assembled, and it is doubtful whether, if provided, such volumes would be widely read. Some consideration of the subject is feasible, and for that I believe there will be acceptance. There was a time, indeed, not yet distant, when the bestowal of intellectual consideration on Actors and Acting, especially in America, was often designated as unprofitable and absurd. That time is gone,— forever. To-day almost every publication, whether newspaper or magazine, devotes to those subjects a considerable section of every issue, and there is no home or social circle in the land that does not, either directly or indirectly, feel and respond to the influence of the Theatre. The study of Shakespeare is widely and closely pursued. I have had abundance of the experience of being asked for guidance and help in that study. I am therefore persuaded that this work will *prove practically useful to all votaries of Acting and lovers of the Drama.*

The task I have proposed to myself is one of oppressive difficulty: to furnish, with reference to each play that is examined, an epitome of illustrative information; to state concisely such facts of Shakespearean scholarship as are essential to spare a reader the trouble of consulting other books on the subject while reading this one; to classify and coordinate a multiplicity of widely scattered, often contradictory opinions and records as to actors; to provide original studies, in few words, of the Shakespearean characters selected for commentary; to comprehend, define, and describe the spirit of diverse embodiments of the same parts, and in each important case to indicate the method of performance that was pursued; to note essential variations of costume, in the dressing of the same parts and plays; to record wherever possible such of the stage business of every influential actor named in the story of Shakespearean acting as is most illuminative and suggestive, without lapsing into inventory and becoming wearisome; to mention the various ideals and some of the various "readings" of many actors, particularly such as have established traditions which are still valid,—and sometimes such as have attempted mere fantastic and confusing innovations; to show changes that have been wrought, in the lapse of time, in methods of stage presentment; and, avoiding repetition wherever possible,—though at times a certain similarity is inevitable in disquisition on the same part as played by different actors,—to unite facts, theories, traditions, opinions, and conjectures into a sequent and interesting narrative. Whether in this attempt I have even measurably succeeded I must learn from others. I believe that the traditions of Shakespearean acting ought to be familiar to every actor and to every theatrical auditor, and I know that, whatever may be the defects of my book, they have not resulted from any lack of care and industry on my part. It now seems certain that, within the next few years, a revival of Shakespearean acting will be effected on the American Stage: my labor will have been indeed well bestowed if it assists in hastening or to any extent promoting that revival.

The selection of Plays considered in this volume may seem capricious. Preference might have been given to the chronological order in which the Plays of Shakespeare are believed to have been written, in which case I must have begun with LOVE'S LABOR'S LOST *and proceeded with the* HISTORIES. *My election fell on six plays which, in themselves as well as in their stage history, provide abundant elements of variety and contrast. Consideration of the commercial interest of my Publishers,—whose confidence and liberality make so large an investment in the enterprise which I have undertaken,—appeared to warrant that choice. Except for those considerations, in planning the Series of works of which this is intended to be the first, I should have arranged the Plays for commentary in the chronological order of their first performance in America, which, as to many of them, is here noted:*

KING RICHARD III.	New York City,	March 5, 1750.
THE MERCHANT OF VENICE	Williamsburgh, Va.,	September 5, 1752.
OTHELLO		December 26, 1751.
KING LEAR		January 14, 1754.
ROMEO AND JULIET		January 28, 1754.
HAMLET		November 24, 1761.
KING HENRY IV., PART I.,		December 18, 1761.
" PART II.,		February 4, 1822.
CYMBELINE		December 28, 1767.

In many books about the Stage, especially in old ones, there is a vexatious negligence of form, clarity, and accuracy, causing much loss of time and patience. The searcher of such books, if in quest of exact and particular information, must often waste hours in seeking for a correct date or the full name of an actor or an author or a play, details sometimes most important, which a contemporary writer might have furnished if he had taken the trouble to be thorough in his work. I have had occasion to think with sympathy of the exasperated inquiry with which the historian Macaulay embellished the margin of many a page, in books that he had occasion to consult, containing the ambiguous "It was thought" or "It was supposed" or "It was probable"— "Why didn't the fool find out!" In this volume the sections of the several chapters have been disposed in such a way as

*to make them easy of reference, and no point has been left
dubious that could be verified. A* BRIEF INDEX *takes the
place of the customary* TABLE OF CONTENTS, *showing at a
glance the divisions and general scope of this work. The
chapter on* HAMLET *is the longest,—as must always be the
case in any work on Shakespeare's Plays. That wise, gentle
commentator and patient, laborious compiler and editor,
Horace Howard Furness, uttered only the simple truth when
he wrote of* HAMLET *that "upon no throne built by mortal
hands has ever 'beat so fierce a light' as upon that airy
fabric reared at Elsinore"; and the fact that in Furness's
monumental* VARIORUM EDITION OF SHAKESPEARE *two volumes (in all, 922 large pages of small type!), are devoted to
that tragedy alone, without exhausting the subject, significantly attests its preponderant importance. In writing about*
HAMLET, *the second play ever read by me and the dramatic
theme which more than any other has engaged my attention all my life, I should have preferred to devote the greater
part of the available space in this book to the two impersonations of its central character, those of Edwin Booth and
Henry Irving, which have impressed me as wellnigh perfect.
The plan of my work enjoined a more comprehensive treatment of the subject, and while omitting nothing essential to
the display of those performances, I have particularly described representations of* HAMLET *less generally known and
esteemed,—several of which were framed for the avowed purpose of destructive innovation. If more ample descant on the
acting of Booth and Irving in the character of Hamlet should
be desired it will be found in my* LIFE AND ART OF EDWIN
BOOTH *which, revised and much augmented, will shortly be
published, uniform with my* LIFE AND ART OF RICHARD MANS-

FIELD, *and in my* LIFE AND ART OF HENRY IRVING, *which has been for some time in process of composition and which I hope I shall live long enough to complete.*

It is my intention to continue the history of the manner in which Shakespeare's Plays have been represented, making each volume of the series that will be required complete in itself, as this one is. My SHADOWS OF THE STAGE,—*in Three Series, comprising biographies and studies of the acting of many players,—have long been out of print: in this book I have utilized, in a re-written form, material contained in those works, sufficient to make about twenty pages. Articles which are fairly described as brief abstracts of six of the chapters in this book were published in* THE CENTURY MAGAZINE, *February to November,* 1911, *and the commendation elicited by that publication of them makes me hopeful of a favorable reception for this one. Like all other writers who venture to treat of Shakespeare's Plays, I am indebted for instruction in the scholarship of the subject to the labors of many commentators, from Rowe to Furness, but especially to the thorough research, ample learning, and sensible commentary of one who, if not the father of Shakespeare Scholarship, is certainly its head and front,— James Orchard Halliwell-Phillipps* (1820-1889). *For biographical information relative to actors I have had recourse to innumerable sources, specified in the text wherever necessary, ranging from the discursive chronicles and memoranda of Downes, Genest, Collier, Dunlap, and Ireland, to fugitive copies of old newspapers and magazines, and I have trusted to my personal knowledge,—naturally extensive after so many years of observation and study,—of dramatists, actors, and devotees of the Theatre. I mention these facts because wishful to avoid any seeming disregard of the labors of earlier writers.*

Responsibility for the substance of my work, the judgments as to plays and characters of Shakespeare and as to the interpretations of them given by actors, must rest entirely upon myself; and, however much my judgments may differ from those of other persons, I earnestly hope that, as in every important instance the reasons for them are stated, they may prove at least usefully suggestive to my readers.

I would here gratefully acknowledge obligation to my son, Mr. Jefferson Winter, for encouragement and for assistance in the protracted drudgery of research imperatively essential to such a work as this, and also for discriminative and useful suggestion,—particularly relative to the play of THE MERCHANT OF VENICE. *The wearisome labor that must be done by any writer who undertakes to treat the subject of* SHAKESPEARE ON THE STAGE *is not likely to be understood by readers. The names of actors mentioned in these chapters, for example, are, comparatively, not very numerous, but, in order to determine what actors ought to be mentioned, and to mention them correctly, in association with the parts selected for comment, I have been obliged to obtain and sift biographical and technical information relative to about 2,000 performers.*

The illustrations in this volume, although numerous, are yet fewer than I could wish them to be: occasion, almost imperative, could be found for at least 250 pictures: my Publishers, naturally, have not deemed it expedient to indulge in such costly profusion of pictorial embellishment. In the selection of the pictures which are used, an earnest effort has been made to provide only such as give a faithful semblance of the actors depicted and which are most necessary to graphic illustration of the text. There are comparatively few portraits, in dra-

matic characters, of actors of the remote past which furnish authentic impression of the originals, and there are many photographs, made in recent years, which are not much better. Pictures of some of the old actors display veritable "guys," such as would be derided from the stage in the present day,— and probably would have met with the same treatment a century ago. The close observer of portraiture and of written testimony, moreover, will find it difficult, sometimes impossible, to reconcile the contrarieties which exist between the printed description and the pencilled or painted delineation of players of the past,—as, for instance, when considering the picture, by J. Boyne, of Charles Macklin as Shylock side by side with Lichtenberg's description of the actor's dress and appearance in that character. Allowance should be made for the inferiority of old-time methods of pictorial reproduction, as compared with methods now available and sometimes used, but the investigator is early forced to reject as valueless many of the portraits designated as "old prints." As to some of them, indeed, a comment would be appropriate which was made by the renowned lawyer and orator Rufus Choate when speaking of certain paintings which were involved in a law-suit: "It would not be a sin to worship them,—for they bear no likeness to anything that is in heaven above, or the earth beneath, or the waters under the earth!" Some collectors of "old prints," theatrical curiosities, and antique portraits, it would seem, habitually indulge in that form of devotion.

It has not seemed desirable that I should, in this work, traverse the much explored ground of manners and customs of theatrical representation in Shakespeare's time, specifying the names and situations of the several London theatres, the use of inn-yards as play-houses, the circumstance of the open *stage, the ill-effect of the presentment of female characters by men or boys, the general lack of suitable scenery, the admission of spectators to the stage itself, and the frequently riotous conduct of vulgar audiences. Although the epoch of the Miracle Plays and Moralities had passed, the Theatre was then in its infancy, and the exhibition of plays was necessarily crude. Diffuse treatment of that subject might interest confirmed antiquarians, like myself; it would not interest the general public, and at best it would only serve to reiterate a truth, already known, namely, that in the matter of appropriate scenic investiture, such as helps to create and sustain illusion, the modern Theatre,—meaning, here, that of the last sixty years,—under capable management, has far excelled, and continues to excel, any Theatre of the past, in any country or any other period of which there is authentic record. If I could feel assured that I have given, within the compass of about 140,000 words, a reasonably comprehensive and satisfactory account of influential treatment which has been accorded to six of Shakespeare's plays, I should be content.*

In arranging the contents of the various chapters of this work I have not adhered to a uniform plan, because the stage histories of the several plays considered present differences and individual peculiarities making it inexpedient, if not impossible, to treat each of them in the same manner. There have been female performers of King Richard the Third, Shylock, Othello, Iago, Hamlet, and Cardinal Wolsey,—but those performers, except as Hamlet, have not required special examination. Although there is, necessarily, some account, often minute, of actors who have come to America from the European Continental Stage and have here attempted to impersonate Shakespearean characters, it is only with regard to Othello and

Hamlet that their performances could be deemed important enough to require separate sections.

It has seemed to me not only desirable but imperative that, in view of the disproportionate favor and the provincial adulation which is customarily bestowed on those and on all foreign performers who appear in America, a word should here be said for English ideals of the characters in English classic Drama, for English methods of acting and for the traditions and usages of the English Stage,—of which the American Stage is the legitimate child, now and for many years past bounteously contributive to the maintenance of its parent. It has been, and it still is, frequently alleged that actors of the European Continental Stage excel English-speaking actors, alike in dramatic aptitude and dramatic faculty. The pretension is not justified. It is true that in the copying of superficial aspects of life, in the minute embellishment of common subjects with common traits, the European Continental actors are frequently more expert than actors of the English race; but excellence in doing great things is more important and more admirable than excellence in doing little ones. No other race possesses as great a Drama as that of Shakespeare,—the Drama in which the supreme excellence of acting has been accomplished. You can carve a cherry stone or you can carve a block of marble, but splendid achievement in the latter medium is greater than any possible achievement in the former. Individuals, particularly of the Latin races, are, as a rule, more volatile than those of Anglo-Saxon origin. They readily become excited, often about trifles. Their discourse, ordinarily, is voluble, their gesticulation excessive. Neither of those characteristics is contributory toward making them necessarily superior actors. The purpose of acting is to

*impersonate character and impressively and helpfully to reveal,
through the medium of action, the workings of the human
mind, the feelings of the human heart, and selected representative experiences of the human race.   Rattling volubility,
profuse gesture, febrile excitement, and facial contortion are
not implements of the highest dramatic art.   No actor from
the European Continental Stage has equalled, in the personation of great Shakespearean parts, the representative actors
of the Anglican race.   Charles Fechter, one of the best players
of the Continental school, bore no comparison with, for example,
Edwin Booth, in Hamlet and Othello, for the reason that he
could not even approximate to Booth's fine method of inter-
pretative art and deep sympathy with the great elemental emotions of human nature.   Rachel, the Swiss Jewess, the greatest
actress of modern times in France (she performed in America
in 1855), never played a Shakespearean part, but it is not
even remotely probable that she would have borne comparison
with Charlotte Cushman as Lady Macbeth or Ellen Terry
as Ophelia or Ada Rehan as Rosalind.   There is, in the
Anglo-Saxon nature, a deep sincerity, a substantiality of
power, which mingles in the operation of the Anglo-Saxon
mind, however exerted.   The German actors have been more
successful than either the French or the Italian in the endeavor
to act Shakespearean parts.   Salvini, incomparably the greatest of the Italian actors who have appeared in America,—
interesting as a person and superb as an executant,—was
remarkable for his capability, on occasion, of iron repose
and controlled emotion; but he did not, because he could not,
show that he had grasped the conceptions of character that
are in Shakespeare's great plays.   In the domain of artistic
method, furthermore,—as to essentials, not superficialities,—no*

foreign actor who has performed on the American Stage within the last half century has equalled such American actors as Edward Loomis Davenport, Henry Placide, John Gilbert, William Rufus Blake, Charles Burke, William Warren, William Florence, Joseph Jefferson, Charles Fisher, Edwin Booth, Lester Wallack, James Lewis, and Richard Mansfield. No foreign female performer—not even the greatest of them—has excelled the late Mrs. G. H. Gilbert,—a dramatic artist to whom full justice was never done. Mrs. Gilbert acted parts as diverse as Lady Macbeth and Betsy Trotwood; Hester Dethridge and Mrs. Candor; Desdemona and Goneril; Cordelia and Regan; and Meg Merrilies and The Marquise, and was excellent in all. Such actors, of the Past, as Charles James Mathews and Horace Wigan and such actors, of the Present, as John Hare, Edward Terry, Forbes-Robertson, Theodore Roberts, Russ Whytal, George Arliss, and John Mason, have not been and are not excelled, in any important respect, by players of the European Continental school. I have seen all the distinguished foreign theatrical performers who have appeared in America since 1855, and reviewing the subject in the most conscientious spirit, I can find no reason to distrust the judgment that esteems English-speaking actors as the best in English drama and especially in Shakespeare. The Continental ideal of Shakespeare's characters is not true to the poet. Shakespeare's Hamlet is not a lachrymose young lover, a gasconading insurgent, a skipping loon, or an expeditious, resolute man of affairs; Othello is not a sensual, dangerous brute; Shylock is not a petty, oily, sputtering Jewish peddler; Macbeth is not a hirsute, brawny, barbarous Norse chieftain. The Continental actors have often been admirable, and they continue to be so, when speaking their native language and performing in plays indigenous to their national literature and therefore fully comprehensible by them. Salvini was at his best when he acted Alfieri's King Saul,—a wonderful performance! Ristori as Queen Elizabeth and as Marie Antoinette, Bogumil Dawison as Narcisse Rameau, Marie Seebach as Margaret, in FAUST, *Sarah Bernhardt as Donna Sol, Mounet-Sully as Hernani, and Ermete Novelli as Corado were competent and splendid,—accomplished actors rightly placed: no one of them truthfully presented or could truthfully present the whole of a Shakespearean conception of character, and the ideals of such characters which they diffused were more or less misleading and therefore detrimental to the public judgment.*

An interesting opinion relative to this subject was given by the writer of the Table Talk in that good old English periodical, ONCE A WEEK:

"We have a trick of taking up every parrot cry, especially if it be against ourselves, and repeating it without discrimination, and so we go on perpetually talking of ourselves as gifted in an inferior degree with the mimetic power. It was first pointed out to me *by the celebrated Delsarte,*—professor of elocution in the Paris Conservatoire and the greatest master of his art,—that England, cold, stiff, and undemonstrative as is the general bearing of her sons, *has yet produced the greatest actors the world ever saw.* He accounted for this (to him, undoubted) fact by the eccentricity of our national character. The typical Englishman does not fritter away his feelings and passions by useless demonstration: he pens them up till they are to be put in action."

The notion that actors from the European Continental Stage are necessarily better actors than those of the English race is one with which many admirers of the Stage begin, and they begin with it because they frequently hear it stated or meet with it in print. I accepted it in youth and continued to entertain it until observation at length forced me to perceive that it is mistaken. Here is an extract from the writings of an expert observer, who had formed a sound judgment on this subject and who stated it as long ago as 1741. That observer was Lewis Riccoboni, actor and stage-manager, associated with the Italian Theatre in Paris, in the reign of King Louis the Fifteenth. Riccoboni reached his conclusion, as he is careful to state, after a study of "the manners, persons, and characters" of the actors of "the Italian, Spanish, French, English, Flemish, and German theatres," and this it is:

". . . As to the Actors, if after forty-five years' experience I may be entitled to give my Opinion, I dare advance that *the best actors of Italy and France come far short of those in England.* The Italian and French Players, far from endeavoring at that happy Imitation of Nature and Justness which forms the Beauty of Action, affect a forced, stiff Manner of Acting, which never fails to mislead the Audience. To form the better Judgment of both, let us compare them impartially. The English Authors copy Truth and are at great Pains not to Flag on the Stage. As for me, I have always thought, nor have I been singular in my Opinion, that pure simple Nature would be cold upon the Stage. Wherefore the Action should be heightened a little, and without straying too far from Nature some Art should be added in the speaking. As a Statue to be placed at a Distance should be bigger than the Life, that, notwithstanding the Distance, it may appear in due Proportion to the Spectators, so the English Actors have the Art, if I may use the Expression, to heighten Nature, so as it ought to be shown at a Distance, to let us *see* that it *is* pure Nature which they represent."

Shakespeare's Plays must necessarily be condensed and in some particulars altered for use in the contemporary Theatre. Even the shortest of his tragedies, MACBETH, contains superfluous passages. The stage editors of To-day, however, are more considerate toward "the original text" than the adapters of the seventeenth and eighteenth centuries were. Nahum Tate and also George Colman mangled KING LEAR. Garrick mutilated HAMLET and ROMEO AND JULIET, abridged THE TAMING OF THE SHREW, extracted material for a Pastoral from THE WINTER'S TALE,—naming it FLORIZEL AND PERDITA,—and converted THE TEMPEST into an opera. Kemble "revised" OTHELLO, MACBETH, THE MERCHANT OF VENICE, HAMLET, KING HENRY V., and KING HENRY VIII. The various adaptations of Shakespeare were accepted and some of them are still in use. Garrick acted King Lear according to Tate, and so did Edwin Forrest. Kemble, when acting Coriolanus, gave a mixture of Shakespeare and Thomson. The custom long prevailed—and has not been entirely abandoned—of shifting effective speeches from one character to another. Thomas Sheridan when acting Romeo appropriated to that lover the blithe words of Mercutio about Queen Mab and dreams. "Purists" of the passing hour, who would "lose no drop of the immortal man" and therefore protest against any change whatever in the poet's text, seem to suppose that an earlier time evinced a more reverent feeling and consequently a more considerate practice in this respect, but they are mistaken—as a more intimate acquaintance with the Past would admonish them. It is well to know what has been done. That fine actor Robert Mantell was recently censured in print for his treatment of KING LEAR, the treatment of that tragedy by Edwin Booth being, at the same time, commended: Mantell, in fact, had used Booth's ver-

sion, restoring a few lines that Booth omitted. Insistence on the literary element in Shakespeare's plays is doubtless right, if it be not carried beyond reason,—as it often is. The literary quality in a play is secondary to its dramatic quality—a truth that is illustrated and enforced by the many and various testimonies accumulated in this book. The excisions which are made from Shakespeare's Plays, in preparing them for the stage, if the work of preparation is done by a competent hand, are found to be, almost entirely, of two kinds: the indelicate and the literary. The student of English Drama, when exploring a subject which is extensive and perplexing, would find it advantageous to remark the presence and the absence of the great, fundamental element of Drama,—namely, Action. The old English dramatists chiefly expended their force on words. The best of their plays abound with ingredients of literature,—poetry, rhetoric, and eloquence,—but they seldom exhibit movement, and for that reason, the present age being exigent in its dramatic taste, they are seldom or never acted. The complaint that contemporary plays do not contain literature might, no doubt, be measurably justified, but it is not material. Literary qualities in a play possess positive, obvious value, but they are not the qualities which, first of all, invest a play with dramatic life and make it practicable. Ben Jonson's tragedy of CATILINE might prove interesting to a studious reader but no audience to-day would patiently endure a representation of it. Addison's CATO and Dr. Johnson's IRENE are opulent with literary qualities but they are not dramatic, and if they were performed now they would justly be deemed tedious. Men of Letters have seldom manifested the faculty of dramatic expression. Some of the best writers that ever lived have failed in the effort to write a drama.

Milton's use of blank verse is wonderful, his style superb, but Milton's COMUS, *viewed as drama, not as poetry, is lethargic and insipid.* *Cervantes could write* DON QUIXOTE, *which, though its author held it in only the slightest esteem, the world regards as a precious, incomparable romance, but his plays, of which he wrote many and upon which he set great value, were practically worthless in his time, and are absolutely worthless in ours.* *Thackeray failed when, in the original form of his* LOVEL, THE WIDOWER, *he endeavored to write a play.* *The number of versified works which, although couched in dialogue and divided into Acts and Scenes, remain for practical stage purposes as quiescent as statues, is legion.* *Henry Taylor's* PHILIP VAN ARTEVELDE *is a noble poem, but if presented on the stage it would prove monotonous and cumbersome.* *It was a failure, even with so fine an actor as Macready in its principal part.* *Byron's plays, of which the most practicable,* WERNER, *is substantially a paraphrase of Sophia Lee's story of* KRUITZNER, *are for the Library much more than for the Stage.* *Browning's plays, though representative of characters and conditions, are not dramatic: his persons make long speeches in labored verse, and, whether male or female, old or young, prince or peasant, they all talk alike—and they all talk like Browning.* *In the plays of Tennyson there are indications that to the inward eye of the poet the persons in them appeared to move, but the fancied movement was seldom liberated into their constructive fabric.* *That great and wise actor Henry Irving, before he could produce* BECKET,—*the subject of which, it is interesting to remember, he had cherished, for dramatic treatment, during a period of twenty-three years before he could produce the laureate's play, —was obliged to cut and adapt it.* *The sagacious, practical dramatist and manager Augustin Daly was obliged to make many changes in* THE FORESTERS, *in order to insure its effective representation. The faculty of the dramatist is an exceptional and peculiar one, and no person can write an actable play who does not possess it. The literary plays, though often good to read, are not good to act. Shakespeare was dramatist as well as poet, but only about half of Shakespeare's plays are customarily acted. The supreme, distinguishing characteristic of his best plays is Action, and that is why they hold the stage. His literature, magnificent as it is, would not have sufficed to perpetuate his existence in the Theatre. The modern dramatists have written plays some of which, while containing story and therefore character, are vital with propulsive movement and consequently are susceptible of effective exhibition by means of the Art of Acting, and though they are not "for all time" they are destined to a considerable longevity. There was a time when the theatrical audience would listen with approval and enjoyment to long, declamatory speeches; when verbal tumults, sentimental exhortations, harangues of hysterical emotion and personifications of the cardinal virtues and vices were admired expedients of theatrical performance. That time has gone. There are long speeches in all the plays of Shakespeare, but those which it is found always necessary to retain are speeches which arise spontaneously out of the action and reaction of character and circumstance, and which are confluent with the movement. No audience is ever fatigued by adequate delivery of such speeches as those beginning "Give me another horse!— bind up my wounds"; "To bait fish withal!"; "The quality of mercy is not strained"; "I had been happy"; "Oh, what a rogue and peasant slave am I"; "Now o'er the one half world," or "Cromwell, I charge thee, fling away ambition." All along the line of theatrical development, and proceeding with more and more of acquired momentum, a movement has been operative to abandon or greatly to modify the declamatory style of acting and to concentrate the resources of histrionic art upon impersonation. The best artistic temperament of the world to-day craves the seeming substance of things,—reality transfigured in ideal forms, the affluence, the sensuous glow, and the coruscant splendor of conscious, exultant life. On the stage, therefore, human beings are preferred rather than abstractions, and the best modern dramatists, obeying at once their inward monition and the deep impulse of the age, have aimed to create characters susceptible of impersonation and diffusive of various forms of enjoyment, and not animated machines for rounding a rhetorical period or reciting a passage of blank verse. The great plays of Shakespeare, meanwhile, are, for practical purposes, as modern as if they had been written to-day, and because of their vitality of action in the exposition of elemental, universal experience, those plays will continue to be modern, when in a distant future many if not all the plays of our age, because they exhibit only passing phases of contemporary life, will be forgotten.*

W. W.

New Brighton, New York,
November 11, 1911.

"*In the first seat, in robe of various dyes,*
A noble wildness flashing from his eyes,
Sat SHAKESPEARE. *In one hand a wand he bore,*
For mighty wonders famed, in days of yore,
The other held a globe, which to his will
Obedient turned and owned the master's skill:
Things of the noblest kind his genius drew,
And looked through Nature at a single view:
A loose he gave to his unbounded soul
And taught new lands to rise, new seas to roll,
Called into being scenes unknown before
And passing Nature's bounds was something more."

—CHURCHILL.

I.

"SHAKESPEARE SPELLS RUIN."

*"But we worldly men
Have miserable, mad, mistaking eyes."*
—SHAKESPEARE.

FACT *VERSUS* FANCY.

IF you wish that a statement should be believed and established as a permanent truth, make it, and keep on making it.   There is scarce any force as potent as the Parrot Cry, and nowhere has it been used more liberally or more effectually than in the management of theatrical business.   Much contemporary theatrical reputation rests upon it.   With a Parrot Cry the Press Agent can accomplish almost anything.   Select a girl with a pretty face, a piquant demeanor, a winning way, the charm of youth, sufficient self-assurance to maintain composure when in the presence of an audience, and, by means of liberal advertisement, newspaper interviews, and copious distribution of three-, twenty-, and thirty-sheet posters, proclaim that she is a marvellous being and a superlative dramatic artist, persist in your proclamation, and the result is inevitable. The Parrot Cry allures the Public, and in a little time a new leading actress has been created, to irradiate the Stage!

The Parrot Cry is as potential to mar as it is to make. In 1910, in London, the death occurred of an exceptionally able and accomplished actor, whose professional career had been, practically, blighted by it. His name was Herman Vezin. He passed away at the age of eighty-one. In his time he played many parts. He was the original representative of *Harebell,* in "The Man o' Airlie." He was the first performer of *Dr. Primrose,* the *Vicar of Wakefield,* in Wills's fine play "Olivia." His impersonation of *Jaques,* in "As You Like It," was superb. He was admirable in the character of *Othello.* Once, when Henry Irving was disabled by severe illness and could not continue to act, he took the place of that actor, as *Macbeth,* and gave a poetical performance of that great and exacting part. Every part that he played was played well. His elocution, in particular, was excellent. He was a charming man, and in private life exemplary and much respected. Early in his career, however, it chanced that he participated in two or three plays which were accounted failures, and thereupon a newspaper writer designated him "a Jonah." The epithet was repeated, was echoed, was reiterated. It stuck to him. It generated a prejudice against him. Announcement that he would act in a new play seemed to establish a presumption that the new play would fail. He was customarily slighted. He was driven to the expedient of teaching as a means of obtaining subsistence. All possibility of a great career was destroyed for him. He spoke of the injustice with, naturally, a bitter resentment. " They have called me ' a Jonah,' " he said, " and they have ruined my life."

Many years have passed since the London theatrical manager, Frederick Balsir Chatterton (1835-1886), proclaimed the opinion that "Shakespeare spells Ruin,"—doing so for the reason that he had (1873) made a costly production of Shakespeare's superb tragedy of "Antony and Cleopatra" and lost a large sum of money by it. That, as it has proved, was a particularly mischievous statement, for Chatterton, as manager of Drury Lane Theatre, occupied a commanding position, and his misleading deliverance was at once taken up and widely echoed, and the persistent iteration of it, which still continues, has been instrumental in disseminating error and impeding good enterprise. Nothing could be further from the truth than the statement that "Shakespeare spells Ruin." *Incessant* representation of Shakespeare's plays, indeed, never has been, is not, and never will be either financially advantageous or in any way desirable. Excess is tiresome, and an excess of Shakespeare would be inexpressibly tedious, especially to those persons who are constrained to pass the greater part of their lives in attending theatres and studying plays. The plays of Shakespeare, however, are the best that the English-speaking race possesses; they are a fountainhead of modern drama, they give abundant pleasure and benefit when properly presented, and knowledge and practical use of them are essential to the dignity, influence, and welfare of an intellectual stage. A judicious presentment of Shakespeare is not only salutary but imperatively essential to the general good. The American theatregoing public is the most liberal in the world. It deserves well of the theatre, and, being entitled to see the best that can be shown, it is entitled to see the plays of Shakespeare acted, and to see them acted well. Whenever they are acted well they succeed,—that is to say, they not only please the "judicious few" but they "make money," and they have been known to succeed, commercially, even when acted ill. The Parrot Cry, "Shakespeare spells Ruin," nevertheless, has had the deleterious effect of discouraging even a judicious use of that author, and of prompting much vacuous and harmful comment on his plays when any of them have been presented. At this time, in America, only three actors of major importance and influence customarily present any of the plays of Shakespeare, while several of those plays,—which it would be a delight to see,—are, practically, unknown to our stage. It is deplorably true, likewise, that, although fine individual impersonations become occasionally visible, no complete "all 'round" performance of a Shakespearean play can anywhere be seen in America. The custom of acting Shakespeare has been permitted to dwindle. The necessary and valuable traditions have been, in a great measure, allowed to die. There should be a revival, before it is too late. Experience warrants it, and taste requires it.

On February 3, 1869, that great actor and greater man, Edwin Booth, opened Booth's Theatre, in New York,—at the southeast corner of Sixth Avenue and Twenty-third Street. Booth,—a dreamer, gentle, trustful, and eager,—was unfit for commercial ventures. His theatre, instead of costing about $500,000, all told, as he had expected, cost more than $1,000,000. He managed it for three years, and, contrary to a generally accepted belief, his *management* of that theatre was, financially as well as artistically, successful,—the first year showing a net profit of $100,-000, the second a net profit of $85,000, and the third a net profit of $70,000. But the burden of debt that unhappily had been imposed on him in its *construction* was exceedingly heavy. His health was impaired. He

decided to retire from management, and he did so, in
June, 1873.   Seven months later,—January 26, 1874,
—he was, unwisely and needlessly, induced to go into
bankruptcy.   In March, 1877, he was released from
legal meshes by the action of James H. McVicker,
of Chicago, who bought all Booth's debts, and allowed
him the necessary reasonable time in which to pay
them.   This he did, at the rate of $75,000 a year.
His burdens, meanwhile, were continuous and exhausting.   He did not much like to act, but preferred to
sit in a corner, and smoke, and ruminate.   He had
sunk his second fortune in the building of his theatre.
In 1886 he formed a partnership with his friend
Lawrence Barrett, who became his business manager.
During their first season they acted separately, but
in 1887, beginning at Buffalo, September 12, they
acted together, and they continued so to act,—Madame
Helena Modjeska joining them, for a time, in 1889,—
until the sudden, lamentable death of Barrett, March
20, 1891.   On the afternoon of April 4, 1891, at the old
Academy of Music, in Brooklyn, Booth made his last
appearance on the stage, acting *Hamlet*.   On June 7,
1893, he died, at The Players, No. 16 Gramercy Park,
New York City.   He had founded that club, on
December 31, 1888, and given to it the building in
which it is housed, with furniture, library, and all need-
ful accessories.   When his estate had been settled it

was found that he had left a fortune of $605,000. He had paid to J. H. McVicker all the balance of his huge indebtedness, incurred in the erection of Booth's Theatre; he had borne the heavy expenses of his large theatrical company,—scenery and dresses for his plays, and transportation; he had supported himself; he had handsomely endowed his daughter, on her marriage; he had endowed The Players; and he had left more than half a million dollars: and he *earned* all the money with which to do those deeds by practice of his profession, between 1874 and April, 1891,—and he earned it by presenting a repertory of sixteen parts, all told, of which eleven were Shakespearean; those upon which he chiefly relied, except *Richelieu,* were *all* Shakespeare's,—namely, *Hamlet, Brutus, Macbeth, Shylock, Lear, Iago,* and *Othello!* That is a form of "Ruin" to which most persons would be resigned! And all this, it should be remembered, was accomplished by a man in fluctuating health, who, in the course of the period specified, had suffered a severe, almost fatal, accident—the breaking of one arm and two ribs (1875),—and a stroke of paralysis (1889).

In 1871 Henry Irving, after a long period of exacting and exhausting labor, had been recognized as an actor of auspicious ability,—but nothing more. He was then engaged by H. L. Bateman, and he began

his career at the London Lyceum Theatre. On
November 25, 1871, he, for the first time, appeared
as *Mathias,* in "The Bells," giving a performance
which clearly revealed him as an authentic dramatic
genius and which caused a public sensation such as
had not been known in the London Theatre since
the memorable night when Edmund Kean flashed
on the stage as *Shylock.* From that hour he steadily
advanced in artistic authority and public esteem,
contemning detraction, defeating enmity, and sur-
mounting every obstacle. For thirty years he held
the fortunes of the British Theatre in the hollow
of his hand. He did more than any other individual worker has ever done to advance the stage in
essential, intrinsic worth and in the esteem of intellectual, reputable society, and his name, therefore, is
the most illustrious in the history of the Theatre.
His experience in dealing with the plays of Shakespeare is especially instructive. During his twenty-
seven years of association with the Lyceum Theatre
thirteen of Shakespeare's plays were produced there,
of which only three were financial failures, while the
others were abundantly remunerative. "Hamlet" had
200 successive and paying performances,—the longest
run ever made with that play,—and when reproduced
later it was acted 108 consecutive times. "Romeo and
Juliet," when brought out at the Lyceum, in 1882, had

130 consecutive representations. "Much Ado About
Nothing" was acted 212 consecutive times, when Irving
first produced it,—and acted to a *profit* of £26,000,
or, approximately, $128,000. "King Henry VIII."
had a run of 172 consecutive performances. Most of
Irving's Shakespearean productions were frequently
revived and several of them were retained in his regular repertory till the last. "The Merchant of Venice,"
when he first produced it at the Lyceum, had 250
consecutive performances,—the longest run ever made
with any one of Shakespeare's plays, in any country,
at any time; and *Shylock* remained in Irving's
repertory to the end of his career. His last appearance at the London Lyceum was made in that
character, and he acted it, at Bradford, for the last
time, only four nights before his death,—which befell
in that town on October 13, 1905. Irving's management of the Lyceum extended from August 31, 1878,
to June 10, 1905, and his gross receipts, in that time,
were £2,261,637 10*s.* 1*d.*—approximately $10,500,000,
—and *at least* one-third of that sum was earned by his
productions of plays of Shakespeare.

Augustin Daly, the most brilliant, indomitable, and
resourceful manager America has produced, who
adopted theatrical management in 1869, and, except
for a brief interval,—part of the years from the
autumn of 1877 to that of 1879,—remained in that

vocation till his death, in 1899, produced many of
the plays of Shakespeare, and almost invariably he
prospered in his productions and subsequent revivals
of them. At Daly's Theatre, in the years from 1887
to 1899, he presented "The Taming of the Shrew,"
"As You Like It," "All's Well That Ends Well,"
"The Two Gentlemen of Verona," "A Midsummer
Night's Dream," "Twelfth Night," "Much Ado About
Nothing," "The Tempest," and "The Merchant of
Venice." With "The Taming of the Shrew," in which
Ada Rehan gave a puissant and brilliant performance
of *Katherine,*—developing, for the first time in the
long record of stage interpretations of that part, the
lovely, lovable, tractable woman out of the shrill
pugnacious, impetuous vixen,—his gross earnings, first
and last, amounted to about $2,000,000,—for that
comedy was presented by him during long periods and
in many cities, throughout America, in Paris, Berlin,
and Hamburg, and in London and the British provinces. With "Twelfth Night" and "As You Like It,"
also, he had extraordinary prosperity,—Miss Rehan
giving the most poetic performance of *Viola* that had
been seen since the golden day of Adelaide Neilson,
and giving the most evenly sustained and pervasively
sparkling performance of *Rosalind* that has been
shown in our time, or, as far as studious inquiry
ascertains, in any time.

The views of Augustin Daly, relative to Shake-spearean productions, were thus stated by him:

" I fully believe that, where the sole purpose in producing a Shakespearean play *is to make money by spectacular profusion,* disaster *is* likely to result. To overload the drama with cumbrous decoration and supplement it with irrelevant show is not to honor the poet, nor to encourage the study of his beauties, nor to please his judicious admirers: It is to bid for a support more readily accorded to the Hippodrome than to the Stage. I believe I have the right to claim a more respectable motive for my own work in reviving these classics of the English Drama. Ever since I began management, now (1887) some eighteen years, I have devoted a period in every season to the production of a Shakespearean play or an old comedy. None of these productions was ever offered by me to the public with the expectation that it was destined to popular favor by reason of the outlay made upon it. Yet my audiences will bear me out that in not one instance has a limit been fixed to that expense which would make the performance worthy of the poet, acceptable to my patrons, and creditable to the theatre. I have been contented, *if for two or three weeks* I have seen full and appreciative houses, and have been content to take off the play when the admirers of Old Comedy had been satisfied. . . ."

Among the most remunerative plays ever produced are "Pizarro," "Rip Van Winkle," "Monte Cristo," "Our Boys," "Drink," "The Old Homestead," "Ben-Hur," and "The Music Master." The profits from presentation of "The Music Master" have, it is said, reached $2,500,000; yet, large as that sum is, it is much less than has been paid to see some of the plays named in association with it. Lord Byron, who had been a director of Drury Lane Theatre, said to Medwin (1822), "Bad as 'Pizarro' is, it has brought in more money than any other play has ever done." The best money-gainer ever produced in modern times is, probably, "Rip Van Winkle." Jefferson, to whose genius it owes its prosperity, used it for many years and presented it many times. The claim, indeed, has been made that he gave more than 15,000 performances of *Rip,* but that is an exaggeration. He did not himself know precisely how many times he had acted the part. I have made a careful computation, and I think it certain that he did not act *Rip* more than about 5,800 times. That, in itself, probably is an unparalleled achievement. In the early part of Jefferson's professional career his impersonation of *Rip* did not attract extraordinary notice and the receipts were comparatively small, but during the middle and latter part of his career he was much followed and the receipts were very large. He received from Edwin Booth, *as his share,* a guarantee of $750 a performance, during the long run of "Rip Van Winkle" at Booth's Theatre, August 15, 1870, to February 7, 1871. On some occasions in late years the gross income of "Rip" exceeded $23,000 a week,—approximately $3,000 for each performance. The sum of $1,200 would seem to be a safely conservative estimate of the average receipts for each performance of *Rip* that Jefferson gave, in the whole course of his professional life, and the total gross receipts, computed on that basis, would be $6,960,000. The seven predecessors and various subsequent imitators of Jefferson's *Rip* have, probably, obtained as much more.

But neither "Rip Van Winkle" nor any other modern play has earned as much money as has been earned, individually, by some of the plays of Shakespeare, nor is there reason to believe that those modern plays possess anything like the intrinsic vitality and "staying-power" of the Shakespearean drama. I have seen nearly or quite a hundred different *productions* of "The Merchant of Venice"; and, probably, each of the actors representative of *Shylock,* in those productions, in the course of his career, acted that part at least 100 times: more than one of those actors must have acted it more than 500 times: Henry Irving acted it at least 2,000 times. Since its first performance, August 25, 1594 (?), "The Merchant of Venice" has been acted throughout Europe, America, and Australia, and it is probable that, in the course of three centuries and more, it has been acted no fewer than 100,000 times, all told, and, if the average of receipts be estimated at only $350 a performance, the total income would amount to $35,000,000. "Hamlet" and "Romeo and Juliet" have been performed even more frequently than "The Merchant of Venice" has. It is safe to predict that Shakespeare will endure.

The reiteration, by persons making themselves public as theatrical "managers," of the statement that "Shakespeare spells Ruin" is so insistent, not to say blatant, that, in the face of the facts, it causes equal contempt and astonishment. A caustic remark made by Cromwell, to the dissenting Commoners, is not inappropriate: "I beg you to believe that it is possible for you to be mistaken." The experience of individual actors in the presentment of Shakespeare's plays has, from the first, been especially instructive, and it has been, in almost innumerable instances, an experience of opulent success. The reader of old theatrical records, whether they relate to the stage of Great Britain or to that of her American colonies or to that of the United States in the early days of the Republic, continually finds that the leading players evince their highest ambition, exert their utmost powers, and are judged by their achievements, in the great characters of the Shakespearean drama. Ingenuity has produced novelties. Taste has fluctuated. Each succeeding generation has evolved a style of drama peculiar to itself. But, notwithstand-

ing the opposition of ignorance and cupidity, there
has been no period, since the revival of the Theatre
toward the end of the seventeenth century, without
Shakespeare, and almost every name of dramatic distinction which has survived in remembrance to the
present day is associated with one or more of Shakespeare's characters. Cooper and Fennell, conspicuous
favorites on the American stage about the beginning
of the nineteenth century, each possessed a varied
repertory, but it was in Shakespeare that both of
them gained their best success. Nearer to our day,
and well-remembered, Edwin Forrest, in his prime,
prospered abundantly with "Othello," "King Lear,"
"Hamlet," and "Macbeth." Charlotte Cushman
gained fortune as well as her greatest fame with the
characters of *Lady Macbeth* and *Queen Katharine*.
Mme. Modjeska was long on the crest of the wave,
fortunate no less than famous, with a repertory that
comprised *Juliet, Rosalind, Imogen, Ophelia, Portia,
Beatrice, Isabella, Queen Katharine, Lady Macbeth,*
and *Constance*. Mary Anderson established herself
as the favorite of two worlds and gained a substantial
fortune with "Romeo and Juliet," "As You Like It,"
and "The Winter's Tale": *Juliet, Rosalind, Hermione,
Perdita, Desdemona,* and *Lady Macbeth* (in one
scene) are the only Shakespearean parts that she ever
played. Richard Mansfield, although he lost $167,000

by his ventures of 1888-89, largely with "King Richard
III.," owed much of his pecuniary prosperity, as well
as much of his fame, to his acting, and to the artistic
fame of it, as *Richard the Third.* During one whole
season, furthermore, he confined his exertions exclusively to "King Henry V.," and during another he
presented only "Julius Cæsar,"—and his profits during
the latter *exceeded those of any other season in the
whole of his professional career,* not excepting even
that of his presentation of "Cyrano de Bergerac."
The late Louis James depended mainly on Shakespeare
during the last and more important half of his life.
Viola Allen was amply successful with her impersonations of *Viola, Hermione,* and *Perdita.* Julia Marlowe
has acquired riches and brilliant reputation by acting
Juliet,—her impersonation of that difficult part being
the best now visible anywhere on the stage,—and
by giving her lovely embodiment of *Viola.* Edward
Hugh Sothern and Miss Marlowe, acting at the
Academy of Music, in New York, in one of the most
disastrous of theatrical seasons (1909-10), attracted and
delighted audiences that packed that huge theatre
to the roof by presentments of "Hamlet," "Romeo
and Juliet," "Twelfth Night," and "As You Like It";
and later, December, 1910, acting in New York, at
the Broadway Theatre, in that repertory,—augmented
by "Macbeth,"—and doing so at prices reduced one-

fourth from the customary charge for an orchestra seat (that is, to $1.50),—they attracted audiences which filled that house at every performance: and aside from being treated, alike by the press and the public, with every mark of distinguished consideration as artists, they gained a financial reward as abundant as even the most profusely advertised of popular "wanted" plays or spectacles has obtained,—their receipts amounting to an average of $16,000 a week. Their prosperity, furthermore, continues.

It is not essential to dilate on the ventures of all the prominent actors who have produced plays of Shakespeare and earned fortune as well as reputation by their enterprise in that field of artistic achievement. Several names, however, suggest themselves for mention. William Charles Macready, in the course of his management of Covent Garden and Drury Lane, —two seasons only at each of those theatres, 1837-39 at the former, 1841-43 at the latter,—produced twenty of Shakespeare's plays, and on them, in after years, he chiefly relied. The most *remunerative* play in his large repertory, when he acted in America (his visits to the United States were made in 1826, 1843, and 1848), was "Hamlet." Samuel Phelps, who managed Sadler's Wells Theatre for eighteen years, 1844-62, produced all the plays of Shakespeare, except "King Henry VI.," "Troilus and Cressida," "Titus

Andronicus," and "King Richard II.," and he was richly rewarded. Charles Kean gained his most opulent success by the presentment of Shakespeare's plays, of which, when managing the Princess's Theatre, 1850-59, he produced thirteen, in a style of unprecedented magnificence. Ellen Tree, Helena Faucit, Mary Amelia Huddart (Mrs. Warner), Adelaide Neilson, Ellen Terry, Isabella Glyn, Fanny Janauschek, Marie Seebach, Bogumil Dawison, Adolf von Sonnenthal, Ernst von Possart, Tommaso Salvini, Friedrich Haase, Ernesto Rossi, Jean Mounet-Sully, Ermete Novelli, are names intimately associated with amply remunerative representations of the plays of Shakespeare.

The most striking of contemporary examples of the value of Shakespeare on the stage is that which has been furnished by the experience of Robert B. Mantell, the actor who, by right of ability, efficiency, and professional achievement, is now (1911) the legitimate leader of the American stage. When Mr. Mantell made his first important appearance in New York, October 1, 1883, at the old Fourteenth Street Theatre, acting *Loris Ipanoff,* in Sardou's "Fédora," he gained signal success, and it was expected that he would long remain one of the most important dramatic figures of the capital. But after a period of growing popularity, disaster befell him. He was ill advised and ill guided,

and soon New York was closed to him. In 1904
he was, as he had been for many years, toiling in the
irksome labyrinth known to actors as " the road."
Much of the time he was acting in "one-night
stands." In November of that year, in Texas, he
received a circular letter, which had been sent out
by the Messrs. Sam S. and Lee Shubert, theatrical
managers, offering "three weeks of choice time in
New York City," those three weeks of "choice time"
being, in fact, the worst of the season, the three
weeks immediately preceding Christmas. The theatre
thus offered was the Princess,—a little box, now happily demolished, at the southwest corner of Broadway and Twenty-ninth Street,—an "up-stairs theatre"
with a reputation of many failures. Mr. Mantell,
being almost desperate, impulsively determined to
try his fortunes once more in the capital, and therefore he hastily made such arrangements as would
permit his reappearance in New York, and engaged
the three weeks of "choice time" at the Princess. On
December 5, that year, he appeared there, in Cibber's version of Shakespeare's "King Richard III."
The stage hands had importuned him for a scene
rehearsal, but their importunity had been disregarded.
"They only wanted to get money out of me," the actor
said, in recounting this experience; "the scenery had
often been used in one-night stands, coming into the

theatre at five in the afternoon, and there was no need of a full scene rehearsal. Besides, the truth is, I couldn't afford the money to pay for that luxury." The consequence was that everything was done that brutal men could do to injure the performance. The diminutive stage (that of the same theatre which had helped to spoil Richard Mansfield's first production of "The Merchant of Venice") was too small for the scenery. During the first front scene Mr. Mantell, who had a space only about three feet wide in which to move between the drop and the footlights, was almost precipitated into the orchestra by persons behind the drop who "accidentally" stumbled and lunged against him. A single mishap might ruin his venture, and it meant everything to him to recover a foothold in the capital. While momentarily absent from the scene he had warned the stage hands of serious danger if the persecution was continued: " 'Some one will get badly hurt,' I said" (so he related the incident), "and I meant what I said: my house, though not crowded, was attentive; many writers for the press were in front: I was trying 'to come back.' When I had returned to the scene I heard some jeering and laughter in the wings, and presently I was aware of some one feeling along the drop to find where I was standing; a jolt with his shoulder would have toppled me into the orchestra pit. I drew my dagger, and as I felt the man come directly behind me I drove it backward through the canvas. There was a cry and a fall, then some confusion, then silence,—and I finished my scene in peace. When I came off one of the 'hands' came blustering up to me. 'Say,' he said, 'do you know you've killed a man here?' I turned on him in fury. I was utterly regardless of consequences. 'I sincerely hope I *have*,' I said (the fellow was lying on a sofa, groaning and piling on the agony; he had a nasty cut in his leg, as I afterward learned, but nothing serious), and I turned to my dresser. 'Go and get me my last-act gauntlet,' I told him. My little Jap bolted for it and was back in a moment. I wear an iron-shod glove in that act, heavy enough to fell an ox. I drew it on and turned to the 'grip.' 'Now see here,' I said to him, 'I'm a strong man; I can hit hard, at any time. I'm going to wear this glove through the rest of this performance, and if there's any disturbance while the curtain is up I'll leave the stage and brain the man that makes it, with this.' I meant it: and I never acted on so quiet a stage as that one was for the rest of that night."

Such treatment was enough to disconcert and ruin any performance, but Mr. Mantell persevered, and his ability and determination conquered. "King Richard III." was followed by "Othello." A shrewd

manager, Mr. William A. Brady, observed the effect
created by *acting,* even though hampered by wretched
scenery and costumes and a miserable company, saw
the opportunity, and speedily formed an alliance
with the intrepid actor. The next year Mr. Mantell played at the Garden Theatre, New York, and
his receipts were, approximately, $4,000 a week. In
Harlem they rose to $4,500. Later he was able to
secure a little time at the spacious, fashionable New
Amsterdam Theatre,—where, although in the spring
and almost at the end of the season, his receipts
were $8,317.25 for the first week and $9,519.75 for
the second. During four weeks at the Academy
of Music, although he played at what are called
"popular prices,"—the highest priced ticket costing only $1.50,—the gross receipts were $39,939, or
practically $10,000 each week. Then for a year or
more the capital was again closed to him, because
satisfactory terms could not be obtained from the
arbitrary Theatrical Syndicate, a tyrannical monopoly
in those days, well representative of the gross and
base spirit which proclaims that "Shakespeare spells
Ruin." That unjust power, however, had begun to
totter. First one and then another of the vulgar
spectacles that are supposed to "spell Success" failed.
There was a public outcry against indecency on the
stage,—an outcry in which many of the best elements

in the community participated. Soon the Broadway Theatre, and then the New Amsterdam, were opened to Mr. Mantell, for it had become evident even to dull, shop-keeping perception that a return to legitimate drama was "wanted" and demanded by the public. On March 9, 1909, Mr. Mantell began an engagement in the capital, at the New Amsterdam Theatre, acting *King John,* and giving the best impersonation of that part of which there is record in the history of the American Stage. That engagement, first at the New Amsterdam and then at the Academy of Music, lasted until May 29, and in the brilliant course of it more than one hundred performances were given of plays of Shakespeare. With a repertory that "spells Ruin" (a repertory comprising *Othello, Iago, Hamlet, Richard the Third, King Lear, Macbeth, King John, Brutus, Shylock,* and *Romeo,*—Shakespearean characters all), Mr. Mantell, in the period of less than five years raised himself from the comparative obscurity of, *commercially speaking,* a third-rate star, and from the poverty which could not afford a full scene rehearsal, to independence, fortune, and the honorable position rightfully his due in the boun- teous acceptance of the American people.

It is not meant that Shakespeare necessarily spells Fortune. The many dismal failures which have been made in presentations of his plays are not forgotten or ignored. But whether in such instances as those of Booth's presentment of "The Winter's Tale," or Irving's of "Twelfth Night" (in which, however, he gave a great performance of *Malvolio*), or Miss Maude Adams's melancholy venture in "Romeo and Juliet," or Mr. N. C. Goodwin's abortive endeavors in "The Merchant of Venice" and "A Midsummer Night's Dream," or the decisive failure of Mr. Sothern and Miss Marlowe in "Antony and Cleopatra," or the disaster that attended the recent (1910) presentation of "The Merry Wives of Windsor" at the New Theatre,—bad judgment as to the play, the time, and the place, and, most of all, the incompetent acting of vitally important parts, precipitated disaster. The ship did not split on the rock of Shakespeare. Such mishaps only tend to prove the contention that Shakespeare's plays, well acted and at the right time and place, never "spell Ruin,"—for all those plays, adequately and wisely produced, have had ample success, notwithstanding the failure of the ventures just mentioned. Painting is not the only art in which the colors must be "mixed with brains."

Good acting may carry a bad play to financial success, but bad acting will, generally, kill almost any poetic drama, however fine. The reason why managers decry and oppose,—as many of them do,—the presentation of Shakespeare is not obscure. As a rule, *less* profit can be gained in a given time by presenting Shakespeare's plays than by presenting some modern plays, especially such modern plays as require only one or two simple sets of scenery and only six or eight or ten actors to represent them. None of Shakespeare's plays can be presented in fewer than four acts, each containing several scenes. A fairly large company is essential, and considerable scenery and many dresses are required. Under those circumstances,— the control of the American Theatre being largely in the hands of persons who care only for monetary gain, —a reasonable profit is deemed insufficient. The plays of Shakespeare, furthermore, cannot be produced by janitors; they must be acted, and the actors of to-day, as a class, are inadequate to the demands of Shakespearean parts, because they have little or no suitable training to enable them to act those parts.

A success in Shakespeare is far more enduring than a success in most other plays. The plays of Shakespeare can, *in every instance,* be presented at less cost than is often lavished on "musical" abominations now current,—in order to pay for which prodigality it has been seriously urged that managers must tax the public through the dishonest medium of "theatre-ticket speculation"! H. L. Bateman's Lyceum revival of "Hamlet" in which Henry Irving acted the *Prince* cost only £100; Irving's production of "The Merchant of Venice" cost only £1,200, and he expended only £861 during its run, for further embellishments and to "keep up" the scenery and other accessories: but he *acted Hamlet* and *Shylock;* while all the other parts in those plays, when he produced them, were acted in a competent manner.

The custom that ought to be restored and faithfully followed is one that would provide for an adequate, comprehensive training in the technicalities of the art of acting.   No reasonable person wishes to see the production of good new plays restricted or that the community should fail to recognize and applaud those plays and the fine acting that is sometimes seen in them.   But the new plays are not all.   The highest form of acting is impersonation in poetic drama,— tragedy or comedy,—a form of acting almost unknown on the contemporary stage, in any splendid instances. Yet the public is entitled to see such acting and the public "wants" it,—as much as it wants, for example, John Mason's noble impersonation of *Doctor Seelig,* or George Nash's sympathetic embodiment of *Wilbur Emerson,* or Russ Whytall's delicate, winning, lovable *Judge Prentiss,* or David Warfield's *Herr von Barwig,* or Maude Adams's *Peter Pan,* or Mrs. Fiske's *Leah Kleschna.*   Such performances as Forrest's *Lear,* Booth's *Richelieu,* McCullough's *Virginius,* Irving's *Shylock,* Davenport's *Macbeth,* Salvini's *Gladiator,*

Charlotte Cushman's *Queen Katharine*, Ellen Terry's *Beatrice*, Ada Rehan's *Rosalind*, Adelaide Neilson's *Viola*, and Mary Anderson's *Hermione* and *Perdita*, would pack any theatre of the present day for a long time, and also would make a reputation that would endure for generations. No performances of that calibre are visible now, nor are there actors visible who seem capable of giving them if they had the opportunity. It is not the lack of natural ability that causes an impoverished condition of our stage; it is the lack of opportunity for the development of actors,—and the lack of that opportunity has been brought about, at least in part, by the parrot-like repetition and the selfish or supine acceptance of the radically false and injurious assertion that "Shakespeare spells Ruin."

II.

KING RICHARD III.

"And all complexions act at once confusedly in him:
He studieth, striketh, threats, entreats, and looketh mildly grim,
Mistrustfully he trusteth, and he dreadingly doth dare,
And forty passions in a trice in him consort and square."
—WARNER.

HISTORICAL COMMENT.

THROUGHOUT four centuries the memory of King Richard the Third has been persistently blackened by the ascription to him of a sinister character, a malignant will, and the ruthless commission of infernal crimes. An occasional word, indeed, has been spoken in his vindication,—Sir George Buck, Horace Walpole, Sharon Turner, Caroline A. Halstead, and the learned and eminently judicious commentator, Alfred O. Legge, in particular, having ably espoused his cause,—but historians in general, in their narratives of his life, have followed, as Shakespeare did, in his play on that subject, the authority of the chroniclers Hall and Holinshed, who followed that of Sir Thomas More; and it is incontrovertible that More's account of King Richard the Third was inspired, if not actually in great part written, by John Morton, whom King Henry the Seventh, Richard's successor, made Archbishop of Canterbury, and who was one of the most inveterate of Richard's foes. More was a boy five years old when Richard fell, at Bosworth. In youth he became a member of Morton's household at Canterbury, and he was educated virtually under the supervision of that primate. It is possible that Morton may have told him, and that he believed, a story of Richard's career. There is authority for the statement that Morton wrote, in Latin, a narrative of Richard's life, which at his death, in 1500, fell into the hands of More. The "Tragical History" which served to make Richard's name infamous was begun by More in 1513, and he left it unfinished at his death, in 1535. It was completed by Holinshed and Hall.

It has generally been maintained, and the opinion seems to be contemporaneously accepted, that neither the cursory reader nor the scrupulous student of Shakespeare's "Historical Tragedy" is for any reason necessitated to consider anything except the Text. That would, perhaps, be a satisfactory method of reading or study for persons already familiarly acquainted with a complex period of English history; it is not a satisfactory method for persons, naturally and necessarily a numerous class, who are not thus informed, and my acquaintance with actors and other theatrical students has led me to believe that a brief rehearsal of historical facts relative to the subject of Shakespeare's "King Richard III." will be of practical service.

The story, as told by him, is supposed to begin almost immediately after the battle of Tewkesbury, fought May 4, 1471, in which the house of York crushingly defeated the house of Lancaster, and to terminate with the battle of Bosworth Field, fought on August 22, 1485. The actual period covered is, accordingly, fourteen years. Shakespeare seems to have designed that the historical, or pseudo-historical, incidents which he has illustrated should be viewed in a compressed group, and that the action should be confined within a brief limit of time,— possibly within that of a single summer. P. A. Daniels, in his "time analysis" of this play, allots eleven days, with intervals, as the period represented on the stage, and the total dramatic time as "within one month (?)." That, I believe, is too short an allowance. Tewkesbury was fought in May. King Henry the Sixth died a few days thereafter. It would be in August, 1471, according to the dramatist, that Glo'ster wooed and won Lady Anne. The killing of the Duke of Clarence did not occur till 1478, and King Edward the Fourth did not die till April

9, 1483. Edward the Fifth—with his uncle, Glo'ster, as Protector,—was nominally King from April 9 to June 22, 1483. Richard was proclaimed King on June 26, and he and Anne, his Queen, were crowned, in London, at Westminster Abbey on July 16, 1483. Hastings, at the Tower, was slain on June 13, that year, and Rivers, Vaughan, and Grey had already suffered death. The Princes were then lodged in the Tower, and their alleged murder occurred in August. Buckingham perished on the block, at Salisbury, in November, 1483. Richard's Queen died, at Middleham Castle, Yorkshire, March 16, 1485. The Earl of Richmond landed at Milford Haven, August 7, 1485, and Richard was slain fifteen days later. Those events were arranged to the poet's hand, but he has presented them as closely sequent upon one another. Most of the difficulties in the way of a perfect unity, however, are overcome—certainly for stage purposes—if all these occurrences are assigned to the last year of *Richard's* life,—for the dramatist has, in fact, condensed the scattered occurrences of fourteen years, 1471 to 1485, and unfolded the motives and conduct of several lives in a work of action which, practically, can be illustrated within three hours. It is noticeable that throughout this tragedy the weather is summer and that most of the action proceeds by day. For the purpose of stage presentation it is possible and right to assume that it begins in May and ends in August, and that is the assumption upon which is founded the arrangement of, perhaps, the best stage version of the tragedy ever prepared,—that, namely, which was made by Edwin Booth.

Brief consideration of the relationship, personality, and age of the principal characters will also be of service. *Queen Elizabeth* is the wife, afterward the widow, of *King Edward the Fourth*. Her maiden name was Elizabeth Woodville, or Wydevil. She was the daughter of Sir Richard Wydevil, and was first married to Sir John Grey, of Groby, a Lancastrian, who fell at the battle of St. Albans, 1455. She was considerably older than King Edward and she had been nine years a widow when, in 1464, she became his wife. She was a woman of great beauty. After she became Queen her kindred were invested with rank and titles. The *Earl Rivers* of this tragedy, Anthony Woodville, one of the most learned and accomplished men of his time, was her brother, and Lord Grey and the Marquis of Dorset were her sons, by her first husband. She had, by King Edward the Fourth, three children, Elizabeth, Edward, and Richard. The sons are the Princes, Edward and Richard, whom Glo'ster is said to have caused to be murdered in the Tower, but of whose fate History does not afford authentic information. The daughter, Elizabeth, became, in 1486, the wife of Henry, Earl of Richmond, then King Henry the Seventh. Evidence has been adduced that King Edward the Fourth, prior to his union with Elizabeth Woodville Grey, had been privately married to Lady Eleanor Talbot Butler, daughter of Talbot, Earl of Shrewsbury, and widow of Lord Butler, Baron of Sudeley. If that evidence can be trusted, he was a bigamist, his children by his Queen, Elizabeth, were illegitimate, and, upon his death, his brother Richard possessed a clear title to the crown.

The *Duchess of York* is the mother of *Edward, Glo'ster,* and *Clarence; Queen Margaret* is the widow of *King Henry the Sixth.* She was a woman of great ability and of a formidable, warlike character. She defeated in battle Glo'ster's father, the Duke of York, and caused his head, surmounted by a paper crown, to be affixed to the battlements of the City of York. She was captured by King Edward the Fourth soon after the battle of Tewkesbury, was held in captivity during five years, and was then ransomed by King Louis the Eleventh of France. She died, in Anjou, in 1482. She is the *Cassandra* of Shakespeare's tragedy, and there is not in poetic literature a fiercer strain of invective than that which Shakespeare has put into her mouth.

Lady Anne is, first, the widow of *Edward, Prince of Wales,*—son of *King Henry the Sixth,* and *Queen Margaret,*—who was killed in the battle of Tewkesbury: some historians declare he was slain by Hastings and Dorset after that battle. She was the second daughter of Richard Neville, the great Earl of Warwick, surnamed "the King-Maker." It is noted that she was only betrothed to King Henry's son, not actually married to him, and was only fourteen years old when that betrothal occurred. She became the wife of Glo'ster, and died in 1485. Her grave is in Westminster Abbey, near the entrance to the chapel of Henry the Seventh. The inscription on the stone that covers it has been obliterated by time.

Henry the Sixth appears as a character in Cibber's version of "King Richard III." and in that made and used by Richard Mansfield, the scene of his death being taken from the Third Part of Shakespeare's (reputed) tragedy of "King Henry VI."—but he does not occur in the original. He was the predecessor of King Edward the Fourth upon the English throne. He founded King's College, at Cambridge, and Eton College, near Windsor.

Edward the Fourth came to the throne of England in 1461, at the age of 20. He was one of the handsomest, most luxurious, and most licentious kings of whom history preserves a record. He died in the forty-second year of his age and the twenty-third of his reign. He was buried at Windsor, and near to his royal dust was laid the decapitated body of the gallant, brilliant, dissolute Lord Hastings.

Henry Tudor, Earl of Richmond, who succeeded Richard as King Henry the Seventh, was, on the father's side, a descendant from Theodore Tudor, a Welsh brewer, whose son, Owen Tudor, married Katherine, widow of King Henry the Fifth; and, on the mother's side, a descendant, by an illegitimate branch,—afterward, however, legally declared legitimate,—from John of Gaunt, the fourth child of King Edward the Third. He was haughty, peremptory, austere, and avaricious. He accumulated great wealth. He permitted the decapitation, for alleged treason, of Sir William Stanley, who had, probably, been the savior of his life, when personally attacked by Richard, at Bosworth Field. He disliked his wife, Elizabeth of York, and they led an unhappy life. He died of consumption, in his palace at Richmond. His tomb is in the beautiful chapel, in Westminster Abbey, built by his command and under his supervision.

The title to the English Crown during the Wars of the Roses inhered in the house of York. King Henry the Fourth, who deposed his cousin, King Richard the Second, was a usurper, and it was he

who thus caused the subsequent mischief. When King
Richard the Second, "hacked to death," or starved, at
Pomfret Castle, had ceased to live, the crown should
have passed to the line of Clarence, the third child of
King Edward the Third, and not, as in fact it did,
to the line of his fourth child, John of Gaunt.

The house of Plantagenet—of which King Edward
the Fourth, Clarence, Glo'ster, and the Princes,
Edward and Richard, were members—sprang from
the royal house of Anjou. The name of Plantagenet was bestowed on one of the ancestors of the
line, either from the fact that he wore in his bonnet
a sprig of the broom, *planta genista,* or from the
fact that he had done penance by scourging his body
with a whip made of that plant. The last of the
Plantagenets were Edward, son of the Duke of
Clarence, beheaded in the reign of King Henry the
Seventh, and his sister, the Countess of Salisbury,
beheaded in the reign of King Henry the Eighth.

The following passage from Sir Thomas More's
"Tragical History" conveys instructive suggestions
as to the character and feelings of Richard, *as viewed
by his detractors:*

"I have heard, by credible report of such as were secret
with his chamberers, that after this abominable deed" [the
murder of the Princes, his nephews] "he never had quiet
in his mind; he never thought himself sure. When he went

abroad his eyes whirled about, his body privily fenced, his hand ever on his dagger, his countenance and manner like one always ready to strike again. He took ill rest at night; lay long waking and musing; sore wearied with care and watch, he rather slumbered than slept. Troubled with fearful dreams, suddenly sometimes started he up, leaped out of his bed, and ran about the chamber. So was his restless heart continually tossed and tumbled, with the tedious impression and strong remembrance of his most abominable deed."

In the chapel of King Henry the Seventh, in Westminster Abbey, stands a little altar, which was placed by King Charles the Second, to commemorate the Princes. The inscription upon it, in Latin, is as follows:

"Here lie the remains of Edward V., King of England, and Richard, Duke of York, who, being confined in the Tower, and there stifled with pillows, were privately and meanly buried, by order of their perfidious uncle, Richard, the usurper. Their bones, long inquired after and wished for, after lying 191 years in the rubbish of the stairs, were, on the 17th of July, 1674, by undoubted proofs, discovered, being buried deep in that place. Charles II., pitying their unhappy fate, ordered these unfortunate princes to be laid among the relics of their ancestors, in the year 1678, and the thirtieth of his reign."

The place where those bones were, by alleged "undoubted proofs, discovered" is a recess under the winding stairs that lead up to St. John's Chapel, in the White Tower. Miles Forrest and John Dighton

are said to have confessed that they murdered the
Princes, but they were not punished for their crime.
They said that they had "obeyed their King's command," conveyed to them by Sir James Tyrrel, and
it was a doctrine of King Henry the Seventh that
the King's command ought always to be implicitly
obeyed, never questioned.   Tyrrel was beheaded, by
the order of King Henry the Seventh, for treasonable
association with the rebellion of the Duke of Suffolk,
in 1502.

The last moments of King Richard are thus described by Hume:

"The intrepid tyrant, sensible of his desperate situation,
cast his eye around the field, and descrying his rival at no
great distance, he drove against him with fury, in hopes that
either Henry's death or his own would decide the victory
between them.   He killed with his own hand Sir William
Brandon, standard-bearer to the Earl; he dismounted Sir
John Cheyney; he was now within reach of Richmond himself, who declined not to combat, when Sir William Stanley,
breaking in with his troops, surrounded Richard, who, fighting bravely to the last moment, was overwhelmed by numbers,
and perished by a fate too mild and honorable for his mul-
tiplied and detestable enormities. . . . The body of Richard
was found on the field, covered with dead enemies, and all
besmeared with blood.   It was thrown carelessly across a horse,
was carried to Leicester, amidst the shouts of the insulting
spectators, and was interred in the Grey Friars' church of
that place."

The ages of most of the characters in the tragedy can be nearly ascertained. *Richard* is 33; *Richmond,* 28; *King Edward the Fourth,* 41; *Clarence,* 29; *Rivers,* 41; the *Bishop of Ely,* 75; *Prince Edward,* 12; *Prince Richard,* 10; *Queen Elizabeth,* 48; *Queen Margaret,* 59; the *Duchess of York,* about 60. *Lady Anne* died at the age of 28.

For the actor the text of Shakespeare is the arbitrary guide in undertaking to impersonate *Richard the Third* as drawn in Shakespeare's play, and in Shakespeare's play *Richard* is represented as an incarnation of craft, treachery, cruelty, and heaven-defying wickedness, not, however, without conscience and some of the usual attributes of humanity. It is desirable, though perhaps it is not essential, that the actor of *Richard* should be acquainted with every fact ascertainable relative to the actual character, aspect, and conduct of the man; for the reason that such comprehension of him might tend to augment weight, authority, and sincerity in an embodiment of even a wrong conception of him. It certainly is essential that every student of Shakespeare's play should bear in mind its gross inconformity to ascertained facts of Richard's life.

Francis Bacon, although he wrote in the time of Queen Elizabeth, granddaughter of King Henry the Seventh, and wrote like the servile courtier that he was, nevertheless declared of King Richard the Third that he was "jealous of the honor of the English nation, and likewise a good law-maker for the ease and solace of the common people," adding, however, in the mean spirit of political detraction, that Richard's motive was not the purpose of doing justice to his subjects, but that of winning popularity. In fact, Richard relieved the English people of an unjust, extortionate taxation; caused the laws of England to be printed in the English language, and thus made them accessible for the first time; ordained and encouraged the free importation of books into his kingdom; fostered the arts, particularly those of printing, acting, and music (before he had ascended the throne he had organized a company of actors, to perform in his service, and after he became King he made a special point of assembling singers for his entertainment), and throughout his career strove to advance civilization.

Minute inquiry into the history of King Richard the Third educes material facts showing that Shakespeare's portrayal of that prince is a fabric of the imagination, reared on a basis of calumny. Edward, Prince of Wales, was not murdered, but was killed, as other soldiers were killed, in battle, "in the field by Tewkesbury." King Henry the Sixth, who had become half imbecile, died of disease, aggravated by grief, and not by the hand of an assassin. No evidence exists *proving* that the young princes, Edward

From an Antient Original Painting on Board at Kensington Palace.   G. Vertue del. & Sculp.

RICHARD THE THIRD, KING OF ENGLAND

and Richard, sons of King Edward the Fourth, were
murdered, a reasonable probability being that one of
them died, in the Tower, of disease, and that the other
was privily sent out of the kingdom, and reappeared
later, in the person of Perkin Warbeck. Queen Anne,
wife of King Richard the Third, died of consumption, her demise having been precipitated by sorrow
for the sudden death of their only child, Edward,
and not, as Richard's enemies, at the time, whispered,
or declared, and as Shakespeare darkly insinuates,
by the criminal contrivance of her husband. The Duke
of Clarence was put to death by his fierce and cruel
brother, King Edward the Fourth, who distrusted and
hated him, as also did Edward's wife, Queen Elizabeth
(Woodville), and her numerous relatives and partisans,
—Richard being innocent of complicity with that
merciless deed. Lord Hastings was slain because
Richard knew him to be a political opponent and
suspected him of being privily implicated in a plot
to frustrate the protectorate and assassinate the
Protector. Richard loved his mother, "the Rose of
Raby," and he was at all times much under her influence; and also he loved his wife Anne Neville, and
when he became a widower he never entertained the
purpose, but publicly and officially disavowed it, of
wedding his niece Elizabeth, the princess whom subsequently the astute, crafty, avaricious King Henry

the Seventh took to wife, in order to fortify his usurped title to the English crown. In almost every particular, although he was a stern ruler and a fierce, sanguinary, ruthless antagonist, King Richard the Third was literally the reverse of the man whom Shakespeare's tragedy has blazoned as a monster, for the lasting execration of the world.

Richard was not deformed, except that one of his shoulders was a little higher than the other. He was of short stature, slender in figure, and possessed of uncommon strength. His neck was short, and habitually his head was slightly inclined forward. His face was of aquiline cast, his features were regular, and he had the large nose of the Plantagenet family. His eyes were dark and brilliant. His complexion was olive, his hair dark brown, and his cheeks were a little hollow. His voice was notable for placidity and sweetness. He was fond of rich apparel and customarily wore magnificent garments. He was nervous and restless, as shown by his habit of sheathing and unsheathing his dagger, and of sliding a ring off and on one of his fingers—the third finger of his left hand. He was an expert, graceful dancer, a proficient horseman, and in battle his expedition, agility, valor, and prowess were extraordinary. As a qualifying fact touching his alleged "deformity," it might be remembered that, according to apparently authentic

chronicle, he could, and did, when accoutred in full
armor, leap to the back of his horse without touching
foot to stirrup.

THE TEXT.

The text of Shakespeare's play of "King Richard
III." is an eclectic one, taken partly from the First
and Third Quartos, 1597, 1602, and partly from the
First Folio, 1623. The text of the Folio reveals
alterations of the putative original, not, it is supposed, made by the author, but by the actors either
at the preliminary tavern reading of the play,
which was of usual occurrence, or in the processes of
rehearsal and performance during many years. It has
been ascertained and recorded that "there are about
one hundred and twenty new lines introduced in the
Folio" (Knight), and that "the Quartos contain
important passages which are not found in the Folio,
while the Folio, on the other hand, supplies passages,
no less important, which are wanting in the Quartos"
(Dyce). A justifiable inference would seem to be that
the world does not, and never can, possess the text of
"King Richard III." exactly as Shakespeare wrote it.

Henry Irving caused a book to be printed of
Cibber's alteration of Shakespeare's tragedy, in which,
by the use of inks of different colors, the lines known
or believed to be exactly those of Shakespeare were

shown, in contradistinction to the lines selected by
Cibber from other plays by Shakespeare, namely,
"King Henry IV., Part One and Part Two";
"King Henry VI., Part One, Part Two, and
Part Three"; "King Richard II."; and "King
Henry V."; and from lines original with Cibber.
Among Cibber's verses the most ambitious is the
speech declaring, "Conscience! 'tis our coin; we live
by parting with it." The statement put into the mouth
of *Richard,* "I've lately had two spiders crawling upon
my startled hopes," etc., and the commandment, "Get
me a coffin full of holes," etc., are Cibber's,—and not
likely to be mistaken for Shakespeare's. Three of
Cibber's lines, however, are generally supposed to
occur in the original: "Off with his head! So much
for Buckingham!" "Conscience, avaunt! Richard's
himself again!" and "A little flattery sometimes does
well." Coarse as it is, Cibber's version of Shakespeare's play was finally approved, for practical use,
by both Henry Irving and Edwin Booth, consummate
masters of their art, after each of them had made the
experiment of producing the original in a condensed
form. Neither of them, however, reverted to the use
of the Cibber play. Both of them believed, and
several times declared, in conversation with me, that
Cibber's version is more directly *effective* than the
original is, upon the *average public taste.* I disagree

with that opinion, but I think it important to remember that Cibber's version held the stage, *to the exclusion of the original,* for 121 consecutive years, and that it is still preferred and used by several actors.

The first attempt to restore Shakespeare's tragedy to the stage, even in a partial form, was made by Macready, at Covent Garden, March 12, 1821, that great actor impersonating *Richard,* with Mrs. Faucit, mother of Helena Faucit, afterward Lady Martin, as *Queen Elizabeth.* The attempt did not succeed; that is, the play did not please the public, and it was withdrawn after a few performances had been given.

Old votaries of the theatre—such, at least, as have obtained any considerable experience of that institution—are aware of the manner in which within the last fifty years *Richard* has usually been represented. The notion of the conventional "tragedian" has been that *Richard* is "a part to tear a cat in, to make all split," and accordingly the stage has often been the scene for tiresome display of a scowling, mugging, ranting creature of extravagant deformity, as distinct from nature as a nightmare is from sense. The number of actors who have assumed the part of *Richard* is prodigious, but the number of actors who have presented him as a possible and interesting human being, and not as a monstrosity, is few.

THE FIRST *RICHARD.*

The first performer of *Richard* was Burbage, but nothing is known of his method of acting the part or of the dress he wore. The anonymous elegy on that actor's death,—a composition consisting of eighty-six lines of heroic verse which, having long existed in manuscript, was first published in 1825,—mentions *Crookback* as one of the characters in which he excelled, and intimates that when he died that character, among others, died with him; a form of demise frequently named in theatrical memoirs.

Authentic record declares that neither Shakespeare's tragedy nor any alteration of it was acted between 1660 and 1710,—a period covering the last fifty years of Thomas Betterton's life. In 1667, however, Betterton acted *Richard,* not in Shakespeare's tragedy, but in a play called "The English Princess, or the Death of Richard the Third," by John Caryll, a person who in later years was secretary to Queen Mary, wife of King James the Second, and who is agreeably remembered as having suggested to Pope the subject of that poet's exquisite work of fancy, "The Rape of the Lock." Pepys saw the first performance of "The English Princess," and in his "Diary" designates it "a most sad, melancholy play, and pretty good, but nothing eminent in it." Better-ton's acting, as *Richard,* seems to have been excellent. Downes, a principal authority as to the Betterton period, commends it by implication, but does not describe it.

CIBBER AND HIS VERSION.

Colley Cibber's alteration of Shakespeare's "King Richard III." was first produced July 9, 1700, at Drury Lane, and Cibber appeared as *Richard,* giving a performance which was accounted weak, and even ridiculous. The merit of Cibber as an actor consisted in his talent for comedy: as a tragedian he appears to have been a conspicuous failure. In his story of his performance of *Richard* he declares that he acted the part as he supposed that it would have been acted by Samuel Sandford, one of his contemporaries, and he describes Sandford as a man who "had sometimes an uncouth stateliness in his motion, a harsh and sullen pride of speech, a meditating brow, a stern aspect, occasionally changing into an almost ludicrous tri-umph over all goodness and virtue; and from thence falling into the most assuasive gentleness and soothing candor of a designing heart." When first presented, Cibber's alteration of the play had been shorn of its whole First Act, which the Master of the Revels refused to license, on the ground that its portrayal of the distresses of *King Henry the Sixth* was impolitic, because it might prove a reminder to "weak people" of the misfortunes of the fugitive King James the Second, then living in exile at Paris. Several years passed before the whole of Cibber's version was permitted on the stage. From the time of Burbage to that of Cibber's venture the history of the play is a blank.

DAVID GARRICK.

The first unequivocally fine embodiment of *Richard the Third* of which authentic description exists was that presented by David Garrick, at Goodman's Fields Theatre, London, October 19, 1741, when he acted that part for the first time. The important later performances of *Richard,* without exception, have been more or less affected by knowledge of that example. Garrick unquestionably blazed the path for John Philip Kemble, who was twenty-two years old when Garrick retired from the stage, and for George Frederick Cooke, Edmund Kean, Junius Brutus Booth, William C. Macready, Edwin Forrest, and their successors,—the inspiring, enduring magic of his method being vitality of impersonation combined with brilliancy of executive art.

Garrick astonished his public by following a course which in our time would not astonish anybody;

DAVID GARRICK AS *KING RICHARD THE THIRD*

AFTER THE PAINTING BY WILLIAM HOGARTH

transmitted to succeeding actors, has survived and is still used. Investigation of the chronicles of Garrick's acting ascertains that he was remarkable for "natural impetuosity, warmth of speech, and energy of action," and that he excelled in parts which involve "anger, resentment, disdain, horror, despair, madness, convulsive throes, and dying agonies": it is, therefore, not difficult to understand his greatness as *King Richard the Third.* Without doubt he set the example, and it was not alone his art that conquered, but his genius. The spirit that was in the man is indicated by words that Tobias Smollett wrote about him, mentioning "the sweetness and variety of his tones, the irresistible magic of his eye, the fire and variety of his action, the elegance of his attitudes, and the whole pathos of his expression." Garrick's *Richard* has been characterized as "a vulgar assassin." William Hogarth said to him, referring to his widely contrasted impersonations of *Abel Drugger* (in Ben Jonson's "The Alchemist") and *Richard the Third,* "You are in your element when begrimed with dirt or up to your elbows in blood." Garrick's costume, as *Richard,* was fanciful and without even the pretence of correctness, while the actors who coöperated with him in the representation of the tragedy wore court dresses, of the time of King George the Second.

DAVID GARRICK AS KING RICHARD THE THIRD

AFTER THE PAINTING BY WILLIAM HOGARTH

that is to say, he spoke, as far as effect is concerned, naturally, not rhetorically, and he acted naturally, not artificially. It is not meant that he was
a photographer,—no one of his biographers conveys
that impression,—but he concealed his mechanism, he
abjured the formal declamation which had been customary, he projected himself into the character, and
he caused the effect of nature by a judicious and
expert use of art. The stage version of the play
that he presented was Cibber's, and in his employment of it he seems to have made almost all the
"points" that have been made by his successors. On
his first entrance he presented, in face, person, and
demeanor, an image of seething vitality, dangerous
force, sardonic humor, and smiling menace. His
performance was marked by incessant variety. His
question, "What do they in the *North?*" was
shot forth with frightful celerity and rage. His
action and delivery in the Tent or Dream Scene
expressed a frenzy of horror, fear, agony, and conflict,
interpenetrated with the furious courage of desperation. Abundant contemporary testimony designates
the impersonation as wonderfully brilliant. Garrick
was the first of the actors of *Richard* to employ a
joyous chuckle of sardonic delight, when vociferating
"Off with his head! So much for Buckingham,"
which, copied by Cooke and then by Kean, and thus

transmitted to succeeding actors, has survived and is still used. Investigation of the chronicles of Garrick's acting ascertains that he was remarkable for "natural impetuosity, warmth of speech, and energy of action," and that he excelled in parts which involve "anger, resentment, disdain, horror, despair, madness, convulsive throes, and dying agonies": it is, therefore, not difficult to understand his greatness as *King Richard the Third*. Without doubt he set the example, and it was not alone his art that conquered, but his genius. The spirit that was in the man is indicated by words that Tobias Smollett wrote about him, mentioning "the sweetness and variety of his tones, the irresistible magic of his eye, the fire and variety of his action, the elegance of his attitudes, and the whole pathos of his expression." Garrick's *Richard* has been characterized as "a vulgar assassin." William Hogarth said to him, referring to his widely contrasted impersonations of *Abel Drugger* (in Ben Jonson's "The Alchemist") and *Richard the Third*, "You are in your element when begrimed with dirt or up to your elbows in blood." Garrick's costume, as *Richard,* was fanciful and without even the pretence of correctness, while the actors who coöperated with him in the representation of the tragedy wore court dresses, of the time of King George the Second.

JOHN PHILIP KEMBLE.

It does not appear that John Philip Kemble interpreted the character with any notable comprehensiveness or power. He played *Richard* at a time (1783) when Garrick's performance was still remembered, and the impression that he made was comparatively faint. He was innately princelike in manner, and he pleased fastidious taste by his consistently aristocratic bearing and his felicitous subtlety not only of inflection in delivery of the text but of bland suggestiveness of the craft of the character. Sir Walter Scott records that Kemble argued (and this intimates the essential quality of his performance) that *Richard,* "being of high descent and breeding, ought not to be vulgar in his appearance or coarse in his cruelty," —certainly a correct inference as to Shakespeare's *Richard,* but not as to Cibber's. Macready, one of the most discriminative of critics of acting, says of Kemble that his limbs were not supple and that his style was statuesque,—in which case, naturally, he must have been hampered in the part of *Richard,* which imperatively requires, at many points, celerity, and at all times flexibility. Imagination sees Kemble in the grandeur of *Coriolanus* and the pathetic solemnity of *Penruddock,* not in the volcanic passion of *Richard the Third.*

GEORGE FREDERICK COOKE.

George Frederick Cooke, far less scholarlike and accomplished than Kemble ("Black Jack," as he called him), but far more formidable and self-assertive, completely eclipsed that noble actor, in the character of *Richard*. Cooke unhappily did himself lamentable injustice and irreparable harm by hard drinking; but he was a man of sturdy constitution, great force of character, and of wild, discordant mental brilliancy. According to his journal, he seems to have considered himself to be at times a dweller on the verge of insanity, and probably his view of his condition was correct. He acted many parts. He shone as *Falstaff*, but he records that he never played that part to his complete satisfaction. He excelled in *Sir Giles Overreach, Shylock, Iago,* and *Richard*. As *Hamlet* he failed, because of decisive incompatibility. He was a stalwart person, of commanding figure. His nose was large, long, and slightly hooked; his forehead, high and broad; his eyebrows were strongly marked and very flexible. His demeanor was bold, his gesticulation awkward: he made much use of waving arms and of the extended forefinger of his right hand. His vocalism was exceptionally varied. Sometimes his voice was harsh and grating, sometimes dulcet and insinuating, and often his coarse tones

suddenly alternated with his smooth ones. He could
discharge the barbed arrows of sarcasm with scorch-
ing malignity and cruel effect, and he could utter
hypocritical kindness with the soft accent of ingratiating sympathy. He lacked innate refinement of
mind, yet there is authentic testimony that his manner could, on occasion, be mild and agreeable and his
conversation interesting. He could dissimulate well.
Charles Lamb declared of him that his dissimulation
was predominant and masterly, but his hypocrisy too
glaring and visible. A capital portrait of him as
Richard was for many years one of the adornments
of the vestibule of Daly's Theatre, New York. That
picture exhibits *Richard* at the moment when, in Cibber's version of the tragedy, he hears the bell that
sounds the death-knell of the *Princes* in the Tower, and
when his visage, naturally, would reveal exultation
in his accomplished wickedness, and thus it coincides
with authentic testimony as to the actor's appearance. He expressed the joyous malignity of *Richard*
with a fidelity that was terrible, but also, he expressed,
from time to time, the man's sporadic consciousness of the heinous character of his crimes,—as
when, in suggesting to *Buckingham* the murder of
the *Princes,* he evinced what Macready called "a
gloomy hesitation." Cooke's utterance of *Richard's*
"Well, as you *guess?*" was venomous with sarcasm,

and he enunciated "Off with his head!"—the doom
of the captured *Buckingham,*—with a riotous chuckle
of exultant hatred. His face seems not to have been
one well trained to convey a perfect impression of
plausibility, yet it is difficult to determine, from inspec-
tion of the several portraits of him which exist, precisely what his countenance might have revealed. The
face of even such a man as Cibber's *Richard* would not
be always an index to his evil mind. Cibber's best bit
of invention is that which makes *Richard,* on entering
the throneroom after the death of *King Edward,* and
on observing the grief of the company, apply a handkerchief to his eyes and murmur aside: "With all my
heart! I'll not be out of fashion!" At such a point
as that Cooke was an actor certain to excel, and it is
probable that he did greatly excel when speaking
Richard's explicit, comprehensive summary of his own
character, in the lines transferred by Cibber from
"King Henry VI., Part Three," Act III., Sc. 2:

> " Why, I can smile, and murder while I smile,
> And cry content to that which grieves my heart,
> And wet my cheeks with artificial tears,
> And frame my face to all occasions."

Cooke, as *Richard,* wore, for court dress, a doublet
fastened by a broad, jewelled belt, a short cloak
edged with ermine, trunk-hose, pointed shoes, and a

small, close-fitting velvet hat turned up in front and embellished with a tall plume. Around his neck he placed a narrow, pleated, white ruff and a broad ribbon sustaining an Order. At his side was a rapier, depending from a shoulder-belt incrusted with jewels. The face was clean-shaven, except for short, narrow side-whiskers and a small moustache and chin-tuft. The hair was short. In the latter part of the play, armor necessarily was substituted for the court dress.

EDMUND KEAN.

Edmund Kean, whose personation of *Richard* was accounted wonderful, was acquainted with the Garrick tradition as to the acting of the part, and he had seen Cooke on the provincial stage before either Cooke or himself had appeared in London. In 1787 Cooke acted once in London, for some person's benefit, but he did not formally and successfully appear in that capital till 1800, when he was in his forty-fifth year. Kean was on the scene there as a child and as an obscure youth, but he first appeared there prominently in 1814, when he was twenty-seven. The comedian George Fawcett Rowe (1835-1889) many years ago told me that his father, resident in Exeter, had been acquainted with Kean, and that Kean had said to him, "I have the style of Cooke; but nobody will

notice it, because I am so much smaller." The almost
fanatical admiration that Kean felt for Cooke is
recorded in the memoirs of both of them, and
remembrance of it seems to justify credence
that to some extent Kean truly was a disciple
of that singular genius. In youth every actor has
a model.

Cooke died in New York in 1812, and Kean, on
the occasion of his first visit to that city, in 1820,
caused his remains to be removed from a vault beneath
St. Paul's Church and buried in the churchyard, and
likewise placed a monument there, which still stands
at Cooke's grave. The story that Kean took the
forefinger bones of Cooke's right hand, carried them
to England, had them wired together and hung upon
his parlor wall, and made such an ado about the
relic that Mrs. Kean finally became disgusted and
threw it away, has long been in circulation and is
known to be true. To what extent Kean modelled
his acting on that of Cooke it would be impossible
to judge. Each of those actors was, obviously,
of a turbulent nature, much given to tremendous
outbursts of passion, but no men could be more
dissimilar than they were in physical constitution
and appearance. Cooke's face could exceptionally
well express the evil passions. Kean's features
were regular and handsome, and while his face and

EDMUND KEAN AS *KING RICHARD THE THIRD*

FROM A MEZZOTINT

person comported perfectly, as he guided and used them, with the terrible characters of *Richard the Third* and *Sir Giles Overreach,* they were made to suit equally well with those of the loving *Octavian* and the melancholy, pathetic *Stranger.* Cooke was robust, while Kean was slender, and his height was only five feet and four inches.

Kean's acting, in general, and in particular his acting of *Richard,* has been extolled, by competent authorities, to such an extent of enthusiasm that inquiring judgment becomes perplexed in the presence of a multiplicity of adulation. "Just returned from seeing Kean in *Richard,*"—so wrote Byron to Moore, February 19, 1814,—"By Jove! he is a soul! Life—Nature —Truth—without exaggeration or diminution. Kemble's *Hamlet* is perfect, but *Hamlet* is not Nature. *Richard* is a man, and Kean is *Richard!*" The opinion thus expressed, if viewed as criticism, is worthless, *Hamlet* being at least quite as much Nature as *Richard* is, and as much a man; but viewed as indicative of the effect produced upon a poet of marvellous genius by an actor of kindred poetic sensibility it is instructive. Kean appears to have been the originator of the practice, which was customary with Edwin Forrest, John McCullough, and Thomas Keene, when acting *Richard,* of causing him to protrude the lower lip,— probably supposing that the facial expression was thereby made more resolute and savage. In the Wooing Scene with *Lady Anne* he lifted her veil to observe the changes in her face while he was speaking, —a piece of stage business which savors of absurdity, but which, nevertheless, has found commendation. Hazlitt's encomium of Kean's acting in that scene, happily designated the spirit and defined the charm of it, in saying that by his action, voice, and eye, he finely marked the progress of "wily adulation" and "encroaching humility."

Kean's principal dress, as *Richard,* consisted of garments similar to those worn by Cooke—trunk-hose, doublet, ornamental cloak, and ribbon with an Order on it; but he wore top-boots, his hat was shaped like a toadstool, and his wig was made of curly, black hair, somewhat thick. In his right hand he carried, during a part of the play, a military truncheon. The deformity of the figure was indicated by disproportion of the left shoulder. Kean's costume, as noted, is that which he wore after the *Duke of Glo'ster* had become *King.* Kean's stage business as *Richard* was extraordinary for diversification and expressive intelligence. His thoughtful, absorbed demeanor when, preliminary to the terrific Dream Scene, on the night before the furious encounter on Bosworth Field, he traced upon the ground, with the point of his sword, the plan of battle, is remembered and recorded as having had a wonderfully impressive effect. The personation was animated by a dominant, buoyant, electrical, thrilling spirit. The dying *King's* frantic thrusts with his naked arm, as though he still held his sword, after he had been struck down, mortally wounded, in the combat with *Richmond,* were sinister and terrible: that business has reappeared in the performances of many later actors.

JUNIUS BRUTUS BOOTH.

The renown of the elder Booth as *Richard* was great in his lifetime, and the tradition of his astounding performance of the part still survives. Booth was a mild, reticent, modest, unpretentious man, whose aspect and customary demeanor in private were calm, dignified, and reserved. I have never forgotten the thrill of dread that was imparted by his baleful aspect, his incisive, sonorous voice, and his evil demeanor as *Pescara,* in "The Apostate." Persons who acted with him when he played *Richard* have favored me with descriptive recollection of his performance of that part, and in several instances they have declared that at first sight of him they thought him insignificant, but, on seeing for the first time his impersonation of *Richard,* they were not merely astonished, but completely overwhelmed with amazement, by his revelation of a prodigious force and an impetuous, fiery, terrible passion, of the capability of which nothing in his appearance and deportment had given them the slightest hint. In the opening scenes he was comparatively tame, no doubt intending that the character, under the stress of continually changing circumstances, should evince itself gradually, and preparing the way for a brilliant effect of contrast when he became completely aroused. In the succeeding passages of storm and fury he was stupendous. That accomplished actor John Sleeper Clarke,—who married the tragedian's daughter Asia,—told me that nothing could exceed in the effect of terror Booth's aspect, action, and delivery when he said:

> " What do they in the *North,*
> When they should serve their sovereign in the *West?* "

Among the recorded peculiarities of Booth's performance, mention is made of his slow entrance, long stride, and self-communing delivery of the opening speech, in which his elocution was exceptionally elaborate. His tones were varied to suit each figure of speech. He pronounced the word "ocean" as one of three syllables, and he gave a rising inflection to the phrase "glorious summer," as if to suggest a flood of radiance by means of sound. He maintained a watchful, crafty, specious, beguiling demeanor until the crown had been gained, and then he assumed the imperial manner of royalty. He restored to the text the questions "Is the chair empty? Is the sword unsway'd? Is the *king* dead?" and he delivered them in a rising torrent of mingled scorn and passion, and with intense energy. From the moment of the *King's* outset to meet rebellion till the moment of his death on the field of battle he was like a whirlwind, and he carried all before him. Edwin Booth, writing about his father, whom he loved and well understood, thus summarized judgment: "His expressions of terror and remorse were painful in the extreme, his hatred and revenge were devilish, but his tenderness was exquisitely human. At his best he soared higher into the realm of Art sublime than any of his successors have reached, and to those who saw him then it was not credible that any of his predecessors could have surpassed him."

WILLIAM CHARLES MACREADY.

Macready played *Richard* for the first time in London in 1819, at Covent Garden, appearing in the Cibber version of the tragedy. His success with the public was decisive. He had played the part five years before at Bath. Critical opinion on the subject was various, but in effect it was favorable. The actor's method in the wooing of *Lady Anne* was commended for winning sincerity,—the dissimulation not having been variegated by any gleams of sarcasm. His feverish, executive promptitude in directing the disposal of the bodies of the murdered *Princes* was essentially tragic. Leigh Hunt specified the exact spirit of the performance, intimating that it was marked by ardent, sanguine *gayety*. That, in Cibber's arrangement of the play, is a pervasive attribute of the character, for Cibber's *Richard* is not at any moment till the Dream Scene shown as a man capable of sensibility, and his anguish in that scene is as unwarranted as it is unexpected, whereas Shakespeare's *Richard,* long before he is shaken by his mother's curse, speaks of himself as "so far in blood that sin will pluck on sin," and while declaring that " Tear-falling pity dwells not in this eye," has made it clearly evident that he is conscious of his wickedness, apprehensive of its punishment, and therefore vulnerable to retribution. On the occasion, already mentioned, of Macready's treatment of "King Richard III." in a partly restored state (1821), his acting caused a thrilling effect, at the moment when, in the Council Scene, *Richard* bares his withered arm and pronounces the doom of *Hastings*. The burst of fury was electrical. Cooke, and later Kean, had done this, before Macready did it. The version

of the play then used by Macready was one made by
"Mr. Swift of the Crown Jewel Office" and improved
by the actor himself, but it did not in fact very
widely differ from that of Cibber. The advertisement
of it referred to Cibber's alteration as "ingenious."
If it really were so there would,—as remarked by
the sensible and caustic Genest,—have been no reason
for reverting to the original. Shakespeare's tragedy
is impracticable, as a whole, chiefly because of its
great length.

EDWIN FORREST.

Edwin Forrest, acting *Richard,* was burly, loud,
and violent, presenting a transparent villain. He
was jocosely exultant and strongly effective in the
expression of sardonic irony. His representation of
Richard's nightmare was correctly and effectively
attended with convulsive struggles and with tremendous blows at the air, significant of contention with
phantoms of armed enemies. He specially approved
of his acting in the scene of *Richard's* wooing of
Lady Anne, in which he laid great stress upon animal
magnetism. In conversation with John McCullough
he particularly called the attention of that actor to
what he deemed his "invincibility" in that passage,
and McCullough long afterward mentioned the

matter to me. McCullough, who greatly liked and admired Forrest, was for some time a member of his theatrical company, and his anecdotes of him were often happily illustrative of the veteran's peculiar character.

The principal dress of Forrest as *Richard* comprised a belted doublet; a cloak, with a heavy fringe of ermine; knee-breeches; low-cut velvet shoes; a velvet hat studded with jewels and garnished with long plumes; a thick, black wig from which long curls depended, reaching to the shoulders; a dress sword, and leather gauntlets. The doublet was open on the bosom, showing a white, ruffled shirt. The Order of the Garter was worn, as customary. The face was, as usual in that actor's scheme of "make-up," provided with a moustache and a chin-tuft, and it bore no resemblance to any portrait of the actual *Richard*. In the Battle Scene he wore spangled armor. One of Forrest's professional satellites was an eccentric actor named Andrew Jackson Allen (1776-1853), who owned and used a patent for ornamenting leather with gold and silver, and on the occasion of some little dispute with Forrest he astonished that formidable tragedian by the inquiry: "What in hell would your *Richard* be without *my spangles?*" If the exasperated satellite meant to intimate that the performance of *Richard* by the athletic actor consisted

JUNIUS BRUTUS BOOTH AS *KING RICHARD THE THIRD*

more of glittering show than of significant substance, his question implied a sound judgment.

JOHN EDWARD McCULLOUGH.

McCullough's ideal of *Richard* was correct, comprehending intellect, conscience, sardonic humor, latent sensibility, and fiery physical vitality, and his execution of it evinced abundant structural skill,— the faculty, in dramatic art, which differentiates character. McCullough was nearest to himself in *Virginius* or *King Lear* and furthest from himself in *Richard,* —yet he was equally truthful to the substance of each, and especially excellent in method of expression. Morbid parts and parts largely exactive of subtlety clashed against the limitations of his nature and his experience; but in parts involving elemental feelings he moved to victory with the assured step and spontaneous ease of an ordained conqueror. Two qualities were conspicuous in his performance of *Richard,*— elevation of state and simplicity of style. The performance was remarkable for consistent, sustained identification. *Richard* was clearly manifested, at his first entrance, as a consummate type of wicked force. His face was marked with heavy lines and the blight of deformity was seen and felt to have diffused itself through every fibre of the mind and

being. Commingled with attributes of the villain
were attributes of airy duplicity and affected good-
nature. McCullough's *Richard* was a man of evil
purpose,—vigilant, alert, propulsive,—wearing the
bluff aspect of an engaging, martial man-of-the-world.
Cibber's version was used, but the light that the actor's
art irradiated was largely caught from Shakespeare's
original. In the earlier part of his career McCullough
was content to "play for points,"—as he once
declared in conversation with me,—but there came a
time when, persuaded by friendly counsel, he gave
close attention to the *entire drawing* of the characters
in which he acted, and thereafter his delineations of
them were more carefully articulated and made more
nearly complete. His performance of *Richard,* at
first, was imitative of the points made by Forrest,
and therefore was fragmentary: it is here considered,
as it later became, sequent, continuous, and compact. In the scene of the wooing of *Lady Anne*
the glamour that *Glo'ster* exercises was singularly
well employed,—the delusively potent hypocrisy of an
ardent, seemingly remorseful man,—and the spectator
could almost credit the widowed *Lady Anne's* beguilement. McCullough's *Richard* was of flesh and blood,
and vibrant with ruthless spirit, yet there was in it,
perceptible at an early stage in the action, the suggestion of a nature that preys upon itself and has

begun to suffer the pangs of gnawing remorse. The
terrible aspect of that side of the character was clearly
shown in the Night Scene before the battle, involving
the haunting horrors of the Dream, but the power of
those passages of presentiment and torture and the
artistic beauty of their portrayal were augmented
and enforced because the imminent possibility of them
had been foreshadowed. To perceive the opportunity of making that distinction and to use it with
adequate effect was to rise to a great occasion, and
that adequacy McCullough exhibited, in the whole of
his treatment of the latent human attributes of *Glo's-
ter's* complex nature. In the delirium of the awakening the spasmodic action and the almost inarticulate
cries were such as chilled the blood of the listener; the
illusion at that point was complete.

EDWIN THOMAS BOOTH.

The *Richard* of Shakespeare, like the *Iago* of that
same marvellous delineator of human nature, knows
himself, and for himself he wears no disguise. His
mien, when he is communing with other persons, is
habitually that of specious duplicity until his ambition
is achieved. When alone he does not scruple to avouch
himself a villain and to exult in his villany. That
contrast was scrupulously made and shown by

Edwin Booth, whose assumption of hypocritical goodness when acting *Richard,* whether in the Cibber version or in the original,—which, suitably cut, he restored in 1876,—was indeed so deftly ingratiating that it might have deceived the most astute observer, and whose contrasted wickedness was so frank, entire, and cheerfully sinister as to be literally diabolical. The soft, sweet, resigned, melancholy tone in which he said to *Catesby,* in the scene with the *Lord Mayor,* "Call them again," made the use of deceit artistically beautiful, and caused in the listener a singular commingling of dread, amusement, and admiration, while the shocking note of blasphemy and sardonic scorn in his ejaculation, "Let not the heavens hear these telltale women *rail* on the *Lord's anointed,*" caused a shudder. Edwin Booth was the only actor I ever saw who made absolutely credible the winning of *Lady Anne;* and, as nearly as I can ascertain, from careful study and inquiry, he was the only actor of *Richard* who ever accomplished that effect. Compared with him, in the Wooing Scene, Edwin Forrest became ludicrous. Booth even made the physical deformity of *Richard*—deformity which in his embodiment was slight—only another attribute to interest and attract. In that scene he was an image of poetic beauty, at once gentle and fiery, passionate and tender, brilliant, melancholy, eager, satirical, frank, loving, and *noble*. The brilliant, icy contempt and scorn with which he spoke the words: "Was *ever* woman in this humor wooed? was ever woman in this humor *won?*" baffle description. Even to remember that performance, as given when he was in his prime, is to be thrilled and almost frightened; and that performance was the more admirable because it was entirely a calculated, prepared, controlled work of *art*. Never have I been more startled in a theatre than when, having one evening entered the house after the play had begun, I took a place in the front row and at the extreme verge of the audience, and Booth suddenly perceived me, as *Lady Anne* spoke the words: "Come, now, toward Chertsey with your holy load." Standing so that one side of his face was not visible to others in the audience, he bestowed upon me a cheerful grimace and wink, and instantly flashed toward the centre, exclaiming: "Stay, you that bear the corse, and set it down!" He was indeed a marvellous actor, always dominating his artistic faculties and himself, knowing his purpose and confident of its fulfilment.

Whenever excessive emotion has induced a strong physical enthusiasm, the natural craving of the spectator is for a violent outburst of physical power. Edwin Forrest was usually supreme at such moments. Tommaso Salvini excelled in them. The fulfilment of them is generally accepted as *greatness* in acting, whereas, in fact, it is no more than a "limb and outward flourish." Edwin Booth, spiritually a higher actor than either Forrest or Salvini, sometimes,—but seldom,—failed to fulfil them, from lack of volume of voice and muscular strength. The same deficiency was visible in the acting of Henry Irving. The physical power requisite to the making of a whirlwind of expression is a rare gift, though sometimes it exists with little or nothing behind it—as it did with James Hudson Kirby and John R. Scott. When it exists in association with fine intelligence and fiery feeling, as certainly was the case with the elder Kean and the elder Booth,—it is a gloriously potent gift. It was frequently manifest in the acting of Edwin Booth, and, in him, it was governed by taste and guided by discretion. He was often inspired and tremendous in the Death Scene of *Sir Giles Overreach,* the Curse Scene of *King Lear,* the Curse Scene of *Junius Brutus,* the awful midnight Triumph Scene of *Bertuccio,* the Anathema Scene of *Richelieu,* and, especially, in the awakening from the haunted sleep of *King Richard,*—putting forth astonishing power and creating terrific effect. His frenzied force, however, was fitful, and there are moments in some of Shakespeare's plays to which it was not always adequate. In *Richard* as embodied by him the observer recognized a man consistent with human nature and with himself,—false, cruel, wicked, almost demoniac, yet a human being, with brain, heart, conscience, imagination, and passions; not merely a stage ruffian, but a possible man, whose ambition is intelligible, whose conduct proceeds from considerate motive, the workings of whose conscience are visible even in the pains he takes to avow his dissimilarity from other men, whose remorse treads on the heels of his crimes, and whose last hours are agonized by terror and awful with warning. He was the image of an infernal power, playing a great part upon a great stage in human affairs, and while he struck upon every pulse of fear, he also smote the deep springs of pity. The observer, while constrained to rejoice over the defeat and ruin of such a fiendish force, was compelled to deplore the appalling agony, the ultimate bleak wretchedness, and the fearful doom of such an imperial mind. In the electrical fire and facile mechanism of Booth's *Richard* the observer was thrilled by the mysterious faculty of genius and delighted by the beauty of exquisite art. The exceptional character of certain types of the human race was more impressively suggested by Edwin Booth than by any of his predecessors ever seen by me. All the details of his performance of *Richard* were subordinated to the central design of embodying a man beneath whose bright, plausible, handsome, alluring exterior sleeps a hellish tempest of passion, a smouldering flame of malevolence, a fountain of deadly purpose. The prevailing external attribute was specious ingenuousness. Perfect craft assumed the air of perfect simplicity. All along the current of the performance there was an atmosphere of alarming suspense,—as of impending disaster, vague but ominous,—and when at last the fatal lightning of avowed and exultant evil leapt through the mist of smooth deceit, its blaze and shock were frightful. In the Tent Scene, on the eve of the battle, Booth displayed, with agonizing effect, the conflict between mortal weakness and unconquerable will, and revealed the action of supernatural influence upon a haunted, remorseful, but still undaunted soul. His delivery of *Richard's* awakening speech was an afflicting utterance of the agony of remorse. He rolled, affrighted, from the bed to the ground, sprang forward and crouched upon his knees, staring and gasping with horror. In the combat his jaws worked convulsively, like those of a furious wild animal. He seemed like some grisly reptile, turned at bay, desperate and terrible. Hatred and ferocity gleamed in his countenance. When disarmed of his sword he fought with his dagger, and on receiving his death blow he fell precipitately, plung-

EDWIN BOOTH AS *THE DUKE OF GLO'STER*

AFTER THE PORTRAIT IN OIL BY JARVIS McENTEE

ing headlong to the ground,—a ghastly, terrific image of conquered ferocity and ruined power. Cooke, I believe, on the sum of the testimony, was the best representative of Cibber's *Richard:* the best representative whom I have ever seen of Shakespeare's *Richard* was Edwin Booth. One of the greatest of Booth's many great attributes was the consummate ability, in the very torrent, tempest, and whirlwind of passion, to "acquire and beget a temperance that may give it smoothness."

BARRY SULLIVAN.

Barry Sullivan, who seems to have been considered in London as "an outsider," but who was an actor of exceptional ability, gave a remarkably potent performance of *Richard*—consistent, sustained, uniform, and effective. Genius he did not possess. Knowledge of his art he did possess, in a remarkable degree, and he notably evinced it in his acting of this part. There was an air of plausibility about his demeanor and proceedings when *Glo'ster* was in company with other persons that might have imposed upon anybody, and there was a gay, soaring complacency in his demeanor when alone that conveyed a complete impression of incarnate wickedness delighted with itself. He acted in Cibber's version, which he had modified. He was common in fibre, and his delivery was at times spasmodic, but he presented a formidable, distinct image of an ambitious, cruel, evil, crafty, dangerous person. His ideal of *Richard* was a man of fiery, regnant intellect, possessing a moral sense which always *informs* but never *controls;* who, in the middle stream of a ruthless, sanguinary career, is checked and appalled by his mother's curse, and presently is shattered by terrific visitations from the spirit world. His impersonation lacked electrical fire, but it possessed clarity of design, consistency of execution, and abundant and sustained force. It followed, substantially, the tradition not of Edmund Kean, but of Macready. Sullivan was superlatively effective in expressing the grim, sarcastic, pitiless humor of *Richard,* particularly in the scenes with *Lady Anne.* His mechanism was peculiarly subtle— as when he allowed expressions to flit over his face, accordant with the effect upon his mind and feelings of every word spoken to him. That merit was prominently obvious when, in the Wooing Scene, with *Lady Anne,* he listened to her prayer that, should her late husband's murderer ever have a child born to him, it might be deformed. Sullivan's performance was thickly studded with beauties of that description, and therein it was a consummate work of art.

Henry Irving's embodiment of *Richard,* often and brilliantly exhibited in England (he produced the tragedy, according to Shakespeare, at the London Lyceum, January 29, 1877; revived it December 19, 1896; revived it again, February 27, 1897), was never fully shown before an American audience; but, on one occasion, (November 24, 1883, at the Star Theatre, New York), he acted the part, in the opening scene, and afforded a signal evidence of his perfect comprehension of the spirit alike of the character and of the play. The scene displayed a street of old London, with many quaint buildings and the Tower in the background, and was brilliantly illumined, as with the brightest of summer suns. The buildings were gayly decorated. The air was flooded with the melodious clangor of many silver chimes. Upon that brilliant scene *Glo'ster,* clothed in bright raiment, entered through an archway, and paused and glanced around and listened to the merry bells before he began to speak, in tones of airy mockery, the soliloquy prompted by those surroundings:

> " Now is the winter of our discontent
> Made glorious summer by this sun of York."

By the air of *inevitable predominance* with which
he invested the figure of *Richard,* signifying conscious power and foreshadowing triumphant victory,
he struck the key-note of a personation which, in its
day, elicited the highest praise from the most accomplished of contemporary critics.   That key-note was
designated (1897), by Sir Edward Russell, as the
humorous enjoyment of intended villany.   In the
Wooing Scene the specious hypocrisy of his *Richard*
made the auditor almost believe that such a man
might really cajole a weak woman, in the circumstances prescribed.   In the Tent Scene he was, being
alone, observed to be a broken, prematurely old man,
—affording, in this contrast, says Russell, "as on the
reverse of a medal, the full meaning of all the high-
spirited revelling devilry which he has kept up before
the world."

VARIOUS PERFORMERS.

An English actor distinguished in his prosperous day as *Richard the Third* was James Bennett.
He visited America, making his first appearance, as
Richard, at Niblo's Garden, New York, but his acting
—correct, conventional, uninspired—attracted little
attention.   His embodiment of *Richard* evinced
scholar-like comprehension of the subject and ample
professional capability.   His engagement was pre-

cipitately closed. He was not generously or even fairly treated. I have been assured that, when old and poor, that worthy and excellent man was maintained, to the end of his days, by Henry Irving, at a lodging in Stratford-upon-Avon.

Among the many actors who have presented *Richard* on the American stage were John Hodgkinson, Lewis Hallam, Charles Kean, Henry James Finn, Sheridan Knowles, Charles Henry Eaton, James William Wallack, Edward Loomis Davenport, William Creswick, Gustavus Vaughan Brooke, Wyzeman Marshall, Thomas Sowerby Hamblin, Charles Kemble Mason, Edwin Adams, James Edward Murdoch, Lawrence Barrett, Thomas Keene, Richard Mansfield, and Robert Bruce Mantell. Many years ago James Booth Roberts was conspicuous in the part, till he laid it aside to identify himself with that of *Mephistopheles*. Mr. Roberts was a man of diminutive figure but dignified bearing, and a scrupulous stickler for correctness and decorum—such a man as mischievous youths would naturally select as a subject for a practical joke. The great comedian Joseph Jefferson, although in his maturity he strongly condemned the practice of "guying," did not in his youth wholly abstain from that form of frolic. Thus, he told me that when on one occasion he was playing *Catesby* to the *Richard* of Roberts, he rushed upon

the Battle Scene exclaiming,—instead of the correct
line, "Behind yonder thicket stands a swift horse,"—
"Behind yonder *swifet* stands a *thick* horse!" "Mr.
Roberts," he added, "was much incensed, and he
rebuked me, after the play, in strong language. I
told him that I was very sorry and had not meant
to misread the line; that it had been repeated to
me in transposed form, and I had become confused.
'I do not believe you, sir!' rejoined the angry
tragedian. 'You are a damned mischievous young
man.'" Mr. Roberts, born in 1818, was one of the
comparatively few actors of American birth who
gained distinction in the first half of the nineteenth
century. He was first seen in New York on February
22, 1847, at the New Chatham Theatre, in Chatham
Street, where he acted *Richard* and made a decisive
success. His Shakespearean repertory included,
among other parts, *Lear, Iago,* and *Othello.* He was
an excellent "all 'round" actor and an accomplished
elocutionist. His career was long, and he outlived
popularity as an actor and ultimately became a
teacher. He died, September 14, 1901, esteemed by
all and sincerely lamented. His personation of
Richard is remembered as definite in ideal, fiery in
spirit, and smooth in execution.

RICHARD MANSFIELD.

That remarkable actor Richard Mansfield made for himself a stage version of Shakespeare's tragedy and produced it in a costly and magnificent setting at the Globe Theatre, London, on March 16, 1889, then acting *Richard* for the first time. Later he made his performance known throughout the United States. His ideal was that of the "laughing devil," and in the exposition of it he indicated a novel theory. *Richard* is nineteen years old when he kills *King Henry,* in the Tower, and thirty-three years old when he is slain, on Bosworth Field: his *progress* in evil, the actor maintained, should therefore be exhibited, each of his murderous deeds being made to react upon him mentally and physically, and the effect of that reaction being shown in gradual but distinct changes of condition, aspect, expression, and voice. Pursuant to that theory, he made *Richard* youthful and gay at the beginning, and caused him to become grave, stern, massive, ruthless, and terrible, as time lapsed and the action proceeded, till at last, prematurely old, he was seared, haggard, agonized, and desperate, yet undaunted. One of the effective devices of pictorial stage business invented and employed by Mansfield was the use of a ray of red light which, streaming through the stained glass of a window in the throneroom, when the *King* was sitting alone upon the chair to which he had made his way by murder, fell upon his hand and seemed to bathe it with blood, causing him for a moment to shrink and shudder, and to crouch, dismayed, in the shadow of the throne. Several renowned actors of this part denoted the entrance of the iron of remorse into the soul of *Richard* at the moment of his mother's denunciation of him. Mansfield showed it as early as that scene upon the throne. The most effective business he employed was that of mistaking *Catesby* for yet another apparition, when that officer enters, at the culmination of the Dream Scene. No one who heard it will ever forget the shrill, agonized sound of Mansfield's voice when he spoke the words: "Zounds! *who's* there!" Indeed, the whole of his action and delivery in that scene was magnificently expressive of tumultuous anguish, horror, and frenzy, the haunted murderer leaping wildly from his couch, whirling an imaginary sword, plunging forward as if in battle with frightful forms invulnerable to mortal blows, and finally stumbling to his knees, as he uttered, in an appalling shriek, the supplication "Jesu, have mercy!"

Mansfield, before producing the tragedy in London, had bestowed much thought upon his plan of accomplishing a correct, elaborate, and beautiful presentment of it. His chief counsellors, in prepara-

RICHARD MANSFIELD AS *THE DUKE OF GLO'STER*

*"For God he knows, and you may partly see,
How far I am from the desire therefor."*
Act III., Sc. 1 (R. M.'s arrangement)

tion for the enterprise, were Walter Herries Pollock and J. G. Waller,—the former a noted Shakespearean scholar, the latter a learned antiquarian. The requisite scenery was painted for him by William Telbin and other artists. The dresses and armor were designed by Seymour Lucas. The incidental music was composed by Edward German. Nothing was neglected and nothing omitted that could enrich the setting or augment verisimilitude in the picture. The result was a pageant perhaps unsurpassed in the stage history of this play,—and, in recording this opinion, it is not forgotten that modern productions of "King Richard III."—notably those of Macready, Charles Kean, Barry Sullivan, Edwin Booth, and Henry Irving,—have far excelled those of the Garrick period, in pictorial splendor as well as in thoroughness of detail.

MEANING AND VALUE OF THE PLAY.

Much fine scenery, representative of Old London, was painted by William Capon, for John Philip Kemble, in 1793-94, and Kemble, it is apparent from the records, made the first really important efforts that were made in the British Theatre to set the plays of Shakespeare on the stage in a suitable investiture,—this tragedy being one of the several that he revived. No record, however, has been found of any attempt to set and dress "King Richard III." in a comprehensively correct manner before the time of Macready,—whose good example, in that particular, was followed by Charles Kean and Samuel Phelps. The first person to restore this play to the stage, suitably cut, was Phelps,—always a stickler for "the original text,"—who discarded Cibber and produced a condensation of Shakespeare, at the Sadler's Wells Theatre, Islington, London, on February 20, 1844. Aside from imperative omissions, the principal liberty taken with the original was in fashioning a scene, subsequent to the removal of the dying *King Edward,* explanatory of deleted passages, —that scene being composed of lines from other portions of the original. Phelps,—a great actor, an indomitable worker, a felicitous originator, and a splendid stage director,—acted *Richard,* embodying him as a villain equally bold and specious, whose triumphs result as much from ability and artifice as from the violence of power. The Wooing Scene was fraught with fine dissimulation, the denunciation of *Hastings* was fiery and abrupt, the treatment of the exacting later scenes was notable for sustained tragic power,—a quality lacking in most performances of *Richard,*—and the Death Scene was terrific. Phelps, however, abandoned Shakespeare and reverted to Cibber—largely on the advice of his nephew, W.

May Phelps, who felt that Miss Atkinson, a member of his company, could not equal Mrs. Warner's antecedent tragic accomplishment as Shakespeare's *Queen Margaret*. Phelps reverted to the Cibber fabric on November 23, 1861. The first actor to restore Shakespeare's "King Richard III." to the American Stage was Edwin Booth, who brought it out, late in 1876, at Brooklyn, New York. Booth's version, although there are some changes in the distribution of the text as well as in the arrangement of the scenes, presents Shakespeare's work not as it stands in the eclectic library editions, yet substantially as Shakespeare wrote it. No extraneous matter is introduced and only a few words are altered—to suit the exigencies of stage business. Henry Irving's restoration of the original was not effected until after Booth's revival had been made. In each of those splendid settings some latitude had been allowed to fancy. Literal accuracy in the presentment of historical plays, or of any plays, is neither essential nor desirable. We cannot,—as remarked by Thackeray,—have *Caractacus* painted blue, like a veritable ancient Briton, or *Boadicea* with nothing on but a cow-skin—and very little of that. If dresses in every particular correct were used in presenting "King Richard III.," the resultant effect would often be more tiresome and ridiculous than impressive and

dramatic. General conformity to the customs,
implements, and usages of the historic period indicated satisfies every reasonable requirement, and this
conformity both exacts and allows practical remembrance of many points, some of the more important
of which it will be serviceable here to mention. The
colors of the house of York were dark red and blue;
those of the house of Lancaster were blue and white;
those of the house of Tudor were white and green.
The use of purple cloth of gold and of purple silk
was, in England, in 1482, restricted by law to the
Royal Family. No person less in degree than a
duke could wear cloth of gold of tissue, but noblemen of lower rank were allowed to wear plain cloth
of gold. Knights could wear velvet and squires could
wear satin. The state dress last worn by King
Edward the Fourth was one that had very full,
hanging sleeves, lined with rich furs, and this robe
was "so rolled over his shoulders as to give his tall
person an air of peculiar grandeur." In King
Edward's reign short gowns were worn, over closely
fitting body suits, with slits through which came the
arms, while the outer sleeves hung, as empty orna-
ments, from the shoulder. Short-waisted jackets,
thickly padded at the shoulders, were in use. The
boots and shoes of the period, at first, were fashioned
with long, pointed toes, but later the toes were made

broad and round. Men wore caps adorned with gems and feathers. The gowns of women were made with long trains, embellished with broad velvet borders. The waists, in King Edward's time, were very short, but in King Richard's time they were made longer. Broad belts were worn, with buckles in front. The sleeves were long and tight. The steeple head-dress (Norman) was fashionable, but it was superseded by a cap of gold embroidery, covered by a transparent veil, which was stiffened in somewhat the form of wings. The "common people" wore plain tunics reaching to the knees. The robes of the Lord Mayor of London were scarlet in color. Long hair was in fashion, but it was cut straight across the forehead, "clubbed" or "blocked." Ribbed, or plated, armor was used in war.

It was the opinion of *Polonius* that "the apparel oft proclaims the man." It certainly often does furnish sidelights upon the character. The taste of Richard, in this respect, was such as warrants the stage representative of him in use of the most luxurious personal adornment—a warrant reinforced, for stage purposes, by the facts that a man conscious of the disadvantage of physical deformity would be likely to seek, by splendor of appearance, to nullify it, and that such adornment, properly varied, would heighten dramatic effect. There are authentic por-

traits of Richard, one of which depicts him as attired
in a close-fitting suit of scarlet, over which hangs a
robe of cloth of gold and a black cap, adorned with
a pearl, while another presents him in a black cap,
with a body suit of cloth of gold, and a black robe,
with black and red sleeves.   Planché, one of the
highest authorities that could be quoted upon this
subject, gives the following significant view of the
man, in this aspect of his complex, singular, and
interesting character:

"Richard's wardrobe was, at all times, magnificently furnished,—he and the Duke of Buckingham being notorious for
their love of dress and finery.   A mandate still exists, amongst
the Harleian MSS., sent from York, by Richard, to the keeper
of his wardrobe in London,—August 31, 1483,—wherein he
specifies the costly habits in which he was desirous of exhibiting himself to his Northern subjects, with a descriptive detail
which, as Mr. Sharon Turner justly remarks, 'we would rather
look for from the fop that annoyed *Hotspur* than from the
stern and warlike Richard.' "

The subject of King Richard the Third is one of
the most interesting in all the long and various annals
of English history, and its presentation in the theatre
should be encouraged.   False as Shakespeare's tragedy is to history, a judicious version of it and such a
restoration of it to our stage as would compel aban-

donment of the Cibber hash is much to be desired. Great as some of the performances of *Richard* were that actors of an earlier time than ours achieved in Cibber's play, it is ascertained by careful examination that the greatness of them was chiefly due to the powerful passages of the original, selected and preserved by Cibber, in the mosaic which he made out of Shakespeare's text, the opportunities of acting thus provided, and the actor's capability of improving those opportunities. The resistless charm of the authentic theatrical character of *Richard* consists in the union of colossal will with instantaneous promptitude of action. He has been conceived and portrayed by the poet as a complete incarnation of that pernicious force in Nature which never sleeps, never rests, never pauses— the force of Evil, provided, in the mysterious scheme of things, for the production of Good. *Richard* affords startling contrasts, either moving furtively or braving all opposition and trampling upon everything. He is the embodied energy of an infernal spirit. Twice only is he checked, and then for only a moment. But, notwithstanding all his wicked power, *Richard* is human, and though he cannot be reached from without he is finally struck from within. The regnancy of his indomitable intellect, which carries him so high, and which should forecast events and lead him to ultimate victory, crumbles in the flame of its own wickedness. Any expert, capable actor would always have an audience as *Richard*. Given an actor who can provide that personality with a fair and winning exterior and can display it by brilliant expression,—an actor who possesses the lithe body, the luminous face, the piercing eyes, the capacious, sonorous voice, the ruling brain, the fire, the terrible tragic power, and the consummate art which sometimes are combined in one man, as they were in Edwin Booth in his prime,—and Shakespeare's *Richard the Third* furnishes one of the greatest of all opportunities that even such a marvellously gifted actor can seize—the opportunity to interpret and make actual in the theatre a thrilling, terrific conception of intellectual power perverted to the service of Evil and at the same time convincingly to demonstrate its utter futility when at last and inevitably it dashes itself against the adamant of Divine Law.

III.

THE MERCHANT OF VENICE.

"Thou art come to answer
A stony adversary, an inhuman wretch
Uncapable of pity, void and empty
From any dram of mercy."
—Shakespeare.

THE most popular of Shakespeare's comedies, the one most widely known, the one by means of which most abundant success has been obtained on the stage, is "The Merchant of Venice." One reason for its exceptional vitality is the fascinating charm of its style, the simple, direct, fluent, sweet, natural language of human feeling, sometimes irradiated with the fire of poetic thought, and sometimes expanded and elevated with the fervor of noble eloquence. Its more decisive power consists in the felicity of its fable, and in the force, interest, and variety of its happily harmonized and as happily contrasted characters. The love story of *Bassanio* and *Portia* is ingeniously fanciful, and it may be doubted whether, in the whole wide range of the poetic drama, there is any woman who can vie with *Portia,* as a type of blended intellect,

129

brilliancy, and feminine fascination. No characters in Shakespearean comedy are more sharply discriminated or more vigorously drawn than those of *Portia, Shylock, Antonio, Gratiano,* and *Launcelot Gobbo.* Nowhere else is the poet more eloquent than he is in this play, in expressing elemental passions of human nature. *Portia* is a perfect incarnation of love, *Shylock* a perfect incarnation of hate; *Antonio* typifies the temperament of constitutional melancholy; *Gratiano* is embodied glee, and *Launcelot* is an image of drollery and animal happiness. Studies of character that the poet began in his juvenile comedy of "The Two Gentlemen of Verona" are massed and completed in his mature comedy of "The Merchant." *Launce,* in the former, foreshadows *Launcelot* in the latter, *Lucetta* is the germ of *Nerissa,* and *Julia* preludes *Portia.*

Shakespeare may have derived the principal incidents of his plot from Giovanni's tale, called "Il Pecorone," published at Milan, 1558, or he may have found them in the "Gesta Romanorum"; he probably knew the old ballad of Gernutus, which particularly tells the story of the *Jew,* but more probably he built upon the basis of an older play, which was on the stage when he was a boy. That older play is mentioned in "The School of Abuse," 1579, by Stephen Gosson, clergyman and poet, 1554-1623, who says that it was "shewn at the Bull," and that it represented "the greedynesse of worldly chusers and the bloody minds of usurers." The cruel Jew is an ancient denizen of the world of fiction. Dowden remarks that the story of the casket can be found in the mediæval romance of "Barlaam and Josaphat," written by Joannes Damascenus, about the year 800, and that it occurs in Boccaccio, 1313-1375, and Gower, 1320-1402. The choice of materials, however, was not so important as the use of them. Shakespeare was an interpreter, and in this case, as in so many others, the magical touch of his genius transmuted the dross of legendary lore into the pure gold of poetry and lit the still life of narrative with the blaze of action. Astute judges of dramatic art have agreed that Shakespeare, in "The Merchant of Venice," shows himself the absolute master of his art. "The union of the two actions in one event," said Dr. Johnson, "is eminently happy: Dryden was much pleased with his own address in connecting the two plots of his 'Spanish Friar,' which yet I believe the critic will find excelled by this play." "In the management of the plot," said the learned Henry Hallam, "which is sufficiently complex, without the slightest confusion or incoherence, I do not conceive that it has been surpassed in the annals of any theatre."

No record exists stating when and where "The Merchant of Venice" was first produced. It is one

of the twelve plays by Shakespeare mentioned by
Francis Meres in his "Palladis Tamia, Wits' Treasury," 1598. It was entered at Stationers' Hall in that
year, first printed in 1600, reprinted the same year,—
each time in Quarto,—and not again printed till reproduced in the First Folio, 1623. In Philip Henslowe's
diary there is mention of the "Venesyan Comedy" as
having been acted for the first time on August 25,
1594, but the authorship is not stated. If, as seems
probable, that was Shakespeare's play, this comedy
has (1911), in one form or another, been on the stage
intermittently for 317 years. Henslowe, theatrical
manager and play-broker, was the partner of Edward
Alleyn, the distinguished actor who founded Dul-
wich College, where the Diary is treasured,—as it
should be, because it is one of the most informing and
useful of existing records relative to the drama in the
time of Queen Elizabeth. If "The Merchant of
Venice" was first acted on the date named by Henslowe, the performance occurred at Newington Butts,
in Surrey; for the players, at that time, having been
expelled from Southwark, had removed to that place,
not distant from London. Between 1594 and the
period of George Granville, Viscount Lansdowne (1667-
1735), who mutilated the comedy, and whose mutilation of it, first produced January 11, 1701, at Lincoln's
Inn Fields, was used in the theatre for the ensuing

forty years, the stage history of "The Merchant of Venice" is a blank.

THE FIRST *SHYLOCK*.

There is sufficient reason to believe that the first of the many performers who have appeared as *Shylock* was Richard Burbage, though nothing is known of the manner of his performance. It can, however, rightly be inferred from such imperfect knowledge as is possessed of his acting in general that he played the part in accordance with the serious spirit in which it is written. The elegy on his death,—as to the authenticity of at least a part of which there is, however, a reasonable doubt,—provides the information that in his dressing of *Shylock* he wore red hair, and J. Payne Collier declares that he also wore a long false nose, such as was worn by Alleyn, the representative of *Barabas,* in Christopher Marlowe's "The Jew of Malta," acted in 1591. If so, that fact would seem to indicate that Burbage laid particular stress, amounting, indeed, to caricature, on the Jewish physiognomy. It seems credible that the tragic method of playing *Shylock* was not used in the time of the author, for the Jews were disliked in England, in Queen Elizabeth's reign and that of King James the First, and a high ideal of *Shylock* would not have been accepted by the public.

THE LANSDOWNE ALTERATION.

Lansdowne's perversion of Shakespeare's comedy is called "The Jew of Venice." It is provided with a prologue, written by a person named Bevil Higgons, in which the ghosts of *Shakespeare* and *Dryden*, crowned with laurel, deliver an inane colloquy, one illuminative line of which says, "To-day we punish a stock-jobbing Jew." In the Second Act several of the principal characters are assembled at a feast, and *Shylock*, sitting apart from the other persons, drinks a health, saying: "Money is *my* Mistress! Here's to Interest upon Interest!" The festival is prolonged by a dreary masque, called "Peleus and Thetis." There are five acts in the Lansdowne hash, compounded of extracts, often garbled, from Shakespeare's text, and bad verses by the adapter, the dominating purpose being to make *Bassanio* the chief part in the comedy. *Shylock* is made ludicrous and contemptible. The cast with which Lansdowne's jumble was produced included Thomas Betterton, as *Bassanio;* Barton Booth, as *Gratiano;* John Verbruggen, as *Antonio;* Henry Harris, as the *Duke of Venice;* Thomas Dogget, as *Shylock;* Anne Bracegirdle, as *Portia;* Mrs. Bowman, as *Nerissa;* and Mary Porter, as *Jessica,*—by all accounts surely an extraordinary group of players.

Mrs. Bracegirdle and Mrs. Bowman were women of superb beauty.

Betterton, incomparably the greatest actor of his time, never appeared as *Shylock*. Thomas Dogget, of whom it is recorded that he was "the first star" in the annals of the stage, made *Shylock* a low comedy part, especially in the colloquy with *Tubal;* but particular description of his comicality has not been found. He was essentially a comic actor. The remark made by Downes, on that point, is conclusive: "Mr. Dogget, on the stage, he's very aspectabund, wearing a farce in his face; his thoughts deliberately framing his utterance congruous to his looks. *He is the only comic original now* [1708] extant: witness, *Ben, Solon, Nickin,* the *Jew of Venice,* &c." Dogget died in 1721. He was, on the authority of Colley Cibber, highly commendable, among other merits, for care and correctness in the dressing of the characters that he assumed.

MACKLIN TO MANSFIELD.

Among memorable embodiments of *Shylock* that have established themselves in theatrical annals are those that were given by Charles Macklin, John Henderson, George Frederick Cooke, Edmund Kean, Junius Brutus Booth, William Charles Macready, James William Wallack, Edwin Booth, Bogumil

Dawison, Henry Irving, and Richard Mansfield. In the forty years preceding the time of Macklin *Shylock* had been represented, when represented at all, which was not very often, in Lansdowne's version, and always as a low comedy part. Macklin reverted to Shakespeare, revived the original play, discarding the Lansdowne deformity, and acted *Shylock* in a tragic spirit, achieving an immediate and prodigious success. The dress and make-up of Macklin included long, wide trousers, a loose, black gown, a three-cornered red hat, and a piqued beard. He probably wore red hair, as had been customary. *Black* hair was first worn in the part by Edmund Kean. James William Wallack was the first actor to dress *Shylock's* head with literally *gray* hair, which he did at the earnest request of his son, Lester Wallack. The exact age of *Shylock* is indeterminate; but he is a widower, with a daughter of marriageable age; in the Trial Scene he is called *"old* Shylock"; and he so designates himself: "Thou shalt see: thy eyes shall be the judge, the difference of *old* Shylock and Bassanio": in the Street Scene there is still another intimation as to his age. *Solanio,* replying to *Shylock's* bitter reproach of his daughter, "My own flesh and blood to rebel," makes the ribald, punning answer, "Out upon it, *old* carrion! rebels it at *these years?"* It is imperative to depict the Jew as a man of fifty years or more. His visage, moreover, would naturally be marked by the lines of craft and seared by the seething fire of evil passions.

Macklin's embodiment of *Shylock* was grim and terrible. He was a man of sinister aspect. Quin, his contemporary, said that his face was marked not with lines, but with cordage. His eyes were dark and fiery; his nose was aquiline and very prominent; his jaws were large and heavy; his mouth was wide; his lower lip protruded; his complexion was yellow, his figure stout and formidable, his voice harsh, and his temper arrogant. As *Shylock,* he incarnated malice and revenge, and therein he was true to Shakespeare's conception of the character, albeit there is a temptation, to which various actors and commentators have succumbed, to provide the *Jew* with amiable, redeeming human attributes.

THE CHARACTER OF *SHYLOCK*.

The notion that *Shylock* is, or was intended to be, a majestic type of the religious and racial grandeur of Israel appears to have germinated, or at least to have acquired authority, about the beginning of the nineteenth century. The German publicist, Ludwig Bœrne (1786-1837), writing about "The Merchant of Venice," designated *Shylock* "an exalted Jew and an

avenging angel," not persecuting *Antonio* as the foe
of usury, but as the foe of the Hebrew faith. Douglas
Jerrold (1803-1857) said of Edmund Kean, as *Shylock,* that he impressed his audience "like a chapter of
Genesis." Thomas R. Gould, writing about the elder
Booth as *Shylock,* declared that he made the part "the
representative Hebrew." That view is alluring to
imaginative, sympathetic, ingenious students of this
complex subject, and they are prone to read subtle
meanings into the text of Shakespeare; but it is not
warranted by anything in the play. On the contrary,
everything in the play confutes it. No word spoken
by *Shylock,* and no word spoken about him, justifies
the theory that he is "an avenging angel." No part
of his conduct justifies it, and, as an old proverb says,
"Actions speak louder than words." *Shylock* hates
Antonio for several sufficient reasons, which are distinctly specified. He is a revengeful man, and he
purposes to gratify his revengeful desire by committing
murder under the sanction of legal form. Able and
admirable representatives of *Shylock,* subsequent
to the time of Macklin, have deemed it essential
to commend the character to public sympathy by investing it to some extent with paternal feeling and
domestic virtue. Even George Frederick Cooke, the
avowed disciple of Macklin, when delivering *Shylock's*
passionate expostulation, "Hath not a Jew eyes?"

dwelt pathetically on the word *"affections."* Henry
Irving after saying of *Jessica,* "I would my daughter
were *dead* at my foot, and the jewels in her ear! would
she were *hearsed* at my foot, and the ducats in her
coffin!" interjected, in tones of poignant anguish, "No,
no, no, no, no!" Richard Mansfield, at the place where
Shylock leaves his house, to feast with his Christian
enemies (immediately subsequent to his emphatic
refusal to do so!), caused the father to embrace his
daughter *Jessica* and kiss her on the forehead,—that
daughter who describes their house as "hell," and
testifies as to *Shylock's* feeling and purposes revealed
in the privacy of his home.

> "When I was with him, I have heard him swear,
> To Tubal and to Chus, his countrymen,
> That he would *rather* have *Antonio's flesh*
> *Than twenty times* the value of the sum
> That he doth owe him."

Shylock has been grossly ill-treated by *Antonio,*
stigmatized as a "cutthroat dog," publicly spurned,
insulted on the Exchange,—the Rialto,—kicked, spat
upon, habitually reviled, treated as if he were
no better than "a stranger cur"; and *Antonio,*
—"the good Antonio," "the honest Antonio," of
whom it is said by one of his friends that "a kinder
gentleman treads not the earth,"—has explictly

assured him of the likelihood of a continuance of the same ignominious treatment. *Shylock* accordingly hates *Antonio* with an implacable though natural hatred and wishes to kill him; and, opportunity presenting itself, *Shylock* speciously and treacherously induces *Antonio* to make a covenant the breaking of which will, on the exaction of the nominated forfeiture, cost him his life. *Shylock* hypocritically calls that covenant "a *merry* bond," and signifies that even though *Antonio* should "break his day," the penalty would not be exacted; and this he does within a few moments after privately asseverating that, if he "can catch him once upon the hip," he "will feed fat the *ancient* grudge" he bears him. From the first moment when he perceives even a glimmering chance of revenge it is the intention of *Shylock* to murder the man whom he hates and loathes. It is obvious that his reasons for entertaining and pursuing that intention are sufficient to his own mind, but it is also obvious that he is a sanguinary, ruthless villain. Opinion on that point has always differed, and accordingly the numerous representations of *Shylock* which have been provided within the long period since Shakespeare's *Jew* was restored to the stage (1741), by Macklin, have chiefly varied in the particular of morality, some actors endeavoring to present *Shylock* as an austere image of Justice, others presenting him as a baleful image of Revenge, and still others,—James William Wallack, Edward Loomis Davenport, and Richard Mansfield, for example,—striving to make him a composite of both.

CHARLES MACKLIN.

Macklin's restoration of Shakespeare's comedy to the stage was accomplished under circumstances of peculiar interest. The scene was Drury Lane Theatre. The actor, then past fifty, was desirous of making a more distinctive mark than he had ever before made. The manager of the theatre, Charles Fleetwood, had left the direction of the stage and the dramatic policy of the theatre mainly in his hands. Macklin chanced to consider the character of *Shylock,* and, disapproving of Lansdowne's play and the long prevalent custom of making the *Jew* a broadly farcical character, as that play requires that the actor of *Shylock* should do, determined to revert to the original piece, and to act the part as a serious one. Fleetwood consented, and Shakespeare's comedy was put into rehearsal. The actors associated with Macklin, when apprized of his purpose to appear as *Shylock,* received the avowal of it with derision. At the rehearsals, accordingly, the astute player, concealing his full design, enjoined his fellows, speaking in his capacity of stage manager, to put forth their utmost powers; but he himself acted tamely, so that they were all deceived and became persuaded that he would meet with disgraceful failure. Fleetwood, alarmed by their reports, urged him to desist from the attempt, but was reassured by the intrepid innovator's declaration that he was purposely misleading his associates in the cast, and "would pledge his life" on the success of the undertaking. Quin, the *Antonio* of the occasion, said that Macklin would be hissed from the stage. When the night of trial arrived, an eager assemblage, filling Drury Lane, saw *Shylock* attired as he had never before been attired within their knowledge, and likewise saw a presentment of the character which was altogether new. Approval greeted the opening scenes, but when, in the tremendous passion of the Street Scene, the actor liberated all his fire, the astonished audience became wildly enthusiastic, and his triumph was complete. "I had the good fortune," so he said, recounting his memorable experience, "to please beyond my warmest expectations. The whole house was in an uproar of applause, and I was obliged to pause between the speeches to give it vent, so as to be heard. . . . The Trial Scene wound up the fulness of my reputation. Here I was well listened to, and here I made such a silent yet forcible impression on my audience that I retired from this great attempt most perfectly satisfied." It is recorded that the dense monarch King George the Second, who saw the performance, was so completely frightened by it that he was unable to sleep that night. The German traveller and critic George Christopher Lichtenberg, to whom readers are indebted for glimpses of the acting of the Quin-Macklin-Garrick period, wrote of Macklin's *Shylock:* "In the scene when for the first time he misses his daughter he appears without his hat, with his hair standing on end and in some places a finger's length above the crown, as if the wind from the gallows had blown it up. Both hands are firmly clenched, and all his movements are abrupt and convulsive." The comedy, as revived and treated by Macklin, held the stage for a long time and was often performed, always with success. Macklin's embodiment of *Shylock,* judging from the records which survive, while it has been excelled in minutiæ of detail, has never been excelled in ideal or in terrific power. Thomas Davies (the biographer of Garrick, be it remembered!), who had seen and capably observed the acting of Charles Macklin, mentions him as the *only* actor he had ever seen "that made acting a science." On the night of Macklin's signal victory Kitty Clive played *Portia* and Hannah Pritchard played *Nerissa.*

JOHN HENDERSON.

John Henderson, succeeding after many repulses, made his first prominent appearance in London, playing *Shylock,* June 11, 1777, at the Haymarket Theatre, and although, as certified in one contemporary record, "his style being different from Macklin's, critics were divided in opinion," gained brilliant success. "Henderson's *Shylock,*" said John Philip Kemble, "was the greatest effort that I ever witnessed on the stage." George Colman, then manager of the Haymarket, said that "in the impassioned scene with *Tubal* he seemed a black *Lear*" and bore "an odd resemblance of a mad king in a storm"; but Colman objected to his costume, declaring that it looked as if it had been hired from a pawnbroker. Macklin attended the performance, and cordially praised it. "And yet, sir," said Henderson, "I have never had the advantage of seeing you in that character." "It is not necessary to tell me that, sir," replied the veteran; "I knew you had not, or you would have played it differently."

Garrick, who disliked Henderson, remarked, after witnessing the representation, that the part of *Tubal* had been acted well. The renown of Henderson, who in his short professional life of only thirteen years played more than a hundred parts, rests mainly on his impersonations of *Shylock, Falstaff, Iago,* and *Sir Giles Overreach,* although he was also admired in *Hamlet, Macbeth,* and *King Lear,* and in *Horatius,* in William Whitehead's tragedy of "The Roman Father." Among all the players of the shining Garrick period he appears to have been exceptionally versatile, and he possessed distinctively original genius. The testimony is emphatic that his acting was guided by extraordinary acuteness of judgment and vitalized by splendid enthusiasm. He was decisively effective in his sudden transitions from one passion to another, and he excelled equally in the delivery of soliloquy and the pointed ejaculation of abrupt speeches. Minute analysis of his method of representing *Shylock* is not available, but Colman's simile for the embodiment—"a black *Lear*"—conveys instructive significance both as to manner and aspect. He made his way to eminence despite serious physical disadvantages and harsh adversity of criticism. He died November 25, 1785, at the age of thirty-eight, and his ashes rest, near those of Garrick and Dr. Johnson, in the Poets' Corner of Westminster Abbey.

GEORGE FREDERICK COOKE.

George Frederick Cooke, who in his youth had seen Macklin as *Shylock,* followed in general the example

of that distinguished predecessor; yet while embodying *Shylock* as an odious incarnation of the diabolical
purpose of murderous revenge he tempered the
malignity of the character by an infusion of domestic
sentiment and grim piety. That turquoise ring which
Shylock 'had of *Leah* when he was a bachelor,' and
that oath of his, which he declares to have been regis-
tered in heaven, are the chief pretexts for that humanitarian gloss. Cooke's performance of *Shylock* was
first seen in London in 1800, and first seen in New
York in 1810. Mention is made of the savage exultation of his laugh when hearing *Tubal's* statement of
Antonio's losses, the electrical rapidity of his transitions of passion, and his mingled apprehension and
inveteracy when, replying to *Portia's* entreaty, "Bid
me *tear* the bond," the *Jew* ejaculates, "When it is
PAID—according to the tenor!" Shouts of applause
testified to the effect of his utterance of the tremendous
agony and rage of the Street Scene. "I can," wrote
his biographer, William Dunlap, "conceive of nothing
so perfectly 'the Jew that Shakespeare drew' as the
voice, face, manner, and expression of Cooke"; and,
according to that authority, "the whole of the Trial
Scene was inimitable in Cooke's hands," defying competition. When *Portia* spoke the line, "It is an attribute to God himself," he reverently bowed his head;
but when she said, "That same prayer doth teach us

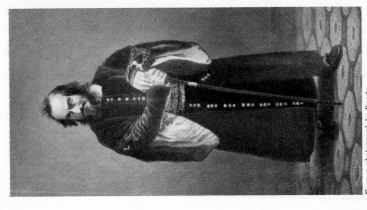

From a photograph by Brady

EDWIN FORREST AS *SHYLOCK*

WILLIAM CHARLES MACREADY AS *SHYLOCK*

FROM AN OLD PRINT

all to render the deeds of mercy," he made a movement
of head and hand to signify his rejection of the sentiment as something completely irrelevant to himself
and his race. Other performers of *Shylock* have used
that business in later years.

EDMUND KEAN.

Edmund Kean, whose great triumph in the part
of *Shylock* was achieved at Drury Lane, on a dreary
winter night, January 26, 1814, presented the *Jew*
as a creature of murderous malice, and yet of distinctively Hebraic majesty, and of what can perhaps
correctly be called Mosaic fanaticism, a relentless
adherence to the dogma "an eye for an eye and a tooth
for a tooth"; captivating the public, however, more by
the spell of terror, exerted in a whirlwind of conflict·
ing passions suddenly loosed out of cold, concentrated,
iron composure, than by a definite, coherent, rounded
impersonation. One of his greatly effective points
was a complete collapse at the climax of the Trial
Scene, when he spoke, in tones of overwhelming agony,
the abject supplication, "Nay, take my life and all,
pardon not that!" Most of the descriptions which
survive of Kean's acting are so charged with enthusiasm and so garnished with superlatives that they
bewilder more than they instruct; but, obviously, he

was a prodigy of genius. Kean was in the twenty-seventh year of his age when he gained this his first success on the London stage. His life had been one of continuous hardship. He was wretchedly poor. He was comparatively unknown. The directors of Drury Lane Theatre, however, had heard of him, and, being in urgent need of an attraction, they sent a person to see him, at one of the English provincial theatres, with authority to engage him, for London, in case his acting should, to that emissary, prove satisfactory. He was engaged, and on reaching the capital, accompanied by his wife and their infant son Charles, he obtained a lodging in the garret of a house in Cecil Street, Strand. Various obstacles were thrown in his way. The directors of Drury Lane patronized him, asking at first that they might hear him "recite," later declaring it would be judicious for him to make his first appearance in a minor part. The terms of his engagement stipulated that he should act only leading parts. He stood on his rights. He declined to recite and he declined to play second to anybody. The part of *Richard the Third* was then contemptuously offered to him, but, as he deemed his figure too diminutive for it, he refused to act in it. *"Shylock,* or nothing" was his final answer, and, after three other actors,—Stephen Kemble, ———— Tokely, and ———— Huddart,—had been put forward as the *Jew,* all of whom failed, he was announced for that part. One rehearsal was allowed to him,— on the morning preceding his first appearance,—at which rehearsal he so restrained his powers and concealed his purpose as to impress all observers with a confident belief that he would fail. The day preceding his crucial effort had been wet, cold, and gloomy; the evening was desolate and bleak. When he left his miserable lodging, to walk to the theatre, through drizzle and slush, he was heard to murmur, "I wish that I was going to be shot!" In a poor, inconvenient dressing-room at Drury Lane, which he was shamefully necessitated to share with two of the minor actors, he put on the gabardine of *Shylock,* and, for the first time in the stage history of that character, a *black* wig,—instead of a red one,—thereby inciting the surprise and the contemptuously expressed pity of the manager. Then came the wonderful performance,—the totally unexpected revelation of tremendous power, terrific tragic passion, imperial authority, and intense feeling,—a performance which had proceeded only a little way when the theatre resounded with the applause of an astounded and delighted audience, and at the fall of the curtain after the Street Scene one of the most signal victories had been gained that ever have been achieved in the history of the Stage. Hazlitt, representing "The London Morning Chronicle," chanced to be present, and he sounded the first note of the resonant acclamation which,—notwithstanding quarrels and qualifications,—ever since has followed the acting of Edmund Kean.

JUNIUS BRUTUS BOOTH.—WILLIAM CHARLES MACREADY.— CHARLES KEAN.

Junius Brutus Booth as *Shylock* took the imaginative, exalted view of the character, laying particular emphasis on those intimations of racial pomp and religious austerity which predilection for the ideal of the pious and majestic Hebrew discerns in such phrases as "our holy Abraham," "at our synagogue," and "An oath, an oath! I have an oath in heaven"; at the same time, like Edmund Kean, he wrought his chief effect by means of the *Jew's* delirium, thrilling his hearers by the tempest of emotion, the frenzied ebullition of commingled impulses and contrasted passions,—avarice, fury, resentment, and snarling, murderous malignity,—in the Street Scene. There is a published letter in which Edwin Booth, writing to the eminent Shakespeare scholar Horace Howard Furness, expresses his belief that Cooke, Edmund Kean, and the elder Booth followed the Macklin tradition and presented *Shylock* as "grotesque in make-up

and general treatment." Cooke, undoubtedly, copied
Macklin's method, and yet even of Cooke it is
recorded that he sounded a note of pathos in the
performance: but Edmund Kean and J. B. Booth
deviated widely from the model set by Macklin. It
was of Kean's *Shylock* that Douglas Jerrold said it
was "like a chapter of Genesis,"—meaning that, in
its stern, bleak simplicity, it was austere, hard,
peremptory, decisive; incarnating the Mosaic idea of
inexorable Law; and Hazlitt, Kean's ardent admirer
and advocate, intimated that his performance of the
Jew was essentially unlike that of Macklin (which
he had never seen: Macklin, who finally retired from
the stage in 1789, died when Hazlitt was only eleven
years old), and superior to it. The elder Booth's
Shylock is specifically described by his faithful and
reverent chronicler, Thomas R. Gould, and obviously
it did not resemble that of Macklin. "He made
it," says Gould, "the *representative Hebrew:* the
type of a race as old as the world. He drew
the character in lines of *simple grandeur,* and filled
it with fiery energy. In his hands it was marked
by pride of intellect; by intense pride of race; by a
reserved force, as if there centred in him the might
of a people whom neither time, nor scorn, nor political
oppression could subdue; and which has, at successive
periods, even down to our own day, drawn the atten-

tion of mankind towards its frequent examples of intellectual power."

Macready's ideal of *Shylock,* which he presented in his customary admirable style of minute elaboration and complete symmetry, was not, as historic commentary has sometimes declared, the majestic Israelite, intent to avenge upon the Christian the accumulated wrongs of his "sacred nation," but a creature compact of austerity and murderous malice. He declared the opinion that the character is "composed of harshness," and that *Shylock's* anguish relative to the loss of the ring of *Leah* is only the suffering of wounded cupidity. His delivery of one sentence, *"Nearest his heart*—those are the very words," which was horrible in its expression of hatred and exultant cruelty, signified the intrinsic spirit of his performance.

Charles Kean not only made *Shylock* a *quaint* character but also he made him, at some moments, noble and winning,—a condition absolutely incongruous with Shakespeare's *Jew.* His ideal, accordingly, was measurably incorrect: his execution was deft and admirable. In aspect and demeanor Kean was austere and formidable, and he employed in his performance many of the striking devices of stage business which had been used by Edmund Kean, his father. His delivery was generally correct, but occasionally it was marred by his "pudding voice" enunciation,—as when, in the Trial Scene, he besought the *Duke of Venice,* saying:

" Nay, take my life and all; pardon not *dat:*
You take my house when you do take *de* prop
Dat doth sustain my house; you take my life
When you do take the *beans* whereby I live."

Edwin Forrest sometimes acted *Shylock,* but early in his career he discarded the part, as also he did that of *Iago,*—"on account," says his chief biographer, Alger, "of his extreme distaste for the parts, and his unwillingness to bear the ideal hate and loathing they awakened in spectators." There is a record which alleges, on the authority of "an old actor of the Bowery Theatre, New York," that Forrest, in his early days, when playing *Shylock,* was accustomed to include in his equipment for the Trial Scene a small whetstone with which to sharpen his knife preparatory to the cutting of the "pound of flesh."

EDWIN THOMAS BOOTH.

Edwin Booth, in his younger days, when acting *Shylock,* endeavored to express the same ideal of that character which had been shown by his father, but later he discarded that ideal and presented *Shylock* as the relentless revenger of personal indignities,—an injured, insulted, bitterly resentful man, animated by a vindictive, implacable hatred, intensified by racial and religious antipathy. In his letter to Furness, already mentioned, Booth wrote:

"I think Macready was *the first* to lift the uncanny Jew out of the darkness of his native element of revengeful selfishness into the light of *the venerable Hebrew, the Martyr, the Avenger.* He has had several followers, and I once tried to view him in that light, but he doesn't cast a shadow sufficiently strong to contrast with the sunshine of the comedy. . . . *'Twas the money value of Leah's ring that he grieved over,* not its association with her, else he would have shown some affection for her daughter."

It is notable, as a coincidence of thought, that Macready, many years before Booth thus expressed his judgment, had not only written, of *Shylock,* that the part is "composed of harshness," but also had set forth the identical conclusion reached by Booth relative to *Shylock's* interest in Leah's ring.

Booth's first great revival of "The Merchant of Venice" was effected at the old Winter Garden Theatre, New York, on January 28, 1867, when he accomplished a production of that comedy not before equalled and not surpassed until Henry Irving revived the play, November 1, 1879. The scenery, painted by Henry Hilliard and Charles Witham, from original pictures of streets and buildings in Venice, not only presented a faithful transcript of selected beauties of the "Sea Cybele," but constituted a magnificent pageant. The principal scenes were the Rialto, the Church of San Giovanni, the Place of St. Mark, a Hall in *Portia's* House at Belmont, and the Hall of the Senate. The first Rialto scene was animated by the passage to and fro of many persons, intent on various occupations, and it was happily suggestive of the actual life of the city. On April 12, 1869, Booth effected another fine revival of "The Merchant of Venice," this time at Booth's Theatre, New York. In making an acting version of "The Merchant" he followed a custom which had long prevailed, cutting the play in such a manner as to make it serviceable chiefly to the prominence of *Shylock* and ending it with the *Jew's* exit, at the close of the Trial Scene,—the last words spoken being those of *Gratiano,*—"To bring thee to the gallows, not the font." That version he used for many years, but after forming his professional alliance with Lawrence Barrett, in 1887, he rectified his stage copy, and, influenced by the example of Henry Irving, restored the end of the Fourth Act, and also the whole of the Fifth Act,—excepting only those few lines in it of indelicate speech, which good taste does not tolerate and always must exclude.

It was my privilege, in association with Edwin

Booth, to edit,—1877-78,—the sixteen plays that constituted his customary repertory, and those plays
were subjects of our frequent discussion. At that
time my views of the character of *Shylock* were
colored by the ingenious and persuasive but fanciful
expositions of it that had been set forth by such
authoritative writers as Hermann Ulrici, Ludwig
Bœrne, and Victor Hugo, and I urged Booth to present
a majestic Hebrew of the old Bible. I was mistaken.
His ideal, on the contrary, had been then derived
exclusively from Shakespeare, and it was correct.
There was pathos, at certain moments, in his personation of *Shylock,* but it was the spontaneous, involuntary ebullition of his innate sensibility, and in
particular it evinced itself in the exquisite melody of
his sympathetic voice: he touched the hearts of his
hearers because he could not help doing so. At certain times, indeed, the delivery of Booth was perfunctory, languid, tame: he was an uneven actor and of
many moods, not a machine: but no words can
describe the glow of his spirit and the music of his
tones when once his feelings had been fully aroused
through that sympathy with which a powerful imagination can inspire the mind. His impersonation of
Shylock blended subtle craft with grim humor, but
also it blended burning passion with Oriental dignity;
and his method was, in various particulars, original.

The custom had been for *Shylock* to make his first entrance following *Bassanio*. Booth began the scene with a picture: *Shylock* was "discovered" standing, midway, on a short, broad flight of steps, where he had at that moment paused, at mention of the sum of money which *Bassanio* wished him to lend to *Antonio,* and *Bassanio* was visible, in the act of turning away, as if impatient at the *Jew's* hesitation. Thus poised, *Shylock* spoke his first words, "Three thousand ducats—*Well?*" Then, as the colloquy proceeded, *Shylock* advanced, *Antonio* entered, and the climax of the scene was reached in Booth's fervid delivery of the apostrophe to the *Merchant*, in which suppressed passion burned and glowed beneath a glitter of sarcasm. The First Act was ended with another picture,—*Antonio* and *Bassanio* departing together, and *Shylock,* at first, moving in the contrary direction, then pausing to turn and gaze after them, with a look of horrible hate and gesture of menace, as he spoke the lines, transposed from the *Jailer's* Scene (Act III., Sc. 3):

> "Thou call'dst me dog, before thou hadst a cause;
> But, since I *am* a *dog*, BEWARE my fangs!"

The humanity of the man he embodied was vitiated by evil, but it was humanity. The thrilling dramatic effects that he caused were provided in the tremendous speech which begins "To bait fish withal" and ends with "It shall go hard but I will better the instruction," and in the horrid ejaculation of wicked triumph, —exultant, jubilant, inexpressibly terrible,—of *Shylock's* joy on hearing of *Antonio's* losses: "I thank God! I thank God!" In the Trial Scene his movements were slow, precise, exact, predominant, massive, as of inexorable power; his face was rigid and pale; his eyes burned darkly; there was an occasional tinge of grisly humor in his delivery: the total effect was that of the vibrant, observant poise of a deadly reptile, aware of its lethal potency, and in no haste, although unalterably determined, to make use of it.

The dress that Booth wore when acting *Shylock* was distinctively Hebraic and strikingly expressive of Oriental character. It comprised a long, close-fitting gown, dark green in color; a dark brown gabardine, with flowing sleeves and a hood; a scarf, of variegated colors, twisted around the waist so as to form a girdle; a leather pouch, dependent from the scarf; pointed shoes, of red leather; a Phrygian cap, having a turned-up rim, about two inches wide; ear-rings; several finger rings, and a ring on the thumb of the left hand. The face was made up thin and haggard. The beard was grizzled. The head,—in the actor's earlier days,—was dressed with a "black-bald" wig; later, with a gray wig, bald on the crown.

EDWIN BOOTH AS *SHYLOCK*

FROM THE DRAWING BY W. J. HENNESSEY

In his right hand he carried a long, gnarled staff. His appearance, as fittingly described by himself, was "grotesque," but also it was tragic. The picture of Booth drawn by that conscientious, sympathetic, felicitous artist William J. Hennesy, in 1872,—one of a series made to illustrate a book of mine called "Edwin Booth in Twelve Dramatic Characters,"— shows exactly his make-up and appearance in the part, and especially it exhibits the "grotesque" aspect which, especially in early life, he imputed to the *Jew*, and which he intentionally emphasized in present-ment: but that picture, useful and instructive though it is, does not convey any impression of Booth's final ideal of *Shylock,* or signify in the least the lurid passion and terrific power with which that ideal was embodied by him.

VARIOUS PERFORMERS.

Many assumptions of *Shylock* have been shown on the stage, in England and America, since the time of Macklin, some of which might repay a studious examination, even though commentary on them should compel a monotonous ringing of the changes between miscreant and martyr,—*Shylock* having been presented in both ways. Names that are more or less con-spicuously associated with the part in the annals of the

English Theatre are those of Colley Cibber, Lacy
Ryan, —— Rosco, Richard Yates, William Smith,
John Philip Kemble, Joseph George Holman, Edward
Shuter, West Digges, Thomas Sheridan, Thomas King,
Stephen Kemble, George Bennett, William Dowton,—
who is said to have assumed the *Jew* by request of Lord
Byron, and who was practically laughed off the stage,
—George Bartley, Thomas Ryder, John Harley,
Robert William Elliston, Charles John Kean, Gus-
tavus Vaughan Brooke, Samuel Phelps, John Ryder,
and Herman Vezin. On the American Stage "The
Merchant of Venice" was performed for the first
time, September 5, 1752, at Williamsburg, Virginia,
—being the second of the plays of Shakespeare acted
in America. Notable performers of *Shylock* in the
early days of the American Theatre were John Henry
and Thomas Abthorpe Cooper. Later representatives
of the part were John Vandenhoff, 1840; James
Booth Roberts, 1846; Charles W. Couldock, 1853;
James William Wallack, 1855; Edward Loomis
Davenport; John McCullough, Lawrence Barrett,
Richard Mansfield, Robert Mantell, and Edward
Hugh Sothern. *Shylock* was acted in New York
by Macready in 1844, and by Charles Kean in
1845. Couldock, when first he played the part in
the American capital, appeared at Castle Garden.
When "The Merchant of Venice" was produced at

Wallack's Theatre,—the old Broadway and Broome Street house,—in 1858, it held the stage thirty-three nights and that was recorded as "a longer run than ever before enjoyed by a Shakespearean production." The elder Wallack acted *Shylock,*—his son Lester Wallack acting *Bassanio,* and Mrs. Hoey (Josephine Shaw) *Portia.* Many years afterward, Lester Wallack, speaking to me of that performance, said that his father "was best in *Shylock,*" representing him as an injured, suffering man, and deeply affecting the feelings of his audience. That method of acting *Shylock* has been pursued by most of the foreign actors who have essayed the part in America.

FOREIGN ACTORS.

BANDMANN.—DAWISON.—NOVELLI.

Among the presentments of *Shylock* which have been given upon the American Stage by European actors, speaking foreign languages, the most notable were those of Daniel Edward Bandmann,—who, however, acted the part in both German and English,— Bogumil Dawison, Ernst von Possart, and Ermete Novelli. Bandmann, a Jew, of German lineage, asserted the majestic Hebrew racial ideal, and being, in his youth, a wild enthusiast, gave a performance that was fraught with hectic, ever-varying emotion and physical force. Possart presented a similar ideal with better art. Dawison,—who, on the German Stage, was accounted second only to the renowned Devrient,— much excelled them both. He acted the part in such a way as to exemplify the concrete results obtained in the portrayal of it according to German theatrical custom. Novelli illustrated the Italian view of the character.

The first performance of *Shylock* given in America by Dawison occurred at the Stadt Theatre, New York, September 30, 1866, and by his compatriots it was received with enthusiastic approbation and extolled as one of eminent worth. The chief merits of it were authority and executive skill. The chief defect of it was an indefinable yet clearly perceptible pettiness in the quality, fibre, or essence of the character. Whatever else *Shylock* may not be, he *is* terrible. Dawison's embodiment evinced duplicity, greed, and implacable malignity, but, notwithstanding his uncommon advantages of physical stature and intellectual force, it was not terrific. In the nature of a man who, —at great risk, in the centre of a community bitterly hostile to his race and specially inimical to himself,— will, at the sacrifice of almost every advantage he might please to exact, continuously persist in a course of murderous cruelty, intent to "have the heart" of his victim, there is nothing puny. Dawison's expression of his ideal was generally beautiful in its skill: the dress was skilfully fashioned to accentuate the height and leanness of the figure; the elocution was exact, fluent, and consistent, marked by a slight accent, intended to denote that *Shylock* is a foreigner in Venice, and that accent was intensified in moments of vehement utterance. The business with the knife, in the Trial Scene, when, after fumbling for it, *Shylock* produced it from a pouch, was artificial and clumsy, yet the modelling, the process of sculpture, was, in general, superb. There was no use of transparency,—no impartment of the *Jew's* subtle, deadly venom, making it obvious to the spectators, while concealing it from the dramatic interlocutors. Dawison's *Shylock,* like many others which have been seen, did not, in facial aspect, disclose any trace of the ravages of evil passions long privately indulged and more fiercely convulsive of the mind because pent up and hidden. The making of his bargain with *Antonio* was shrewd and tricky, rather than speciously crafty. In the Second Act he was unimportant. In the Street Scene he was fiery and effective. In the Trial Scene he concentrated attention upon himself not only by his personal magnetism, but by an arrangement of the stage which crowded the other characters into the background and the corners. As a whole the personation remains in memory as an able and effective display of an incorrect and inadequate ideal.

The attempt to act *Shylock* that was made by the Italian comedian Novelli was mournfully abortive. That eminent foreign performer made his first appearance on the American Stage, in Boston, in 1907, and on March 17, that year, appeared for the first time in New York, at the Lyric Theatre, acting in a play called "Papa Lebonnard." Later he presented himself in a concoction which was obtruded as Shakespeare's tragedy of "King Lear," and still later he produced a version of "The Merchant of Venice," understood to have been made by himself, and appeared as *Shylock*. His dress comprised long trousers, a short jacket, a cloak, a large turban, and a profusion of long gray hair and beard. His ideal of the character was seen to be simply ignominious, his *Shylock* being nothing more than a trivial Jew pawnbroker. He was neither tremendous as the representative of inexorable Mosaic Law nor terrible as the pursuer of a murderous revenge. The fable of the original play remained; the conduct of it had been so materially altered that all continuity was broken and nothing survived but a hybrid, tediously episodical patchwork. *Shylock* was converted into an eccentric low comedy part, a trivial trickster, a sly contriver of mischief, a commonplace creature of low cunning and petty spite. The method pursued in the action was that which is miscalled "natural." The style was finical, a confused style, full of spasmodic gesture and grimace, inclusive of much spreading and pointing of the fingers, much shaking of the legs, much teetering, much pulling of mugs and wagging of beards, much facial contortion, much confidential whispering, and generally inappropriate detail. *Shylock* first appeared on the balcony of his house, in response to a call from *Bassanio:* he then descended and came into the street to discuss the business of the loan. He snared his Christian oppressors,—who were easily snared,—in a vein of coarse pleasantry. While conferring as to the desired loan he fumbled a string of gems, which were a part of his apparel,—the apparel, that is, of a wily usurer who, in Shakespeare's play, is scrupulous to declare that he must *borrow* money in order to lend it. After he had agreed to lend the money he departed, arm-in-arm, with *Bassanio* and *Antonio,* as though, in amity and social equality, they were going to "the notary's": in Shakespeare's text, it is expressly appointed that they shall *meet* there. When *Shylock* gave his keys to *Jessica* he hitched them to a string that she had let down to him, from the balcony, and by that same string *Jessica* presently let down the box of ducats and jewels which she steals, in her elopement. Signor

Novelli's *Shylock* was also a highly sensitive father, shedding copious tears over his daughter's flight. Much of the tempestuous Street Scene was played by him in a sitting posture, the *Jew* telling beads while he gasped, hissed, and wheezed,—the sequence of the scene being destroyed by transpositions. When *Shylock* recited the passage, "if a Jew wrong a Christian," Signor Novelli rose from a seated attitude, moved into the centre of the stage, and beckoned to *Salarino* and *Salanio,* twiddling the four fingers of each hand, palm down, with a crab-like motion, to summon them,—to which summons those Christians, with a compliance truly wonderful in the Venice of the period, at once obediently responded: and then he delivered the great speech as though arguing about the price of a second-hand waistcoat. When he heard of the losses of *Antonio* his expedient was to dance, infirmly, with senile joy. At the parting with *Tubal* he pursued that Israelite, shouting "At our synagogue" while off the stage, and then returned, prancing and teetering, in the manner of Pantaloon in the pantomime. In the Trial Scene he sat on the steps, before the desk of *Balthasar,* and, removing one of his red morocco slippers, laid it across his lap, sharpened his knife on it, and then, plucking a hair from his beard, tried the edge of the knife, in the manner of a barber. When he was offered the choice between death and apostasy, he allowed spittle to drool over his beard; then, almost in collapse, he tottered out of the Court, but immediately returned, strong and insolent, and hurled a defiance at the Doge such as would have caused his instant incarceration if not his doom of death. If an English-speaking actor were to offer such a performance as Novelli did and call it *Shylock,* he would be overwhelmed with ridicule. Presented by an Italian actor it was considerably applauded and not a little commended in print.

DAVENPORT.—McCULLOUGH.—BARRETT.

Davenport was one of the best of American actors, and, in point of versatility, one of the most extraordinary actors of whom record exists,—having been equally proficient and admirable in tragedy, comedy, and farce. His impersonation of *Sir Giles Overreach* nearly equalled that of the elder Booth,—with whom, in youth, he acted and whose example he followed, in that part,—and it has not been rivalled. His impersonation of Shakespeare's *Brutus* remained peerless until Edwin Booth assumed that character. As *Duke Aranza,* in "The Honeymoon," he was perfection. His *Hamlet* was, for many years, accepted as a true embodiment of the melancholy Dane. His performance of *Macbeth* blended poetry of ideal, imaginative treatment, and competent physical power, and it was one of the most impressive portrayals of that supremely difficult part ever given on our stage. Davenport acted *Shylock,* in a four-act version of the comedy, but his ideal was contradictory, and his expression of it lacked consistency. In the earlier scenes his *Shylock* was a crafty, evil schemer; in the middle scenes he became an image of incarnate ferocity, —the actor then yielding himself to the tragic mood and employing the tragic method, liberating a frenzied fury of wounded avarice and savage, murderous hatred, and causing an effect of wild excitement; at the last, abruptly, he assumed the guise of the majestic Hebrew, the authentic representative of his "sacred nation," the ordained avenger of an outraged race and religion. The portrayal, accordingly, while full of professional talent, exemplified only a fruitless effort to blend and unify opposed and irreconcilable attributes. The words of *Shylock* were, to Davenport, as familiar as the alphabet, yet in utterance he often jumbled or transposed them. He did not much care for the part and his best powers were not evoked by it. In person he was tall, massive, and handsome, having a thoughtful face, regular features, blue eyes, a strong, melodious voice, and an engaging manner. Like many other tragedians whom I have known, he was, in private life, genial and humorous.

John McCullough's repertory included *Shylock,* but his performance of the *Jew* was conventional and, comparatively, unimportant. Like Davenport, he was, by temperament, antipathetic to the character, and he could not get inside of it. He copied the model set by Edwin Forrest, employing the customary business and making the customary points. Both McCullough and Davenport required, for absolutely the most predominant, winning expression of which they were capable, parts which implicate the heart, the affections, the noble, the manly, the heroic, the magnanimous conditions and aspects of human nature,—such parts as *Othello, Virginius,* and *Damon.* Davenport, indeed, by means of his thorough, practised art and his keen, perceptive intellect, triumphed also in other realms, but his most influential achievements were those of good, not evil.

Lawrence Barrett's impersonation of *Shylock* was among the best that have been seen. He had profited by the example of Edwin Booth, and he was, indeed, one of the most conspicuous examples of the active influence of that wonderful man. He rejected the theory which would endeavor to make the *Jew* an austere image of retributive Justice, and embodied him correctly, as the implacable avenger of personal wrongs,—presenting, at first under a cold, crafty yet specious exterior but later without disguise, a fierce and dangerous nature, full of hatred and malice, a darkly and wildly passionate man, intent on revenge and inexorable in his resolve to obtain it. His personation, however, is chiefly memorable for exactness and beauty of execution, not for originality of ideal or treatment. He had studied the traditional business devised by Edmund Kean and also that of the elder Booth, practically all of which, at one time or another, was transmitted by Edwin Booth, and in using much of that business, and in following the examples selected, he splendidly evinced that fine intellect, intense feeling, and copious nervous energy for which he was remarkable. His delivery of the speech beginning "To bait fish withal!" was a whirlwind of passion: his demeanor throughout the Trial Scene was that of invincible authority, deadly purpose, and secret exultation, which contrasted with his final exit and made it finely pathetic in effect. In the death of Lawrence Barrett, which was sudden,—befalling on March 20, 1891, almost at the moment when he could have commanded and shaped the destiny of our Theatre, which he would have done, had he lived, as absolutely as Henry Irving did that of the British Theatre,—the American Stage suffered a prodigious, an afflicting, and an almost irretrievable disaster.

CHARACTER OF *SHYLOCK.*

Two considerable reasons for the enduring popularity of *Shylock* are the startling authenticity of the character as a complete exponent of human hatred, and the absolute excellence of the part as a medium for dramatic impersonation. That celestial humility which, when wrongfully stricken upon the face, can and does "turn the other cheek" involves a wondrous element of self-control and lovely patience, and, theoretically, it is practicable. The iron doctrine of the Law, "An eye for an eye and a tooth for a tooth," on the other hand, is eminently human, and unregenerated humanity cordially approves and generally acts upon it. The notion that *Shylock's* conduct can be justified is preposterous, notwithstanding the vindicatory arguments that have been put into his mouth. There is abundant reason for his conduct. Persecuted the "sacred nation" unquestionably had been, when Shakespeare wrote "The Merchant of Venice," and persecuted it continues to be, in some places,—although, in America, it is rapidly coming into possession of its inheritance, the Earth,—and certainly it is no longer remarkable for sufferance or humility. *Shylock,* enduring with patient fortitude and without rancor the insults and injuries heaped upon him, would be one of the noblest and most sympathetic characters in literature. The wrongs to which he is subjected neither justify nor extenuate his proceedings, but his rehearsal of them does irresistibly appeal to the sense of "fair play," and that tremendous speech beginning "Hath not a Jew eyes?" is overwhelming in its cogent reasoning and lurid eloquence: it crystallizes the whole being of *Shylock* into a gem of light, and it remains, and will always remain, the final word on the subject of his character. It is a marvel of rhetoric. It scorches like devouring flame. It shrivels and annihilates all the sentimental sophistry with which mistaken theorists have tried to invest the character. It is superlative, whether for logic, passion, or the spontaneous, fiery ejaculation of inveterate malignity: and it prevails. It states *Shylock's* motive,—Hate, inspired by wrong: and it states his purpose,—Revenge, not Vengeance. The *Jew* is abhorrent and detestable, but he is "within his rights"; and whenever he is greatly represented, notwithstanding his infernal wickedness, he possesses a horrible grandeur, as the emblem of terror and the example of that retributive ruin which inevitably overtakes those persons who seek revenge. " 'Vengeance is mine,' saith the Lord: 'I will repay.' "

Those strenuous efforts which were begun long ago, on the stage, to read into the character of *Shylock*

various genial attributes which are alleged to be
elemental in humanity,—affection, parental solicitude,
pious devotion, and the like,—have been industriously
continued in recent times. The *Jew,* it is asserted,
has been an ardent lover and a good husband; is a
good father; is devout; is fraternal with other Israel-
ites; is exemplary as a citizen; keeps a "sober house";
frequents the synagogue, and respects the laws. Those
assertions are transparently irrelevant. Aside from
the allusion to Leah's ring,—"I would not have given
it for a wilderness of monkeys,"—there is nothing in
the play to suggest affection on the part of *Shylock*
for his dead wife: his daughter specifically describes
their home as "hell," and there is no word spoken
or action performed to warrant the ascription to *Shylock* of any qualities except such as appertain to a
bigoted, perverted mind, an embittered heart, a
nature saturated with guile and malice and cor-
roded by resentful suffering through long years of
oppression and by the consuming fires of evil passion.
Shylock deceitfully cajoles *Bassanio* into consenting
that *Antonio* shall sign the bond, by declaring that he
would not, under any circumstances, exact the penalty. He expressly declares that the transaction is
a jest,—"a merry sport." When suggesting this
"merry bond" to *Antonio,* he carelessly specifies
that,

" If you repay me not on such a day,
  In such a place, such sum or sums as are
  Express'd in the condition, let the forfeit
  Be nominated for an equal pound
  Of your fair flesh, to be cut off and taken
  In what part of your body pleaseth me " ;

but when the bond has become forfeit and is produced in Court the fact appears that, in the actual
execution of it, the *Jew* has been scrupulously careful
to insert in it a deadly exactitude of specification: the
pound of flesh is to be cut from the merchant's
"breast";—*"Nearest his heart: those* are the very
words!" He plainly declares his purpose in com-
passing the death of his enemy: that purpose is not
only Revenge but the obtainance of a clear field for
usury. "Were *he* out of Venice, *I* could *make what
merchandise* I would." Whatever *Shylock* may
originally have been (and in every form of evil that
comes through human birth there is some admixt-
ure of good), he has become incarnate wickedness,
and he is not the less a monstrous villain because he
is an insulted man and a legal creditor.

HENRY IRVING.

The most thoroughly consistent, absorbingly interesting, and decisively paramount impersonation of *Shylock*

that has been seen within the last sixty years,—and, in
its maturity, as I believe, after weighing the recorded
evidence, the best ever given,—was that of Henry
Irving. That great actor had studied the subject with
microscopic scrutiny, and he knew every fibre of it. His
opinion relative to the earlier performances of the part
was expressed to me in the remark that, as far as his
reading and observation had enabled him to judge,
Henderson was the greatest of the actors of the Garrick period, and I believe he considered that Henderson gave the true ideal. *"Shylock,"* he said, in my
presence, "is a bloody-minded monster,—but you
mustn't play him so, if you wish to succeed; you
must get some sympathy with him." In old times
"The Merchant of Venice" was invariably offered for
the sake of *Shylock* alone, and with that purpose it
was cut and condensed. In Henry Irving's version it
was given for the sake of all that it contains, and
given, substantially, as Shakespeare wrote it; and
when it is thus given,—that is, not merely with single
design to display the semi-tragical *Jew,* but also with
intelligent purpose to exhibit and enforce its constituents of pure, high comedy,—the romantic story of
Portia becomes the most engaging part of it, and the
character of *Portia* becomes conspicuous. In Irving's
presentment of it a fine equilibrium was preserved
between the parts, and while the bloodthirsty *Jew,*

intent on obtaining his pound of flesh, was kept at a proportional level, the serene presence of *Portia* dominated an enchanting picture of friendship vindicated and love fulfilled,—the massive weight and propulsive force of *Shylock,* nevertheless, remaining unimpaired: *Portia* was the fascination: *Shylock* was the power.

Irving's production of "The Merchant of Venice" was first effected at the London Lyceum Theatre, on November 1, 1879, and it was first shown in America, at the Star Theatre, New York, on November 6, 1883. The expenditure of money on this revival was small,—only $60,000,—but the setting was made with exact knowledge, sound judgment, and superlative taste, and artistically it was the most elaborate and complete presentment of this play that has been seen. Special felicities of investiture and detail in it were the pictures of the Place of St. Mark; the passing and repassing of traders on the Rialto; the almost spectral gondolas, gliding along a shadowy canal; the opulent variety of the scenes in *Portia's* House, at Belmont; the use of clashing cymbals, making wild, Oriental music, to signalize the arrival and departure of the *Prince of Morocco; Shylock's* grim return to his desolated home, which, during his absence, had been despoiled by his treacherous daughter and her lover,—a return effected in gathering gloom, immediately after an episode of tumultuous revelry, the distant sounds of music being still faintly audible, —a poetically effective treatment, devised by Irving, which has since been copied in almost every representation of the comedy; the restoration of *Shylock's* scene with the *Jailer* and *Antonio,*—time and opportunity being thus, by implication, duly allowed for the marriages of *Bassanio* and *Portia* and *Gratiano* and *Nerissa;* the opulent pageantry of the Venetian Court; and the lovely, moon-lit summer-night picture of *Portia's* Garden.

When Irving first acted *Shylock* he manifested a poetically humanitarian ideal of the part, and, like those eminently pictorial actors, his predecessors in the character, Robert William Elliston and James William Wallack (whom he had never seen, but of whom, naturally, he possessed the tradition), he indicated the *Jew* as the venerable Hebrew patriarch, the lonely, grieved widower, and the affectionate, while austere, father. He failed not, indeed, to present *Shylock* as the *vengeful* representative antagonist of intolerant Christian persecution of the Jewish race and religion, but he personated a man, originally humane, who had become embittered by cruel injustice, without having entirely lost the essential attributes of average humanity. His garments were scrupulously arranged, his aspect was neat, his demeanor was formal,—even to the extent of suggesting the "smug" decorum at which he sneers, when describing *Antonio* ("That used to come so *smug* upon the mart"), his action was restrained, and in the fundamental, propulsive motive of his performance there was more of racial oppugnancy than of personal hatred. As time passed, however, a radical change in the personation was, little by little effected, till at last, without entire abandonment of a purpose and power to awaken sympathy, it became the true *Shylock* of Shakespeare—hard, merciless, inexorable, terrible. Thus matured, Irving's *Jew* was a man upon whom,—while his every thought was colored and every purpose directed by racial antipathy and religious fanaticism,—social oppression had so wrought as to develop only the most radically evil propensities; a representative Hebrew, who, while revering "our sacred nation," swearing by *"our* holy Abraham," and *"our* holy Sabbath," having "an oath in heaven" and urging the sanctity of it, is animated by the wicked purpose of a murderous personal *revenge.* The work of art which shows the possible depravity of human nature should justify its exhibition by an impartment of warning, by an inherent admonitory exposition of the bleak, miserable loneliness of the soul that has succumbed to Evil, the corrosive, withering effect, alike upon the physical system and the spiritual being, of that fatal surrender to sin which

abandons the heart to wicked passions. Irving's
mature, final embodiment of *Shylock* imparted that
warning, and in such a way as to impress it on the
memory forever: and it was by means of the moral
influence thus exerted in association with the charm of
his magnetic personality that the actor excited pity
and gained a certain rueful sympathy with a character
that is terrible, displayed in conduct that is monstrous.
The consummate skill of Irving, informed by profound knowledge of human nature and guided by
unerring judgment, wrought every essential detail,
however minute, into every fabric of dramatic art that
he presented, but perhaps his portrayal of *Shylock,*
more distinctively than any other single work of his,
excepting *Becket,* exemplified his marvellous faculty
of impersonation,—that faculty as to which, considering breadth of range, wisdom of choice, precision
of touch, and uniformity and thoroughness of execution, he was unequalled in our time, and, probably, has not been equalled in any period or in any
land.

Irving's *Shylock* entered, for the first time, preceding *Bassanio,* who, obviously, had found him in
the mart and spoken to him about a loan of money.
He was seen to be a man stricken in years—his
shoulders a little bowed, his knees a little bent,
his face lined and wrinkled, his hair gray,—*"old*

Shylock" in every detail,—but hardy, resolute, formidable, possessing the steel-sinewy, nervous vitality of the Hebrew race, and animated by indomitable will. His aspect was distinctively Jewish, and it was Orientally pictorial. His demeanor revealed a mind intensely interested, veiling that interest by a crafty assumption of indifference. His detested enemy had applied to him, to borrow money: that fact was singular, was astonishing; there might be no consequence in it, or there might proceed from it the opportunity, for which he had long hungered and thirsted, to strike that enemy dead. *Bassanio* must be made to repeat his request, and the matter must be carefully considered. One skirt of the *Jew's* gabardine,—a garment of rich material but of sober hue and well-worn,—was caught up at the side and held in the right hand, which also held a black crutchstick, grasping it near the middle and more as though it were a weapon than a prop. Throughout the opening scene the mention by *Shylock* of the ducats desired by *Antonio* was made in a lingering, caressing tone, involuntarily expressive of his love of money, and the thumb and first two fingers of whichever hand happened to be free,—for he shifted his staff occasionally from one hand to the other,—were, from time to time, moved slowly, as though in the act of counting coins. The first speech, "Three thousand ducats—

From a photograph by Lock and Whitfield

HENRY IRVING AS *SHYLOCK*

Well?" only noted the sum, with an accent of inquiry;
the second speech, "For three months:—Well?" indicated watchful expectation of something to follow;
but the third speech, "*Antonio* shall become *bound*,"
was uttered with a strong emphasis on the merchant's
name and on the word "bound," accompanied by a
momentary flash of lurid fire in the dark, piercing,
baleful eyes, a quick contraction of the muscles of
arms and hands, instantly succeeded by a perfect
resumption of self-control, as the calm, cold voice,
reiterated the recurring question, "Well?"   The utterance of the declaration "I *will* be *assured* I may" was
sharp, incisive, almost fierce, but the tone quickly
softened in delivery of the words that immediately
follow.   The rebuff beginning "Yes, to smell pork,"
was ejaculated in a bitter tone of contemptuous protest, till the close, when the words "nor *pray* with you"
were spoken in accents of deep solemnity. Then *Shylock* saw and recognized the approaching figure of
Antonio,—a fact signified in the expression of his
face, before he asked, with an entire change of manner,
in a nonchalant, indifferent way, "What news on the
Rialto?"   He then raised his left hand, as though to
shade his eyes, and gazed intently into the distance,
saying "Who is he comes here?"   There was in the
action of Irving's *Shylock,* at that and at some other
points, a viperous impartment of the *Jew's* inherent

treachery and deep-seated malice—the duplicity which
is characteristically false in circumstances in which it
would be much easier to be true. *Bassanio* left the
scene, to meet his friend *Antonio,* while *Shylock,* alone,
delivered the self-communing speech which follows,
not as an "aside," but as a soliloquy, gazing malevo-
lently at the Christian friends, and contemptuously
mimicking their greeting of one another. The line "How
like a *fawning publican* he looks!" was spoken with
a loathing sneer, a peculiar long, soft emphasis of contempt and scorn being laid on the word "fawning,"
but that sneer instantly gave place to a glare of
reptile hate, as the avowal of bitterest animosity
was harshly snarled forth, with significant and appropriate stress on the second word of the second line:

> " I *hate* him, for he is a Christian,
>   But MORE, for that, in low simplicity,
>   He lends out money *gratis.*"

Shylock was shown to be aware of the *Merchant's*
approach, but also he was shown to assume, because of
sheer, innate duplicity, an air of preoccupation, as
though ignorant of the contiguity of the man whom
thus he hated and denounced. His greeting to
Antonio was that of cringing humility, and when he
mentioned the feasibility of borrowing money from
Tubal, "a *wealthy* Hebrew" of his tribe, he lapsed into

the condition of the sordid, specious, wily money-lender, incapable, from force of the habit of trickery, of anything like fair and open dealing. His manner became formal and his articulation sharply incisive, when saying "I had forgot—three months,"—a pause, and then an intent look at *Bassanio,—"You* told me so." The *Jew's* defence of usury was made with a slow, ruminative insistence on the details of the Biblical story of Jacob's thrift. The trenchant rebuke to *Antonio* was begun with an assumption of judicial restraint, a certain dignity, but, as the delivery of it proceeded, the feeling became intense, the utterance bitter, mordant, and fiery, such as might well incite the *Merchant's* angry retort; but at "Why, look you, how you storm," the manner of the *Jew,*—his rage repressed by a sudden exertion of will,—became meek and ingratiating. When he said, "Your single bond," *Shylock,* over-eager, touched the breast of *Antonio,* who thereupon drew back, wrapping his cloak around him, as though the touch of the *Jew* were a contamination, and in the brief pause which ensued *Shylock* was seen to curb his resentful exasperation at being treated as if he were a leper, the obvious effort being followed by a copious glow of cordiality, in the offer of "kindness" and in the insidious proposal of the "merry bond." There was, in Irving's peculiar intonation and manner, when his *Shylock* said, "An

equal pound of *your fair flesh*," a suggestion of
latent, sinister meaning, as if his secret thought were,
"If my touch contaminates you, perhaps I shall soon
give you reason, indeed, to dread it!" His delivery of "O father Abraham, what these Christians are!"
was so convincingly honest and earnest, in its apparent
candor, that it might have beguiled even the most
distrustful of hearers. At the close of the scene,
Antonio and *Bassanio* having parted from him, *Shylock* turned away, moved a few steps, paused, turned
back, glared after his foes, raised his crutch-stick and
shook it, in menace, with a look of frightful hatred,
making such an illuminative picture of the character
as only the brush of inspired genius could convey.

In Irving's arrangement of the comedy the Second
Act contained three scenes, the second being devoted
to *Lorenzo's* love affairs, and the third, exceptionally
picturesque and illuminative, devoted to *Shylock,*
in his relation to the incident of *Jessica's* elopement. In this latter scene the place represented was
a street in front of *Shylock's* house. At the back a
finely painted drop afforded a spacious view of
romantic Venice, in the dim starlight. A high bridge,
spanning a canal, extended across the stage, from the
upper left-hand corner to a point forward on the right.
The bridge was accessible by steps. At the right of
and below it was a building, fashioned with a pro-

jecting hood above the door,—the "pent house" mentioned by *Lorenzo*. At the left of the stage, in the
foreground, bordering the canal, was placed the house
of *Shylock,* on the front of which was a prominent
balcony. *Launcelot* and *Shylock* entered from that
dwelling, the former in haste and perturbation, as if
retreating from his harsh employer. *Shylock's* speech
of dismissal to him,—"Well, thou shalt see,"—was
spoken by Irving in a strain of censorious sarcasm, and
the *Jew's* parting from his daughter, immediately
before her flight, was effected in a mood of
querulous anxiety, *Shylock* showing himself oppressed
by presentiment of impending disaster: "There is some
ill a-brewing towards my rest." At mention of
Bassanio, when *Launcelot* said, "My young master
doth expect your reproach," there was a quick accession of severity in *Shylock's* face and demeanor, and
the tone in which, to the menial's blundering speech,
he replied "So do I—*his*"—was grim with expectancy
of revenge. When he ended his authoritative delivery
of the mandate, to *Jessica,* "Lock up my doors," he
entered the house, was absent for a moment, and then
returned, wearing a cloak and an orange-tawny,
turban-like head-dress, and carrying a lantern and a
staff. Hearing the voice of *Launcelot,* who was
speaking in a hurried undertone to *Jessica,* but not
hearing the words, he swiftly advanced to his daughter,

as *Launcelot* sped away, seized her by the wrist, looked suspiciously upon her face and harshly put the question to her,—pointing with his stick after the departed servant,—*"What says* that fool of Hagar's offspring—ha?"　Reassured by *Jessica's* ready lie, he turned from her, murmuring, "The patch is kind enough," and then, with the old proverb about the wisdom of precaution on his lips, ascended to the bridge and passed across it, out of sight.　The elopement of *Jessica* with *Lorenzo* was then effected, in a gondola, which moved smoothly away in the canal, and the scene became tumultuous with a revel of riotous maskers, who sang, danced, frolicked, and tumbled in front of *Shylock's* house, as though obtaining mischievous pleasure in disturbing the neighborhood of the *Jew's* decorous dwelling.　Soon that clamorous rabble streamed away; there was a lull in the music, and the grim figure of *Shylock,* his staff in one hand, his lantern in the other, appeared on the bridge, where for an instant he paused, his seamed, cruel face, visible in a gleam of ruddy light, contorted by a sneer, as he listened to the sound of revelry dying away in the distance.　Then he descended the steps, crossed to his dwelling, raised his right hand, struck twice upon the door with the iron knocker, and stood like a statue, waiting—while a slow-descending curtain closed in one of the most expressive pictures that any stage has ever presented.

Irving did not follow the Macklin tradition as to the acting of *Shylock* in the tremendous Street Scene of the Third Act,—the stage tradition, that is, which prescribes as imperative in that scene almost incessant movement, explosive vociferation, and lamentable and furious delirium. His reason, probably, was that he did not consider himself physically equal to the effort required by that method of treating the situation, or he may have deemed, and probably did deem, another method more effective upon the feelings of an audience. The treatment which he devised and employed was wonderfully potent. The convulsive passion, liberating the man from every restraint of prudence and every expedient of duplicity and bursting forth in torrid eloquence, the derascinating conflict between outraged parental authority and the animal instinct of paternity, the overwhelming access of religious fanaticism, the terrific wrath of despoiled avarice, and the savage determination to have a hellish revenge—all those shattering forces were implicated and displayed in Irving's acting of *Shylock,* in this tempestuous scene, with a spasmodic energy of natural emotion, transcending, in its power to excite pity while diffusing a sense of terror, any possible manifestation of mere physical excitement. When he entered, the "out-

rageous passion" immediately consequent on his
daughter's thievery and flight had somewhat abated.
His dress was disordered. His gown (the cloak or
gabardine had not been put on) was torn open at the
throat, his hair was dishevelled, his hands were
clenched, his movements were swift,—the mental
tempest venting itself in physical agitation,—and as
he approached, the jeers of his Christian persecutors
being faintly audible in the distance, he was snarling
and muttering to himself. When he perceived the
Christians, *Salanio* and *Salarino,* the comrades of
Lorenzo and *Bassanio,* his fury flamed forth again,
and the glare of hatred which he bent upon them
was shocking in its infernal intensity. The exclamation, "My own flesh and blood *to rebel!*" commingled relentless anger with astounded incredulity.
There was comparatively little movement on the
part of *Shylock,* throughout this scene,—there was no
yelling, and there was no rushing to and fro. The
utterance of "There I have another—*bad match*"
expressed the infinite of loathing. The ominous words,
"Let him look to his bond," were spoken in a lower
tone than was used in speaking the associated
sentences, and in the final iteration every word
was uttered separately. "Let—him—look—to—his—
bond!" The furious response to *Salarino's* question
about the flesh, "What's that good for?" came like a

lightning flash,—"To bait fish withal!" and then, after a pause of suspense, ensued the torrid invective, the greatest of all *Shylock's* speeches, uttered at first in an almost suffocated voice,—"If it will feed nothing else it will feed my revenge,"—but presently in the fluent tones of completely liberated passion. As the infuriated *Jew* proceeded the Christians involuntarily shrank from him and he slowly moved toward them, until he had fiercely enunciated the reply to his own question, "Why, revenge!"—at which point he whirled away and came down the stage in the opposite direction, twice ejaculating the word "Revenge," as if convulsed with delirium, and then he stopped and again turned on his enemies. Throughout that exacting scene Irving never lost control equally of the situation and the audience, but held both in complete thrall, not pausing to allow the destructive interjection of applause, after the word "Revenge,"—an interruption frequently permitted by performers of *Shylock*,—but commanding his auditors till the superbly rounded close, "It shall go hard but *I* will *better* the *instruction!*" which always elicited a tremendous burst of enthusiastic fervor. The awful picture of wrath which he had thus created was held by him for a moment, and then *Shylock* seemed to become oblivious of the Christians, and, turning from them, encountered his associate and emissary, *Tubal.* That person came

from the left of the stage, as *Salanio* and *Salarino*
vanished at the right, and *Shylock,* meeting him, laid
his left hand on *Tubal's* right arm, at the elbow, and
his right hand on *Tubal's* left shoulder, and, so holding
him and leaning on him, three times spoke his name:
"How now, Tubal, Tubal, Tubal,—*what* news from
Genoa?"   Then, holding him off at arm's length, he
asked, "Hast thou found *my daughter?*"   The revelation of the indurated selfishness of *Shylock's* nature,
in Irving's utterance of "The *curse* never fell upon
our nation *till now*—*I* NEVER *felt* it till now," was so
complete as to be absolutely shocking.   There could
be no doubt relative to his perception of the character.
When *Shylock,* in the overwhelming anguish of self-
pity, dwelt on the magnitude of his losses, he plucked
open his robe, with the left hand, while with the right,
firmly clenched, he convulsively smote himself, many
times, delivering slow, heavy blows, on his naked breast.
The momentary revulsion of feeling that Irving permitted the *Jew* to indicate, after his frenzied invective
relative to *Jessica's* ignominious robbery of his treasure
and flight from his home, seemed to be an involuntary
impulse not so much of human nature as of the animal
propension toward its young.   A kindred emphasis
was placed on "No tears but of my shedding"; but
the tears of *Shylock* are those of rancorous rage and
furious desperation, not of wounded affection or grief,

and that was the meaning Irving conveyed. The
ejaculation, "What, what, what? *ill* luck, *ill luck?*"
was given with ferocious animation and joyous expectancy, and the wicked outcry, "I thank God, I
thank God," with a horrible exuberance of delight,
immediately succeeded by almost piteous doubt,
at *"is* it true? *is it*—TRUE?" An effect of contemptuous amusement followed his agonized groan, at
Tubal's mention of *Jessica's* extravagance and the
abject meanness of the accents in which he moaned, "I
shall never see my gold again." The repetition, "four-
score ducats," was spoken in a semi-bewildered undertone, as though the *Jew* could not credit the possibility
of such wanton waste by his child. The supreme
climax of the situation was reached and shown by
means of sudden contrast,—fury abruptly succeeding
lamentation, in the thrilling celerity with which he
cried, "I am very glad of it:—I'll *plague* him: I'll
torture him: I am *glad* of it," and the subsequent, "I
will have the *heart* of him, if he forfeit." Persons who
truly saw that frightful figure,—an authentic and
terrific image of tragedy,—can never forget it,—the
tall, attenuated form, the ghastly, pallid face, the deep-
sunken, dark eyes, blazing with wrath, the jaws
champing, the left hand turning the sleeve up on the
right arm as far back as the elbow, and the fingers of
the right hand stretched forth and quivering, as if

already they were tearing out the heart of his hated enemy. The scene was rapidly rounded. Irving, although exceptional among actors for the perfect poise and massive authority which take fully and exactly the time required, be it ever so long, for the accomplishment of a purposed artistic result, never marred effect, whether great or small, by lingering unduly on an achievement once completed.

Some time had been supposed to elapse prior to the scene of the *Jew's* colloquy with the *Merchant,* when *Antonio* walks abroad, in the *Jailer's* custody. *Shylock's* excitement had given place to cold, concentrated determination of murder. In that scene Irving was incarnate cruelty. His attire was orderly, sober, correct; his demeanor obdurate. He evinced a calm, revolting pleasure in the rejection and suppression of the miserable *Antonio's* appeals, together with hectoring censure of the *Jailer's* clemency, in allowing his prisoner "to come abroad" for exercise. Throughout the Trial Scene his acting was perfect in symmetry, particularity of expressive detail, cumulative power, and tragic effect. All indication of passion had disappeared from his visage and person. He seemed the authentic personification of the Mosaic Law, the righteous minister of Justice; the ordained avenger. In the presence of that majestic Hebrew the observer became, for a moment,

completely oblivious that *Shylock* is not only a
villain but a trickster; that his nature, like his quest,
is abhorrent; that the "bond" to which he appeals,
and by virtue of which he so ostentatiously craves
"the law," was obtained by the hypocritical pretence
of friendship and magnanimity; and that he is now
proceeding in his actual character, that of a dis-
sembling scoundrel, to do a murder, under the compulsory sanction of a Court of Justice. The illusion,
however, was only momentary. Every evil passion
poisons the mind that harbors it, till, if the inevitable
degradation be not stayed, the character is vitiated,
the body is ravaged, the soul is polluted. That
truth was legibly written in the countenance of
Irving's *Shylock,* and as the *Jew* stood there, in the
Courtroom, no thoughtful observer could fail to
read it. There was a horrible yellow pallor of the
skin. The lines in the face had been deepened. The
cheeks were hollow. There was a faint glow of
hectic color around the sunken, burning eyes. The
body was emaciated. On entering the Court *Shylock*
advanced a little way, paused, and slowly gazed
around until his eyes found *Antonio,* upon whom
his look then settled, with evident gloating satisfaction,—a cruel, deadly look of sanguinary hatred,—
and then he stepped a little forward and gravely
bowed toward the *Duke's* throne. The address of

that magistrate was heard by him with patient but wholly unmoved attention, and his reply was spoken with dignity and decisive force. The words, "What judgment shall I dread, doing no wrong?" were so spoken that they seemed those of honesty, and almost carried conviction of right intent. The contempt with which *Gratiano's* appeal was answered was of withering indifference. That voluble intercessor's denunciation was totally disregarded, except that, after it had ended, *Shylock,* with the point of his naked knife, touched the bond, which had been thrust into his girdle in the form of a roll, and made his curt answer in a cold, level, sinister tone, expressive of a scorn so profound as to be devoid of all feeling. In the peculiar emphasis that he laid on the word "law" there was a latent sarcastic mockery, as if, in his thought, he were deriding the folly of a law that could be made to serve such a purpose as the murder which he intended to commit. There was bland simplicity in his question, "On *what* 'compulsion' *must* I?" and he listened with weariness and growing impatience to the speech about "The quality of mercy," feeling it to be irrelevant, futile, and tedious: his answer to it was abrupt and decisive. When *Portia,* in pitiful entreaty, said, "Bid me *tear* the bond," he laid his left hand heavily on both of her hands, to stay the action, and answered,

without even a tremor, "When it is *paid,* according
to the tenor." At "So says the bond—doth it not,
noble judge?" he laid the point of his knife on the
words in that document, held open by *Portia,* and
when she inquired, "Are there balance' here, to weigh
the flesh?" he caused an hysterical laugh, by the
grisly promptitude with which he brought forth the
"balance" from his bosom,—an action which seemed
to imply that he had carried the implement there, to
comfort him by its touch, with assurance of his certain revenge. The relentless statement "'Tis not *in*
the bond" was horrible in its icy implacable resolve,
and he uttered with infernal exultation the summons
to the *Merchant,* "A sentence!—*Come!* PREPARE!"
In the subsequent resolute, persistent effort to
extricate himself with at least financial profit from
the ruins of his defeated scheme of murder the stalwart force of the *Jew's* character was splendidly maintained, and at the final catastrophe, the collapse,
both physical and mental, was denoted with consummate skill. In making his exit from the Court *Shylock* moved slowly and with difficulty, as if he had
been stricken by fatal weakness and were opposing
it by inveterate will. At the door he nearly fell,
but at once recovered himself, and with a long, heavy
sigh he disappeared. The spectacle was intensely
pathetic, awakening that pity which naturally attends

upon despoiled greatness of character and broken, ruined power, whether that character and that power be malignant or benign.

Irving's dress, for *Shylock,* comprised a brown gabardine, girdled by a parti-colored shawl, a black, flat-topped cap with a yellow band across it, and square-toed shoes, of soft leather. He dressed the head with gray hair, long behind, the crown of the skull being bald. One lock of hair, being brushed forward, appeared on the brow, projecting from beneath the hat. He carried a black crutch-stick. In the Second Act he slightly changed the costume,—as already noted. In the Third Act he wore a long robe, but neither hat nor gabardine. In the Trial Scene, his dress was scrupulously correct, neat, and formal, his hair carefully smoothed and arranged, his aspect that of a priest going to the altar, to offer sacrifice: a more composed aspect could not be imagined,—the aspect of a lethal monster, sure of his prey, because bulwarked behind the pretence of religion and law,— and nothing at once as imposing and terrible had before been shown on our stage by any actor of *Shylock.* When Irving first presented "The Merchant of Venice," in London, it had a run of two hundred and fifty consecutive performances, a record never equalled with any play of Shakespeare's. He restored the Fifth Act, which, after the time of Edmund Kean, had frequently been omitted.

RICHARD MANSFIELD.

Richard Mansfield assumed the character of *Shylock* for the first time on October 23, 1893, at Herrmann's Theatre, New York, and retained it in his repertory till the last. His ideal of it was not absolutely definite, but in the main it was correct. At first he endeavored to infuse into the performance a strain of sensibility,—judicious, perhaps, from one point of view, but unwarranted. His purpose then was to emphasize every redeeming human characteristic that ingenious reasoning can attribute to Shakespeare's *Jew,* and thus to win, particularly from a Hebrew audience, active sympathy with a despised, persecuted, injured man, pursuing a justifiable course to avenge the wrongs which had been heaped, not only on himself, but on his tribe. Later he partly eliminated sensibility and laid the stress chiefly on evil power, but he never reached a decisive attitude toward it. At the time of his first appearance as *Shylock,* he had, as he assured me, never seen a performance of the part, and he declared that he had approached the subject "with a white mind." He also said that the play of "The Merchant of Venice" appeared to him to be "a fairy tale,"—an opinion which, con-

sidering certain inconsistencies and fanciful elements
in its plot, is not, perhaps, entirely indefensible.
His dressing as well as his acting of *Shylock* underwent various changes, from year to year. Some
of the stage business that he used at first,—
as when he, literally, spat upon the stage, after
saying, to *Antonio*, "Your worship was the last
man in our mouths,"—was subsequently discarded.
His original dress, which consisted of such profuse
drapery that his rather short figure seemed nearly as
broad as it was long, was, in time, much improved by
closer adjustment of the robe to the person, but he
could not be induced to reject a queer cap, having flaps
upon it, resembling the wings of a bat. The heavy
long gray beard, diversified by a tuft of black hair
beneath the lower lip, with which, at first, he obscured
Shylock's face, was dismissed, and first a long, iron-
gray beard, without moustache, and then a thin, short
beard, with moustache, both of the latter nearly white,
—were substituted for it, allowing facial expression
to become visible. A ballet of "fairies," with which
he had caused the Fifth Act to be opened, was soon
cast aside. In his final arrangement of the comedy
Mansfield cut, altered, transposed, and condensed the
text, till the original form of the piece was greatly
marred. One of the Casket Scenes and the Garden
Scene were retained. The supreme moments in Mans-

RICHARD MANSFIELD AS *SHYLOCK*

FROM A PAINTING BY EDGAR CAMERON

Э

field's impersonation of *Shylock* were those that include the delivery of the *Jew's* speech on usury, the sudden change from malignant volubility to simulated geniality of humor, at "Why, look you, how you storm!" and the delirium of the Street Scene, a passage in which he wrought a tremendous effect by means of his frenzied action and his exceptionally copious and resonant voice. In the delivery of the text he used the expedient of cadence, producing the effect of dialect,—therein subscribing to a practice long prevalent in the Continental Theatre of Europe, but first employed on the English Stage, I believe, by the elder Booth. At the close of the Trial Scene he made *Shylock* place the point of his curved knife, inside his dress, at the throat, intimating the purpose or act of suicide, and he spoke the words, "I am not well," in a weak, thin voice, as though to signify that the *Jew* was bleeding to death, from a stoically self-inflicted wound,—a piece of business not merely unwarranted but preposterous. It is remembered that an unfortunate, partially demented man, James Owen O'Connor,—who undertook to be an actor, and eventually died in a mad-house,—appearing at the Star Theatre, New York, April, 1888, when presenting himself as *Shylock,* caused the *Jew* to commit suicide in the Court, at the climax of his discomfiture. As a whole Mansfield's portrayal of this part,

while superb at certain points, remains in memory,—
like Aladdin's tower,—unfinished.

LATER PERFORMANCES.

Since the time of Macklin, the character of *Shylock*
has been, for the most part, left to actors distinctively
serious, but, of late years, several comedians have
undertaken to play it,—among others, Herbert Beerbohm-Tree and Arthur Bourchier, in England, and
Sidney Herbert, Nathaniel Cheever Goodwin, and
Edward Hugh Sothern, in America. The performances of the part given by Mr. Tree and Mr.
Bourchier have not (1911) been seen on the American Stage. Mr. Herbert's performance was given
at Daly's Theatre, New York, on November 19, 1898,
when the late Augustin Daly revived "The Merchant
of Venice," with the lovely Ada Rehan as *Portia*.

AUGUSTIN DALY'S REVIVAL.—SIDNEY HERBERT.

Daly's first venture with this comedy was made
at the New Fifth Avenue Theatre, New York, on
January 11, 1875, when he presented a version, in
four acts and four scenes, such as had been performed at the Prince of Wales Theatre, London.
E. L. Davenport acted *Shylock* and Carlotta Leclercq

acted *Portia*. Daly's revival in 1898,—the last production of a Shakespearean play that he ever made,—was his consummate contribution to stage endeavor with this comedy. It was at that time, and at other times, alleged by censors of Daly's management (and, being a man of dictatorial character, indomitable will, peremptory manners, and extraordinary achievement, he had many enemies),—that his revivals of Shakespeare were "irreverent" and "over-elaborate." That charge was both false and contemptible,—the mean detraction, bred of envy and spiteful animosity, which must ever asperse merit. It gained, however, a shadow of justification in his final presentment of "The Merchant of Venice," in which, conscious of the prevalent acceptance of Irving's artistically matchless setting and interpretation of that play, Daly made prodigious endeavor to overwhelm comparison,—setting the piece in scenery of extraordinary magnificence, and dressing it with a splendor of costly apparel unprecedented in its stage history. The luxury of environment was carried beyond the limit of necessity, the comedy being decorated to excess. The consonance that should exist between raiment and character was not scrupulously considered, though historical accuracy was earnestly sought. The occasional attempts at verisimilitude in every-day life,—street scenes, frolics, riots, and the like accessories,—sometimes ended in commonplace prosiness of detail. The presence of a throng of vocal spectators during *Lorenzo's* assignation scene with *Jessica* and their elopement was both incredible and ludicrous. On the other hand, the acting, throughout the performance, was noble in purpose and often splendid in fulfilment, the setting comprised many elements of beauty, the humorous points of the play were made specially effective, and the atmosphere of romance that should accompany its presentation was, in general, admirably preserved. The public benefit which accrues from an earnest, adequate presentment and interpretation of any one of Shakespeare's great plays could not be overestimated. Daly richly deserved, on that occasion, public gratitude and a generous recognition of his superb accomplishment, but, although the comedy was acted fifty-two consecutive times, he did not receive his merited reward. A competent performance of "The Merchant of Venice" is a public service, of exceptional and specific importance. In no other play, except in that marvel of felicitous diction, "King Richard II.," has Shakespeare written in a vein of such exquisite poetry and splendid eloquence as are found in certain passages of this comedy,— such, for example, as *Shylock's* rebuke to *Antonio; Bassanio's* apostrophe to *Portia's* portrait, *Portia's* speech when plighting her troth, and *Lorenzo's* pæan

to the stars in the midnight sky. "The Winter's
Tale" excels "The Merchant" in imagination; "As
You Like It" is richer in fancy, pensive philosophy,
quaintness, and sprightly mirth; "Twelfth Night"
contains more humor and more wealth of diversified
character; "Much Ado About Nothing" is more brilliant and crisp; but neither of those comedies is the
equal of "The Merchant of Venice" in human interest
of plot, passionate intensity of feeling, absorbing
dramatic action and suspense, or the perfect harmony
of concurrent and contrasted tragical and comical
ingredients, symmetrically united and made propulsive to a perfect artistic climax and fulfilment.

Daly invariably assumed the function of the
instructor as well as that of the *manager*,—often with
advantageous results, equally to actors and auditors,—
and the observer of performances given on his stage
was, therefore, necessarily often in doubt as to whose
ideal was disclosed. The anxiety of that manager as
to his production of "The Merchant of Venice" was
extreme. The play was in rehearsal, intermittently,
for more than one year,—a fact unprecedented in
his management. He was perplexed to find an actor
for *Shylock,*—the election at one time inclining
toward Tyrone Power, at another toward George
Clarke, since deceased, and finally lighting upon
Sidney Herbert. Mr. Herbert's ideal,—or rather the

ideal that he presented,—was, at first, blurred by
nervous trepidation, but his performance, after a time,
became definite, coherent, and consistent, evincing
thought, feeling, and force. Viewed as the first
attempt of a comedian in a character that contains
elements of tragedy, it certainly was the best performance, of its class, seen on our stage for many
years. It again, in some measure, presented *Shylock*
as the austere, majestic avenger of the wrongs of
Israel, but it employed a method of feverish flurry
which is not warranted by the text and which was
not justified by its practical result. "Never move"
was the precept of Mrs. Siddons, in acting the
Sleep Walking Scene of *Lady Macbeth*. "Move
continually" appeared to be Mr. Herbert's precept,
in acting *Shylock,* although he gradually abated his
activity. The *Jew* was not shown as self-centred
and authoritative, but generally as in a state of
splenetic bustle,—a scorpion in venom, but a scorpion
also in celerity. During the Bond Scene with *Bassanio*
and *Antonio* Mr. Herbert chiefly impressed his audience by his superb make-up, which would have been
a fit subject for a painting, his deft expression of
veiled craft, his suppressed animosity, and his fluent
delivery of the sarcastic speeches. In the Second Act
he copied much of the business of Henry Irving.
Not till the Street Scene did he become approximately

free, though even there he seemed inexplicably desirous to keep himself down and to substitute a squall for a tempest. His achievement in that trying situation would have had more potency of effect but for the needless and disturbing presence of a rabble of children, racing at the *Jew's* heels and deriding him,—an incident mentioned in the text but not shown, and neither essential nor desirable to be shown. He revealed considerable and unexpected resources of power, and notwithstanding a partially defective method, as of an actor mistakenly curbing his natural spirit and his freedom of expression, he gained a substantial success, by sincerity and intense feeling. No comedian of Mr. Herbert's order since the time of Thomas King,—as far as stage records testify,—has endured such a test. In the Trial Scene he was comparatively unimpressive, partly by reason of the incomplete method of his expression, partly because the premature disruption of the Court marred his climax, but more because of his weak, causeless prostration of himself upon the floor. The *Jew* is, indeed, broken at the last, but even at the last he exerts his will, and when he departs from the Court in which he has been so disastrously defeated and despoiled he will go away to sign that "deed of gift" and to die,—if die he must,—alone.

NATHANIEL CHEEVER GOODWIN.

Mr. Goodwin assumed the *Jew* for the first time in New York, on May 25, 1901, at the Knickerbocker Theatre, in a presentment of the comedy which was made with much of the accoutrement that had been devised and employed by Daly. In eccentric comedy Mr. Goodwin has used good abilities with good effect, but his personality is not commanding and he is destitute of tragic power. The actor who would impress an audience as *Shylock* must be, in himself,—whatever be his ideal or his method,—authoritative and formidable. No performer of flimsy character, slender fibre, finical make-up, and frivolous manner can create and sustain an illusion in that or in any kindred part. Among the anecdotes of Napoleon there is one which relates that a person who had hidden himself in a picture gallery for the purpose of shooting that great soldier was so completely overwhelmed with terror when the Emperor fixed his gaze upon him that he became temporarily paralyzed. Certain parts in the drama require, in the actor, stalwart individuality, fiery intellect, massive physical force, and great inherent facility of tragic expression. *Shylock* is one of those parts. Mr. Goodwin did not rise to that height, because he could not. His performance commingled craft, sarcasm, bitterness, splenetic humor, and malice, and that conglomerate was tempered with a singular old-gentlemanly complaisance, as though *Shylock* were apprehended as a possibly benign person.   His level speaking was smooth, he skilfully indicated the duplicity of the *Jew's* bargain with the *Merchant,* and he caused a momentary ripple of dramatic effect by his delivery of *Shylock's* sarcastic address to *Antonio,* on past indignities and present solicitations; and that effect he made, while showing himself to be neither correct nor fluent in the delivery of blank verse.   In the Street Scene he was merely vehement, and in the Trial Scene he was colloquial and commonplace, signifying nothing of *Shylock's* smouldering passion and concentrated hatred, and, at a supreme moment, showing his inconsequence by turning his back upon his victim.   His voice was thin, his action tame, his identification with the character very slight, and his performance, as a whole, crude, spasmodic, and insignificant.   In the ideal there was some manifestation of humanitarian design.   The beginner in study of *Shylock* is often misled by that mirage, but the mature student is forced to reject it.   *Shylock* is strength, not weakness; hate, not love; cruelty, not mercy; incarnate wickedness,—having abundant reason for being the villain that he is; intent on a sanctioned murder, possessed of a sufficient cause, and confident in his purpose and himself. The comedian signified comprehension of him as only the well-meaning "man in the street." The garments worn by Mr. Goodwin dwarfed his somewhat squat figure, and by their ornamentation suggested that *Shylock* was, perhaps, a dealer in feathers. One new but ineffective piece of business was introduced, at the end of the Second Act,—another of the several futile efforts which have been made to better the instruction of Henry Irving. *Shylock,* on returning to his house, after the incident of *Jessica's* flight, was made to knock on the door, thrust it open, rush in, and, presently, being unseen, to utter cries of distraction and rage, and then to emerge, distraught and dishevelled, bearing in his hand a letter, presumably left for him by his fugacious daughter, and as he ran across the stage to blurt the words which, subsequently, *Solanio* says "the dog Jew did utter in the streets":

> " ' My daughter!—O my ducats!—O my daughter!
> Fled with a Christian!—O my Christian ducats!
> Justice! the law, my ducats, and my daughter!' "

EDWARD HUGH SOTHERN.

Mr. Sothern's performance of *Shylock,*—first shown in New York, February 16, 1907, at the Lyric Theatre,—was so incorrect and ineffective that it would

require no mention but for the fact of that comedian's
prominence in the contemporary American Theatre,—
an honorable prominence, gained by ambitious, conscientious, continuous labor, during many years, and
by fortunate association with the best Shakespearean
actress of the present period on the American Stage,
Miss Julia Marlowe. Allusion occurs in the writings
of Fanny Kemble,—who certainly was an authority
on Acting,—to "those rare gifts of Nature without
which Art is a dead body." Mr. Sothern's *Shylock*
was "a dead body" indeed. Professional skill was
indicated, together with some results of study, but the
ideal was false and the expression of it was weak.
Once more the wearied beholder discerned an abortive effort to blend greed with benevolence, the crafty
usurer with the majestic Hebrew patriarch, the
bloodthirsty schemer for revenge with the noble,
loving father, the would-be murderer with the austere,
righteous minister of Justice, and once more the
union of those antagonistic components was seen to
be impossible. The comedian concealed his face,—a
face which, when fully disclosed, is not remarkably
expressive,—by a superabundance of hair and paint,
and in his speech he affected a thick, nasal "pudding"
voice utterance. One instance of his stage business
should alone suffice to prove how completely unworthy
his performance of *Shylock* was of particular examina-

tion and record: like his foreign predecessor, Ermete Novelli, he seated himself in the Street Scene!

ROBERT BRUCE MANTELL.

Mantell wisely followed the tradition established by Macready. His method was marked by simplicity. He did not endeavor to invest *Shylock* with religious austerity or place him in a sacramental attitude toward his Christian rival and insulter and the Christian community of Venice. He presented a formidable, revengeful Jew, bitterly resentful of the injuries that he had personally suffered; his expression of mingled rage and anguish over his losses and of cruel and frantic exultation over the supposed losses of his hated enemy was expert and effective; and his maintenance of a coldly diabolical purpose of murder, at the culmination of *Shylock's* treacherous contrivance against the life of *Antonio,* was massive with authority, determinate with inflexible purpose, and consistent and fine with the fluent procedure of studied art. There was not, in his acting of the *Jew,* an overwhelming whirlwind of passion. There was no peculiar ingenuity in his stage business. Mantell's costume was Hebraic and appropriate: his excellence as an actor has been shown in parts that transcend *Shylock* in many ways.

PORTIA.

It is not possible to sympathize with a fortune-hunter who purposes to rectify his financial affairs by marrying a wealthy heiress, but it is easy to perceive that *Bassanio* is substantially a good fellow, and that he is truly in love with *Portia,* as *Portia* certainly is with him, and, so perceiving, it is pleasant to follow the course of their love-story to its happy close. *Portia,* unhappily, has often been performed by elderly or obviously mature women, and made unduly old and even masculine. She is a young and lovely girl; she lives in the season when love is essential and delicious; and when she says, to her intimate companion *Nerissa,* "My little body is a-weary of this great world," she unconsciously indicates her desire for love—her weariness of a life that is incomplete. The words that *Portia* speaks immediately after *Bassanio* has made his fortunate choice of the leaden casket utter the very heart of love and reveal the whole soul of the woman.

The *Portias* of the stage have been numerous. When Burbage acted *Shylock,* the part must have been misrepresented by a male, according to the custom of that period. Kitty Clive and Peg Woffington were among the first prominent actresses to appear as *Portia,* after Macklin had revived Shakespeare's comedy. Kitty Clive, in the Trial Scene, when disguised as *Balthasar,* was accustomed to imitate the manner of one or another well-known lawyer of the day. Peg Woffington, who acted *Portia* for the first time, May 1, 1743, at Drury Lane, is said to have been excellent in the part, but there is no detailed description of her performance. Mrs. Yates acted *Portia* in 1770. Mrs. Siddons,—advertised as "A Young Lady," and making her first London appearance,—played the part for the first time in 1775. Then, in the old records, follow the names of Miss Macklin (daughter of Charles), Miss Barsanti, Elizabeth Farren, Elizabeth Younge (afterward Mrs. Pope), Eliza Kemble, Anne de Camp, Miss Ryder, Mrs. Pope 2d, Miss Murray, Mrs. Glover, Miss Smith, Mrs. Ogilvie, Miss Jarman, Mrs. Morris, Mrs. Henry, and Mrs. Merry (Anne Brunton). Nearer to the present time come Ellen Tree, Helena Faucit, Fanny Kemble, Julia Bennett Barrow, Mrs. F. B. Conway (Sarah Crocker), Bella Pateman, Ellen Terry, Helena Modjeska, Ada Rehan, and Julia Marlowe. Mme. Modjeska gave a delicious impersonation of *Portia,* upon which memory delights to linger. She specially revealed, and exulted in, the tender, ardent, intrinsic womanhood of that golden girl of Italy, and I remember that the love-light in her eyes when *Portia* looked at *Bassanio,* while he was making choice among the caskets, was one of the most expressive, artistic, fascinating beauties of her beautiful performance,—a seemingly spontaneous but perfectly ordered achievement in acting, which irradiated with the light of genius the whole fine love-story of Shakespeare's exquisite comedy,

"Where every something being blent together
Turns to a wild of nothing save of joy."

ADA REHAN.

Ada Rehan, as *Portia,* gave a performance combining innate loveliness of spirit with a fine aristocracy of demeanor. It happens that among all Shakespeare's heroines *Portia,* in the affection of that actress, has ever been the favorite. She merged herself in the character; she was, in person, the dazzling white and golden beauty whom the poet has drawn; and in her acting she diffused the double charm of exquisite grace and deep feeling. The resemblance of *Portia* to *Rosalind* was discerned and indicated by her, but also she discerned and indicated the difference between them. *Portia* combines exceptional mind with irresistible feminine allurement. She is more intellectual than *Rosalind,* and at the same time more passionate, but, like *Rosalind,* she is expert in kindly banter and playful, almost satirical, mockery: like *Rosalind,* she assumes man's apparel in order to accomplish a purpose, and, like *Rosalind,* she is self-contained, holding all her feelings in control. Unlike *Rosalind,* on the other hand, she is concerned in high, serious employment; she confronts a situation of tragic import, a situation fraught with enormous responsibility and agonizing suspense, and throughout a long and painful ordeal of conflicting emotions she is self-possessed, authoritative, and competent, manifesting a force of character such as *Rosalind* nowhere indicates, and such as would not be expected from any other of Shakespeare's comedy women, except the gentle but resolute *Imogen.* Ada Rehan, who had given the best representation of *Rosalind* that has been seen in our time, evinced, in her acting of *Portia,* an exact discrimination between the qualities of the two characters, emphasizing the intellectual element in the lady of Belmont, while freely and fully depicting the romantic, exalted, tremulous and various conditions and emotions appurtenant to love. Her *Portia* could be coldly dignified, but also she could be meek and gentle; she could be radiantly merry, and she could be fervently passionate. There was, in her temperament, a constitutional winning sweetness that not her most sparkling raillery could wholly conceal, and in the archness of her innocent mischief,—

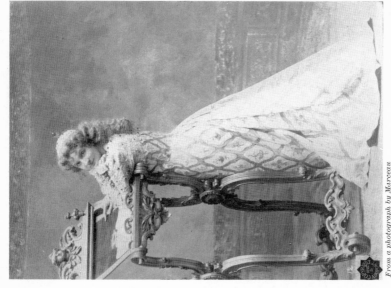

From a photograph by Marceau

ADA REHAN AS *PORTIA*

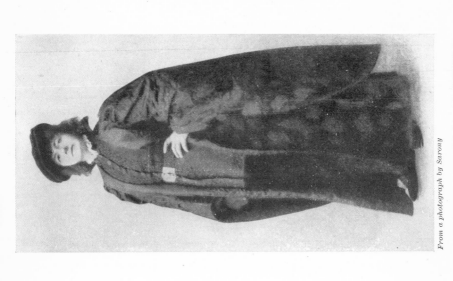

From a photograph by Sarony

HELENA MODJESKA AS *PORTIA*

as when she said, in the first colloquy with *Nerissa,* "I know it is a sin to be a mocker,"—an exquisite charm. During the Casket Scenes she expressed a tremulous solicitude, peculiarly animative of sympathy, and her simulation of delight, combined with feminine delicacy and a maidenly restraint of ardor, in *Portia's* self-surrender to the fortunate *Bassanio,* was supremely artistic. The reply to *Nerissa's* reminiscent remark about the Venetian scholar and soldier who came in company with the Marquis of Montferrat, "Yes, yes, it was *Bassanio,*" being spoken with eager joy, which instantly became reserve, tinged with a delicate self-consciousness, when she added, "As I *think*—so was he called," and turned to sweet gravity as she concluded, "I remember him well, and I remember him worthy of thy praise." Happiness, however, is not (at least, it is not in great natures) the chief object of life. *Portia* is unselfish. She thinks of others, and cares for them. It was one of the felicities of Ada Rehan's impersonation that it showed a solid sense of duty to be the basis of *Portia's* nature, and indicated her capability of being sufficient to herself, and, should adversity of fortune require the sacrifice, of living without love. The sacrifice, happily, is not required. *Portia* loves and she is beloved, and thus she was shown in this portrayal,—not less the inspiration of love than the ecstatic personification of it. Her demeanor in the Trial Scene, when *Portia* meets *Shylock,* was completely surcharged with goodness. She met him on the ground of their common humanity, not believing possible such wickedness of purpose, such diabolical cruelty, as had been imputed to him. The reminder, "Shylock, there's thrice thy money offered thee," was spoken very gently, confidentially, in a way to appease the hardest of angry men. When the test failed her indignation made her implacable, and from that point to the end she was the rigorous administrator of the exact law, committing the cruel *Jew* to his ruinous doom without one moment of compunction. Ada Rehan's appearance, in *Portia's* early scenes, was exceptionally beautiful. She wore pearl gray raiment, exceedingly becoming to her tall, lovely figure, and her hair was golden red. Later the dark robe of the *Doctor of Laws* was worn with perfect grace. It is especially memorable that this actress was the first and the only *Portia* of our time or, as far as stage history shows, of any time, who, when appearing before the "strict court of Venice," evinced and consistently maintained the anxiety not to say the solemnity inseparable from the situation and feelings of a person who is to adjudicate upon a question of wealth or ruin and life or death.

ELLEN TERRY.

The masculine objection to women who are distinctively and severely intellectual expresses itself in the reproach that they are "mannish." No real man likes a "mannish" woman, any more than a real woman likes an effeminate man. In old times *Portia* was frequently played by heavy formidable females, unlovely, unromantic, hard, cold, practical, matter-of-fact, some of them provided with the stalwart legs of a piano and the booming voice of a trombone, and the part, as presented by those executants, naturally, diffused no charm. That sophisticated stage *Portia* was an image of artifice in the sprightly scenes, and of masculinity and declamation in the scene of the Trial. She cared more for herself than for her lover, and her function in the performance had been fully accomplished when once she had delivered the speech on Mercy. She was an incident to *Shylock*. In later times all that has been changed. It might almost be maintained that the true *Portia* has only in comparatively recent years been discovered. In her latter presentations of the character on our stage Ellen Terry occasionally disfigured her performance of *Portia* by irrelevant and farcical interjections, but the most spontaneously feminine, completely symmetrical and absolutely enchanting embodiment of that part was the one given by her, as she presented it in the earlier days of her professional association with Henry Irving. All the gayety and all the poetry of the part were elicited by her, and she was the first among players to show *Portia* as a lover,—a woman in love, a woman knowing herself to be loved, and radiant with happiness because of that knowledge. One piece of her stage-business, in particular, was an inspiration. After *Bassanio* had made his fortunate choice she crumbled some roses and allowed the leaves to flutter down into the leaden casket from which the happy lover had taken her picture, and then, bending over it, seemed to consecrate it with a kiss. Ecstasy has not, within my observation of acting, been better expressed. The melody of Ellen Terry's speech, the clarity and sweetness of her articulation, the fine intelligence and unerring precision with which she gave to every word its exact shade of meaning, and the spontaneity and grace of her action had the inevitable result—and could have no other—of making her,—in Ben Jonson's felicitous phrase,—"Mistress of arts, and hearts, and everything." The lovely lines about Mercy came from her lips in a strain of golden melody,—for she could and did speak blank verse so as to make it seem the language of nature; and, a little to vary Wordsworth's fine couplet,

The music in our hearts we bore
Long after it was heard no more.

When Ellen Terry thus embodied *Portia* the
observer saw a woman of fine mind as well as of
enchanting beauty; an imperial woman, yet one essentially feminine, possessing a deep heart and a passionate temperament, and, at the same time, possessed
of that arch, buoyant, glittering piquancy and play-
fulness which are fluent from health, innocence, and
kindness toward all the world.

Portia is a "rich heiress." She has been reared in
luxury. Her state is that of a princess. All things
around her are sumptuous, and her mind, like her
environment, is superb. Every word of her speech is
noble; every part of her conduct is free, generous,
and fine. That ideal cannot be made actual by a commonplace person. Ellen Terry had only to be herself in order to make it real. In *Portia's* scenes with
Nerissa, Morocco, and *Arragon,* during the first half
of the play, Shakespeare's heroine conquers not by
action and not by much speaking, but by condition;
she is incarnate enchantment. Her period of active
expression begins with the scene of *Bassanio's* choice
of the leaden casket. But *Portia* is, from the first, a
lover. Her eyes have told it to *Bassanio,* and her
heart has told it to herself. That note was sounded

by Ellen Terry, in her assumption of *Portia,* with the
first word that she uttered, and that was ever the great
felicity of her embodiment. When love is at the heart
every object upon which the gaze of the lover falls
is hallowed; every experience of life is tremulous with
the sweet excitement of that divine fever,—for true
passion is ecstatic and it makes humanity, in its finer
types, almost celestial. The consummate art of Ellen
Terry was never better shown than in her impartment
of the condition that accompanies a cardinal emotion.
She invested *Portia* with all the requisite vivacity and
with the pretty craft that veils her passionate longing
beneath smiles, banter, and raillery, but also she made
Portia romantic, tender, ardent, and keenly sensitive,
—irradiating her being with sensibility and allurement. In her utterance of *Portia's* playful satire on
her motley suitors there was no acerbity, but only
archness, sparkling over grave and gentle preoccupation. Her illuminative by-play, during the Casket
Scenes, was governed by the instinct of perfect
courtesy toward *Morocco* and *Arragon,* and it disclosed, as no words could ever do, at the moment of
Bassanio's choice, depth of heart and ample poten-
tiality of imparting bliss.

Portia's fertility of resource and expedition of movement with respect to *Antonio's* perilous condition in
the scene of the Trial are winged with love, yet her

impetuosity is speedily curbed by the refinement and the poise which are attributes of her noble nature. Few of the women of Shakespeare denote as broad a vision or such a wide capacity of thought as *Portia* does, and there again the acting of Ellen Terry satisfied the Shakespearean standard. There was nothing puny in it; nothing narrow; nothing indicative of inadequacy and effort. An alluring presence, great mental fervor, and the absolute sincerity which befits an occasion of almost tragic suspense constituted her, in the Trial Scene, an image of righteous authority, and her delivery of Shakespeare's melodious verse, some of the sweetest of which is put into the mouth of this heroine, made it still more beautiful. Ellen Terry was the first to dress *Portia,* for the Trial Scene, in a beautiful, flowing scarlet robe,—incorrect, according to authority on the costume of a Paduan doctor of laws of the period of the play, but delightfully effective. By Henry Irving's wise restoration of the long disused last act of the comedy *Portia* was shown in her triumphant happiness, when the wolfish *Jew* had been discomfited and her husband and his friends were assembled at Belmont. The glee of Ellen Terry, in that act, was the sunshine of a guileless, happy heart, and it made that lovely Garden Scene radiant. There is no reason to suppose that we shall ever again see *Portia* so truly and entirely incarnated as she was by that great actress. If the acting of Ellen Terry in the character of *Portia,* when that actress was in her prime, was not perfect dramatic art there is no such thing,—

> "And there is nothing left remarkable
> Beneath the visiting moon."

ELLEN TERRY AS A LECTURER.

Twenty-seven years, almost to the day, after her first dramatic appearance in New York,—October 30, 1883, at the Star Theatre, as *Queen Henrietta Maria,* in Wills's picturesque and pathetic play of "King Charles I.,"—Ellen Terry made her first appearance in that capital as a Lecturer and, at the Hudson Theatre, November 3, 1910, delivered a discourse, diversified by readings, on "Shakespeare's Heroines—Triumphant." Many things, in that interval,—during which she had given about 1,500 performances in America,—had changed and broken: there was but little change in her. Time, it was seen, had only touched with a pensive grace the affluent beauty which it had not the heart to spoil. Her figure was still imperial. Her movement still evinced the buoyant freedom of the curling wave. Her smile still flashed like a sudden sunbeam. Her rich voice was

ELLEN TERRY AS *PORTIA*

still a strain of music. Her gestures still possessed the
ease, breadth, and spontaneity which always made
them absolutely appropriate and expressive. She
still was Ellen Terry, the foremost inspirational
actress of her time; a woman of authentic genius,
whose dramatic art,—often exquisite, more often lawless and wild,—derived an unpremeditated, enchanting felicity from her opulence of womanhood,
tenderness of heart, unerring intuition, and passionate
ardor. Not in any period,—as far as can be learned
from historic records, certainly not in our period,—
has the stage presented such a striking example as
was shown by Ellen Terry of the union of wild
genius with practical sense in the conduct of professional life, and trained skill with vagrant, intuitive
impulse in the art of dramatic expression. She had
rivals in specific walks of the drama, but essentially,
as a personality and as an actress, she stood alone.
When she was on the stage in her rightful, natural
environment she was an acknowledged Queen: the
supreme, unapproachable *Ophelia;* the perfect *Beatrice;* bewitching and pathetic beyond description as
Goethe's *Margaret;* like a lily of loveliness as Tennyson's *Rosamund;* exquisite in the simplicity and purity,
and heartbreaking in the ardent passion and natural,
womanlike grief, of Wills's *Olivia;* the veritable
rough diamond of humor and goodness as *Nance*

Oldfield. The honor roll of her fine artistic achievements would be a very long one, and full of light. On the Lecture Platform she was not able to reproduce those images of dramatic power and beauty which long ago she had revealed in the Theatre and left as a benediction in the public remembrance. The most that she did as a Lecturer was to impart an occasional suggestion of some of them,—as in a recital of *Portia's* exposition of the quality of Mercy; but to remember her delivery of that and kindred speeches is to be reminded of the lovely lines by Ben Jonson,

> "The voice so sweet, the words so fair,
> As some soft chime had stroked the air,
> And, though the sound was parted thence,
> Still left an echo in the sense."

To see Ellen Terry, in her great day, as an actress, was to see a vital creature of beauty, passion, tenderness and eloquence, a being, in *Cleopatra's* fine phrase, all "fire and air": but even to see her as a lecturer was a privilege,—because it is always a pleasure and a benefit to experience mental and spiritual intercourse with a woman of fine temperament and rare personal charm. Ellen Terry, indeed, was not a good lecturer: there is an art in lecturing as well as acting, and she had not learned it. Her method was experimental. She did not speak with conviction, but rather with the dubiety of a person who seemed either to be uttering the thoughts of another mind or uttering thoughts which had not been maturely and thoroughly considered. She overran her "points." She made no sufficient allowance for either laughter or applause. She dropped her voice at the end of sentences, so that some of her words became indistinct or inaudible. She lacked the decisive, dominant quality of authority, being at times uneasy, hurried, flurried, and, at such times, therefore, ineffective. Her views, furthermore (such of them as she made public), were often incorrect, generally commonplace, and, in the matter of thought, superficial. Her hits, as a speaker, were mostly made by quick little flashes of piquant comment and sudden transitions of playful tone,—as when, remarking on the theoretical doubt of Shakespeare's entire authorship of "King Henry VIII.," she "just *knows* that Shakespeare *did* write it, at least *Queen Katherine,*" and thus jauntily laughed the commentators out of court.

The wiser course for her to have pursued as a Shakespearean entertainer would have been to read or recite Scenes from Shakespeare, as once she did, in London, in association with Henry Irving, when they gave an impressive and eminently effective reading of "Macbeth." The most illustrious of her female predecessors on the platform, Fanny Kemble and

Charlotte Cushman, took that course and were brilliantly successful in it. To *act* is one thing; to *expound* is another; and the clangor of controversy that has been sounding on among commentators for two hundred years might well be accepted as a warning against unprepared adventure into the field of Shakespearean Commentary, where, indeed, the speaker must "speak by the card." Ellen Terry's views, however incorrect or trivial, were widely received with unhesitant credence, simply and solely because they were expressed by a great actress who ought to be sure of her facts and was presumed to be so. They were not entitled to any such acceptance. Examination of all her remarks about the many characters in Shakespeare upon which, in her fleeting way, she was pleased to touch would tax a reader's patience. Brief reference to some of those concerning "The Merchant of Venice," while indicating the flimsy nature of her superficial speculations and enforcing the truth that, though she was important as an *impersonator* of Shakespeare's heroines, she was not important as an *expositor* of them, will also indicate some essential traits in the character of *Portia,* and thus find a legitimate and useful place in the stage history of the play. In her descant on "The Merchant" Miss Terry declared that, notwithstanding her "speech of submission" to her lover (which, by the

way, is not "a speech of submission" at all), *Portia*
remains very independent and immediately hits upon
a plan for the rescue of *Antonio,* which, without advice
or assistance, without asking leave or opinion, she
puts into effect.   That is an error.   The scene of
the betrothal of *Bassanio* and *Portia* is, of course,
followed by their marriage.   *Bassanio,* leaving his
wife at the altar, then returns to Venice, provided with
money to pay the bond.   There is an indication of
lapse of time between the departure of *Bassanio* from
Belmont and the subsequent departure therefrom
of *Portia:* "You have a noble and a true conceit of
god-like amity; which appears most strongly in bearing thus the *absence* of your lord."   *Portia's* course
of conduct is clear.   *Solanio* has stated, of *Antonio,*
"It should appear that if he had the present money
to discharge the *Jew,* he would not take it."   *Jessica*
has warned *Bassanio,* in *Portia's* presence, that her
father "would rather have *Antonio's* flesh than twenty
times the value of the sum that he did owe him," and
that "it will go hard with poor Antonio," unless
Shylock is overruled by "law, authority, and power."
In her extremity *Portia,* who wishes to see her husband as well as to save his friend, and who has a
nimble wit, applies for help to her cousin, *Doctor
Bellario,* a learnèd lawyer.   Her first application is
made by letter, asking for instruction as to how to

proceed for *Antonio's* relief, and also asking for assistance in masquerading as a lawyer in the Court of Venice. To her servant she says:

" See thou render this
Into my cousin's hand, Doctor Bellario:
And, look, what *notes* and *garments* he doth *give thee*,
Bring them, I pray thee, with imagin'd speed,
Unto the tranect, to the common ferry
Which trades to Venice."

It is manifestly impossible that at this time *Portia* can have thought of, or planned, the quibble which defeats and ruins *Shylock,* for the simple but conclusive reason that, at this time, she has not seen *Antonio's* bond to the *Jew* and does not know the terms of it. Ellen Terry declared that this quibble "is not a man's idea," but "a woman's"; that it occurs to *Portia* and is employed by her as a sudden, desperate clutching at a last possible means of escape for *Antonio,* and that it is justifiable, if at all, only on the ground that "desperate diseases require desperate remedies"; that it is used for a good purpose; and that "people employ weapons against a mad dog for the use of which they would be condemned if the dog were only wild and unruly." That view of the subject is preposterous.

The quibble employed by *Portia* is, unmistakably, the technical quibble of a lawyer and of a shrewd and tricky one. There is almost positive evidence, in the posture of circumstances as well as in the letter of *Doctor Bellario* to the *Duke of Venice,* that *Portia* has, in person, consulted her lawyer-cousin before appearing in court: "We turned o'er many books *together."* Even assuming that this is only *Doctor Bellario's* thoroughgoing method of imposing on the Court in commending his substitute, essential facts are evident. The *Duke* has submitted the case of *Shylock* v. *Antonio,*—in which he has taken exceptional interest ("twenty merchants, *the duke himself,* and the magnificoes of greatest port, have all persuaded with" the obdurate *Jew),*—to the consideration of counsel learned in the law, and, naturally, to the greatest authority known to him, in the hope of finding some method of escape for the *Merchant.* The *Duke* says:

> "Upon my power, I may dismiss this court
> Unless Bellario, a learned doctor,
> Whom *I* have *sent for* to determine this,
> Come here to-day."

This, obviously, has nothing to do with the plans of *Portia.* It is incontestable that *Bellario* could not write to the *Duke,* as he does, of having received his letter and of having "acquainted" the young doctor of Rome "with the cause in controversy between the *Jew* and *Antonio the Merchant,*" unless *Bellario* had

himself been first made acquainted with it by the
Duke: the young *Doctor* declares in court: "I am
informèd throu'ly of the cause," etc.

The line and plan of *Antonio's* defence have been
thoroughly worked out by *Bellario:* in the pleading
of the case by *Portia* opportunity is given to the implacable Hebrew to withdraw, with great material
advantage to himself: perhaps it was not quite certain in advance that the Court would sustain the
wretched quibble: perhaps there was some decent
repugnance to employment of such chicanery, if it
could be avoided.   But—not only has the ruinous
technical quibble been thought out; the method of
overwhelming the *Jew* and of inflicting fearful punishment upon him has been provided.   The utterance
of the speech beginning "Tarry a little" is no last,
desperate effort to save a forfeited life; it is the deliberate voice of "justice according to law" which speaks,
and it speaks the doom of *Shylock.*   The *Jew* may
take his pound of flesh, but if, in doing so, he shed
one drop of Christian blood his lands and goods are
forfeit unto the State.   That is no sudden effort of
woman's wit,—no "blanket in the alarm of fear caught
up,"—to shield *Antonio.*   It is the letter of the Law.
When *Shylock,* stunned and appalled, inquires: "Is
that the *law?"* the stern answer is immediate and
conclusive: "Thyself shalt *see* the act"; and the loca-

tion of that "Act" in the Criminal Statutes of Venice certainly could not have been known to *Portia,* and it is equally certain that it would naturally be known to, or be found by, "the learned *Bellario,*" when engaged, at the *Duke's* solicitation, in preparing *Antonio's* defence.   Nor is that all: *Portia* has been equipped with additional legal knowledge, the substance of which she states in Court, whereby, for having "indirectly, and directly, too" "contriv'd against the very life" of *Antonio, Shylock's* estate, even in the event of his *not* attempting to cut the forfeiture, is not only forfeit, half to the State and half to the object of his "lodg'd hate," but his life is placed at "the mercy of the Duke only."

The following instructive words were written by the great actress Fanny Kemble, one of the most intellectual women who have graced the stage:

" There is no reason whatever to expect that fine actors shall be necessarily profound commentators on the parts that they sustain most successfully, but rather the contrary," the reason being that " the dramatic faculty lies in a power of apprehension quicker than the disintegrating process of critical analysis, and when it is powerful and the organization fine, perception rather than reflection reaches the aim proposed."

Ellen Terry as a lecturer on Shakespeare provided a conspicuous example of that truth.

IV.

OTHELLO.

"It works! The venom doth corrupt his soul!
And he, who was all goodness, will become
The instrument of Hell,—most terrible
Because most virtuous."

—OLD PLAY.

VIEWED exclusively as a dramatic fabric, that is to say, with reference to the element of action and that only, "Othello" is not only the best of Shakespeare's plays but the best play in the English language. The action of it begins with the first word that is spoken, steadily increases and broadens, culminates at a tremendous crisis, and terminates in a complete tragic fulfilment. The element of pantomime,—that element which is the basis of all drama,—is so abundant, pervasive, and distinct in it that the movement could be carried on and made intelligible to an audience, almost without words. Among its many admirable attributes the one that first particularly impresses the reader or the spectator of it is simplicity and the dominant prevalence of that attribute points to the first requisite in a representation of the play.

The Shakespeare scholar is aware that the poet

232

derived the materials for his tragedy from a tale contained in the "Hecatommithi," by Giraldi Cinthio, Italian novelist, 1504-1573, the details of which are barbarous, and that, according to his custom, he greatly elevated a borrowed subject by his imaginative, poetical treatment of it. By way of exemplifying the attribute of simplicity in this play and directing attention to the supreme skill of the dramatist in employing simple expedients and making them productive of thrilling situations and terrible effects, a brief epitome of the incidents of the story seems appropriate. The scene is Venice; the time 1570. The beautiful *Desdemona,* a motherless girl, is fascinated by the manly *Othello,* a picturesque, eloquent soldier, and she encourages him to become her lover. Both of them abuse the confidence of the girl's father, *Brabantio,* and *Desdemona* elopes with *Othello* and is married to him. *Brabantio* is compelled to recognize the lawful union of the lovers, since it has already occurred, but subsequently he dies of a broken heart because of his daughter's conduct,—described by her as "downright violence and scorn of fortune." *Othello,* commander-in-chief of a Venetian army, appoints *Cassio* to the position of his lieutenant, a position which had been, and continues to be, coveted by *Iago,* another officer, who is assigned to a subordinate place. *Roderigo,* a rich Venetian youth, has long been infatuated with *Desdemona,* and desirous to win her. *Cassio* is smitten by the beauty of *Desdemona,* but his regard for her is that of a chivalrous admirer. *Iago,* who knows those persons and that posture of circumstance, determines to displace and ruin *Cassio,* whom, for no adequate specific reason, he hates, and to obtain for himself the position of *Othello's* lieutenant. Pursuant to that determination he contrives to make *Cassio* drunk, to have him dismissed for inebriety and brawling, to make him the object of *Othello's* deadly jealousy and hatred, to supersede him in his military office, and to cause *Othello* to kill *Desdemona,*—the end of all his scheming being the vindication and reinstatement of *Cassio,* the murder, by *Iago,* of his wife, *Emilia, Othello's* suicide, and his own frightful death, by torture. No story could be more simple, direct, fluent, and elementally tragic; but with what fine contrivance the poet has told it, with what ingenuity of invention, what vibrant vitality of continuous action, what ample and superb drawing of character, what prodigious volume of feeling, what tumult of surging and conflicting passion, and what perfection of poetic style! *Othello,*—not *Romeo,*— is the supreme representative lover, unmatched as such in all Shakespeare and all fiction, and the play is the supreme dramatic exposition of all the tragedy that can be born of love.

The date of the composition of "Othello" has not been determined and, apparently, it is indeterminable. The play was published in Quarto form in 1622 and it is included in the Folio of 1623. The first mentioned presentment of it occurred in the autumn of 1604, at the palace of Whitehall, London, in the presence of King James the First and his court, and the first representative of *Othello* was Richard Burbage. All that is known about his performance is that, according to an intimation in the Elegy on his death,—a composition, anonymous, alleged to have been written immediately subsequent to the sad event, —it was accounted supremely good. These are the words of the Elegy, relating to this subject:

> "He's gone, and with him what a world are dead,
> Which he reviv'd, to be revivèd so
> No more:—young *Hamlet*, old *Hieronymo*,
> *King Lear*, the cruel *Moor*, and more beside,
> That lived in him, have now forever died."

Prior to the demise of Burbage *Othello* was represented by John Underwood, an actor relative to whom the chronicles afford but sparse information. Davenant expressed a very high opinion of him. He had been a member of the company of "The Children of the Chapel," he participated in the first performance of Ben Jonson's "The Alchemist," 1610, and he died in 1624. *Othello* had also been acted by Nathaniel Field, ———— —, 1641, another graduate from the company of "The Children of the Chapel," and by Eylaeward Swanston. The death of Burbage occurred in 1629, the fourth year of the reign of King Charles the First. It seems probable that Joseph Taylor succeeded to the parts which had been played by Burbage. There is authentic record that Joseph Taylor played *Hamlet* and *Iago.* He was "Yeoman of the Revels" in 1639, and he died, aged eighty-two, in 1658, at Richmond, Surrey.

Of the successors of Burbage in *Othello,* during the period of the generation which intervened between his death and the revival of the Theatre, at the Restoration, 1660, scarcely anything is known. Among the leading actors of the English Stage in that period,— actors who were contemporaneously esteemed for brilliancy of talent and achievement,—were not only Burbage's associates John Lowin and Joseph Taylor, but also Michael Mohun, Charles Hart (grandnephew of Shakespeare), John Lacy, —— Clun, and Henry Harris. Most of those players had deteriorated or passed away by the time Betterton reached middle age, and long before he reached middle age that extraordinary actor had taken precedence of his competitors and appropriated to himself most of the greater dramatic parts. The date of his first assumption of *Othello* is not recorded, but probably he added that part to his repertory after the union, in 1682, of the two prominent dramatic companies then existent in London, Killigrew's and Davenant's, the former known as "The King's," and the latter, because patronized by the Duke of York, the King's brother, as "The Duke's."

On February 6, 1669, sometime before the union of those two companies, "Othello" was performed by Killigrew's actors, with a cast which contained —— Burt, as *Othello,* Michael Mohun, as *Iago,* and Margaret Hughes, as *Desdemona.* No account of Burt's acting has been found. He was eclipsed, in *Othello,* by Charles Hart. On January 28, 1707, the tragedy was performed at the Haymarket Theatre, with Betterton as *Othello,* and from that time onward the chronicle of its fortunes is reasonably continuous and clear. On the occasion when Betterton acted at the Haymarket as *Othello* the cast included the shining names of Barton Booth, as *Cassio,* John Verbruggen, as *Iago,* and Anne Oldfield (1683-1730),—an exceptionally delicious and bewitching woman,—as *Desdemona.* Betterton's impersonation of *Othello,* according to Sir Richard Steele's incomplete yet instructive description of it, in "The Tatler," must have been exceedingly noble, powerful, and pathetic. One citation from that account tells much:

"The wonderful agony which he appeared in when he examined the circumstance of the handkerchief, the mixture of love that intruded upon his mind, upon the innocent answers *Desdemona* makes, betrayed in his gestures such a variety and vicissitude of passion as would admonish a man to be afraid of his own heart, and perfectly convince him that it is to stab it to admit that worst of daggers, jealousy."

A supreme merit of Betterton's acting is indicated in one significant sentence by Cibber: "He could vary his *spirit* to the different characters he acted." He made *Othello* black, and, probably, he wore a court dress of his period.

CARELESS INVESTIENT.

The unprovided or wrongly provided condition of the British Theatre in the matter of scenery, and the fatuous negligence as to suitability of costume which generally prevailed in it prior to John Philip Kemble's assumption of the management of Drury Lane Theatre, which occurred in 1788-89, can be inferred from these expressive sentences concerning that subject, written by Kemble's biographer, James Boaden, in 1825:

"The memory of no very aged person may present, if closely urged, some not very brilliant impressions of the miserable pairs of flats that used to clap together on even the stage trod by Mr. Garrick; architecture without selection or propriety; a hall, a castle, or a chamber, or a cut-wood of which the verdure seemed to have been washed away. Unquestionably all the truth, all the uniformity, all the splendor, and the retinue of the stage came in with Mr. Kemble."

The same historian records that Thomas King, on relinquishing the management of Drury Lane, to which Kemble succeeded, significantly remarked that while he had been manager of the theatre he "had not even the liberty to command the cleaning of a coat, or adding, by way of decoration, a yard of copper lace, both of which, it must be allowed, were often much wanted." As illustrative of the habitual indifference to fitness of dress which had long prevailed before Kemble's time mention should be made that, in 1787, when James Fennell, making his first appearance on the stage, acted at the Theatre Royal, Edinburgh, as *Othello,* the garb that he wore, furnished by the manager, John Jackson (author of "The History of the Scottish Stage," 1793), consisted of a coat, waistcoat, and trousers of white cloth, —the coat and waistcoat being profusely decorated with silver lace,—a black "ramillies," that is, a wig, made of black hair, with a tail attached to it, about a yard long, white silk stockings, and dancing pumps.

BARTON BOOTH AND QUIN.

After Betterton's time the first decisively important performer of *Othello* was Barton Booth, who must have been exceptionally well qualified to play that part, his natural demeanor being characterized by great dignity, his temperament being emotional,— beneath an habitually calm exterior,—and his countenance, in which the muscles were prominent and flexible, being well adapted to express the incessant and continually changing play of varied feeling,—a facility much required in the terrible situations contrived in the tremendous Third Act of the tragedy. Colley Cibber, a good judge, notwithstanding his demonstrable bias in some cases, declares that *Othello* was Booth's masterpiece; and Benjamin Victor, a careful theatrical recorder, bears significant testimony to the effect of his acting, in these words: "In all the distressful passages of heart-breaking anguish and jealousy I have frequently seen all the men, susceptible to the tender passion, in tears." Booth, unquestionably a man of genius, was unequal in his acting, sometimes superb, sometimes languid, careless, and indifferent. He vitalized the formal rhetoric of Addison's *Cato* and he gave a profoundly pathetic impersonation of *King Lear*. He was an athletic man, five feet eight inches in height, of a comely aspect, and possessed of a voice of wide compass and peculiar sweetness. Aaron Hill wrote of him, as an actor, that "the blind might have seen him in his voice and the deaf have heard him in his visage." Accessible though incomplete analysis of his presentment of *Othello* indicates that his personality was solid, his demeanor grave, his elocution notable for variety and significant pauses, and his transitions of feeling effected with consummate skill. Like Betterton he made *Othello* black. Booth was utterly indifferent to suitability of costume, on the stage. As the Roman *Cato,* for example, he wore a long gown, figured all over with flowers, and a huge powdered wig. As *Othello* he probably followed the example of Betterton, with whom he had acted and whom he venerated, and wore a court-dress of his time (1681-1733). There is no known description of the costumes used by either of those actors, in that part.

James Quin (1693-1766), the most renowned *Falstaff* of his time, who followed Booth as *Othello* (1738), gave a performance of the part which was recognized by contemporaneous critics as dignified, correct, and respectable. Quin was a man of strong intellect and formidable character. It is not credible that he actually failed in *Othello,* but it is not likely, judging from what is known of his acting in other parts in which he was distinguished,—notably the *Ghost of King Hamlet, Marcus Brutus, Cato, Angelo, Melantius, Bejazet, Pinchwife, Sir John Brute,* and *King Henry the Eighth,*—that he achieved any considerable success in it. He made up his face and hands black, for *Othello,* and wore an English military uniform, a large, powdered wig, and white gloves. When he removed the gloves the sudden disclosure of his sable hands seemed to accentuate the fact that he was showing *Othello* as a Negro. One authority declares that Quin's *Othello* was positively "bad," and condemns by use of the same epithet his *King Lear, Macbeth,* and *King Richard the Third.* On the occasion when Quin first appeared as *Othello,* John Mills exerted his conventional, experienced professional talent in the part of *Iago,* and Mrs. Cibber, —not a beauty, but undoubtedly a woman of dramatic genius, all feeling and fire, with mind to lead and taste to guide,—was the representative of *Desdemona,* and it is doubtful if the part ever had a better one.

Colley Cibber, to whom the student of theatrical
history is indebted for valuable information concerning some of his contemporaries on the stage and also
for information, apparently not always reliable, as
to a few of their immediate predecessors, did not
attempt to play *Othello*, but he played *Iago,* and he
gave a poor performance of that exacting part.
Davies says that he acted *Iago* in a drawling, hypocritical style, and made him such a transparent villain
that *Othello,* "who is not drawn a fool, must have
seen through his thin disguises." He was tolerated,
not esteemed, in tragedy, to which, indeed, he was
not fitted, either by capability of emotion, sensibility
of temperament, dignity of person, or quality of voice.
He could, and did, act old men and fops, and he
acted them well. He rose not beyond that level.
Cibber was not, in talent, the utterly contemptible
person that Pope represents him to have been, but
there is evidence that he was a man of shallow nature,
flimsy character, superficial attainments, and dissolute
life. Success in the impersonation of the complex,
potent, massive characters drawn by Shakespeare
is not possible to persons of frivolous constituence.
Simulation can to some extent beguile, but person-

ality shows itself, and it is decisive in its impartment of final impression.

Iago is incarnate evil but, like every other character in the tragedy, he should be viewed as a poetic type, not as a prosy trickster,—such as, evidently, Cibber made him. He is part of a system of dramatic machinery that operates within the realm of imagination. He was not drawn for the commonplace purpose of showing merely unmitigated depravity. The tragedy of "Othello" tells an awful and agonizing story, of which that ruthless, terrible, but highly intellectual villain is the mainspring of action. The tragedy is made unfit for representation when it is acted in a manner that reduces it to the level of common life. It has been so acted by many players, domestic as well as foreign, whose names it is not essential to mention. Indeed, a complete list of the persons who are known to have appeared as *Othello* and as *Iago* would be almost as prolix and tiresome as the Catalogue of the Ships in the "Iliad."

WILKS AND GARRICK.

The representation of *Othello* given by Robert Wilks, who was more a comedian than a tragedian, seems to have been creditable but not remarkable. Steele intimates that he succeeded in parts of *Othello*, only failing when he tried to imitate Betterton. He made *Othello* black, and he dressed him in a British military uniform and wore a large wig.

The brilliant Garrick, so sympathetic as *Hamlet*, so imaginative and weird as *Macbeth*, and so piteous, affecting, and terrible as *King Lear*, made no significant impression as *Othello*. He acted the part for the first time on May 7, 1745, at Drury Lane. Macklin played *Iago*, and Mrs. Cibber played *Desdemona*. Quin, who did not approve of Garrick's innovating style, attended one of the representations and openly sneered at it, as also did the clever, piquant, satirical, coarse Kitty Clive, an actress of fine ability, a woman of sturdy common sense and one who was accustomed to speak her mind freely on all occasions. To those observers Garrick's *Othello* seemed to be a "little nigger boy." The judgment of Victor, on the contrary, was favorable to Garrick's embodiment, and particularly he extolled that actor's treatment of the piteous scene of *Othello's* epileptic trance,—a scene which, in almost all modern presentments of the tragedy, on the English-speaking Stage, has been omitted. Henry Irving, in his production of "Othello," February 14, 1876, at the London Lyceum Theatre, restored it. Garrick's costume as *Othello* is not particularly described. One of his biographers, Arthur Murphy, says that "he chose to appear in a

Venetian dress,"—in which case he chose aright. Another recorder, of later date, affirms that he wore Moorish garments. It was not his habit to consider correctness of apparel. His venture in *Othello* seems to have been as decisive a failure as Cooke's venture in *Hamlet,* and he discarded the part, after giving only three performances of it. Horace Walpole wrote that Garrick's *Othello* was "ridiculous."

BARRY AND HENDERSON.

Spranger Barry, with his fine, manly person, handsome face, melodious voice, and sympathetic temperament, made the part of *Othello* so much his own that, in the prime of his popularity, 1747 to 1758, no competitor for the public favor undertook to vie with him in it. Colley Cibber esteemed him superior, as *Othello,* to either Betterton or Booth. He dressed the part in a suit of scarlet cloth, decorated with gold lace, and wore a small cocked hat, knee-breeches, and silk stockings, the better to display his shapely legs, of which he was vain,—as men usually are who possess those accidental advantages. He had profited much by the instruction that he received from Macklin, who, if not always able to exemplify his own teaching, was unquestionably an actor of extraordinary intellectual resource and power. Macklin never acted *Othello,* but he acted *Iago,* not only to the *Othello* of Garrick but to that of Foote,—whose performance of the part was given February 6, 1744, at the London Haymarket Theatre, and was a failure. In the opinion of Macklin, Barry's exhibition of the contrasted passions of love and jealous rage was finer than that accomplished by any other actor of *Othello* whom he had ever seen, and Macklin's mature and competent memory of the stage covered the entire period from the time of Betterton to that of Kemble. One enthusiast mentions that when Barry uttered the words "Rude am I in my speech" his tones were "as soft as feathered snowflakes that melt as they fall." Barry made *Othello* a black man, but as his person was tall,—more than five feet eleven inches, —and absolutely symmetrical, his countenance expressive, his smile winning, his voice rich and sweet, and as, being a remarkably expert dancer and fencer, his demeanor and motions were graceful, he was able to overcome that disadvantage. There is no reason for doubt that among all the performers of *Othello* who appeared on the English Stage in the course of the eighteenth century Spranger Barry was the best.

John Henderson did not undertake *Othello* but he played *Iago,* and he was the first among actors of that part to speak the rhymed lines with which *Iago* responds to *Desdemona's* inquiry concerning what would be his praise of "a deserving woman indeed" as if he were slowly and carefully composing them, and not speaking them as a composition which had been committed to memory. He dressed *Iago* in any military garb that chanced to please his fancy, for he was absolutely heedless of propriety of costume. Record is made of the fact that he prided himself on having, in the course of one London season, acted ten different parts in the same apparel. The experienced journalist and competent critic John Taylor, commenting (1833) on Henderson's personation of *Iago,* comprehensively remarked: "He admirably mingled the subtlety of the character with its reputed honesty." To do that was to fill a true ideal.

JOHN PHILIP KEMBLE.—MRS. SIDDONS.

Kemble, in accordance with his custom when performing in a work of imagination, acted *Othello* as a poetic character. "From his first entrance to his last," says Boaden, "he wrapped that great and ardent being in a mantle of mysterious solemnity, *awfully predictive of his fate.*" The same conscientious authority declares that he was "grand, awful, and pathetic, but a European," and adds that he "never so completely worked himself into the character as to be identified with it." The fact that he was "a

European" can scarcely be deemed surprising when it is remembered that *Othello,* although called a Moor, is, unequivocally, drawn as an Englishman, and that whoever plays the part conformably to the text cannot avoid playing it in accordance with that delineation. Kemble's dress, as *Othello,* was strangely incorrect. At one time he wore a portion of the uniform of a British military officer and with that he combined Turkish trousers and a turban! At another time he wore a Moorish costume, obviously inappropriate to a Venetian general. Macready, as a young actor, aged twenty-three, attended (1816) his performance of *Othello,* and saw him in Moorish attire. "His darkened complexion," says Macready, "detracted but little from the stern beauty of his commanding features, and the enfolding drapery of the Moorish mantle hung gracefully on his erect and noble form." The same observer mentions "the dreary dulness of his cold recitation," remarks that "his readings were faultless," and adds that in his acting "there was no spark of feeling." In 1784 William Dunlap, the historian of the early American Theatre (then, as it chanced, a visitor in London), saw Kemble as *Othello,* dressed in a scarlet coat, waistcoat, and breeches, white silk stockings, and a long military cue, and at the same time he saw Robert Bensley as *Iago,* in which part that actor was esteemed very good, dressed in a military uniform of red and blue. When Kemble acted, at Drury Lane, March 8, 1785, as *Othello,* his sister, the wonderful Mrs. Siddons, appeared as *Desdemona,* greatly overweighting a part the predominant and essential characteristic of which is gentleness. Her expert use of the text, in point of inflection, emphasis, and shading of the meaning of words,—examples of which elocutionary felicity have been preserved,—was noted as particularly admirable.

EDMUND KEAN.

The most powerful impersonation of *Othello* that ever was exhibited,—in its effect upon the feelings,— if the numerous and almost invariably enthusiastic accounts of it which exist can be credited, was that of Edmund Kean. The store of superlatives with which the English language abounds has been well-nigh exhausted in the celebration of it. The address that *Othello* delivers to the Venetian Senate was, it appears, as spoken by Kean, a consummate achievement of natural eloquence. *Othello's* greeting to *Desdemona,* on his arrival in Cyprus, was beatific in its expression of love. His dismissal of *Cassio* was noble. His demeanor while his mind was being poisoned by the artful insinuations of *Iago* was such as to communicate to an audience all the afflicting perturbation of an agonized soul. His utterance of the Farewell was the final, overwhelming, surpassingly pathetic impartment of a desolate spirit, a ruined life, and a broken heart. His delirium of jealousy struggling with love was prodigious and awful. His killing of *Desdemona* was sacrificial. His ultimate despair was that of a bleak agony which drowned his being in a sea of grief. His manner of death, making a futile attempt to kiss the face of his dead wife, was unspeakably piteous. Hazlitt designated Kean's *Othello* as "the finest piece of acting in the world."

An opinion generally prevalent among commentators on this subject is that *Othello,* like *Macbeth,* because he is a soldier, has had much experience in warfare, has performed feats of valor and endured many hardships, should be represented by a man of large size. He is called "the Moor," and he declares himself to be of royal lineage. Moors are not, racially, large men. The point is not material. It does not signify whether the actor who appears as *Othello* is tall or short, if he truly is able to act the part. Barry was tall and of large frame; Kean was of low stature and slender figure; each was magnificent as *Othello.*

A question of practical importance, however, is that of *Othello's* color. All the actors who played *Othello* prior to Kean's assumption of the part made him "black," and the text contains phrases which, by some judges, have been thought to justify that usage. Such phrases as "the sooty bosom" and "old black ram" are, it should be observed, spoken by persons hostile to *Othello* and intent on expressing their malicious antagonism toward him. There is no better reason for accepting "black" as literally descriptive of his color than there is for thinking him a four-footed beast because *Iago* calls him so. His own expression, "haply for I am *black*," occurs in a speech in which he is humbly depreciating himself in comparison with the beautiful girl whom he has wedded, and it is figurative, not literal. A Moor is not necessarily black; he is tawny. *Othello* is not a Negro and he should not be represented as one. Kean was the first among actors of the part to recognize that fact and to make that distinction as to color. Furthermore, it is essential that the actor should consider the imperative requirements of facial expression and dramatic effect. The tragedy of "Othello," written mostly in blank verse, and, in general, sustained upon a high level of thought, feeling, invention, and style, if it is to be acted at all should be acted in a poetical spirit. To take a cue from such expressions in the text as "thick lips" and "Barbary horse," and make *Othello* a Negro, is, necessarily, to lower the tone of the interpretation. Kean made him light brown, and his example, in that respect, has been generally followed. It seems not possible fully to depict in words the image of desolation that Kean became,—according to contemporary testimony,—when he reached the climax of that agonizing scene which culminates with the pathetic Farewell. Recorders of his achievement dwell particularly on the quality of his voice,—the thrilling tones, flowing as if out of the depth of a broken heart,—in which he uttered the desolate lines,

> "O now, forever,
> Farewell the tranquil mind! Farewell content!"

and his coincident action, culminating in a complete physical as well as spiritual collapse, when, as he moaned forth "Othello's occupation's gone!" he raised his arms, clasped his hands, and sank back, in the abject misery of ruin. His voice, said Hazlitt, "struck on the heart like the swelling of some divine music." "My father told me" (so wrote Edwin Booth) "that in his opinion no mortal man could equal Kean in the rendering of *Othello's* despair and rage, and that, above all, his not very melodious voice, in many passages, notably that ending with 'Farewell, Othello's occupation's gone!' sounded like the moan of ocean or the soughing of the wind through cedars." His manner of ejaculating, to *Desdemona,*—in the tempest of contention between love and fury that makes *Othello* almost a madman, in the dreadful scene in which he accuses his wife of infidelity,—"Would thou had'st ne'er been born!" is said to have reached the uttermost of pathos. The exclamation, "O fool! fool! fool!" when *Desdemona* is dead and *Iago's* monstrous villany has been revealed came from his lips in a heart-rending whisper of agony. In our time only one actor whom I recall has caused a like effect with it. That actor was Gustavus Vaughan Brooke (1818-1867), a man of deep heart, commanding presence, and rare dramatic ability, whose performance of *Othello* was noble, passionate, and true. Brooke put into the iterated utterance of that little word the whole vast volume of *Othello's* love and woe. The sob with which he accented the last word was afflictive in its excitation of sympathy and grief. Kean's frequent employment of a sob is mentioned in several contemporary accounts of him: when his powers were failing he used it so frequently, indeed, that on one occasion he was hissed for it, and he is said to have remarked, "They have found me out." Brooke could not have been an imitator of Kean. He was only fifteen years old and was resident in Dublin, when Kean, who had long been ill and broken, and whom he had never seen, died, 1833, at Richmond, near London. He had, however, acted with Forrest, who had learned much from Kean and who, rightly and naturally, made use of what he had learned, and thus, no doubt, transmitted much to Brooke. An illuminating remark about Kean's acting was made by the poet Southey, who said that, when inflamed with passion,—which he could simulate with terrifying fidelity,—he looked "like Michael Angelo's rebellious archangel." His voice, by some writers said to have been deficient of melody, was, on the contrary, according to musical authority, one of exceptional range, and could be loud or low, piercing or soft, as his will directed: William Gardiner, in his "The Music of Nature," first published during Kean's life, said, "Mr. Kean possesses the greatest number of effects, having a range of tones from F below the line to F above it, the natural key of his voice being that of B♭, a note lower than Talma's."

JUNIUS BRUTUS BOOTH.

The elder Booth gave a performance of *Othello* which, by some contemporary admirers of his acting, was esteemed kindred with that of Edmund Kean in nobility and pathos. Those two actors, while presenting various points of difference, resembled each other in important particulars, so that, in dramatic history, their names have become almost inseparable. As to Booth's impersonation of *Othello* there are many wild stories. One declares that he acted the part arrayed in an old yellow faded dressing-gown; another that, on one occasion, having no black stockings, he blackened his legs as well as his face and hands, and thereby, in the course of the performance, soiled the white dress of the fair *Desdemona.* The fact is he bronzed his face and hands for *Othello,* as Kean had done, and he presented him not as a Negro but as a Moor. Booth did not, at any time, give scrupulous heed to costume, and at all times he was more or less erratic; but he was a great actor,—greater in *Sir Giles, Pescara,* and *Richard* than in *Othello.* His practice of fitting the sound to the sense, in the delivery of a poetic text, was felicitously evinced in his speaking of *Othello's* address to the Senate, and contemporary celebration of his acting commends as exceedingly beautiful his utterance of the lovely passage,—so peculiarly illuminative of *Othello's* nature,—beginning "If it were now to die, 'twere now to be most happy." Clarity of articulation and careful distribution of accent were among the conspicuous merits of his delivery,—as, indeed, they were among those of the speech of many actors of his period, such as James W. Wallack, William Warren, James E. Murdoch, John Gilbert, John E. Owens, Henry Placide, W. H. Smith, and William Rufus Blake. It is recorded as an excellence of his *Othello* that he dismissed *Cassio* without any denotement of wounded

affection, whereas that was a manifest fault,—because
Othello is deeply grieved. "Cassio, I love thee;
but nevermore be officer of mine" is not the language
of a mere military martinet. In uttering the Farewell, at "Othello's occupation's gone!" he stood erect,
gazing into space, spellbound in misery. As usual
with him, it was not until he had made a considerable
progress into the play that his power and fire were
fully liberated,—the great, surging outburst coming,
in his *Othello,* at the terrible conflict of passion in
the Temptation Scene, in the dreadful Third Act.
He spoke the passage beginning "Like to the Pontic
Sea,"—a passage always omitted by Edmund Kean,
whose strength was not equal to it,—and he made it
tremendously effective. When, at the last, he entered
the chamber to do the killing of *Desdemona* he
carried a lighted lamp in one hand and a naked
simitar in the other, and he maintained an aspect of
deadly calm. The design of the actor apparently,
from the first moment when *Othello's* jealousy had
been awakened, was to allow an Oriental temperament
to show itself, slowly prevailing over the adopted
customs of the Christian. Booth's final business,
which was exceedingly artificial, was to throw a silken
robe across his shoulders and draw from a turban,
on his head, a dagger which had been concealed in
it, with which he stabbed himself to the heart. His

son Edwin wrote of him that his treatment of *Othello* was "eminently Shakespearean and profoundly affecting," and gave also this singular information: "If 'Othello' were billed for the evening, he would, perhaps, wear a crescent pin on his breast that day, or, disregarding the fact that Shakespeare's Moor was a Christian, he would mumble maxims of the Koran."

KEAN AND BOOTH.

Three years after Kean had made his dramatic conquest of London and when he was at the summit of his renown, acting at Drury Lane, Junius Brutus Booth appeared at Covent Garden, February 12, 1817, as *Richard,* and astonished the public not less by his striking resemblance to Kean than by his magnificent performance. Much attention instantly concentrated itself on this surprising newcomer; the adherents of Kean became worried, thinking that a rival to the god of their idolatry might have arrived, and measures were taken by them to bring the question of rivalry at once to a test. Kean called on Booth and invited him to leave Covent Garden and come to Drury Lane, the purpose being, as alleged at the time, to bring him out, at the latter theatre, in a disadvantageous position, and thus to check his advancement. Booth, being young and inexperi-

enced,—he was only twenty-one years old,—accepted
the invitation, and on February 20 "Othello" was
presented, Kean acting *Othello* and Booth acting
Iago. A person, now dead, who was in the audience
that night told me that both actors put forth all
their powers; that the representation was exceptionally
brilliant; that Kean acted with more splendor of
passion and melting charm of pathos than he had
ever shown before in the part of *Othello,* completely
excelling himself; and that Booth, although admirable,
was obliterated. A prominent theatrical writer of
the period, William Oxberry, recorded that "Kean,
on this occasion, outdid all his former outdoings, and
Booth, though *Iago* is not a part for applause, elicited
it in every scene save the drinking one." Booth
accepted his reverse, returned to Covent Garden,
where, after several riots, he was allowed to act, and
continued his career,—coming to America in 1820-21.
The performance of "Othello" in which those two
wonderful actors coöperated must indeed have been
extraordinary, and its occurrence is a memorable fact
in the history of the play. Kean's last appearance
on the stage was made as *Othello,* March 25, 1833,
at Covent Garden,—his son Charles acting *Iago*. He
died, May 15, 1833, at Richmond, and his grave is
near to that of Thomson, the poet of "The Seasons,"
in the old church of that storied town.

MACREADY AND PHELPS.

Macready seems neither to have satisfied himself
(he was a judicious and stern critic of his art), nor
deeply moved his auditors, in the acting of *Othello,*
but he particularly excelled as *Iago.* That result
might have been expected. It is not unjust to his
memory to say that his intellectuality exceeded his
tenderness. Writing in 1835 Macready made this
comment on his *Othello:* "I do not find that I yet
give that real pathos and terrible fury which belong
to the character," and also he described his personation as "elaborate but not abandoned." The part had
then been included in his repertory for nineteen years.
His make-up for *Othello* was Venetian and correct.
Othello is not only an officer in the military service
of the Venetian government, but he has abjured
the religion of Mahomet and become a Christian.
There can be no question as to the costume that
he should wear, and Macready was too much a
scholar and thinker and too scrupulous an executant
to have made a mistake as to *Othello's* raiment.
Hazlitt, generally a discriminative but sometimes
a splenetic, censorious critic, tartly remarked (1816),
relative to Charles Mayne Young and Macready,
who were then acting together in this tragedy, and
alternating the two great parts, that "Young, in

EDWIN FORREST AS *OTHELLO*

Othello, was like a great humming-top, and Macready, in *Iago,* like a mischievous boy whipping him." The greatness of Macready's acting was exhibited in the thrilling revealment of *Macbeth's* agonized and haunted soul, and in the full denotement of the terrific frenzy of *King Lear,* but not in *Othello,*—his performance of which, nevertheless, gained praise for "condensation of vigorous utterance and masculine expression."

Samuel Phelps, while he seems to have followed in a conventional track when acting *Othello,* seems likewise to have given a judicious, potent, and effective performance. He followed old stage traditions in causing *Othello* to strangle Desdemona behind curtains, in an alcove at the back of the closing scene. An English critic, of judgment and taste, F. C. Tomlins (he died in 1867), wrote, of Phelps's *Othello:* "The great and pathetic speech of the Farewell was given with consummate art and force; the images rose one after the other into a grand climax, till they were all scattered by the last, despairing line."

EARLY AMERICAN STAGE.

Among the performers of *Othello* on the American stage, in early times, were Robert Upton, David Douglass, William Hallam, and John Henry. The first representation of the tragedy given in America occurred at the theatre in Nassau Street, New York, December 26, 1751. Upton played *Othello.* The performance given by John Henry, a handsome man, six feet in height, was thought to be more than ordinarily good. He wore the uniform of a British military officer of the period. His face was black and his hair woolly. He made *Othello* a Negro. James Fennell (1766-1816) long retained the part in his repertory, and his personation of it, when he acted in America, was highly extolled. "His appearance in the Moors, *Othello* and *Zanga,*" says Dunlap, "was noble. His face appeared better and more expressive and his towering figure superb." Fennell had light-gray eyes and yellow eyebrows and eyelashes, and he needed "make-up" to produce facial effect, but he was judiciously accounted one of the best tragedians of his day. John Hodgkinson, one of the most versatile actors of whom there is record, while better suited for comedy than tragedy, nevertheless attempted tragic parts, but his performance of *Othello* was neither authoritatively commended nor particularly described. He acted the part, February 6, 1793, at the John Street Theatre, New York, with that excellent actor Lewis Hallam, second of the name, nephew of William Hallam, as *Iago.* Thomas Abthorpe Cooper, whose career was brilliant and whose repertory comprised two hundred and sixty-four parts, obtained his brightest laurels in *Macbeth* and *Virginius,* but the veteran John Bernard, a critical observer not prone to effusive encomium, records the opinion that Cooper's performance of *Othello* was equal to that of Barry,—which, of course, he had seen, —and S. C. Carpenter, writing in 1810, declared that, in the last act of the tragedy, Cooper's acting was "superlatively great." Cooper was an actor remarkable for intrinsic majesty of bearing and deep tenderness of feeling as well as lively imagination and exquisite taste. He made *Othello's* complexion brown and he wore a Venetian dress. He also acted *Iago,* and his performance is recorded as "insidious and pliant in manner, the complete, smooth, varnished villain."

EDWIN FORREST.

Edwin Forrest (1806-1872), who formed his style largely on that of Cooper and somewhat on that of Edmund Kean, with both of whom he had acted and both of whom he fervently admired, gave a potent performance of *Othello,* not, however, free from that animal coarseness which was more or less apparent in all his acting. To deprecate that coarseness was, in Forrest's time,—and, to some extent, is now,—to incur the reproach of being puny, or over-fastidious, or literary, or undemocratic, or prone to "silk-stocking" views of life and art. The Rev. William Rounseville Alger, the principal biographer of that great actor, —for a great actor he was, in his peculiar field and within his obvious, specific limitations,—informs his readers that Forrest's portraiture of *Othello* was sometimes subjected to "censorious criticism" for the reason that "the scale and fervor of the passions bodied forth in it were so much beyond the experience of average natures; they were not exaggerated or false, but seemed so to the cold or petty souls who knew nothing of the lava-floods of bliss and avalanches of woe that ravage the sensibilities of the impassioned souls that find complete fulfilment and lose it." Much fustian, of which that is a specimen, was written about Forrest, in his lifetime, and it has been occasionally written about him since his death. The fact is that he lacked refinement, and that until late in life, when he had greatly suffered, and when his *King Lear* became a royal and deeply pathetic impersonation, his best acting was exhibited in parts that permitted a liberal display of muscularity. He lacked spirituality, and, as a general thing, he lacked poetry. His acting was radically literal. He was a robust man, he possessed a magnificent voice, and always in *Sparta-*

cus, Jack Cade, and *Metamora,* and often in parts
of higher range, such as *Virginius, Damon, Othello,*
and *King Lear,* he acted with a tremendous vigor that
stirred the multitude, more particularly the "average
natures," much as a tempest stirs the waves of the
sea. He impressed his style on the acting and on
the popular taste of his generation, he inspired numer-
our imitators, and when at his meridian he was the
most widely and generally admired actor in America.
Upon the part of *Othello* he bestowed exceptional
attention, and his performance of it was the most
symmetrical, rounded, and finished of his achievements,—unless, indeed, that distinction should be
awarded to his *Febro,* in "The Broker of Bogota."
His appearance in *Othello* was imposing, notwithstanding the ridiculous attire with which he invested
himself, and his acting was powerful and at times
fraught with a barbaric splendor of distinction all
his own. He wore, as *Othello,* a tunic, cut low in the
neck, dark-colored tights, low shoes fastened with straps
and adorned with buckles, an ample silk mantle
spotted with large gilt leaves, a turbanlike hat,
resembling an inverted saucepan, and a dress sword.
His face was clean-shaved, except for his usual mustache and tuft of hair under the lower lip, and his
color was dark brown. In the opening scenes he bore

himself with a fine, solid dignity, suitable to a massive person and a composed, deliberate mind. In the passion and agony of the Third and Fourth Acts he put forth his powers with prodigious effect. His delivery of the Farewell was a sonorous, various, skilful achievement of elocution, and at that point his rich voice was heard with delight. The ensuing transition was made suddenly and with startling effect, when, with a wild, insane fury, he turned upon *Iago,* clutching him by the throat, and in the speech beginning "If thou dost slander her and torture me" he reached a supreme altitude of frenzy. In the last scene he so arranged the stage business that he was "discovered," *Desdemona,* meanwhile, being asleep in bed. The killing was done quickly and with judicious, artistic avoidance of coarse and horrible literalism, an avoidance as effective as it was unusual in his acting. The subsequent action, on the revelation of *Iago's* treachery, was nobly tragic. No player could ever have spoken with more effect "Wash me in steepdown gulfs of liquid fire." The suicide was accomplished with one blow of a dagger, and the death was immediate.

EDWIN THOMAS BOOTH.

On the American Stage the sceptre that slipped from the hand of Edwin Forrest was grasped by the hand of Edwin Booth. It was my fortune to see Booth many times in *Othello*. His performance varied greatly; it was sometimes defective by reason of a certain element of unfitness,—namely, the involuntary infusion into it of a mentality too keenly perceptive and intuitive for the character; but the performance was invariably a skilful, fascinating work of art. It especially excelled in the expression of *Othello's* love for *Desdemona*,—a love which contemplates its object as invested with sanctity; and also in the winning denotement of *Othello's* magnanimity. On one occasion, at Booth's Theatre, it was my privilege to see him act the part to perfection. No affluence of emotion and no skill of beautiful artistic treatment could have improved the performance. I talked with him after the last curtain had fallen and told him that I had never seen him act the part as well. "I have never played *Othello* so well before," he said, "and I shall never play it so well again." He had, though greatly agitated, succeeded in maintaining absolute control of himself and of the part and, at the same time, in creating an effect of complete spontaneity and abandonment. His feelings,—for he was a man of tender heart and acute sensibility, notwithstanding the exceptional dominance of intellect in his nature,—had been so completely aroused that, after the self-contained, majestic opening, he seemed to be swept along upon a veritable tempest of passion, and he carried his auditors with him as leaves are swept by the whirlwind.

In the killing of *Desdemona,* which, terrible though it be, is, in her husband's belief, a righteous immolation, *Othello* is like a priest at the altar. There is then no anger in his conduct. The man has passed through a hell of anguish and passionate conflict, has fallen in epileptic fits, has barely survived an ordeal of maddening torture, and at last he is calm, in the concentration of despair. *Desdemona* must die, because, as he believes, it is necessary and right. He is not doing a murder; he is doing what he thinks to be an act of justice. He confidently supposes himself to be fulfilling a sacred duty of *sacrifice.* He is the wretched victim of a horrible delusion, but in that awful moment he is a sublime figure, an incarnation at once of rectitude and misery. That was the eminence to which Edwin Booth attained in his personation of *Othello,* and his acting, in that scene, on that occasion, has not been surpassed by any performer of our time.

DAWISON AND BOOTH.

One of the most pathetic moments in acting that I have known, or that, as I believe, was ever known by anybody, was the moment when the German tragedian Bogumil Dawison (1818-1872), playing *Othello,* raised the dead body of *Desdemona* in his arms, and, swaying to and fro, in utter, abject, unspeakable misery, with excruciating sobs, three or four times, in accents of heart-rending lamentation, moaned out her name. The Dawison performance of "Othello" was given December 29, 1866, at the old Winter Garden Theatre (which stood on the west side of Broadway, nearly opposite to the end of Bond Street, New York), in association with Edwin Booth, as *Iago,* and Mme. Methua-Scheller, as *Desdemona.* Dawison spoke German, Booth and the members of his company spoke English, and Mme. Methua-Scheller spoke both languages. That was the first of the polyglot representations of Shakespeare with which the American Stage has been disfigured, but it discovered some remarkably fine effects. Dawison was, at that time, fulfilling a professional engagement at the old Stadt Theatre, in the Bowery. In the production of "Othello" which was made for him by Booth, at the Winter Garden, the colloquies that begin the Fourth Act,—comprehending *Othello's* epileptic fit and *Cassio's* contemptuous reference to his mistress, *Bianca,* which *Othello* overhears, supposing it to be allusive to *Desdemona,*—were restored. That part of the tragedy, containing the final and decisive stroke of *Iago's* deadly artifice, contains also such foulness and such excess of agony that, commonly, it is omitted. Many lines of "Othello," indeed, must be discarded in order that it may be made endurable, not to say decent, in a public representation, and, matchless though it is as a piece of dramatic construction, the community, perhaps, would not suffer an irreparable loss if it were altogether relegated from the stage to the library. There can be no doubt, however, that it exactly fulfils the purpose of tragedy as defined by Aristotle,—the excitation, namely, of pity and terror. No adequate presentment of it ever yet failed to provide a solemn warning against the passion of jealousy—always cruel in its operation, and often appalling in its consequences.

Booth made a fine production of "Othello," October, 1862, at the Winter Garden Theatre (which was burned down March 22, 1867), and another, more elaborate and splendid, at Booth's Theatre, April 12, 1869. On the later occasion *Iago* was acted by Edwin Adams, while Mary McVicker (she was married to Booth in the following June) appeared as *Desdemona,* and, in the Fifth Act, sang the Willow Song, the effect of which was ominous and sadly beautiful. It had not, I believe, been heard on the dramatic stage before that time, and it has not been heard there since.

EDWIN BOOTH AS *IAGO*

BOOTH AS *IAGO*.

Booth gave incomparably the best performance of *Iago* that has been seen on our stage within the last fifty years. His *Iago,* when in company, was entirely frank and not only plausible but winning. The gay, light-hearted, good-humored soldier whom he thus presented would have deceived anybody, and did easily deceive *Othello,* who, as Kemble truly and shrewdly remarked, is "a slow man,"—meaning a man slow to those passions which shatter the judgment. Nothing could be more absolutely specious and convincingly sympathetic than Booth's voice, manner, and whole personality were when he said, "There's matter in 't *indeed,* if *he* be *angry!"* The duplicity of the character, when visible in association with others, was made evident to the audience by the subtle use of gesture and facial play, by perfect employment of the indefinable but instantly perceptible expedient of *transparency,*—and it was only when alone that his *Iago* revealed his frightful wickedness and his fiendish joy in it, and there was, in that revealment, an icy malignity of exultation that caused a strange effect of mingled admiration and fear. Although we must detest *Iago* even while we admire and shudder at him, he not only supplies the motive and inspires the action of the tragedy, but also he is the most interesting figure in it, even if the interest be akin to the fascinated loathing inspired by a deadly reptile.

BOOTH AND HENRY IRVING.

Henry Irving acted *Othello* for the first time on February 14, 1876, at the London Lyceum, giving a performance which, if it had been given at a later period in his astonishing career, would have commanded high respect for scholarship, taste, and feeling, but which then was savagely censured in many newspapers: it was withdrawn in April. There could be no doubt of the actor's complete comprehension of the part: Irving knew the great characters of Shakespeare and the great feelings of humanity, through and through: but it was thought that his personal idiosyncrasy made him unfit for the part of *Othello,* and he laid it aside. In 1880 Edwin Booth appeared in London, at the Princess's Theatre, where he gave 119 consecutive performances, his repertory on that occasion including *Hamlet, Richelieu, Iago, Othello, King Lear, Bertuccio,* and *Petruchio.* After his engagement had ended he conceived the idea of giving a series of afternoon performances, and he communicated to Irving his wish to give them at the Lyceum Theatre. His proposition was accepted, but Irving was of opinion that a production of "Othello" in which Booth and himself should appear, alternating *Othello* and *Iago,* would strongly attract the public and prove largely remunerative. That plan he suggested and Booth cordially concurred in it. "Othello" was produced at the Lyceum on May 2, 1881, Booth acting *Othello* and Irving acting *Iago,*—for the first time. Ellen Terry was the *Desdemona;* William Terriss the *Cassio;* Thomas Mead the *Brabantio,* and the now celebrated dramatist Arthur Wing Pinero the *Roderigo.*

The intimation was, after a time, duly supplied, relative to the alliance of Irving and Booth in their production of "Othello" at the London Lyceum, that Irving had formed a sinister scheme for the ruin of Booth as an actor. Irving, no doubt, would have been glad to prove himself a greater actor than Booth in two of the best acting parts in Shakespeare, and Booth, on the other hand, would have been glad to excel Irving and to find himself hailed as the better actor of the two. I was intimately acquainted with both of them, and I can testify, from positive knowledge, that each of them regarded the other as, intrinsically, the only formidable rival on the stage of their time. The rivalry between them, however, was not less honorable than natural. It was the rivalry of emulation. The charge that Irving either attempted or wished to injure Booth in the esteem

of the English public was, and is, ridiculous. The
trial that Irving proposed was eminently a fair one,
and, if disadvantageous to either party, disadvantageous to himself. Booth had been for many years
habitually acting both *Othello* and *Iago*. He was
thoroughly "up" in each part, and he had been victorious in both, in London as well as in America.
Irving had not acted in "Othello" for five years,
when he had, for a short time, "put up" that play
and appeared as the Moor, and he had never acted
Iago. It was necessary for him to "recover" *Othello*
and to learn *Iago,* and that work he was constrained
to accomplish while attending to the business of his
theatre, providing for an entirely new production
of the tragedy, rehearsing the company,—a duty
which Booth, with characteristic inertia, was glad to
escape,—and acting at night, as *Synorix,* in "The
Cup," and as *Doricourt,* in "The Belle's Stratagem."
Booth, meanwhile, was resting. A more liberal
arrangement than that proposed by Irving could not
have been conceived, nor a more intrepid, self-
confident spirit displayed than was displayed by
him.

The opening performance was accounted remarkably brilliant. The two chieftains were liberally
extolled, public opinion, in general, placing them on
about the same level. On May 4 the exchange of parts

first occurred, Booth assuming *Iago* and Irving assuming *Othello*. The dominance of the American actor on that occasion was incontestable,—not that Booth's *Iago* was universally thought to excel that of Irving, but that Irving's *Othello,* compared with that of Booth, was ineffective and decidedly inferior. The engagement lasted from May 2 till June 11 and it was continuously prosperous: the tragedy was acted, however, only three times each week during that period. The prices of seats were raised. More than £4000 had been paid into the Lyceum treasury before the first performance was given. Irving's *Iago,* which was a positive novelty, was picturesque in appearance, genial and winning in manner when in company, openly sardonic, villanous, and odious when alone and speaking the soliloquies, marked by supreme identification, and, as to details, beautifully finished. While watching *Cassio* and *Desdemona,* "Ay, smile upon her, do," he stood aside, unnoted, and as he spoke the soliloquy slowly picked rich, ripe grapes and ate them, spitting out the seeds, between phrases. In the scene at Cyprus, on the "court of guard," when *Iago* makes *Cassio* drunk, his vigilant but veiled craft and light, bantering demeanor were especially effective. In relating to *Othello* the incidents of the drunken brawl his bearing and speech were aptly and happily expressive

of friendly solicitude and grieved affection,—a consummate display of perfect, victorious hypocrisy. In
the distressing scene of *Iago's* beguilement of *Othello*
his insidious deceit and his maintenance of a deadly,
persistent, exultant joy, artfully restrained and hidden from his victim, caused both admiration and
horror. In the night scene in Cyprus, in which *Cassio*
is attacked by *Roderigo* and subsequently stabbed by
Iago, at "Who's there? whose noise is this that cries
on murder?" Irving came on alone, before *Lodovico*
and *Gratiano,* and the business which he used was
commended as "singularly happy." One observer
described it thus:

"It is the last scene of the Fourth Act, a narrow, dimly-
lighted street, made darker yet by the tall houses that close it
in. *Roderigo* lies dead (sic) upon the ground, and *Cassio*
wounded and alone with his deadliest foe. As the scene is
here played, no others are with the two. The night is dark,
and the town very silent. As *Iago* bends over the wounded
man the thought flashes across him, 'Why not get rid of the
two at one happy stroke?' and with the thought he raises his
sword. Another moment and *Cassio* is gone to join *Roderigo,*
but, ere the moment can pass, the called-for succor comes, and
the murderer's hand is stayed. Whether there be warrant for
this in any of the texts we know not, but the effect is very
fine."

The effect *was* very fine,—but the arrangement of
the scene and the illustrative business were invented

and first used by Edwin Booth, years before that
Lyceum revival: they had been seen, and they were
copied from Booth, by Irving. Booth's "Prompt
Book" of "Othello" was published in 1878.

After the Lyceum engagement had ended Booth
publicly declared, June, 1881:

"I was never received more heartily in all my life than by
the audiences drawn together when I played in London. I
have had a most delightful experience, socially, professionally,
and in every respect, with exception of the unfortunate illness
of my wife. . . . My engagement with Irving was one of
the most agreeable that I have ever played. He is one of
the most delightful men I have ever met: always obliging, and
always kind in every possible way."

And in writing to me (Booth never hesitated to free
his mind to me, on any subject) he said, relative to
his Lyceum season:

"Its success is very great, in all respects, and only my
domestic misery prevents it from being the happiest theatrical
experience I have ever had. I wish I could do as much for
Henry Irving in America as he has done here for me!"

Booth's *Othello* costumes were,—First Dress: A
long gown of cashmere, wrought with gold and
various colors. This was looped up on the hip, on
the left side, with a jewelled fastening. A Moorish
burnoose, striped with purple and gold. Purple
velvet shoes, embroidered with gold and pearl. A

sash of green and gold. A jewelled chain. Second
Dress: Steel plate armor. A white burnoose, made
of African goat's hair. Third Dress: A long
white gown, Moorish, with hood and scarlet trim-
mings. A white sash made of goat's hair. Scarlet
velvet shoes. Pearl earrings. These dresses were
intended by Booth to depict a gorgeous barbaric
taste, modified by partial conformance to Christian
and Venetian custom. They were, substantially,
incorrect.

Irving made *Othello,* practically, black. Ellen
Terry has recorded, in her "Recollections," that he
used much pigment, and that on every occasion when
she acted *Desdemona* to his *Othello* her dress and
arms were soiled by contact with him. His dress was
rich and significant of an Oriental taste. In the First
Act he wore a capacious scarlet cloak, with a hood.
Later, he wore a loose, amber-colored robe, a purple
gabardine heavily brocaded, and a small white turban—the latter somewhat similar to that shown in old
prints of Barry as *Othello.* Irving's *Iago* adorned
his person with raiment distinctly unsuitable, because
of its opulence, to either the character of the man
or the rank of the officer. His dress comprised,
among other trappings, a crimson and gold jerkin,
a cloak, of dull dark green color, and a scarlet
mantle. *Iago* is, comparatively, poor and necessitous,

according to his statement about himself, and he is
occupied, aside from other nefarious business, in
swindling, and he follows the wars for "present
living."

Booth's acting of *Othello* and *Iago,* although it
elicited earnest and cordial commendation, in print,
was by some London writers unjustly, ignorantly,
and impertinently disparaged. One censor emitted
the sapient observation that, in speaking, he "gobbled
like a turkey"—a remarkable discovery, indeed, to
have been made relative to one of the best elocu-
tionists that ever spoke, whether on the Stage or
off. Another pundit ascertained that Booth lacked
distinction, at the same time affirming that Irving,—
who, of course, possessed it, as everybody knows
who ever saw him,—much resembled Booth! Such
prattle of mean detraction, not intelligent enough
to be even logical, is worth notice only as a detail
of historical record. Irving himself, who in early
life was a careful student of elocution, considered
Booth to be the finest reader he had ever heard, and
often expressed that opinion. Booth has been dead
eighteen years, and in that time much is forgotten, but
persons still living who heard the music of his tones
and were moved by the exquisite beauty of his utterance will never forget the charm of his speech.
More than half a century ago, in Boston, I chanced

to see him, in the crowded street, dark, straight, lithe as an Indian, and I marked, as he walked swiftly through the crowd, that many persons turned to gaze after him, so remarkable was his aspect of dignity, so distinguished his demeanor. Edwin Booth and Henry Irving unquestionably were rivals, but there never was the slightest need that either of them should be disparaged for the glorification of the other. At a time when German critics were contending as to the relative greatness of Goethe and Schiller, Goethe disposed of the subject by exclaiming, "Let them be thankful that they have two such fellows to talk about." The supremacy of Booth in "Othello" is settled by one decisive fact. Irving, who lived till 1905, never acted either *Othello* or *Iago* after June 15, 1881. Booth acted both parts, in Great Britain, Germany, the United States, and Canada, until nearly the close of his life—his last appearance in the tragedy being at the Broadway Theatre, New York, March 20, 1891,—and always to crowded houses and with great success.

EDWARD LOOMIS DAVENPORT.

An exceptionally fine performance of *Iago* was that given by Edward Loomis Davenport (1815-1877). The maintenance of a bluff manliness of demeanor and an aspect of jovial good nature, in *Iago's* colloquies with *Cassio*, was, in Davenport's assumption of the villanous *Ancient,* so easy, spontaneous, and engaging as entirely to account for *Cassio's* beguilement. His plausibility, in *Iago's* subtle, wicked instillation of jealousy into the mind of *Othello,* was perfect. No actor of the part could ever have more completely justified the confidence of his deluded victim:

> "This fellow 's of exceeding honesty,
> And knows all qualities, with a learnèd spirit,
> Of human dealings."

Virtue, candor, sympathy, and sincerity made up the outward show of the personation, beneath which, revealed in the soliloquies and in the sinister treachery of the action, surged a frightful spirit of odious malice and devilish delight. Strange indeed it seemed that the man who could act *William,* in "Black-Eyed Susan," in such a way as to touch every heart and win not only admiration but affection could also act *Iago* in such a way as to inspire horror and loathing. As to the style of Booth and Davenport, no competent judge of acting ever questioned its spontaneity, flexibility, and absolute consonance with Nature. No actor of the present day (1911) has surpassed, very few have equalled, either of those actors in the matter of being "natural" without ceasing to be artistic and interesting,—and they thus excelled, it should be remembered, in poetic tragedy, not by the employment of photographic copies of the surface aspects of vulgar life. If Davenport's personation of *Othello,*—for he also acted that part with abundant success,—had been as true in pathos as it was symmetrical in form it would have been perfect.

JOHN EDWARD McCULLOUGH.

Behind the artist stands the individual, the personality, from which the artist, however imaginative and however expert in assuming guises that imagination frames, can not and does not escape. John McCullough, intrinsically, was a noble person, and the inherent nobility of his nature was the basis of the greatness of his embodiment of *Othello,*—one of the best embodiments of that character which have been seen in our time, or, as I believe, in any time. The man was a rock of truth and he possessed absolute poise of self, at once royal and simple. His acting was pervaded by a profound and lovely sincerity. He was of commanding stature, his features were bold and regular, and he possessed unusual strength and a melodious voice. With the incarnate magnanimity of *Othello* he was naturally sympathetic, and his potent and winning personality, combined with a perfect command of his rare, diversified, and cultivated dramatic faculties and his capability of rising to great occasions, made him supremely true and deeply affecting in that part. His ideal was poetic, his execution plain, direct, and decisive. At the beginning he did not, even remotely, suggest a man predestined to a tragic fate, and in that particular his *Othello* was, practically, unique,—Salvini alone resembling him in treatment of the first entrance. He was of "a free and open nature," absolutely happy, —his manner that of dignified authority, but manly, confiding, and attractive. The right note was exactly sounded in the manner of that entrance, for when the mind of such a man as he displayed is shattered by jealousy,—when that cruel, fatal passion has torn his heart,—the contrast which is afforded becomes vivid and afflicting, and the inevitable ruin will be no less pathetic than terrific. The calm glance of surprise, at *Iago,* as that miscreant uttered his lie about having thought to have "yerk'd" *Roderigo* under the ribs, the composure of "'Tis better as it is," the modesty of "Let him do his spite," the easy dominance with which he quelled the turbulent disputants, at "Keep up your bright swords," and at "Hold your hands," were perfectly accordant with the equanimity and sweet gravity of the character, and finely effective. In the explanatory speech to the Senate he was open, ingenuous, eloquent, essentially noble; in the meeting with *Desdemona* gentle and tender, almost awe-stricken,—as if it were not possible that such happiness could be found on earth; imperious and majestic in subduing the riotous tumult on "the court of guard"; dangerous and threatening, though restrained at "My blood begins my safer guides to rule"; thrilling and terrible at the climax of the colloquy with *Iago,* "If thou dost slander her and torture me"; piteous in the heart-rending delivery of *Othello's* "Farewell content"; and rightly and pathetically sacrificial in the awful scene that culminates in the killing of *Desdemona.* His cry of anguish when the wretched man becomes aware of his fatal error was more deeply fraught with the delirium of a half-crazed mind and the misery of a broken heart than any words of mine can say. Throughout the performance there was no element of self-consciousness. The identification was complete. The *Othello* was a soldier, so inured to "battles, sieges, fortunes," "hair-breadth 'scapes," "moving accidents," "the flinty and steel couch of war," the command of fierce men and the perils of combat that they had become the custom of every day, and he was as unmindful of them as of his own strength and poise. And, above all, the *Othello* was a lover reverent of the

JOHN McCULLOUGH AS *OTHELLO*

FROM A CRAYON DRAWING

object of his love. Nothing could exceed in pathetic
effect in those cruel scenes of agonized jealousy the
quick relapses into momentary sweet, blind belief in
Desdemona's purity: "If *she* be false, then Heaven
mocks itself." Finer tragic effect could not be
imagined than was wrought by McCullough in
Othello's final utter surrender to the spell of *Iago's*
treachery, when that fiend exclaims "I'm bound
to thee forever!" The Italian tragedian Salvini
expressed the workings of the passion of jealousy, in
the scene of *Iago's* treacherous beguilement of *Othello*,
as I earnestly hope never to see them expressed again,
but it was the jealousy of an infuriated brute, not that
of a noble, generous, tender, loving man—which is the
jealousy of *Othello*. The English ideal is much the
better, because the true one. McCullough filled it;
and in the essential attributes of power, solidity,
elevation, passion, pathos, manly grace, competent
vocalism, and fluent continuity of artistic treatment
his impersonation of *Othello* ranked among the best
dramatic achievements of our time.

The dresses that McCullough wore, one of which
was decorated on the back with the head of a wild
beast, were devised for him by his friend Dion
Boucicault. They were Oriental, not Venetian, and
therefore they were incorrect. Whatever barbaric
impulses may be assumed to slumber in the Christian-

ized Moor there is no warrant for making him considerate of the adornment of his person.

Charles Fechter (1824-1879) within his appropriate professional field was a remarkably fine actor, but Fechter when performing Shakespeare was such an eccentricity as imposed a severe tax on critical patience. The Shakespearean parts that he assumed were *Hamlet, Iago,* and *Othello,* and of his performances of those parts *Iago* was the best. He failed as *Othello.* He lacked dignity; he was weak, fantastic, and unimpressive. In his utterance of the Farewell he rose from a chair and declaimed the lines as if delivering an address,—the bad effect of which proceeding was intensified by his sing-song delivery and execrable utterance of the English language. The business with which he began the last scene should, alone, suffice to prove his lack of comprehension of the character. He went to a mirror and stared into it at his countenance and then spoke the words which *Othello* utters relative to the necessity of killing *Desdemona,*—

> "It is the cause, it is the cause, my soul,—
> Let me not name it to you, you chaste stars!—
> It is the cause—"

meaning to indicate that *Othello* ascribes *Desdemona's* supposed infidelity to the fact of her husband's black color and racial difference. In the killing of *Desdemona* Fechter's *Othello* pursued his terrified wife to the chamber door and dragged her back to the bed, to smother and strangle her. At the supreme moment of *Othello's* desperation, when he said "I took by the throat the circumcisèd dog," he seized *Iago* by the throat, forced him to his knees, made a show of stabbing that miscreant, and then turned the death-blow on himself. His performance, though it deserved no admiration, did not lack admirers. Foreign misrepresentations of Shakespeare's characters seldom suffer from lack of praise.

TOMMASO SALVINI.

The question as to the representation of *Othello* is a simple one: Should the character and experience be interpreted before the public as poetry or as prose? Discussion of that subject was much stimulated when the eminent Italian actor Tommaso Salvini first made his appearance in New York, September 16, 1873, at the Academy of Music,—acting *Othello*, and presenting an Italian ideal of the part. The excellence of Salvini as an executant in the practice of his art has not been doubted or denied. He was a great actor, one of the greatest that have ever lived. In the characters of *Conrad*, in "La Morte Civile," and *Niger*, in "The Gladiator," he surpassed competition. In *King Saul*, a grand and terrible figure as drawn by Alfieri from the old Hebrew scripture, he was artistic perfection. Those parts, and others which could be named, appertain to the dramatic literature of his native land, and they were wholly within his comprehension. In the great characters of Shakespeare, because they do not truly exist in the Italian language, he was always and necessarily obstructed by his lack of a full understanding of the conceptions of the English poet. His performance of *Othello* was tremendously effective as a piece of dramatic execution, but it was radically and ruinously false in ideal. The love of *Othello* for *Desdemona* is devotional, not sensual. When they meet at Cyprus he hails her with the expressive words, "O my *soul's* joy!" The keynote is struck in that greeting:

> "If it were now to die
> 'T were now to be most happy; for I fear
> My soul hath her content so absolute
> That not another comfort like to this
> Succeeds in unknown fate."

The exquisite poetry of that speech has not been conveyed into the Italian language. Salvini not only did not express it but did not even indicate any knowledge of it. Already, in the First Act of the play, he had made it clearly manifest that his impersonation of *Othello* would be prose and not poetry, for when *Brabantio,* after the dispersal of the Senate, warned him, with the words "She has deceived her father and may thee," he introduced a denotement of coarseness and jealousy, giving a violent start, and looking from father to daughter with a quick, flickering, tigerish glare,—proceedings obviously unwarranted in a man "not easily jealous," and whose very next words are, "My *life* upon her *faith!*" Prose the impersonation was when first revealed and prose it continued to be. Salvini caused a startling effect by rushing in and beating down with his naked hands the drawn swords of the combatants in the night brawl, but in so doing he lapsed out of massive poise and lost control of the situation. When, in the dismissal of his lieutenant from the command, he said, "Cassio, I love thee, but never more be officer of mine," he shook his fist in the face of that officer,—his dearest friend, who had gone a-wooing with him,—and thus he disclosed an innate plebeian quality of character completely foreign to *Othello,* as drawn by Shakespeare. As the performance proceeded that quality became more and more conspicuous. The manifestation of jealousy was animal and vulgar, affording no suggestion of the noble mind and loving, trusting heart which should bend and break under the conviction of a base betrayal. In the furious assault on *Iago,* after the speech of Farewell,—which, as spoken by Salvini, was no more than a flourish of rhetoric,—he seized that dangerous man, hurled him to the floor, and lifted his right foot as if to stamp upon his head, a proceeding which Shakespeare's *Iago,* being what he is and being armed, would endure for about two seconds. The whole conduct of that frightful scene was very striking, artfully planned to cause great excitement, and it nearly always produced the effect that the actor had intended. He became an incarnation of animal fury, huge, wild, dangerous, and horrible, but he was consistently common and bestial. The innate grandeur of Shakespeare's *Othello,* which had been measurably suggested in the delivery of the speech to the Senate, had completely disappeared. In the last scene, when *Othello* came into *Desdemona's* chamber, and when he should be, for a considerable period, self-controlled, deliberate, grandly solemn, Salvini was robed in a yellow gown, and he prowled to and fro like an enraged tiger about to spring upon his prey. *Desdemona* attempted to escape from him, but *Othello* seized and dragged her to the bed and there killed her, in the most extreme violence of snorting fury, after which deed of massacre he circulated to and fro about the bed for some moments, disregarding the calls of *Emilia* and seeming demented with rage. When *Iago* was brought in, bound, *Othello* snatched a sword from one of the several attendants present and delivered upon him such a stroke as would have killed him,—ignoring the guidance of the text, *Iago's* "I bleed, sir, but not killed." The sustained, uniform, correct, artistic execution of his ideal could not be overlooked, and it could not be regarded as other than the admirably ample and exact fulfilment of a clearly formed design. The defect was in the design, and it was a fatal defect, pervading the entire performance. Salvini's *Othello,* however, has, throughout the principal countries of Europe and America, been accepted and extolled with prodigious enthusiasm, and, only because of the excitement that it diffused throughout the nervous systems of the multitude, it possesses a worldwide renown. Offered as Shakespeare's *Othello,* it was repugnant equally to judgment, scholarship, and taste. In fact, it was a desecration of the poetic original.

Salvini's dressing of the part, throughout, was Moorish and therefore wrong. His business at the end was to cause *Othello* to kill himself by hacking open his throat with a curved knife,—a proceeding totally at variance with Shakespeare's text:

"I *took* by the throat the circumcis'd dog,
And *smote* him—thus!"

No ingenuity can turn a *blow* into hacking open the throat, nor could a man with his throat chopped open utter the last words of *Othello*:

"I kiss'd thee, ere I kill'd thee:—no way but this,
Killing myself to die upon a kiss."

There are characters and passages in the poetry of Shakespeare relative to which a reasonable ground exists for difference of opinion. There is no ground for difference of opinion as to certain qualities in the character of *Othello* and certain passages in the tragedy,—notably the scene at Cyprus and the last scene. Shakespeare's *Othello* is neither sensual, animal, nor ferocious: he is manly, magnanimous, fearless, confiding, noble, romantic, and tender, and at the culmination of his terrible experience he is an authentic type of woful grandeur. The last scene of the tragedy might well be selected as a test scene. There stands the poetic text, and it cannot be evaded. *Othello* has been so ravaged by contending passions and by grief that he has twice fallen in epilepsy. "He looks gentler than he did." When he enters the bed-chamber he comes as the minister of Fate. He is absolutely quiet. "It is the cause." The death of *Desdemona* has been ordained. She is lovely and greatly loved, "yet she must die, else she'll betray more men." The wretched man is about to extinguish the light burning in the chamber but pausing a moment, gazes at his beautiful wife, quiescent in slumber, and doing so murmurs his thought in words of solemn beauty:

"If I quench *thee*, thou flaming minister,
 I can again thy former light restore,
 Should I repent me:—but once put out *thy* light,
 Thou cunning'st pattern of excelling nature,
 I know not where is that Promethean heat
 Which can thy light relume. When I have pluck'd the rose
 I cannot give it vital growth again,
 It needs must wither."

Three times he kisses the sleeping *Desdemona,* but so gently that she knows it not and does not waken. The exquisite loveliness and the innocence of his wife, in which he has believed, and a dreadful wickedness of her conduct which he has been beguiled to credit, unite to overwhelm him, and he weeps:

"But they are cruel tears: this sorrow 's heavenly;
 It strikes where it doth love."

Here is no fury, no tigerish convulsion. It is the soul that speaks. "Have you prayed to-night?" he asks, when at length the poor child has wakened. "I would not kill thy unpreparèd spirit." It is not until, as he believes, she utters a falsehood, even in the presence of death, when he has bade her make her peace with Heaven, that *Othello's* wildness momentarily returns upon him:

> "Thou dost stone my heart,
> And mak'st me call what I intend to do
> A murder, which I thought *a sacrifice.*"

And even in the very commission of the dreadful deed there is mercy: "I would not have thee linger in thy pain." The student who can find in that awful and pathetic scene any warrant for such acting as Salvini and various other foreigners have provided for its illustration must be peculiar in the faculty of discernment.

ERNESTO ROSSI.

The advent on the American stage of the distinguished Italian actor Ernesto Rossi (1829-1896), occurred at Booth's Theatre, New York, October 31, 1881, and was effected in *Othello.* The Italian ideal of the part had been made known by his illustrious predecessor, Salvini, and it was known to be completely wrong. Rossi's performance only served to accentuate its deformity. His *Othello* was a common man, at first intoxicated by sensual passion and after-

TOMMASO SALVINI AS *OTHELLO*

ward infuriated by demoniac jealousy. In person
the actor was large and stout, having a round face,
regular features, dark eyes, and a strong, resonant
voice, neither melodious nor very flexible, but, in its
hoarse, broken tones, effectively expressive of painful
emotion. As an actor he was authoritative, distinct,
definite, continuously animated, profoundly earnest,
and so entirely masterful of the instrumentalities of
his art as to create the effect of complete spontaneity.
His acting was especially competent and effective in
moments of half-crazed perplexity,—the oscillation
between confident belief and distracting doubt,—when,
as at the summit of the scene of *Iago's* poisonous
distillment, it seemed that neither body nor mind
could endure the strain of conflicting passions, and
also in the frenzy that culminates in the epileptic
trance. The situations thus indicated present no
obscurity to an able and experienced actor. The
difficulty is to make apparently actual a clear, rounded,
finished, true ideal of Shakespeare's conception.
Rossi's delivery of *Othello's* speech to the Senate,
while accompanied by much expressive and commendable gesture, was devoid equally of simplicity and
dignity,—the speaker destroying illusion by turning
his back upon the Senators and addressing the audience. The greeting to *Desdemona* at Cyprus was
expressed in a spirit of gloating, uxorious animal-

ism, inconsistent equally with the character and the situation. The delivery of the rebuke to *Cassio* was exasperated, and neither dignified nor sorrowful,— the words "Cassio, I love you" causing no effect. The demeanor and gesture, when *Othello,* becoming surprised and a little bewildered by *Iago's* innuendoes, exclaims "Thou dost mean something," signified only sneaking suspicion. The pathetic Farewell was a burst of hysterical garrulity. The denunciation of *Iago,*—who, yelling with fear, had been hurled to the floor, Rossi, like Salvini, raising his foot over the *Ancient's* head as though about to stamp out his brains,—was snarled forth with merely blatant vehemence. The killing of *Desdemona* was effected with hideous brutality, and in the act of suicide *Othello* was made to emit spasmodic gurgling sounds, as of a person choked by blood. The several facts, which, in treating this subject, cannot be over-emphasized, that, in Shakespeare's tragedy, *Othello* is a poetic creation, a consummate type of nobility and magnanimity; that his love for *Desdemona,* while humanly passionate, is awed in the presence of its idolized object and exalted by its ecstasy, and that the killing of his wife is a sacrifice, not a butchery, were not comprehended by Rossi, any more than they had been by Salvini, and his embodiment,—unredeemed by such personal magnetism and such colossal individuality as those of his predecessor,—was radically wrong and supremely repulsive.

Ermete Novelli presented himself in the guise of *Othello,* for the first time on the New York Stage, on March 25, 1907, and, while manifesting his unquestionable ability, succeeded only in misrepresenting the part and again proving what had been proved already,—that the Italian ideal of it is radically false to Shakespeare and obnoxious to good judgment and good taste. As *King Louis,* as *Corado,* and as *Geronte,* in "The Beneficent Bear," Novelli showed himself to be an excellent comedian, but the endeavors that he made in tragedies of Shakespeare evinced no decisive tragic capability. His ideal of *Othello* was seen to be substantially identical with that which had been revealed by Salvini and Rossi, while his mechanism was, in every way, inferior to that of both his compatriots. He looked like a buck Negro, and when rushing wildly to and fro, glaring backward over his shoulder, as he did almost continuously in the crucial scene in the Third Act, he seemed like an infuriated gorilla. By enthusiastic admirers (for always "The present eye praises the present object") Novelli was hailed as another Salvini, but in fact he no more resembled that great actor, who, among other merits, possessed repose, than a powder-mill resembles a volcano.   His stage business was even more unsuitable than that of his predecessors.   After using *Iago* as a floor-mop,— according to the Italian stage custom,—he indicated a quick revulsion of feeling and assisted his officer to rise.   *Othello* respects and trusts *Iago,* being duped by that scoundrel's hypocrisy, insidious pretence of candor, and specious assumption of loving friendship, yet the demeanor of Novelli's *Othello* toward *Iago* was, almost invariably, the careless, contemptuous demeanor of an arrogant master toward a servile lackey.   There is a moment in the play when *Othello* says that his blood begins his safer guides to rule: in Novelli's performance *Othello's* blood began that operation at the first and continued it almost incessantly till the end,—his habitual behavior being that of an irritated bully.   On *Roderigo,* whenever he beheld that silly dupe, he glowered like an angry mastiff.   He introduced a grimacing pantomime signifying to *Desdemona,* who coincidentally indicated solicitude lest *Othello* might speak harshly to her sire, that he could not possibly be disrespectful toward that venerable person.   In the Senate Scene he kept his back turned upon his audience much of the time, so that his voice could not always be distinctly heard nor his face be seen, but when addressing the Sena-

tors (who were arranged across the back of the
stage from left to right centre) he occupied the
middle of the scene, turned his back upon the "potent,
grave, and reverend signiors," and apostrophized the
audience. Toward *Brabantio,* after the old and
broken father had spoken his warning, "Look to her,
Moor," his attitude became that of wrath and menace;
he rushed after him to the door of the chamber, bawl-
ing the words, "My life upon her faith,"—words
that should be spoken with the dignified composure
and sweetness of happy, confident love. When he
came upon the scene of the brawl at Cyprus he rushed
in looking like a Negro, arrayed in the military uniform of a Zouave, wildly waving a naked simitar and
whirling 'round between the combatants with an aspect
of fury. He omitted "Silence that dreadful bell,"
and when he said "Cassio, I love thee, but nevermore be officer of mine" he kept his face turned from
the audience and he twiddled a forefinger of his right
hand under the nose of his "loved" friend, and after
Desdemona's entrance he shook his fist in *Cassio's*
face. When uttering the heart-broken Farewell he
seized a large, high-backed chair, and, clasping both
hands on one corner of its back, bent his body
forward and to the right, and poured out all but
the last three or four lines of that agonizing speech in
a stream of prosy colloquialism, and then ran

"up-stage" and spouted the conclusion to the back drop. In the Oath Scene, after "I here engage my words," his expedient was to rise half-way and then sink back, at *Iago's* "Do not rise yet," and remain, with his hands lifted to his face and joined as if in prayer, while *Iago,* standing over him, delivered the impious apostrophe "Witness, you ever-burning lights." In the last scene he came on, carrying a huge silver lamp, lighted—the distinctly specified requirement being that *Desdemona* shall be asleep, in her bed, with a light burning in the room. His grunting and growling aroused *Desdemona,* who left the bed and came down the stage, to act the scene with him in front, where, finally, he seized her around the throat, with both hands, dragged her across the whole depth of the stage, in a violent struggle, threw her upon the bed, springing upon her and dropping the bed-curtain; whereon ensued a vocal emission of horrible snarls, gasps, growls, and gurgles, degrading that deed of "sacrifice" to a beastly *Bill Sikes* murder of *Nancy.* When he killed himself he cut his throat, as Salvini had done, and died, rolling down steps in front of the bed.

Novelli's dressing of *Othello* was Moorish, that fact giving decisive proof of either ignorance or disregard of the correct dressing of the part. *Othello* has become a Christian and he is a general in the service of the state of Venice. The studious commentator Charles Knight remarks that *Othello's* marriage to a Christian lady is, in itself, conclusive proof that he must have ceased to be a Mohammedan. The testimony of *Iago* is explicit on this point:

> "To win the Moor—were 't to *renounce his baptism*,
> All seals and symbols *of redeemèd sin*—
> His soul is so enfetter'd," etc.

And *Othello* himself says (Act II., Sc. 3):

> "Are *we* turned Turks, and to ourselves do that
> Which Heaven hath forbid the Ottomites?
> For *Christian* shame, put by this barbarous brawl."

The correct dress for *Othello* is that of a general in the service of the Venetian Republic. It is recorded by Paulus Jovius that the Venetian generals were always foreigners, selected for that office "lest any of their own countrymen [Venetians] might be puffed up with pride and grow too ambitious." On the day of his election to office the Venetian general assumed a distinctive dress: a full gown of crimson velvet, with loose sleeves, over which was worn a mantle of cloth of gold, buttoned upon the right shoulder with massy gold buttons; a cap of crimson leather; and a silver baton, ensigned with the lion of St. Mark. In action he would wear full armor of the period (1750), which was much the same over all Christian Europe. Such is the information supplied by Planché, one of the best authorities extant on costume.

As *Othello,* Novelli arrayed himself in the remarkable garments here specified. First dress: trousers of dark blue or black, with white embroidery about the ankles: a light, parti-colored vest, heavily embroidered with gold: a sash of parti-colored silk, twisted into a heavy roll, around the waist: a richly jewelled dagger, thrust into the middle of the sash; a surcoat, the ground color of which was purple, incrusted with gold, while on the back, across the shoulders and reaching almost to the waist, was gold embroidery; a red turban, embroidered with gold, the centre and top of the turban being white; and a spray-like plume of feathers, rising from the turban. Second dress (at Cyprus): A chain-mail tunic and mail covering for the legs: a breastplate of gleaming steel, with a large gold spike in the centre of it: A red under-dress embroidered with black,—which he wore throughout the rest of the play: that dress reached from his neck to his ankles; the cuffs of it were parti-colored silk, hanging from each wrist about three inches: it was moderately close-fitting on the body, loose and baggy from the waist to the knees, close-fitting from the knees to the ankles (the *color* of his under-dress was, when Novelli made his second tour of the United States, changed to *blue*) : a parti-colored scarf, round the waist, in a roll: a white cloak, heavy with gold embroidery; a steel helmet, with a Moorish parti-colored turban round it, and a plume of spray-like feathers in its front; a huge "two-handed" sword, which he carried unsheathed: the top of his helmet was ornamented with a gold *crescent*—the emblem of the Moslem faith, which *Othello* has abjured, and likewise the distinctive blazon of the Turk, against whom he is, at the time, in arms!

Novelli was not satisfied to present his perversions of Shakespeare (he appeared as *King Lear, Shylock, Hamlet, Petruchio, Othello,* and *Macbeth*) and allow them to stand for what they were. He deemed it necessary and judicious to publish instructions as to what actors and acting should be, and he appeared in print to justify his performance of *Othello* in the Italian alteration of the play. If his performance had left any doubt as to his complete misunderstanding of *Othello* his published remarks would have removed it, while also disclosing radical defect in his artistic principles and method.

"Never do I upon the stage,"—so he wrote,— "anything I have not *seen done, in like circumstances, in real life.* I hold the mirror up to nature, which is truth, which is *realism.*" Exactly: it *is* realism, while

Acting is Dramatic *Art.* "The blood leaped from his gashed neck," continued Novelli, describing an act of suicide in a public place, "like a fountain of wine. He held the razor—thus: and he bent forward—so. I shoulder (*sic*) my way to the front of the crowd, and, as I do it, I hear the dying man give a gurgle in the throat—a gurgle like this—s-s-s-r-r-r-r-R-R-r! And then I say: '*That* is the way! *Now* I know how the Moor died. *At last* I can play the part!' And that night I begin rehearsal of 'Othello.' "

What relation does a street-suicide committed by an Italian barber who cuts his throat with a razor bear to the tragedy of "Othello"? "Never do I upon the stage anything I have not seen done, *in like circumstances, in real life,*" was Novelli's declaration, and he killed *Othello* by causing him to cut his throat according to the model he described. What *likeness* exists in the circumstances of the two deaths? And what must be the mental calibre of an actor who cannot "play the part" of *Othello* until he has looked on the hideous and vulgar spectacle of an actual suicide; who waits to begin rehearsals of "Othello" until he has seen a death that he thinks can appropriately be copied into that play,—two minutes before it ends! "In acting," he added, "the days of artifice have gone; the day of truth has dawned." Sublime discovery! Beneficent impartment! But, who were the practitioners of

"artifice" on the benighted English-speaking Stage
that, happily, have passed away? Were they, perhaps, Garrick, Barry, Henderson, Kean, Booth,
Macready, Phelps, Forrest, Brooke, Davenport,
Edwin Booth, McCullough, Barrett, Wallack, Burton, Finn, Warren, Gilbert, Irving, Mansfield?
"With Shakespeare," said Novelli, "I did only some
cutting which was necessary to make him, *for the
first time,* popular in Italy." That claim indicated
the modest disposition of its maker, and, incidentally,
of course, rectified serious error. An impression had
long prevailed that, while Ermete Novelli was still
a youth, his illustrious leader, Salvini, however
inadequate his performances may have been to the
requirements of English ideal, had, at least, accomplished something by way of making the Shakespeare
alterations "popular" in Italy. On the whole,
Novelli's printed deliverance respecting *Othello*
afforded an admonitory example of the injury which
proceeds from a hurtful custom, prevalent among
actors, of publishing views about their performances
and about the art of which they are ministers. Acting
which requires elucidation by diagrams and foot-notes
by the performer is not good acting. Foreign
actors, in particular, visiting America, show themselves to signal disadvantage, often creating a harmful impression of ill-breeding, when they indulge in

that form of literary industry. There are persons, indeed, considerable in number, who admire all foreign forms of art only because they are foreign, and who accept with meek and humble provincial gratitude the patronizing precepts of foreign performers; but the American community, as a whole, naturally regards as an impertinence the top-lofty attitude of foreign visitors to the American Stage who assume to dispense instruction as to the function of dramatic art and the meaning of English dramatic literature. It should be remarked, furthermore, that the writings of those peripatetic players are, in general, not only impertinent but ridiculous. Some of the views promulgated by foreign actors and some of the performances exhibited by them would speedily exile any English-speaking actor to the obscurity of the backwoods.

AN OFFENSIVE THEORY.

The tragedy of "Othello" has not escaped indignity in print. One peculiarly offensive view of the subject, and one that is not less absurd than it is offensive, was set forth in a treatise on "The System of Shakespeare's Dramas," by D. J. Snider, and, strange to say, it has not only been tolerated but sometimes even approved. That view maintains that jealousy between *Othello* and *Desdemona* must necessarily

From a photograph

ERMETE NOVELLI AS *OTHELLO*

occur because of the racial difference between them
(which is to look at the subject through the eyes of
Iago), and furthermore that *Othello*, in the poet's
scheme, must be assumed to have committed adultery
with *Emilia*, the wife of *Iago*, and for that reason,
being aware of the possible fact of infidelity in the
married state, is the more credulous of *Iago's* insinuations and affirmations relative to unchastity on the
part of *Desdemona*. No extravagance of misunderstanding could be more monstrous. *Desdemona* is
never jealous. The last words that fall from her
lips as she dies,—words spoken in order to shield
Othello,—ascribe her death to her own hand,
and express absolute fidelity of love to her husband: "Commend me to my kind lord." *Othello's*
jealousy is no ethnological consequence but a passion
artfully inspired by the hellish ingenuity of an intellectual monster. What except folly could suppose
that *Othello*, if he had been guilty of debauching
Iago's wife, would deliberately and needlessly select
Iago as the guardian of his bride, and appoint *Emilia*,
—his paramour, as in the case assumed, she would
be,—as his bride's special attendant and companion?

> "Honest Iago,
> My Desdemona must I leave to thee:
> I prithee let thy wife attend upon her
> And bring them after in the best advantage."

And what except ignorance of human nature could believe that, under the circumstances which would exist, consequent on a criminal intimacy between *Othello* and *Emilia,* an affectionate friendship could ensue between *Emilia* and *Desdemona,*—as it *does* ensue,—causing *Emilia* to serve *Desdemona* implicitly, to defy *Othello,* to oppose and denounce *Iago,* and to endanger and lose her life by proclaiming *Desdemona's* innocence and exposing *Iago's* guilt?

> "Moor, she was chaste: she lov'd thee, cruel Moor:
> So come my soul to bliss as I speak true,
> So speaking as I think, I die—I die."

To allege that *"Iago's* suspicion of *Othello* is true" *(sic,* meaning justified), only because *Iago* entertains it, is to crown folly with nonsense. *Iago* is, by nature, an utterly selfish man, and jealous as well as licentious and envious. It is, first of all, his knowledge of himself which has assured him that "trifles, light as air, are, to the jealous, confirmation strong as proofs of holy writ." He is jealous of all goodness and all merit in other persons, and his perception of goodness and merit is immediate, exact, and profound: he perceives them and he hates them. His suspicion of *Othello* is the suspicion of an evil mind, conscious of its evil. His surmise as to the likelihood of *Cassio's* love for *Desdemona* proceeds from the same fountain of turpitude in himself. He abhors both those men, and he will ruin them if he can. When he says, of *Cassio,* "there is a daily beauty in his life that makes me ugly," he expresses his characteristic animosity toward everything in the world which he sees and knows to be better than himself. Motive for *Iago's* malignity is not more obscure than that of the wary, deadly rattlesnake, that strikes whatever obtrudes on him, because it is his nature to envenom and kill. There are precisely such men and women in the world. Furthermore, belief in the possible criminal conduct of other persons operates on the mind of *Iago* exactly as positive knowledge would operate. No man in actual life and no man depicted in fiction ever knew and understood himself more thoroughly, or could describe himself more exactly, than that miscreant does in Shakespeare's page, and of his views relative to *Othello* and *Emilia* and *Cassio* and *Desdemona* he makes, in soliloquy, a definite exposition, together with the reasons for them, an exposition which it is difficult to understand how any examiner can so distort as to make them in any degree substantiatory of Snider's preposterous doctrine.

Consideration of the different ideals of *Othello* which have been proclaimed and the different methods of acting the part which have been illustrated on the stage could be much prolonged, but not to instructive purpose. Many actors of *Othello* whom I have seen, and many of whose endeavors in the character I have read, contributed practically nothing more than professional skill in the exposition of ideals and methods originated for them by others. Reputable, sometimes admirable, performances of the part, in Great Britain and America, have been given by Thomas Ryder, Alexander Pope, George Bennett, James Robert Anderson, John Ryder, Charles Dillon, Herman Vezin, Wilson Barrett, Wyzeman Marshall, James Booth Roberts, Charles Barron, Louis Aldrich, Lawrence Barrett, Louis James, Frederick Warde, Barton Hill, George Edgar, and Robert D. MacLean.

Mention should be made, as of a curiosity, of Ira Aldridge (1804-1867), a Negro, whose performance of *Othello* was accepted and admired by considerable audiences, and by persons of critical pretension, in Great Britain and in Germany, 1826, 1833, 1852. Accounts of the life of that performer are various and dubious. One narrative designates him "the

African Roscius" and states that he was descended
from "Princes of Senegal." I have heard that in
boyhood he was employed at the Chatham Garden,
New York, as a dresser, attendant on Henry Wallack.
His first appearance on the stage appears to have
been made in London, at the Royalty Theatre.
Approval of his acting was ascribed to Edmund Kean
and also to the popular actress Eliza O'Neill (Lady
Wrixon Becher). He seems to have been a man of
talent, and probably his performance of *Othello*
attracted particular attention and was considered the more remarkable because of his being a
Negro. He was born in Maryland, and he died in
Poland.

The best, indeed the only important, impersonation of *Othello* recently shown (1911) on the American Stage was that given by Robert Bruce Mantell.
It was pervaded by the right spirit,—that of martial
authority, innate dignity, simplicity of mind, and a
sweet, confiding magnanimity,—and it possessed the
artistic beauties of symmetrical form and fluent
expression. The style of Robert Mantell was formed
by close study and severe practice, on the English
provincial stage, at a time when the influence of "the
old school of actors," as it is customarily called,—an
influence which compelled strenuous endeavor,—had
not perished. Like Henry Irving, he derived lasting

benefit from professional association with Charles Mathews, a performer who, though he did not adventure in tragedy, was a master of the art of dramatic expression. As *Othello* Mantell struck the true note of pathos in a heart-breaking show of the terrible struggle between love and doubt in a generous mind and in depicting the fanatical, almost maniacal, prepossession of a deceived, bewildered, cruelly afflicted man, intent to achieve justice by inflicting death. His expression of *Othello's* frenzy when deluded by *Iago* was ample and terrible, and his management of the whole closing scene was marked by a controlling sense of the solemnity, the terror, the pathos, and the appalling misery which are its dramatic constituents. He used the text as arranged in Edwin Booth's "Prompt Book," slightly modified, and he followed, as to business, in the traditional path.

IAGO.

The name of the first performer of *Iago* is unknown. The name first associated with the part in theatrical annals is that of John Taylor. Mention is made by Halliwell-Phillipps of a legend that *Iago,* when first acted, was assumed by "a comedian," and that Shakespeare "adapted some of the speeches to the peculiar talents of the actor." In Glidon's "Reflections" (1694) there is an intimation that "Shakespeare put several words and expressions into his part, not so agreeable to his character, to make the audience laugh." The legend has no adequate ground and the intimation is absurd. Enough is known of the actors of Shakespeare's time to warrant the belief that many of them were competent to perform in both serious and comic parts. The humor of *Iago* is sometimes affectedly jocular and sometimes sardonic. No man in the whole wide range of dramatic literature expresses himself in a manner more absolutely consistent with his character than *Iago* does. His levity of speech is as genuine as his villany of conduct. There was not, and could not have been, need of insertion of any words to cause laughter. The chronicle of early representatives of the part includes, beside Cibber, Macklin, and Henderson, already mentioned, ——— Clun; Michael Mohun, 1668; John Verbruggen, 1706-07; Lacy Ryan, 1722; John Mills, 1738; David Garrick, 1750; William Havard, 1761; Richard Sparks, 1762; ——— Sowdon, 1769; John Palmer, 1773; Robert Bensley, 1774; Thomas Ryder, 1787; George Frederick Cooke, 1797; Edmund Kean, 1815; Junius Brutus Booth, and Thomas Abthorpe Cooper. Kean, according to some, if not all, contemporary testimony, was as fine in *Iago* as in *Othello*. Hazlitt declared Kean's *Iago* to have been the most thoroughly sustained of all his performances: other first-hand testimony has ascribed that superiority to his performance of *Sir Edward Mortimer,* in "The Iron Chest." It does not seem surprising, in view of the contrast between the two characters, that a superb actor should succeed in causing even a stronger effect with *Iago* than with *Othello,* for the reason that, in point of propulsion,—a continuity of *doing* something,—*Iago* is the better part. *Iago* acts: *Othello* is, to a great extent, acted upon. Were it not that *Iago's* proceedings keep *Othello* continuously before the "mind's eye" *Iago* might be made to absorb all attention. Kean, according to Hazlitt, whose accounts of his acting are detailed and specific, made *Iago,* throughout, "an excellent good fellow and lively bottle companion," "a pattern of comic gayety and good-humor,"—not, however, sufficiently grave to satisfy the judgment of that observer, who pointed out, as a radical distinction between *King Richard the Third* and *Iago,* that the former is "a princely villain" who misuses his power, in contempt of mankind, and should be represented in "the regal jollity and reeling triumph of success," while the latter is "an adventurer in mischief" who cannot assume superiority as if he were entitled to it.

Nearer to the present time, among the many actors who have performed as *Iago,* a few who gained distinction in the part were James Robert Anderson, John Henry Barnes, George Bennett, Gustavus Vaughan Brooke, William Creswick, Leigh Murray, and Samuel Phelps, in Great Britain, and Edwin Adams, Lawrence Barrett, John McCullough, Barton Hill, William E. Sheridan, George Jamieson, Charles R. Pope, James William Wallack, Jr., and Frederick Warde, in America.

TIME AND "DOUBLE TIME."

Inquiry as to the Duration of Time in the action of "Othello" opens a wide field of speculation and enjoyment to those numerous investigators who delight in the exposure of discrepancy in the mechanism of Shakespeare's plays, and to them it should especially be commended. Not indeed because it has been neglected,—for more than once ingenious commentary has riddled the structure of "Othello" by presentment of incongruity between its events and the time of their occurrence,—but because it presents such ample opportunity of floundering in needless and useless argument. There, for example, is the wonderful "DOUBLE TIME" theory, propounded by Professor Wilson,—a doctrine which even the saving humor of the sagacious and gentle Furness did not prompt him to reject,—which Æschylus is thought to have known and sanctioned, and which, as applied to "Othello," produces a muddle, perspicuous only to the elect. "If we find those effects in their dramas," says Furness,—meaning the dramas of Æschylus and Shakespeare,—"their hands put them there, and to imagine that we can see them and that the mighty poets themselves did not, is to usurp a position which I can scarcely conceive of any one as willing to occupy." It may be presumptuous to believe, but I cannot escape the conviction, that enthusiasm, especially when it has a theory to sustain, habitually discovers, in the works of "the mighty poets," many things of which they would have been astonished to hear. Pope has told us that

> " Whoever thinks a faultless piece to see
> Thinks what ne'er was, nor is, nor e'er shall be " ;

and, after many years of Shakespeare study, inclusive of much diligent reading of learned, ingenious, often instructive, sometimes sophistical commentary on the subject, and after making more than one contribution to the medley of Time Analysis, I humbly resign the task of trying to harmonize flat contradictions and convert into intended beauties the obvious faults in Shakespeare's plays. I remember the evidence which proves that he often built on the basis of old materials;

that there *is* such a thing as poetic license, of which, manifestly, he took advantage; that, although it was his custom to "strike the second heat upon the Muse's anvil," he wrote for the stage, and, considering the quality and number of his plays, must have written very rapidly; and I reach the comforting conclusion that it is rational and right to accept for what they are the obvious imperfections in the literature with which he enriched the world,—a literature which, whatever be its faults, is supremely beautiful. The great plays of Shakespeare, written by a man who was not only a dramatic poet but an actor and a theatrical manager, are adequate to every practical requirement of the stage—and to a great deal more!— and of those great plays "Othello," dramatically the best, requires no justification by wire-woven theory or hair-splitting argument.

THE POWER OF THE PLAY.

In the pathos of its picture of human life, in the terror which it causes, the pity which it inspires, and the consequent chastening influence which it exerts "Othello" is only a little less than "King Lear," and thus only a little lower than the highest. The difference is in degree. *Lear* sacrifices himself before he is sacrificed by his children. *Othello* is despoiled and ruined by his enemy. The old *King* comes a little nearer to the heart, therefore, and the spectacle of his anguish is somewhat more pitiably desolate, for that reason. In the tears which we shed over that venerable ruin there is a blind submission to fate, a dazed sense of the weakness of man when at strife with nature, an infinite sorrow for the utter helplessness of the human race. Our grief is so great that it drowns our anger, and *Regan, Goneril,* and *Edmund* are forgotten, with the rest of the lumber of the commonplace world. The spectacle of *Othello's* misery may be equally agonizing, but the emotion it inspires is not as ineffably piteous. In our tears for him there is fire—the fire of an immitigable rage against the diabolical intellect that has destroyed him. He represents magnanimous virtue, simple, stalwart goodness, leonine power, commingled with the trustful candor of innocent childhood. He has not outlived his time nor the sunshine. He is not yet, in any sense, due to death. There may be autumnal tints in the foliage of his garden, but it is not amiss that he should gather the ripe fruits of life, love, and happiness, and we feel that he ought to possess them. When, therefore, his grandeur is broken by the adverse will of a malignant genius,—against which, because of his confiding nature, he is powerless and defenceless,— our rage strikes hands with our sorrow, and the tide of our hate rises equally with the tide of our love. But, though in the scale of emotion a little lower than the highest, these feelings are high, grand, sacred, and our minds resent the least approach toward trifling with sensibilities so acute and experiences so vital and tragic. Just as no soul that really feels will endure a light mention of the names of the beloved dead, so no soul that really feels will endure a vain, casual meddling with those immortal ideals in which Shakespeare has expressed the sum of human greatness and human misery.

V.

HAMLET.

> " *There is an order*
> *Of mortals on the earth, who do become*
> *Old in their youth, and die ere middle age,*
> *Without the violence of warlike death;*
> *Some perishing of pleasure—some of study—*
> *Some worn with toil, some of mere weariness,—*
> *Some of disease—and some insanity—*
> *And some of withered, or of broken hearts;*
> *For this last is a malady which slays*
> *More than are numbered in the lists of Fate,*
> *Taking all shapes, and bearing many names.*"
>
> BYRON.

THE tragedy of "Hamlet," current on the stage for more than three centuries, has been acted thousands of times, and scores of actors have performed as the *Prince of Denmark*. Almost every actor who loves his profession wishes to act the *Prince,* and it is natural that he should wish to do so, the character being irresistibly attractive. Attributes fascinating to the imagination are combined in *Hamlet,* and, furthermore,—a fact which intensifies the inherent fascination,—he is the central figure in a romantic story which involves the awful mystery and sublimity

of preternatural environment. The list of actors who
have played the part, if it were possible to obtain
a complete one, would be prodigious; even an incomplete one would be very long, and it would include
many forgotten names, with, of course, a few that
still retain some lustre of traditional renown. Authentic intimation, sometimes becoming description, of the
manner in which *Hamlet* was dressed and acted by
eminent actors of the past did not begin to glide into
contemporary records until about the end of the
seventeenth century, and until a recent time it
remained meagre.

BRITISH STAGE.—THOMAS BETTERTON.

The first representative of *Hamlet* was Richard
Burbage, concerning whose performance no specific
information has been found. The part was also acted
in Shakespeare's lifetime by Joseph Taylor, and it
is known that Shakespeare personally imparted to
Taylor his views of the manner in which it ought to
be played, that Taylor performed it "incomparably
well," and that Sir William Davenant, who had
seen Taylor's performance, described it to Thomas
Betterton.

The performance of it by Betterton, which is, to
some extent, specifically depicted by Colley Cibber,

provided the traditional method of acting it,—a method which, more or less diversified, has survived to the present day. Betterton's performance, in 1661, appears to have been illumined by transcendent genius. One remark about it indicates its excellence: "When I acted the *Ghost* with Betterton," said Barton Booth, "instead of my awing him, he terrified me: but divinity hung round that man." Betterton was twenty-six years old when he first played *Hamlet,* but he seems to have made the part his own at once, and all his life he was peerless in it. At about the age of seventy he was still able to play it, and even then his performance elicited cordial commendation. Steele, in "The Tatler," praised it, signifying that the aged actor had not lost his vigor, but appeared as "a young man of great expectation, vivacity, and enterprise." The dress of the *Prince,* as presented by Betterton, according to an authentic portrait which hangs in the Garrick Club, London, was almost ecclesiastical, particularly in the detail of a conspicuous white neckcloth. One account of that actor's appearance mentions as parts of his *Hamlet* attire a cocked hat, shoulder-knots, and a full-bottomed wig, trappings obviously and ludicrously inappropriate to the character: but the dress was that of Betterton's period and the audience was accustomed to it.

DAVID GARRICK AS *HAMLET*

AFTER THE PAINTING BY BENJAMIN WILSON

COSTUME.

Correct dressing on the stage, whether historic or æsthetic, came into vogue by slow degrees. It has not been customary, and it is not now, to modify the dress of *Hamlet,* in the course of a representation of the play, so as to make it entirely consistent with the varying conditions of the man portrayed in Shakespeare's text. Prior to the time when *Hamlet* first enters he has not seen or heard of the apparition of his murdered father. *Ophelia,* who subsequently describes the *Prince's* appearance and attire, is not present in his first scene. In that scene he should be clothed in raiment befitting his rank and princely condition. He wears black, whereas the *King,* the *Queen,* and the courtiers have discarded mourning robes; but, although a settled melancholy possesses him, his apparel should not be dishevelled nor his person unkempt nor his visage distraught. The final shock—the vision and impartment of the *Ghost* —is yet to come. The unhappy man, indeed, is weary of life and has contemplated suicide, but his mental balance has not yet been vitally disordered. It is not till after the awe and terror of the midnight encounter with the *Ghost* that he breaks down altogether, and comes before *Ophelia,*

" With a look so piteous in purport,
As if he had been loosèd out of hell,
To speak of horrors."

From that time his aspect, naturally, would be that of
a man whom anguish, corroding the heart and distracting the mind, has made heedless of dress and
appearance, except in as far as innate, habitual delicacy
would involuntarily prompt care of the person. He
suffers acutely and continuously. He is incarnate
misery. *Ophelia's* description of him,—

" With his doublet all unbrac'd;
No hat upon his head; his stockings foul'd,
Ungarter'd, and down-gyvèd to his ankle;
Pale as his shirt; his knees knocking each other,"—

suits with that condition. She, with cause, believes
him to be mad, and later she laments to behold

" That noble and most sovereign reason,
Like sweet bells jangled, out of tune and harsh."

The general custom of the stage, however, has been
to present *Hamlet,* throughout every scene of the
tragedy, as "the glass of fashion and the mould of
form." The reason for that custom is obvious: if
he were presented as continuously in the condition
described by *Ophelia* he would be, to the general
public, less an object of sympathy. A spectacle of

abject misery becomes tedious to the multitude. The wretched are soon forsaken.

INSANITY OF *HAMLET*.

Actors habituated to deep study and to thought would naturally, in their dressing and acting of *Hamlet*, be influenced by the conclusions they reach relative to the question of his "madness." No Shakespearean student is warranted in assuming that *Hamlet* is a victim of "maniacal-depressive insanity" and in need of a straitjacket, or, with all due respect to the many ingenious medical arguments which have been advanced, that Shakespeare intended the character as "a study in madness." There is no reason to believe that the poet possessed exceptional scientific, physiological, or medical knowledge, or that when he wrote "Hamlet" he wrote as an alienist. There is some reason to believe that he founded his "Hamlet" on an earlier and bad play derived from the French "Hystorie of Hamblet," in Belleforest's "Historie Tragique," of which there was an English translation accessible in his time. It is certain, from the testimony of all his works, that he thoroughly knew human nature. In *Hamlet* he exhibited a representative image of pathetic experience, common in a greater or less degree to the human race, and the human race has therefore continuously manifested intense interest in it. John Philip Kemble noticed that any volume of Shakespeare which had been habitually read would show signs of having been more frequently opened at the play of "Hamlet" than at any other. Commentators who maintain that *Hamlet* is drawn as consistently sane have pushed their contention to excess: that impassioned thinker and caustic writer Charles Reade, for example, intimated that a belief in *Hamlet's* "madness" is a symptom of insanity in the person who entertains it. But what are the facts? *Hamlet,* noble and gentle, a Prince, invested with extraordinary charm and placed at the summit of his social world, loving and beloved by a girl of singular spiritual and physical beauty, is suddenly stricken by the mysterious death of his father, whom he idolizes. He suspects foul play. He knows himself deprived of his royal inheritance. He sees his mother wedded with indecent haste to his uncle, whom he dislikes and instinctively suspects. He is prone to melancholy, and that predisposition, accentuated by bereavement and affliction, prompts him to brood on suicide and death. In that woful condition he is confronted by a spirit from beyond the grave, apprised that his father has been murdered, that his mother has committed adultery with the murderer, to whom she is now married, and that the murderer wears the crown; and he is enjoined to execute revenge. Such an accumulation of anguish and horror, descending like an avalanche upon an already broken spirit and bringing with it an overwhelming access of doubt and perturbation, might well be expected to paralyze the will. This it does, and the conduct of *Hamlet,* thereafter, under the stress of that awful experience, conclusively manifests a condition which would be fairly designated as "intermittent compound-confusional insanity," involving morbid emotional and mental disturbance "consequent upon shock." The wretched man wanders in the borderland between reason and madness. His scene with *Ophelia* is a heartrending exhibition equally of hopelessness of love and despair of reason. His projects of revenge contemplate not only slaughter of the bodies of his enemies but provision for the eternal damnation of their immortal souls. *Claudius* is to be slain in such a way that "his heels will kick at heaven" and his "damn'd and black soul" go to "hell." *Rosencrantz* and *Guildenstern* are to be killed without allowance of time even for shrift. To infer that the condition and proceedings of *Hamlet* are invariably sane is surely to misapprehend the meaning of the tragedy.

DAVID GARRICK.

David Garrick, when acting *Hamlet,* whom he represented as a sane man assuming insanity, wore a court-dress of his time, that of King George the Third. His impersonation of the *Prince* was first given in 1742. There is emphatic testimony that it was princely in spirit and consistent and sustained in execution. Particular emphasis was laid by Garrick on the expression of filial love, and he caused an effect of prodigious emotion by his delivery of the passionate speeches, such as the passage beginning "Oh, what a rogue and peasant slave am I!" At the climax of the Play Scene, when *Hamlet* wildly vociferates the lines

> "For some must watch while some must sleep,
> So runs the world away!"

he pulled out a white pocket-handkerchief and, walking rapidly about the stage, twirled it spasmodically in the air. That "business" was long afterward repeated by Macready, with whom it seems generally to have been thought original, and it was for using that "business," not inappropriate though rather finical, that Edwin Forrest hissed Macready, at the Theatre Royal, Edinburgh, in 1846. In the interval between the time of Betterton and that of Garrick

Hamlet's counsel to the *Players* was not spoken on the stage, but Garrick restored it. His treatment of the play in general, however, was not judicious. The tragedy is long, and for representation it must be cut. Garrick for a time omitted the *Grave-diggers;* and he discarded mention of the fatal catastrophe that befalls *Ophelia,* rejected the expedient of poisoning the *Queen,* causing her to become insane from remorse, and introduced a combat between *Hamlet* and the *King,* in which the *King* was killed. His version was a mutilation.

EARLY ACTORS.—KEMBLE.

Robert Wilks, Spranger Barry, Thomas Sheridan, and John Henderson, all of the period extending from the time of Queen Anne into that of King George the Third, gave performances of the *Prince* which were variously commended, without being minutely described. Barry's musical, sympathetic voice was extolled, and the extraordinary ability of Henderson, who must have been, indeed, extraordinary, since he excelled in such widely contrasted parts as *Iago, Falstaff,* and *Shylock,* was warmly celebrated.

John Philip Kemble was the first exceptionally popular representative of *Hamlet* (1783) subsequent to the time of Garrick. The portrait of him in that character, an artificial, somewhat absurd picture by Sir Thomas Lawrence, is well and widely known in the engraving by H. Dawe. It is said that Jackson, the English pugilist, remembered as Lord Bryon's preceptor in boxing, stood for the figure in that painting. The *Prince* is represented standing,—and the pose is stately,—presumably in a burial-ground in the neighborhood of the Castle of Elsinore, which is shown in the distance. His left hand holds a skull. His arms are drooping at full length. His eyes are upturned in a manner incongruous with either mournful revery or passionate rhapsody. He is arrayed in a suit of black raiment, consisting of a hat with two plumes and several feathers in it, a doublet slashed at the waist, knee-breeches, stockings, low shoes with rosettes on them, a wide sword-belt across his right shoulder, sustaining a heavy sword, a ribbon about the neck, from which is pendent the Danish Order of the Elephant (instituted about 1448), a capacious cloak trimmed with fur, and the Order of the Garter. He wears a loose, open collar, and outside of it something which seems to be a ribbon of esses. His cuffs are white. According to Kemble's biographer, his *Hamlet* wore a black-velvet court-dress, a star on the breast, an Order pendent to a ribbon, the Garter, a mourning sword, deep ruffles, and black shoes with buckles on them. His face was clean shaved and his hair was powdered.

JOHN PHILIP KEMBLE AS *HAMLET*

AFTER THE PAINTING BY SIR JOSHUA REYNOLDS

Kemble indicated the "madness" of *Hamlet* as assumed, and whenever he feigned distraction, he dishevelled his hair. The pervasive quality of his performance appears to have been the hopeless loneliness of immedicable grief, and especially he expressed filial love. When he uttered the word "father," in speaking *Hamlet's* adjuration to the *Ghost,* he simulated affectionate feeling so well as often to move some of his auditors to tears. As he spoke that word he sank to his knees, and upon the disappearance of the *Ghost* he repeated that action. Hazlitt wrote at one time that Kemble played *Hamlet* like a man in armor, but at another time that his *Hamlet* had not been surpassed. Leigh Hunt, an astute observer of mental and spiritual complexities of constitution in actors, wrote that Kemble was best in characters that are occupied with themselves and their own importance. However that may be, his impersonation exerted a greater influence upon the tradition of the part inherited by all his successors in it than has been exerted by any other performance of *Hamlet.*

Among those successors, on the English Stage, native born, most of whom have passed away, were Charles Kemble, Charles Mayne Young, Edmund Kean, Junius Brutus Booth, William Charles Macready, Charles John Kean, Barry Sullivan,

Gustavus Vaughan Brooke, Samuel Phelps, Henry Irving, Wilson Barrett, Herbert Beerbohm-Tree, and Johnston Forbes-Robertson. About each of those names, particularly when associated with *Hamlet,* there has been a lively surge of conflicting critical opinion. Each has been a prominent figure as the *Prince,* and each has been earnestly extolled and as earnestly condemned within comparatively recent years. Those of signal importance who have appeared in America in this character are considered, in chronological order, in the section of this chapter which is devoted to THE AMERICAN STAGE. The *Hamlet* of Charles Kemble lives in the illuminative words of his famous daughter Fanny— "an image of a distracted intellect and a broken heart." His ideal seems to have been absolutely true; his expression of it inadequate, except in parts. Young and Macready were scholars in the character, the latter excelling in the expression of a profound and thrilling sense of *Hamlet's* preternatural experience. Edmund Kean, superb in *Richard* and *Sir Giles,* seems not to have achieved equal success in *Hamlet.* Indeed, a very old man who had seen him in all the great parts that he played told me (in 1877) that Kean's only entirely consistent, sustained impersonation was that of *Sir Edward Mortimer,* in "The Iron Chest." The elder

Booth was deficient in princely grace but winning by reason of exquisite sensibility. Charles Kean, whom I saw often, and found admirable in various characters, was mechanical, unsympathetic, and uninteresting in *Hamlet*.

AMERICAN STAGE.

The first performance of *Hamlet* on the American stage was given by Lewis Hallam at Philadelphia, in July, 1759, and in November, 1761, he acted it at a theatre in Beekman Street, New York. Beekman Street was then known as Chapel Street, and the theatre was then a new one. Hallam has had many successors. Particular account of them would fill a large volume. A glow of renown still lingers on impersonations of the *Prince* by Thomas Abthorpe Cooper, James William Wallack, George Vandenhoff, James E. Murdoch, Edwin Forrest, Edward Loomis Davenport, Edwin Booth, and Lawrence Barrett.

EDWIN FORREST.

Edwin Forrest esteemed himself and was esteemed by his admirers a great representative of *Hamlet*. He wore in that part a black doublet and over that a short, black cape. The doublet was edged at the neck with white, was buttoned down the front, and was fastened around the waist by a belt. The cape, open in front, was allowed to hang loose, and was looped across the chest by a double cord, to which were appended several tassels. Black-silk tights and low shoes with buckles completed the dress. Forrest wore his own hair, slightly curled. His face was clean shaved, except for small, short, black side-whiskers, a short moustache, and a small tuft under the lower lip. His neck was bare. His person was conspicuously stalwart. His calves were huge. His face was pale, and his eyebrows, naturally dark, were blackened. He was, customarily, at the first revealment of *Hamlet,* "discovered" seated under a small canopy at the right of the scene, the *King* and *Queen* being seated under a large canopy in the centre. He spoke in a deep voice. Being a resolute, formidable, athletic man, of combative disposition and truculent aspect, he was as little like *Hamlet* as it would be possible for any person to be. His excellence as an actor, when in his natural and proper sphere, was eminent, and it was duly recognized. The power, passion, authority, and art of his personations of *Othello, King Lear, Coriolanus, Spartacus, Virginius, Febro, Aylmere,* and *Damon,* for example, were in the highest degree convincing and admirable, but his temperamental as well as physical unfitness for *Hamlet* was so radical and obvious as to be painful. The moment he was seen in that character all possibility of any illusion of poetry, pathos, tenderness, and grace was forestalled. He spoke the words, he did the usual business, and sometimes in his burly way he was personally interesting, but he was completely unsuited to the part. In the opening scene of the Presence, his head was held erect, his dark, glowing eyes were fixed defiantly on the *King,* his hands were clenched on the arms of his throne chair, his demeanor was that of menace, not of melancholy, and it was evident that if any "clouds" hung upon him they were thunder clouds. His delivery of *Hamlet's* first line, "A little more than kin and less than kind," was firm, deep, reverberant, and it needed only a sonorous profane expletive to make it superlatively Forrestian. Forrest possessed a magnificent voice, and he was well aware of it. He could perfectly convey the musical quality that is inherent in certain words and cadences of words. In the stage business of Forrest's *Hamlet* there was no salient trait of novelty. He had seen and acted with Cooper, who followed the example of Kemble, and he had seen and acted with Edmund Kean; he knew the tradition and for the most part he followed it. His death-scene was needlessly "realistic," and he was accustomed to say that a man as strong as himself could not expire without decided manifestations of physical agony. There was a coarse streak in the nature of Forrest, and it showed itself on occasion in his acting.

EDWARD LOOMIS DAVENPORT.

The art of Davenport in the performance of *Hamlet* was beautiful. He was one of those rare and charming actors who obey the precept of Shakespeare, and in the whirlwind of passion use all with gentleness, not overstepping the modesty of Nature. Sincerity, delicacy, grace, and fine intelligence pervaded all his impersonations. The vitalizing element that some of them lacked was the magnetic power which arouses feeling, carries conviction, and creates an effect of pathos. It was possible to view his performance of *Hamlet* without being deeply moved. He was fortunate in person: his figure was imposing, his head noble, his countenance expressive, his voice copious and sympathetic, his demeanor dignified, his action fine. Some old pictures represent him as a veritable "guy," ungainly and ridiculous, wearing ample "side-whiskers," —and they do him much injustice. His ideal of the *Dane* accorded with that of Kemble and Macready. *Hamlet,* as played by him, simulated insanity, was an affectionate, sorrowing son, was a lover, seemed entirely qualified to revenge the murder of his father, and exemplified the scholar and the soldier. He was not boisterous; he was not belligerent: yet he appeared a capable *Prince,* and in his presence the observer did not understand why the hand of retributive justice should be stayed. He delivered the soliloquies in fluent, melodious tones, and he used the customary stage business. I knew Davenport well, and greatly liked and admired him. He impressed me, in the latter part of his career, as being a man whom disappointment had somewhat embittered and whose sensibilities had been somewhat blunted by ill fortune, vicissitude, and rough contact with the world. He was, in many respects, a great actor: his *Hamlet* satisfied the sense of form; it did not satisfy the sense of soul.

BARRY SULLIVAN.

Barry Sullivan, who had long been popular on the Irish Stage, made his first appearance in London, February 7, 1852, acting *Hamlet,* and on November 22, 1858, made his first appearance in New York, in the same part. It was a favorite with him, as it is with most actors of tragedy. When he began his second and last tour of America he again presented *Hamlet,* appearing at Booth's Theatre, August 30, 1875, and giving a performance which, in point of definite ideal and artistic finish, was remarkably fine.

I met and conversed with him, about that time, and was impressed by his solidity of character, his scholarship, and his courtesy. His aspect, whether on the stage or off, was leonine, his demeanor stately. He was tall, his face was of that square form observable in portraits of men of the time of Queen Anne, his eyes were gray, bright, keen, and expressive of an impetuous temperament carefully controlled. His *Hamlet* was intellectual, not poetic: a man of action, not a baffled dreamer "thinking too precisely on the event." His ideal evinced imaginative perception, but there was no pathos in his expression of it. He made *Hamlet* a sane man simulating insanity, and he effectively expressed the bitter humor that sometimes flickers through the *Prince's* constitutional melancholy. His elocution was correct, and in delivery of the soliloquies deeply impressive, as illustrative of the art of thinking aloud. He dressed *Hamlet* in black and purple raiment and wore a light brown wig, the hair being parted in the middle, curled and flowing. His method was direct, his art well concealed,—producing the effect of spontaneity. One of his readings attracted attention by reason of its peculiarity. When *Hamlet* is baffling the inquisitive spies, *Rosencrantz* and *Guildenstern,* he grasped a wrist of each of them and exclaimed, "I know a *hawk* from a *heron,*" and then, after a pause, looking from one to the other, and throwing them off, contemptuously added, "Pshaw!" In stage business he generally followed accepted traditions. He employed the expedient of twirling a handkerchief, at "I must be idle,"—the usage introduced by Garrick and continued by Macready. His acting incurred the practical disapprobation of Edwin Forrest, who hissed him, in Philadelphia, as he had hissed Macready in Edinburgh. Sullivan, however,—it was said at the time, and I believe truly,—rejoined by pointing at him, in a stage box, as he spoke the line "That great baby you see there is not yet out of his swaddling clouts." A comic occurrence incident to Sullivan's advent at Booth's Theatre as *Hamlet* (1875) seems worthy of mention. The Band of the 69th Regiment (Irish) of the New York State Militia had been stationed in the theatre to welcome the Irish tragedian, and, by a ludicrous mistake, it pealed forth its joyous greeting upon the first entrance of the *Ghost,* crashing into the silence with "Lo! the Conquering Hero Comes!"

EDWIN BOOTH.

Edwin Booth was essentially a tragedian, and although he liked to act comedy, believing and declaring that it helped to impart flexibility to his style, he never brilliantly succeeded in it. He possessed the princely mind, the gloomy temperament, the introspective propensity, the contemplative disposition, the moody manner, and the slender, nervous physique that are appropriate to the character of *Hamlet*. He could be genial and even gay when in company with an intimate friend, but in general he was reserved and silent. His mind dwelt almost continually on solemn themes. He was constitutionally a melancholy man: even his smile, though very sweet, was sad. On one occasion, speaking to me about the murder of Lincoln by his brother John, he said: "All my life I have thought of dreadful things that might happen to me, and I believed there was no horror that I had not imagined, but I never dreamed of such a dreadful thing as *that*." He was deeply religious, in the broadest sense of that word, and he was credulous of the possibility of spiritual apparitions. He told me that he believed he had seen the face of his first wife, Mary Devlin, looking in at him through a car window, in the night, when he was travelling from New York to Boston, in 1863, to be present at her death-bed, where he arrived shortly after she had died. Such was his temperament, and possessing that temperament he was peculiarly fitted to act such parts as involve grief, gloom, and the element of the preternatural. He was born to act *Hamlet*.

Many years ago Booth related to me how it happened that he undertook to play that part, and in my "Life" of him I have told the story, which has been much copied. He was in California with his renowned father, and they were to act together, for Edwin's "benefit," in "Venice Preserved," the father as *Pierre,* the son as *Jaffier.* When Edwin had dressed himself for *Jaffier* he entered his father's room. The elder actor, looking at him, mused a moment, and said:

"You look like *Hamlet.* Why didn't you play that for your benefit?"

"I will," the youth answered, "if I ever have another."

Later the chance came, and Edwin, remembering that promise, acted *Hamlet,* and he continued to act it all his life. No actor of the many years known to me has more completely entered into and expressed the soul of *Hamlet* than he did. His only peer in the acting of the part was Henry Irving, and in the elocution he had no peer.

Booth's first appearance as *Hamlet* was made on April 25, 1853 (for his benefit), at the San Francisco Theatre. In 1857, after a successful engagement in Boston, he came to New York, for the first time as a "star," appearing, May 4, at Burton's Metropolitan Theatre, afterward the Winter Garden, as *Richard*

the Third, and later he there acted the part for the
first time in that city. After various ventures in
America he acted, in 1861, in a repertory, in England,
and in November that year, he appeared in Manchester,
as *Hamlet,* Henry Irving being the *Laertes.* During
the next three years he filled many engagements in
American cities, and on November 26, 1864, he accomplished one of the most conspicuous victories of his
artistic career,—the first of the superb revivals with
which he dignified the American Stage,—in a production of "Hamlet," at the Winter Garden Theatre,
New York, which remained there until March 24,
1865, enjoying a career of 100 consecutive performances,—the longest run which, at that time, had been
achieved with that or any other Shakespearean play,
and, all things considered, a more remarkable accomplishment than even Irving's subsequent run of 200
performances of "Hamlet" at the London Lyceum.

Booth's revival was effected with every helpful
auxiliary then within the reach of theatrical enterprise. After its withdrawal from the Winter Garden
the tragedy was taken to the Boston Theatre, where
Booth was acting in it, when, on April 14, the insane
murder of President Lincoln by John Wilkes Booth,
the tragedian's brother, appalled and enraged the
country, causing Edwin's retirement. He reappeared, under pressure of necessity, at the Winter

Garden, on January 3, 1866, acting *Hamlet*. On January 22, 1867, he received a *"Hamlet* medal," the gift, publicly tendered, of many citizens of New York, who wished to express their appreciation of his great performance of that part and formally to recognize the importance of his service to the public. He effected many subsequent presentments of the play,—one of the best of them being its first presentation at Booth's Theatre, New York, January 5, 1870.

Edwin Booth was an inspired tragic genius, and for that very reason his acting was uneven: the mechanism of his art was always under his control, but he could not always inflame his imagination and liberate his feelings. I have seen him act when his performances were lifeless, but even his worst was better than the best of many other actors, and his best, in tragedy, was sublime,—and it is at his best that every artist should be judged and remembered. In acting *Hamlet* he carried "naturalness" of method to the fullest extent that is possible in the treatment of poetic tragedy, and the effect of his personation was that of perfect truth. The arrangement of "Hamlet" which he presented in 1870 formed the basis of his final revision of the acting text, which was published in 1878. The enthusiastic commentator Charles Cowden Clarke affirmed that Shakespeare "never wrote a line that did not harmonize with and tend to define, the portrait he was limning,"—a statement aptly exhibitive of the extravagance of adulation which would accept the defects in Shakespeare's writing as equally precious with its transcendent beauties, and which has prompted some of the most erroneous critical estimates of his plays. Booth's arrangement of "Hamlet" was designed to clarify obscurity and rectify error, and it was made with the reverence of a loving disciple. It consists of five acts, containing fourteen scenes. The curtailments were made with a view to accelerate movement, eliminate description, and avoid repetition. Offensive words and passages were invariably excluded by Booth from all his stage versions of the plays in which he acted. In "Hamlet" a few lines were transposed and a few words were changed, but without alteration of the sense. The announcement of *Ophelia's* madness was allotted to *Marcellus* instead of *Horatio* because, if *Horatio* had been aware of *Ophelia's* affliction and of her subsequent death, he must have communicated the knowledge to *Hamlet,* previous to the Burial Scene, in the Churchyard. The general method of Shakespeare, in displaying action long past, is to display it as proceeding in the present, and his plays are customarily embellished with illustrative accessories or references appertaining either

to his own period or to others, long subsequent to
the historic period of the action displayed. *King
Claudius*, for example, is furnished with cannon, like
King John (1199), though cannon were not in use
until the battle of Cressy (1346). As a dramatic
editor, however, Booth considered the vital necessity
of effect, and in making his "Prompt Book" of "Hamlet" refrained from all attempt to reconcile Poetry and
irrelevant History. In particular he did not revert
from the poet's text to the ancient chronicle, con-
verting the *Prince* into a burly Dane, of the Middle
Ages, and degrading a poetic ideal to the level of
commonplace. He treated the tragedy, from first to
last, as a poem, and he dressed it in conformity with
idealized usages and customs of an early period in the
history of Denmark, such as he found conducive to
the preservation of a pictorial atmosphere without
sacrifice of an effect of reality. His stage business
was elaborate, various, and carefully considerate of
every detail. Full description and analysis of it and
of his readings would fill a volume. A few particulars will suffice. He used, as his father had done,
various readings and business expedients original with
John Philip Kemble,—such, for example, as a stress
of pathetic enunciation of the word "father," when
entreating the *Ghost* to speak; a strong emphasis on
the word "you," in *Hamlet's* question to *Horatio*,

"Did *you* not speak to it?"; an expressive shading of words in *Hamlet's* reply to *Horatio,* "Sir, my good *friend;* I'll change *that* name with *you,*" and also in his "And for my *soul,* what *can* it do to *that?*"; and the greeting of *Bernardo,* obviously a person whom *Hamlet* has not met before, in a courteous but markedly formal manner. Kemble, when making *Hamlet's* exit, following the receding phantom, allowed his right arm to droop, so that the sword, held by the right hand, was trailed behind him. The stage usage had been to present the point of the sword toward the spectre. Booth reversed the sword, so as to present the hilt, which, being in the shape of a cross, might be supposed protective against a spirit possibly evil, which had assumed "a pleasing shape," and, as far as I can ascertain, he was the first to do so. The business certainly was original with him.

The main structure of Booth's performance, after it had been matured, that is from about 1870 till the last, remained unchanged, but he sought relief from the monotony of repetition by the expedient of varying details of business. Thus, in the Closet Scene, he sometimes caused both the picture of the dead *King Hamlet* and that of the living *King Claudius* to be hung upon a wall of the room; at other times, the picture of *King Claudius* was pendent on the breast

From a photograph by Sarony

EDWIN BOOTH AS *HAMLET*

of the *Queen,* while that of *King Hamlet* hung upon
the wall; at others, and this was his usual custom,
Booth, as *Hamlet,* wore a medallion picture of his
father, suspended on a chain worn about his neck,
while that of his uncle was either placed upon the
wall or worn by the *Queen:* sometimes no actual
pictures were used, both being upon "the fourth wall,"
and left to the imagination of the audience.

One of Booth's important innovations was intelligent treatment of the use of the skulls in the
Churchyard Scene. The *Grave-digger* is making a
grave for *Ophelia,* and as he digs he throws up several
bones and skulls. Booth caused him to pause in his
labor, to look carefully at one of the skulls, to which
had adhered a fragment of soiled leather,—the tattered
remnant of a fool's cap,—to pat it in a kindly, jocose
way, and to lay it aside, and later when he said
"This skull has lain in the earth three and twenty
years," to take it up and designate it as "Yorick's
skull,—the King's jester." Prior to Booth's invention
of that expedient no means had been provided of dis-
criminating among the several skulls that were thrown
out of the grave.

Booth, like Macready, and indeed like the majority
of actors, held the opinion that the "madness"
of *Hamlet* is assumed. The question of *Hamlet's*
"madness" appears to be largely one of definition.

What is meant by the word when associated with this character? The inevitable consequence of the terrible experience which befalls *Hamlet* in his condition of exaggerated sensibility and morbid gloom would be a shock almost destructive of perfect sanity in any organization, certainly productive of temporary frenzy in one as tremulous as his. The "madness" of *Hamlet* is a distraught condition of the nervous system in which he will vacillate, doubt, believe, brood, dream, suffer, resolve, hesitate, be strong at one moment and weak the next, accomplish nothing, and wither in despair. Booth aimed to present *Hamlet* as consistently sane. "I do not consider *Hamlet* mad," he said, "except in craft." Nevertheless, when he acted *Hamlet,* an instillation of "madness" found its way into the performance, and made it wonderfully effective, because absolutely true. It is the word from which so many minds recoil.

Valuable as a showing is of an actor's expedients of expression there is a richer revealment of his art, especially when he is acting this part, which it is more difficult to describe,—the revealment of his soul. It is easy to say that Booth, as *Hamlet,* seemed "haunted." It is far from easy to depict the means he used to cause that effect. Mere description of his movement would not suffice. The analyst should, if possible, reveal, or, certainly, indicate, the workings of the actor's mind, the quality of his spirit, and interpret that superlative power of the imagination which enables certain exceptional persons to assume wildered or tempestuous or agonized states of mind and feeling, and to undergo stress of experience which it would be ruin and death actually to feel. The supreme excellence of dramatic art is the coincidence of perfect ideal and perfect expression: that excellence was shown in Booth's *Hamlet,* at its best. He possessed a peculiar physical fitness for the part; a slender figure, a noble head, expressive dark eyes, mobility of countenance, grace of movement, dignity of bearing, a smile that was sadder than tears, and a voice that could express every variety of serious emotion. He possessed also the innate melancholy of temperament that comports with *Hamlet,* together with a facile style of expression that made his acting spontaneous and, without sacrifice of its melody, caused blank verse to seem a natural form of language. In the spirit he disclosed there was the mournful incertitude of a mind that is overwhelmed by the mystery of life and death, appalled by the vastness of man's environment in the boundless universe, and dazed in his baffled effort to penetrate the darkness of inscrutable destiny. His definition of the part illumines, to some extent, his

personation of it: *"Hamlet* is the epitome of mankind," so Booth wrote, "not an individual; a sort of
magic mirror, in which all men and women see the
reflex of themselves." Millions of human beings have
passed, and millions are passing, more or less exactly,
through the spiritual experience exemplified in *Hamlet,*—their minds conscientiously enthralled by the
sense of duty to live a rational life, their hearts
broken by affliction, their thoughts and feelings perplexed and confused, their hopes alternating with their
fears, their faith shaken by their doubt, their desolated
souls longing for the relief of death, and yet dread-
ing the something—or the nothing—after it. Booth's
personation of *Hamlet* was intuitively comprehended
rather than mentally grasped by multitudes of persons
who saw it, and it helped them to a better understanding of themselves. Few of them either tried or
cared to analyze it, to ascertain and designate its
alluring or subjugating attributes, but the charm and
the power of those attributes were universally felt,—
the princely dignity; the exquisite sensibility; the
filial affection; the haunted condition,—so expressed
in the Ghost Scenes as to thrill the imagination with
a shuddering sense of spiritual surroundings;—the
agonizing pathos of the renunciation of *Ophelia* and
therewith the abandonment of all hope of solace in
woman's love; the quick suspicion,—furtive, tremulous,

painful,—of every human being except the beloved *Horatio;* the anguish of outraged veneration for the sinful mother; the misery that broods on thoughts of suicide; the fateful, terrific, involuntary impetuosity of the killing of *Polonius,* with the wild, madly hopeful cry *"Is* it the KING?" and the sublimity of resignation in the hour of death. No element was omitted, whether of the character or the experience, and the art was so fine that it could better be described as living than as acting.

LAWRENCE BARRETT.

Lawrence Barrett, early in his professional career, was much influenced by the acting of Booth, with whom, as leading man, he was associated at the Winter Garden Theatre in 1863, and when, in the following year, at New Orleans, he appeared as a star, he directly and admittedly imitated Booth as *Richelieu* and *Hamlet,* though later he matured his style and became distinctively individual. He was a great interpreter of poetic ideals of human nature. Parts in which specially he excelled,—*Cassius, Yorick, Gringoire,* and *Lanciotto,* for example,—are those in which passion at times breaks loose in tumult of action and splendid eloquence. He rose to a noble height in a character which has long been discarded in our theatre, that of *King James the Fifth,* in "The King of the

Commons." As *Hamlet* he followed in the beaten
track, dressing and acting the part according to the
example of Booth. His final method in it, though,
was his own, and it was characterized by continuous
tremor and nervous excitement, restless movement,
and strongly accentuated bitterness of feeling—"the
torture of the mind." The business of allowing *Hamlet*
to perceive that the *King* and *Polonius,* "lawful
espials," are eavesdroppers in the *Prince's* scene with
Ophelia was used by him,—as it had been by all
other performers of the *Prince,* at least, in our
time, except Fechter,—and that was a blemish on a
scene in which he reached a supreme altitude of passion and pathos. Such a girl as *Ophelia* could not
succeed in acting deceit. *Hamlet,* at that crisis,
intuitively surmises treachery somewhere, and he is
at once shocked into a wild, bitter, resentful passion, on
perceiving the poor girl's attempt at a duplicity which
wellnigh breaks her heart. There are few situations
in Shakespeare more agonizing, and Barrett was touchingly true in his interpretation of its agony.

JOHN EDWARD McCULLOUGH.

In McCullough's performance of *Hamlet* the
Kemble tradition of the part, as to business and
readings, was perceptible, modified by the influence

of Edwin Forrest, from the force of whose example
he never entirely freed himself. The spirit of the
performance was mournful, the form distinct, the
method robust and confident. The only conspicuously
novel attribute of it was absence of ornamentation—
such as had been, and continues to be, customary:
it was severely simple and therein excellent. At the
climax of the Play Scene and at the killing of
Polonius,—essentially great moments, and treated as
such by that actor,—his spirit seemed to struggle for
a freedom of expression that it could not reach: he
knew precisely what to do and he knew precisely
how to do it, but he could not accomplish it. Once,
and only once,—which was in the Closet Scene,
after the appearance of the *Ghost,*—did he embody
the *Hamlet* of Shakespeare. In situations that are
haunted and weird, involving mystery and dread,
McCullough was impeded by insuperable obstacles,
both physical and spiritual. His face could express
perplexity and distress of the mind, anguish aris-
ing from the human affections, more readily than it
could express intellectual conflict and spiritual misery,
while his voice was attuned to the heroic and exultant
emotions more than to the sombre gravity of philo-
sophic or introspective meditation and the moodiness
of melancholy. It was essential that McCullough's
heart should be touched,—as it was by *King Lear,*—

in order that his powers as an actor might become fully liberated, and *Hamlet* did not touch his heart. Like his exemplar, Forrest, however, he formed and expressed a definite ideal of the character. He correctly presented the Prince and the scholar, he simulated insanity, and he fulfilled an artistic design with a precision that was beautiful in its grace and its absolute proficiency. He knew *Hamlet* as actors in general know him, but he did not possess any natural affinity with the part, and his performance, while highly creditable to the actor, was of no considerable import to the auditor.

HENRY IRVING.

Irving first acted *Hamlet* on June 20, 1864, at Manchester, England, on the occasion of a performance for his benefit. In dressing the part he then wore a wig of flaxen hair, as Fechter had done. That device is generally supposed to have been original with Fechter, but, in fact, it had been used, many years before he used it, by E. L. Davenport, in America, and Frederick C. P. Robinson had resorted to it, when, as a beginner, he was acting in provincial theatres of Great Britain. It is not effective and Irving soon discarded it. The great success of that wonderful actor as *Hamlet* was gained ten years after his first per-

formance of the part. On October 31, 1874, at the
London Lyceum Theatre, then managed by Hezekiah
Linthicum Bateman, "Hamlet" was produced, with
Irving as the *Prince* and Miss Isabella Bateman as
Ophelia. The setting was meagre. Only two new
sets were provided,—scenery which had been painted
for "Eugene Aram" and other plays being impressed
into service to make up a passable display. The
cost of the production did not exceed $500. Irving
himself must have known his strength and Bateman implicitly trusted his genius, but expectation,
in general, as to the result of the venture was not
sanguine. Two hundred performances were given,
the run terminating on June 29, 1875. That opulent
and brilliant victory,—for such it was, both financial and artistic,—was due exclusively to the acting
of Irving. The interest that his performance aroused
was not restricted to any one class of the public.
The whole community participated in the excitement that his enterprise had caused and exulted in
the triumph by which it had been crowned. The
character of *Hamlet,* long a favorite theme of the
essayist, was discussed far and wide, more than it
ever had been before or ever has been since, and
Irving's greatness as an actor, while not entirely
undisputed,—although he had triumphantly acted
Mathias, Charles the First, Eugene Aram, and

Richelieu,—was then generally recognized, his leadership acknowledged, and his rank adjudged. Four years later, Bateman having died and Mrs. Bateman, who succeeded her husband as lessee of the Lyceum, having relinquished that theatre, Irving became its manager, in which office his first achievement was a revival of "Hamlet." This was effected on December 30, 1878, and the play then kept the stage until April 17, 1879. An important feature of that presentment was the appearance in it of the consummate actress Ellen Terry, as *Ophelia,*—a character in which she never, in our time, has been equalled or even approached. With reference to the setting, on that occasion, Austin Brereton, the reverent, conscientious, faithful biographer of Irving, has recorded that it exhibited "no oppressive magnificence, wholly out of keeping with the spirit of the play, but a harmony of dramatic and pictorial effect," and that it made actual a dream which the actor told his audience he had cherished all his life. Irving's first appearance in America as *Hamlet* was made at the Star Theatre, New York, on November 26, 1884.

Irving was twenty-six years old when he first appeared as *Hamlet* and he had then been on the stage eight years, playing in various towns as a member of stock companies, and he had seen performances of the *Prince* by several actors, among them Samuel

Phelps and Edwin Booth. In productions made for
Booth, at Manchester, when, in 1861, that actor made
his first professional visit to England, he had participated, and although he was not at any time an
imitator, his acting, in after years, occasionally signified, in subtle, elusive touches, that the peculiar style
of Booth had been suggestive to him. Faint traces of
that style were perceptible in his *Richelieu* and in his
Hamlet. The part of the *Prince* was dear to him, and
he deeply and continually studied it from boyhood
onward. His personation of it cannot readily be
described. It was compact of imagination and feeling,
and it was wildly and strangely beautiful. The condition, at first, was that of enforced calm; the aspect
perplexed, dejected, forlorn; the manner that of
natural courtesy, innate nobility, exquisite elegance.
In the colloquy with *Horatio* and his companions,
about the apparition, Irving's utterance of *Hamlet's*
brief questions was modulated with scrupulous heed
to the necessarily quick, minute changes of feeling,
from the calm wonder of "Saw?—Who?" to the wild
passion of "I'll watch to-night—perchance 'twill walk
again." In the midnight tryst with *Horatio* and the
sentinels his excitement, though controlled, was intense; his glance roved over every discernible object
and searched the darkness, until the apparition came.
In the apostrophe to the phantom there was inexpres-

sible tenderness, mingled with reverence and awe. The
sympathy, pity, and love in his voice, when he half
spoke, half sighed "Alas! poor ghost!" expressed the
soul of *Hamlet* and sounded the key-note of the
impersonation—for Irving, alike in his thought and
his talk about the character, always dwelt on its
intrinsic loveliness. At the climax of the Ghost Scene
he became delirious, plucking tablets from a pouch,
at his belt, and rushing to a pillar of the wall, against
which he placed them, as he began to write. Irving
had made careful study of the principles of elocution
and he was thoroughly well acquainted with them,
but he always contended that, in acting, impersonation should be considered before elocution, and in the
delivery of the soliloquies of *Hamlet* he endeavored
to exemplify thinking aloud: he was ruminative, never
declamatory. At the close of the soliloquy on life and
death he spoke "soft you, now" as if a sequent train
of thought had occurred to him, and then came to
an abrupt stop, with the words "The fair Ophelia!"
uttered as he caught sight of her. In the ensuing
colloquy, which terminates with *Hamlet's* parting
from *Ophelia,* there was a pathetic blending of tenderness with despair, and of the vigilant craft which,
suspecting espionage, assumes disguise of madness,
with the wildness of actual delirium precipitated by
discovery that the suspicion is justified. In the Play

Scene he communicated the effect of agonizing
intensity of emotion with difficulty held in check; his
haggard visage was mournfully expressive of cruel
suffering, and beneath an assumption of crazy levity
there was in his demeanor an intent observance of
every person, incident, and movement, but especially
of *Claudius:* at the culmination of it, when the
affrighted *King* and his courtiers rushed from the
hall, he darted across the stage with a shrill cry, threw
himself upon the throne, and in a tempest of delirium
chanted the lines

> "Why, let the strucken deer go weep,
> The heart ungallèd play,
> For some must watch while some must sleep—
> So runs the world away!"

In the Closet Scene, when the *Prince* has, in some
measure, recovered composure, his austerity toward
his sinful mother was very sweetly tempered by filial
tenderness. The *Ghost,* when it appeared in that
scene, was injudiciously introduced in a kind of robe,
according, it was made known, to the stage direction
in the First Folio, "in his night gown," so that
Hamlet's wild exclamation, "My father, in his
habit, as he *lived!*" seemed to imply that a "night-
gown" was the habitual garb of his lamented sire
when on earth.

The use of pictures of *King Hamlet* and *Claudius* has given rise to much diversity of practice. The old custom of the English Stage was, in the Closet Scene, in which *Hamlet* rebukes the *Queen,* for the *Prince* to produce, out of his pocket, *two* miniatures, "pictures in little," one of his uncle and one of his father, and on them to deliver his passionate descant. In 1794 that custom was first discarded. *Hamlet* continued to wear a picture of his father, but not that of his uncle, while *Queen Gertrude* wore a picture of her new husband, *Claudius,* attached to a bracelet on her arm, or her chamber wall was embellished with a half-length painting, as large as life, of the elder *Hamlet,* her husband deceased. Pictures of *Claudius* seem to have been, from the first, worn by *Rosencrantz* and *Guildenstern.* Irving made no use of actual pictures in that scene, "the counterfeit presentment of two brothers" being left to the imagination of the audience. The pathos of his acting, in that grievous interview of a heart-broken son and a guilty mother, as also in the Casket Scene, when *Hamlet* renounces *Ophelia,* has not been equalled and it could not be excelled. In the Churchyard Scene he caused a piteous effect, such as no other actor of *Hamlet* had ever done, by conveying a shuddering sense of the *Prince's* uncontrollable propensity toward the contemplation of suicide,—often indulged and as often restrained,—into his speaking of those significant lines

" This doth betoken
The corse they follow did with desperate hand
Foredo its own life."

Irving was a man of vast imagination and acute sensibility. He could be stern; he could, and sometimes he did, hate; he was revengeful when he had been injured; but his heart was very tender. A more lovable man never lived. He knew human nature through and through, and his charity for its infirmities was unbounded. His magnanimity was supreme. He possessed essentially a princely nature, and his conduct of life was marked by invariable nobility of purpose, breadth of vision, quick sympathy with mankind in all its aspirations, struggles, and sufferings, and a passionate, unflinching, unswerving devotion to the highest ideals. In his art he was conscientious, laborious, and thorough. Being what he was he could comprehend *Hamlet,* and he could, and did, act the part with essential fidelity to the Shakespearean conception. His treatment of the wonderful Third Act of the tragedy was perfect in every detail: a model and a monument of dramatic art. Within my knowledge, only two actors have entirely justified themselves, to exigent, comprehensive judgment, in their assumption of *Hamlet*—Edwin Booth and Henry Irving.

Irving dressed *Hamlet* in a close-fitting doublet of black silk, black-silk tights, low, black shoes, and a black armhole cloak edged with fur. The doublet was girdled by a belt incrusted with jewels, and from the belt depended a dagger and small pouch at the right side, and a sword at the left. Around the neck was a gold chain, to which was attached a miniature of the dead *King*. He wore his own hair, which was abundant, carelessly parted in the middle, and a slight moustache,—which, ultimately, he discarded. The complete effect of his appearance was that of combined simplicity, refinement, elegance, and poetic wildness. His personality, expressed in his aspect, riveted attention. The eye followed him; the mind dwelt upon him; the imagination was absorbed by him. In his ideal of *Hamlet* the elements were combined of assumed madness and involuntary, sporadic derangement. The *Prince* as impersonated by him was not at any time calmly poised, but at all times the actor manifested that perfection of poise which consists in the steadiness of intense, continuous excitement—burning emotion concentrated at the topmost height of vitality. The pervading spirit of the impersonation was innate, ineffable loveliness of temperament contending with bitterness of feeling which has

HENRY IRVING AS *HAMLET*

FROM THE PAINTING BY SIR EDWIN LONG, A.R.A.

been engendered by wrong, outrage, and a frenzy of
terror and doubt precipitated by preternatural visitation. No other actor of our time made *Hamlet* more
entirely lovable.

WILSON BARRETT AS *YOUNG HAMLET*.

The first line spoken by *Hamlet* is "A little more
than kin and less than kind." That usually has been
understood to mean, "I am a little more than a
kinsman to you, because you, my uncle, have become
my mother's husband; but I am a different sort of
man." The line is a shaft of covert sarcasm. The
shaft, however, is not hurled, because the words are
spoken under the breath and are not intended to
be heard by the *King* and Court. Wilson Barrett, in
speaking that line, made the vowel short in the word
"kind" and sounded that word as if it were a rhyme
for "sinned." The word "kind," he declared, is an
old-country word for "child," and *Hamlet's* meaning
is, "I am more than a kinsman to you but less than a
son." That makes the remark a mere statement of
bald fact, such a statement as *Hamlet,* in his mood of
bitter grief and resentment, would be unlikely to utter.
There are times when the sorrow-stricken *Prince* is
forlorn and gentle; there never is a time when he is
commonplace. Still, it can be assumed that *Hamlet's*

bitterness of feeling underlies his words, whichever way you take them; and the suggested textual emendation may, possibly, be correct. The point has no bearing on the question of ideal.

When *Hamlet* comes upon the platform in the first of his Ghost Scenes, the time being the middle of the night and the night being, apparently, in late autumn, in the harsh climate of Denmark, he remarks that "the air bites shrewdly" and that "it is very cold." Wilson Barrett, speaking those words, turned the last half of the line into a question. "Is it very cold?" he asked; as if the *Prince,* already chilled and therefore aware of the frigid temperature, were inquiring into the state of the court thermometer. There were many other details of verbal modification in Wilson Barrett's reading of the part, all showing a striving after novelty and all insignificant. It was not by his "aitches" that John Philip Kemble became the *Hamlet* of his day. It is not by verbal quirks that any actor ever rose, or ever will rise, to the altitude of that sublime conception.

Shakespeare begins the Third Act of "Hamlet" with a "Room in the Castle," and presently he changes the scene to a "Hall in the Same." In that Hall the play is acted which *Hamlet* has ordered the *Players* to represent before him, and to the prospect of which he has entreated the *King* and *Queen*. That

Play Scene Wilson Barrett presented in a garden. The idea, probably, was derived from a hint in "Coxe's Travels," which mentions "Hamlet's Garden," adjacent to the Palace of Kronberg, near Elsinore, in which tradition says that the murder of the King was committed. The actor thought that he could derive a fine dramatic effect from causing *Claudius* to behold the copy of his monstrous crime upon the actual spot —"within mine orchard"—where it was perpetrated. Upon being told (he wrote) that the climate of Northern Europe is cold, even on a night in summer, for outdoor theatricals, he replied that in the time of "Hamlet" open-air theatres were customary. That position illustrates the fragile texture of his theory. There can be no serious objection to the use of a garden. Whatever will augment the legitimate dramatic effect of a play, without offence to reason, can rightly be introduced, because unless a play is effective it is useless. But the reason should be avowed. No theatres of any kind were in existence in Denmark in the time of the historic Hamlet. Beside, if reference to the time of the play, the eleventh century, is to govern in one particular it should govern in all. If "Hamlet" is to be mounted and dressed according to local custom in the historic period of Fengon and Horvendile, most of the persons in it must present themselves in skins. No authority, furthermore, would remain for the elaborate fencing play that was introduced by Wilson Barrett in the scene of *Hamlet's* combat with *Laertes*. The art of foining, or defensive sword-play with the rapier and foil, did not come into fashion as a courtly practice until about the thirteenth century.

It is a worthy ambition that endeavors, in the stage-setting of a Shakespearean play, to harmonize the work in all its parts and to remove whatever disparities may have been left in it by the author. But that result is not always attainable. In general it can be only approximately reached. Every one of Shakespeare's plays that is acted must be more or less cut, because almost every one of them is too long for representation if left in its original state. "Hamlet," in particular, must be much condensed. Edwin Booth's version of it is the longest in use on the English-speaking Stage, and that version omits nearly one thousand lines of the original. The modern stage accomplishes much by picture that the old dramatists could accomplish only by descriptive words. Wilson Barrett's restorations, most of which were made subsequent to the Closet Scene, while they cast no new light upon the subject, had the effect of retarding the action, and of retarding it exactly at a point where the need of greater celerity has always been felt. Wilson Barrett, however, was an expeditious actor, and his *Hamlet* was notable for celerity.

The evidence derived from the text of "Hamlet" as printed in the First Folio specifically indicates *Hamlet's* age. He is thirty years old. The proof of that is found in the dialogue between *Hamlet* and the *Grave-digger*. Wilson Barrett's method of dispersing that evidence was radical. He declared that it does not exist; that the text has been garbled; that the original language of Shakespeare has been altered; that expressions have been introduced into that conversation between *Hamlet* and the sexton which were not written by Shakespeare, but which were invented in order to make the language conformable to the requirements of various old actors. He maintained that *Hamlet* should be presented and accepted as a youth of about eighteen; that Shakespeare has drawn and described him as "young Hamlet," and that thirty is not "young." He had adopted a theory, and therefore he would have excluded from the tragedy whatever language conflicted with it. That is a convenient method, but its validity is not recognized by Shakespeare scholars. The words of the sexton,—who says that he has been a grave-digger since "the very day that young Hamlet was born," and that he has followed his "business," "man and boy, thirty years,"— are not, indeed, to be taken too literally. "Man and boy," for instance, seems to be no more than a loose phrase of common parlance, used by a quaint Hodge whose general style of thinking and of speech, together with the senility of his fag-ends of mis-remembered song, betoken an elderly man—such a man as, in such an occupation, would be old at fifty; such a man as would be noted rather for sly conceit and dry, waggish humor than for strict accuracy of reminiscence and statement. Still, the text of the Folio, notwithstanding its manifest misprints, is a good basis of the authentic text of Shakespeare. Its editors, Heminge and Condell, affirm it printed from "his papers,"—declaring that they "have scarce received from him a blot" in them,—and therefore a sensible reliance should be placed on it. Obvious blunders in it ought to be corrected, and in good modern editions they mostly are corrected; while reference to the Second Quarto (the First, which was understood to be Wilson Barrett's stronghold, being accounted piratical and untrustworthy) sometimes procures clearer and more felicitous readings. But arbitrary alterations, made without warrant or proof, as restorations of Shakespeare's original words or meanings are never allowable. Wilson Barrett, following a dubious conjecture, maintained that the questionable line in the Fencing Scene, "Our son is fat and scant of breath," was foisted into the text in order to suit the need of a fat actor, and he reasoned that if one line was inserted to suit one actor other lines may have been inserted to suit other actors, and accordingly that the player is justified in rejecting any part of the text that he fancies to have been thus introduced. That is a loose method of reasoning, and if it were applied throughout the tragedy it would produce singular results.

Wilson Barrett seemed to suppose that if the text were altered at points relative to *Hamlet's* age all discrepancies would disappear. That is not true. Indeed, there is not one of Shakespeare's plays that is either free, or could be freed, from discrepancies. *Macbeth,* for instance, in one of his most essential speeches, made at one of the most terrible moments of his afflicted life, suddenly ceases to talk like *Macbeth* and speaks in what is instantly recognized as the characteristic voice of Shakespeare,—introducing the simile of the "poor player." In "Macbeth" also cannon and dollars are mentioned as existing, which in his time had not been made. In "King Lear" there is mention of men who did not live till long after the historic King Lear's time. In "The Winter's Tale" a shipwreck occurs on the sea-coast of Bohemia, which has no sea-coast. In "Hamlet" reference occurs to the University of Wittenberg, an institution that did not exist until 1502, long after the period to which the story of the tragedy is supposed to relate. In "Hamlet," also, ordnance is shot off,—although in the historic age of that tragedy cannon were unknown. Everything in the play is consonant not with the period of its historic basis but with the period of its authorship. One of the speeches in it,—one upon which Wilson Barrett especially relied to prove *Hamlet's* juvenility,—the magnificent lines,

> " Think it no more,
> For nature, crescent, does not grow alone
> In thews and bulk, but as this temple waxes
> The inward service of the mind and soul
> Grows wide withal,''—

is put into the mouth of *Laertes,* a commonplace, shallow, treacherous young man, unlikely to utter any such lofty thought. There again it is the poet who speaks, and not the dramatic individual. Shakespeare was a great poet as well as a great play-maker, and there are times when the copious flow of his poetic inspiration deranges the adjustment of details in the construction of his plays. Artistic consistency and symmetry, indeed, were not wilfully neglected by him. In essential things his plays are coherent and harmonious. But he was careless of pedantic accuracy, and when his soul overflowed, as it often did, he heeded not through whose lips the golden torrent might break.

That *Hamlet* should be regarded as a youth Wilson Barrett chiefly deduced from the fact that his mother, *Queen Gertrude,* is young enough for an amour with her husband's brother, *Claudius.* He made the *Queen* about thirty-six years old, instead of about forty-eight or fifty. *Hamlet* was not young enough to suit his theory at thirty, but the *Queen* was young enough to suit it at thirty-six, and therefore could not be saddled with an adult son. The actor saw no difficulty in the way of making a youth of eighteen the natural exponent and voice of an embittered experience, a fatal grief, and a majestic contemplative philosophy such as never yet were or could be possible to boyhood; but he saw an insurmountable difficulty in the way of making an elderly woman lapse from virtue,— at the solicitation of a lover, obviously younger than herself, who is completely infatuated about her,—and this notwithstanding she is drawn as soft, sensuous, and vain, and is distinctly rebuked by her son, who should know her tolerably well, with conduct utterly inexplicable and senseless at a time of her life when

> " The heyday in the blood is tame, it's humble,
>   And waits upon the judgment."

The actor did not even reflect that the amour of *Gertrude* and *Claudius* may have been going on for a long time prior to the murder of *King Hamlet.*

It is, surely, more probable that a well-preserved and handsome woman of forty-eight or fifty, weary of her too excellent husband and flattered by the passion of a desperate wooer (who thought her so conjunctive to his life and soul that he could no more live without her than a star could move outside of its sphere), should be an amatory sinner than it is that a lad of eighteen should be the mature philosopher, the profound moralist, the representative thinker, the grief-stricken, isolated sufferer, the intellectual, passionate, deep-hearted, supreme man whom Shakespeare has incarnated in *Hamlet*.

In all representations of "Hamlet" the main thing is and should be *Hamlet* himself. The accessories are subordinated in the piece and they should be kept subordinate in the presentment. Wilson Barrett's effort so to assort the ages of the several characters that the amatory relationship of *Claudius* and *Gertrude* might impress his mind as more rational and probable was not, perhaps, unnatural. *Hamlet* himself considered that attachment preposterous,—saying to his mother, "At your age you cannot call it love." But the brisk actor's effort was an example of misdirected zeal. Nobody cares much about *Claudius* and *Gertrude*. Their story, and indeed the story of the play, in as far as it relates to merely mundane affairs, is one that lacks absorbing interest. The essential substance being the spiritual personality of *Hamlet,* when an actor undertakes that part the principal end that it concerns him to accomplish is the revelation of *Hamlet's* soul, not the detail of his environment in the Court of Denmark. The adjuncts should be appropriate and the environment should be harmonious, for all this helps to preserve an illusion; but all this will not avail, unless the actor is able, by virtue of the sovereign quality of his nature, to reach the height of the great argument and embody a true ideal of Shakespeare's conception.

Even admitting that thirty is not young, whereas, in fact, it is, and that "young Hamlet" ought to be figured as a lad of eighteen, what good comes of it? Wherein is the observer enabled, by that means, to bring the experience and signification of *Hamlet* into a more intimate relationship with his own soul? Wilson Barrett—who did not and could not look or act like a boy—presented him as a full-grown, rather athletic man, trying to make himself boyish by acting in an alert manner. If an actor were to succeed, however, in substituting boy for man, he would still be bound to play the part according to the configuration and substance of it as those are found in Shakespeare's tragedy. The essence of *Hamlet* is corrosive misery, and whether it be misery agèd eighteen or misery agèd thirty the personality

remains the same. Call him what age you will, his
words, his conduct, and his nature remain unchanged.
The mystery that enshrouds *Hamlet* is not that of
an inscrutable individuality but that of the agonized
and half-insane condition of a royal and supreme soul
overwhelmed with afflicting consciousness of man's
inexplicable and awful spiritual relation to the universe. From the condition of the character, no matter
what portal of theory be opened, there is no escape.
Much had been said about the limit of *Hamlet's* "madness." Much, at one time, was said about the color of
his hair. It was consistent with precedent that there
should come a season of quibbling on the subject of
his age. By and by, perhaps, there will arise a serious
question as to the length of his nose. Such considerations are immaterial.

In Wilson Barrett's performance of *Hamlet* the
manifestation of filial love was conspicuous for fer-
vency and zeal. But filial love is not the sovereign
charm of *Hamlet* nor is it the dominant impulse of
his character,—an overfreighted, discordant harmony
of all lovable qualities being the one, and the "scruple
of thinking too precisely on the event" being the
other. Filial he is, and filial love is a sweet and tender emotion; but a man may be an affectionate and
devoted son without being, for that reason, an object
of especial interest to the world. Venerable age

overwhelmed with misery is exceedingly pathetic;
but many a father is abused by his children without
therefore becoming an image of the colossal majesty
and ruined grandeur of *King Lear*. Any old man
who is the victim of ingratitude and cruelty is an
object of pity; but *Lear's* experience is possible only
to *Lear's* nature, and, unless that nature be embodied,
the picture of that experience can produce no adequate effect. The world does not love *Hamlet* because
Hamlet loves his father but because he is *Hamlet*.

Wilson Barrett transposed the soliloquy on death
from the Third Act into the Second. He preferred
"a siege of troubles" to "a sea" of them, as Edwin
Forrest did. He referred to a "kindless villain,"
not a "kyndless" one. He addressed the greater
part of "To be or not to be" to the circumambient
air,—a region toward which no human being ever
gazes when his mind is deeply absorbed in rumina-
tion. In the parting scene with *Ophelia* he caused
Hamlet to make a spasmodic discovery of the furtive
King, and immediately thereafter a spasmodic discovery of the furtive *Polonius*—each distinct. He
indicated *Hamlet,* at the close of that parting scene,
as being so passionately attracted toward *Ophelia*
that it is only by a tremendous effort of the will that
he can break away from her; that being, manifestly,
as false a touch as perverse ingenuity could put upon

a mood that incarnates the holiness and pathetic majesty of renunciation. He placed the strongest possible emphasis upon *Hamlet's* hatred and defiance of *King Claudius,* making the *Prince* so resolute and violent in that animosity that he was left without a reason for not having at once accomplished his revenge. He cut the *King* out of "No, his affections do not that way tend," and he closed Act Third with the *Queen's* recital to her husband of the killing of *Polonius,* and the *King's* resolve to send the *Prince* to England. He laid a marked stress upon *Hamlet's* "I essentially am not in madness, but mad in craft," seeming to suppose that this, absolutely and finally, settles the question of *Hamlet's* insanity—whereas this is, perhaps, one of the most characteristic denotements of mental aberration that occur in the tragedy. Persons who have been shocked and dazed and who, while not wholly unbalanced, know themselves to be partially so, are sure, sooner or later, to make a point of asserting their perfect sanity. The most interesting of his restorations was that of the passage in which *Hamlet,* in his delirium, weeps over the body of *Ophelia's* father, whom, in his half frantic mood, he has slain. "I'll lug the guts into the neighbor room" was not spoken; but it ought to be if this scene is to be acted at all, in order to give the situation its rightful effect. *Hamlet* has then become entirely wild, and he breaks down, in a paroxysm of hysterical grief. Wilson Barrett, at that point, and at the exit after the Play Scene (although the action which he there introduced, of striking with a sword at imaginary, lurking foes, was extravagant and tended to make the situation ludicrous), came nearer to being *Hamlet* than anywhere else along the whole line of his performance. Every person in the play who calls *Hamlet* "young" or a "youth" seemed to have been instructed to sound the juvenile designation as with a trumpet; but the *King's* line, "How dangerous is it that this *man* goes loose," was merely murmured. Such were the peculiar views and embellishments that,—with laborious effort and hard and brittle elocution,—Wilson Barrett displayed as *Hamlet*.

At the zenith of his intellectual greatness, the summit alike of his maturity and his fame, and after studying and acting *Hamlet* for more than thirty years, that great actor, Macready,—a wonderful man, to whom the attribute of genius has been unjustly denied, by much of modern criticism, for no better reason than because he was scrupulously thorough, elaborate, methodical, and exacting as an artistic executant,—wrote thus of *Hamlet*: "It seems to me as if only now, at fifty-one years of age, I thoroughly see and appreciate the artistic power of Shakespeare in this great human phenomenon; nor do any of the critics, Goethe, Schlegel, Coleridge, present to me, in their elaborate remarks, the exquisite artistical effects which I see in this work, as long meditation, like long straining after light, gives the minutest portion of its excellence to my view." A remark of kindred significance was made by Betterton, who, at the age of seventy, said to a friend who had praised his performance of *Hamlet* as "perfect": "Perfect? I have played *Hamlet* now fifty years, and I believe I have not got to the depths of all its philosophy yet." Wilson Barrett, comparatively a beginner in *Hamlet,* was troubled by no such scruples. "I have," he declared, "seen *Hamlet* played by every actor who has made a name in that character during the last twenty-five years. I know all their business and all their traditions. . . . When I made up my mind to produce the play in the Princess' Theatre in London, I took up the book to study it, to try to improve on my old performance of the part, and as I read and studied I began to realize slowly how mistaken I had been. . . . For two years I worked on the play, analyzing every line and every word. I arrived at my conclusions after years of study, and the character I have conceived is supported by some of the brightest intellects of our time. This is the outcome of a sincere conviction that I am absolutely right." One of those intellects was the late Clement Scott, a learned, accomplished, competent, and expert dramatic critic. Mr. Scott wrote of Wilson Barrett's *Hamlet,* in an elaborate paper on that subject, these words: "I did *not* find *tenderness, inspiration,* or *imagination.*" What remains in a personation of *Hamlet* from which those attributes are absent?

EDWARD SMITH WILLARD.

Willard possessed attributes as an actor that would give importance to his performance of almost any part he might have chosen to represent. Intellectual concentration, dignity, intensity, weight, power, and melody of voice, copious resonance of delivery, the capacity of quick transition from quietude to trenchant impetuosity,—those, together with fine stature and grace of movement, were blended in him with the self-command and the physical strength essential to sustain an exacting character at a high tension. Those qualities were manifested in his embodiment of *Hamlet,*—a performance which, technically, was often excellent, but which, for reasons partly constitutional and partly capricious, was scarcely ever true to the poet.

Willard seemed to have comprehended *Hamlet* as

an absolutely sane man embittered by painful experience, and to have determined to represent him,—in
the spirit and apart from externals,—as an actual
person of the present day. His performance was based
on "realism," and it was executed in the "natural"
manner. One result only is possible from that method:
"Hamlet" remains a sufficiently effective play but
it ceases to be poetry. The element of *Hamlet's*
nature that Willard expressed was the slightly cynical
bitterness of it,—a quality which, as indicated in
the text, is that melancholy, fretful mingling of
suspicion and sarcasm often associated with mental
derangement. Upon the lovely, dreamlike, pensive,
affectionate, mournful, superstitious, weird, haunted,
desolate, phantasmal aspects of *Hamlet's* mind the
actor cast no light, and, indeed, he seemed to have
bestowed little or no attention upon that spiritual
experience which *Hamlet* was intended to represent.
He played the part like an actor possessed of it;
never like a man whom it possesses and whose soul it
has enthralled.

Among the many sidelights that are thrown upon
the character of *Hamlet* no one is more illuminative
than his mother's description of him, given at the
grave of *Ophelia*. After the fit of madness has passed
his patience is that of the female dove: "his silence will
sit drooping." *Hamlet* has occasional accessions of

frenzied strength, and he is capable of sudden, though intermittent, tumults of action; but, for the most part, he drifts and dreams, and, although he never, for even an instant, ceases to suffer, a dominant attribute of his nature is gentleness. *Hamlet* means spiritual misery. He does not grieve simply because his father has died, or simply because his widowed mother has precipitately married his uncle. He grieves,—and in that grief he contemplates suicide, before the apparition of his father's ghost,—because his mind is overwhelmed with long brooding upon the awful mystery of the spiritual environment. He deeply desires that his relations with that appalling mystery may be adjusted. He is everywhere baffled. His mind is unhinged. And in that condition of agony which conventional criticism would, probably, call "morbid" he receives the shock of a visitation from beyond the grave, and after that experience he is always in the border-land between reason and madness. No actor can gain more than a superficial success in *Hamlet* unless he has comprehended that form of possible human grief, and unless he possesses the intrinsic personal charm that can turn sorrow into enchantment. The slender, handsome gentleman whose elocution neither domestic infelicity nor the paternal spectre can disturb is not Shakespeare's *Hamlet;* neither is the latter-day, agnostical cynic.

Willard did not indicate sympathy with *Hamlet's*
spiritual condition nor even a perception of it. He
was refined, picturesque, interesting, dramatic, modern; a smooth, middle-aged gentleman; a fluent and
flexible actor; a model of executive efficiency and
even of fiery resolution; never the haunted, bewildered,
dejected, mournful, half-crazed *Prince*—never the
authentic oracle of that great message for the soul:
"If it be now, 'tis not to come; if it be not to come,
it will be now; if it be not now, yet it will come:
the readiness is all." *Hamlet* wins and sways by
condition, not by deed, and therefore the more an
actor of him strives after stage-effect the further he
drifts away from the truth. Willard's *Hamlet* was
replete with effective embellishments of professional
mechanism, but it lacked the essential soul. It is
possible, however, that the actor's purpose was to
make himself comprehensible, by commonplace minds,
as a grim and caustic cynic and an apt, scheming,
expeditious avenger, of the purely practical kind.
His advent as *Hamlet* had been heralded with
official promise of "a performance entirely in keeping with the realistic movement of the age,"—
which is exactly what *Hamlet* ought never to be.
It is not, perhaps, surprising that, with such a
design, the haunted *Prince* should first have turned
his back upon the phantom and then violently pur-

sued it, and that, in the supreme scenes of the killing
of *Polonius* and the rebuke of the *Queen,* he should
have caused no effect of frenzy, nor the least feeling
of awe, nor the least sense of pathos.

Willard's stage version of "Hamlet" differed in some
respects from all others known to the theatre. In the
Second Scene of Act First, after *Hamlet* had been
apprised of the apparition, the *King* and courtiers
re-entered, and the subsequent scene, between *Laertes,
Ophelia,* and *Polonius,* passed in the throneroom. By
that expedient the customary front-scene was obviated.
Act Second was amplified by the introduction, from
Act Third, of the soliloquy on death, "To be or not
to be," together with the subsequent colloquy between
Hamlet and *Ophelia.* Those passages were inserted
after "Look, where sadly the poor wretch comes,
reading." *Hamlet* was made to conceal himself behind
curtains, so that he could overhear, in Act Third,
the *King's* instructions to *Rosencrantz* and *Guildenstern,* and also the *King's* soliloquy, before the vain
attempt at prayer. There was a curtain after the
prayer and the Third Act was played in two parts.
Act Third was made to comprise the first three
scenes of Act Fourth and to close with the *King's*
adjuration as to "the present death of Hamlet" in
England,—all the parts being so blended that there
were no front-scenes. Act Fourth included, without

change, the scene of *Ophelia's* madness, that of the passion of *Laertes,* that of *Horatio* and the letter, and that of the compact between *Laertes* and the *King;* while, after the *Queen* had described the drowning of *Ophelia,* soldiers brought in the dead body, upon a bier of hurdles, and it was attended by *Laertes,* weeping. Act Fifth was divided by a curtain, after *Ophelia's* burial,—at "This grave shall have a living monument,"—and the *Osric* and Duel Scenes were made to constitute a Sixth Act, which passed in the courtyard of the castle. The fencing-match was played with both "rapier and dagger." A jester, or court-fool, was introduced, but he did not speak. The double ghost was used, in Act First, in order to give effect to the fugitive character of that illusory spectre, at the exclamatory words " 'Tis here!" " 'Tis here!" " 'Tis gone!" The text was freely cut, especially in the lines allotted to *Horatio, Polonius,* and the *Queen.* There were no new readings. *Hamlet* said "siege of troubles" and not "sea." *Horatio* said "dead waste" and not "dead vast." *Hamlet* said "he wafts me still," and "where thrift may follow feigning," instead of "fawning," and he spoke more than is usually spoken of the speech about Pyrrhus. He likewise repeated in an eager whisper the speech of *Lucianus,* when doing the murder, and instead of "mobled queen" *Hamlet* said "inobled queen,"—a reading taken from the First Folio. Some of those expedients were new; others had long been in use. *Hamlet,* in stage custom, has usually kept a wary watch upon the *King; Ophelia's* dead body has been produced at the end of Act Fourth; the double ghost is old; and the *"in*obled queen" was adopted by Edwin Booth, in 1878, and is so printed in his published "Prompt Book" of "Hamlet," in every edition of it after the first; and it probably is correct,—although "mobled (dishevelled) queen" occurs in both the Quartos, 1603 and 1604, and in the Second Folio, 1632. The most material change made by Willard was the transference of passages from Act Third to Act Second, an alteration for which he had an actor's reason— that it enabled him to create a strong effect at an earlier time in his performance. No Shakespeare scholar could approve of it. In the *Queen's* apartment the portrait of the dead *King Hamlet* was placed behind a curtain, which *Hamlet* drew back to reveal it. Willard sought the earlier prints of Shakespeare, the Quartos, in order that he might obtain his text from a fountain-head; but it should be remembered that the First Quarto is probably piratical, that the Second is dubious, and that all are confused; while the Folio of 1623 is marred with errors, which the later ones only conjecturally emend.

HERBERT BEERBOHM-TREE.

Herbert Beerbohm-Tree performed as *Hamlet,* for the first time in America, at Abbey's Theatre, now, 1911, the Knickerbocker, on February 21, 1895. His impersonation was that of an expert actor; marked by distinction, variety of expressive pose, abundance, if not excess, of gesture, fluency of elocution,—notwithstanding the impediment of a slight lisp,—and an appropriate mystical incertitude; but it was shallow, devoid of poetic emotion, finical in fibre, often marred by inappropriate alertness, and it was metallic in execution.   Of *Hamlet* as the exponent of fatal misery, sequent on long brooding over the awful mystery of the spiritual environment of man, there was no sign.   Every actor of *Hamlet* has a special ideal and a favorite theory.   Mr. Tree particularly denoted his grasp of the subject in his treatment of *Hamlet's* madness,—making the *Prince* by turns mad and sane, yet always keeping him near the borderland between lunacy and reason.   At the climax of the Play Scene he made him delirious, and his strident clamor was theatrically effective.   In his treatment of *Hamlet's* love for *Ophelia* he was not felicitous.   His action, indeed, was gracious and sweet,—the action of furtively kissing *Ophelia's* hair and of pitifully casting flowers upon her grave, but,

since *Hamlet's* love for *Ophelia* is a memory, and
not a passion, those expedients were unsuitable and untrue. No actual lover urges his sweet-
heart to go to a nunnery. Even before *Hamlet,*
with his shocked brain and broken heart, has detected
the weak, docile, frightened *Ophelia* in her forced
falsehood he knows that for him there can be no
refuge in love for woman and no reliance upon it.
His misery is corrosive, bitter, and immedicable.
Mr. Tree placed much stress upon *Hamlet* as a fellow-
student,—upon his "consonancy," his kindness to his
associates at the University,—but comradeship is
a minor element in *Hamlet's* nature. The actor's
postures were often effective, notwithstanding his
angularity, but the full effect of sublimity, terror,
grief, pathos, passion, and delirium cannot be produced by an actor whose face lacks mobility, whose
temperament is cold, and whose voice is hollow and
inflexible. Mr. Tree declared that it is advantageous
for an actor to be substantially ignorant of the stage-
traditions of *Hamlet,*—the usages of earlier representatives of the character. That is an unfortunate
and mistaken view of the subject, because the traditions
of the stage are almost always valuable, and they are
especially valuable to a representative of *Hamlet.*
The readings and business that were approved by
Betterton, Kemble, Kean, Macready, Phelps, Booth,

and Irving ought at least to be known and considered by younger actors. Capricious innovation is not a sign of acute intellect but of poor judgment. Mr. Tree shifted the soliloquy on honor and inaction, expunged important words from the part of the *First Grave-digger,* provided a new term of sepulchre for Yorick's skull, muddled the matter of *Hamlet's* age, curtailed the words of *Laertes,* omitted *Osric,* and absurdly concluded the tragedy with a chorus of distant angels,—those "flights," presumably, which are mentioned in the beautiful apostrophe of *Horatio.*

EDWARD HUGH SOTHERN.

Mr. Sothern appeared as *Hamlet* for the first time on September 17, 1899, at the Garden Theatre, New York, and since then he has repeated his performance in many cities throughout America. There is high critical authority for two opinions relative to the acting of that part,—one, by Hazlitt, that it is the most difficult of all parts for an actor to personate; the other, by Macready, that a total failure in it is of rare occurrence. Both opinions have been confirmed by experience. Stage history records only a few demonstrably faithful embodiments of *Hamlet,* but it mentions many that were acceptable because respectably meritorious. Mr. Sothern's per-

From a photograph by Schloss

EDWARD H. SOTHERN AS *HAMLET*

From a photograph by Lizzie Caswell Smith

JOHNSTON FORBES-ROBERTSON AS *HAMLET*

formance was found to belong in the latter class.
It was, at its best, intelligent, conscientious, and
sincere in spirit, picturesque in appearance, and
methodical and evenly sustained in execution. Some
of its defective points, apparent when it was first
presented, were subsequently repaired—and that is
true of every performance of the part which has
endured at all—but it did not become authoritative
and imposing. Denial of Mr. Sothern's proved
capability in his profession would be foolish and
wrong: he is a fine comedian and an admirable "all
'round" actor, but he has not shown tragic power,
and *Hamlet,* without tragic power, although he may
interest and please an acquiescent multitude, cannot
impress informed judgment and is not important.
Mr. Sothern's lack of tragic power became conspicuously evident in the first meeting with the *Ghost,*
the scene of his parting with *Ophelia,* the delirium
which attends the climax of the "Mouse Trap" play,
and the frenzy of mingled horror and exultation at
the killing of *Polonius.* Those situations require
much more than the expertness of trained talent.
The misery of *Hamlet,* the corrosive anguish which
has sapped the foundation of his mind and which
steadily, inexorably procures his ruin, was not even
indicated. The text was volubly spoken and was
made to convey its superficial meanings, but no con-

viction was imparted of the intense mind and deep heart which are behind the words. The personality was finical, undistinguished, commonplace. Filial tenderness and reverence were well expressed, as also, especially in the Closet Scene, were moral fervor and a withering scorn of evil-doing. In his later representations of *Hamlet,* when he apostrophized the *Ghost,* in the Closet Scene, and when he uttered *Hamlet's* dying words, Mr. Sothern was mournfully pathetic, striking a true note. The elocutionary artifice which, in earlier days, he habitually used, of sudden, explosive, exclamatory delivery, had been discarded, and his radically unsympathetic voice evinced certain good results of training and practice, —possibly, also, of chastening experience. In his stage business there were many peculiarities. After *Hamlet's* first interview with the *Ghost,* at the end of the scene, "Let's *go* together," he stood still and posed, facing the audience, in the obvious glare of a white limelight. In the scene of the espial he placed *Hamlet's* discovery of the eavesdroppers, *Claudius* and *Polonius,* at the first "Go thy ways to a nunnery," not at "now receive them, No, not I," or at "Rich gifts wax poor when givers prove unkind," —at one or the other of which points it certainly belongs, if it is to occur at all. In the scene in which *Hamlet* is brought into the *King's* presence and interrogated as to the concealment of the corpse of *Polonius* the *King,* previous to the *Prince's* entrance, was caused to pick up a naked sword from the floor (not evincing any curiosity as to how it came to be there) and place it on a convenient chair, and when *Hamlet* said, "Seek him i' the other place yourself," he suddenly seized that sword and attempted to attack *Claudius* with it, to kill him. In the same scene, at "I see a cherub that sees them," *Hamlet* was caused to show a miniature of his father, indicating that lamented parent as the "cherub." In the Duel with *Laertes, Hamlet* was made to receive a wound in his wrist, to give an astonished glance at it, to glare at his opponent, perceiving that the foil of *Laertes* was not "buttoned," immediately to engage with and disarm his adversary, to set his foot upon the fallen foil, and then to tender his own weapon to *Laertes,* which that treacherous person was constrained in courtesy to accept, according to "the rules of the game." In Mr. Sothern's earlier presentments of "Hamlet" the indispensable passage, "Now might I do it, pat, now he is praying," was omitted; later it was restored. At first he used the advent of *Fortinbras,*—customarily used on the European Continental Stage and always, wherever used, productive of tediousness,—but later he discarded it. One radical defect of his *Hamlet,*—never cured, and, from deficiency of imagination and of the glamour of genius, incurable,—was its complete lack of weirdness, of any intimation of being haunted. As a whole the performance, whether in its crudity at first or its maturity at last, was circumscribed within the conventional limits of stage utility. It was, however, largely attended and sometimes fervently praised. Every actor has his audience and Mr. Sothern's is a large one.

JOHNSTON FORBES-ROBERTSON.

Johnston Forbes-Robertson adopted *Hamlet* into his repertory in 1897, and his impersonation of it has been accepted and admired in many cities of Great Britain and America. He acted it for the first time in New York on March 7, 1904, at the Knickerbocker Theatre. Mr. Forbes-Robertson is an actor of signal ability, fine achievement, and large experience,— acquired in more than thirty years of almost continual practice of the dramatic art; he early profited by professional association with that versatile, powerful, thorough actor, Samuel Phelps, of whom, in 1886, he wrote and published an instructive biography; he had the great advantage of acting under the example, leadership, and guidance of Henry Irving; he is an artist, a student, a writer, and a thinker; he has

played many kinds of parts, and played them all
well; and it would be strange indeed if, in the maturity
of middle life, he were not able to give a performance
of *Hamlet* that should impress even the most exigent
observers as proficient and respectable. Such his
performance was,—the careful, methodical, competent
achievement of a practised performer, following an
established method and walking, for the most part,
in a traditional path.

The customary denotements of *Hamlet's* agitated
mental condition were duly provided, together with
customary stage adjuncts that heighten and enforce
the elegant desolation of that afflicted *Prince* and help
to diffuse the "luxury of woe." The raiment, as usual,
was of a beauteous dusky hue, and very becoming.
The make-up was immaculate, and thus in the highest
degree creditable to those sartorial and tonsorial
artists who have always manifested such consummate taste and skill at the Stage Court of Denmark:
a miserable man, who sees ghosts and contemplates
suicide, necessarily must be, and always is, more than
commonly scrupulous as to his raiment and personal
appearance. The facial aspect was that of emaciation,
appropriate to an agonized being and significant of
his suffering. The text of the tragedy,—aside from
necessary excisions and capricious restorations,—was
correctly spoken. The Ghost Scenes were made spec-

tral with loneliness and limelight. The Play Scene was deftly carried to a telling climax,—although there, as at the greater climax in the *Queen's* closet, at "Nay, I know not! Is it the *king?*" Mr. Forbes-Robertson manifested more the intention than the faculty of tragic power. *Reynaldo* was retained, providing a little more of the tedious senility of *Polonius,* and *Fortinbras* was restored, to point the contrast between the vacillating man of thought and the expeditious man of action.

Mr. Forbes-Robertson's ideal of *Hamlet* was, as far as comprehensible, seen to be, in most particulars, correct, but it was not made absolutely clear, and his expression of it did not, at any point, except in *Hamlet's* interview with *Ophelia,* immediately after the soliloquy on death, exhibit imperial felicity of art. At the last of that colloquy, however, he manifested, exceedingly well, the wounded heart, the disordered mind, the seething passion, the wild, indefinite purpose, and the bitterness and scorn that are constituent elements of *Hamlet's* paroxysm. Neither there, nor elsewhere, though, did he denote that *Hamlet* is a man who has passed beyond the love of woman, and who, more than once, passes across the limit of sanity—as when, for example, he purposes to take such a vengeance on his enemy as will condemn the soul of the monarch to eternal torture in the depths of hell. The excision of an essential part of *Hamlet's* speech in the Prayer Scene almost vitiated, certainly much perplexed, the purport of the embodiment. As to the larger significance of the character, aside from its various values as a vehicle of dramatic expression,—meaning its piteous exemplification of finite man, dazed, mystified, and overwhelmed in the hopeless endeavor to pierce the mystery of his infinite environment in the awful universe of God,—Mr. Forbes-Robertson's presentment of *Hamlet* made no reference, nor did it indicate that this had been considered. The actor was seen to be introspective, intellectual, pensively sombre, endowed with sensibility and refinement, and professionally capable: but the performance, though uninspired, was, nevertheless, vastly superior to the desecrations of *Hamlet* that have been exhibited on our stage from Germany, Italy, and France, such, for instance, as the elderly, brawny, muscular, and fat, or the fantastic, wizened, and vapid *Hamlets* of such actors as Salvini, Rossi, Sonnenthal, Mounet-Sully, and Mme. Sarah Bernhardt. It lacked the authoritative predominance of a great personality; and in the actor's effort to be modern, colloquial, and expeditious its manner dwindled to that of the preceptor,—as in the argumentative, expository utterance of the great speech about death, the instructions to the *Players,* and the dialogue with the graveyard clown; but it was sustained and sincere, and it was characterized by dignity, feeling, and grace.

There is a silly notion, for some time current and frequently voiced, that no admirer of Edwin Booth as *Hamlet* ever did, or ever could, admire any other actor in that part. Nothing could be more absurd. It is not admiration of Edwin Booth that chills enthusiasm in the observer of Johnston Forbes-Robertson, or Edward H. Sothern, or Robert Mantell, when they are performing as *Hamlet*. It is the lack, on the part of those performers, and others like to them, of the *Hamlet* temperament. Mr. Forbes-Robertson, in this character, had fine moments, but, as a whole, his modern, conversational, impetuous image of *Hamlet* did little more than to show the various values of the character as a vehicle of dramatic performance. *Hamlet* means misery; not the woe of black crape and purple velvet; but the lethal misery from which there is no relief and no refuge but the grave. The actor who does not know this and cannot make this *felt* has not fully comprehended the subject and cannot truly act the part. Every actor has his limitations and, as the Oriental proverb wisely says:

> "Though it poorer be, or richer,
> You can only fill your pitcher!"

The acting of foreign performers, when they assume characters of Shakespeare, is necessarily hampered by their natural, unavoidable ignorance or misapprehension of the spirit of the English language. The characters of Shakespeare, substantially, do not exist for them. There is an indefinable elusive quality in every language, especially in the poetry of every language, that cannot be transferred into any other. Foreign actors,—French, German, Italian, Spanish, and so following,—when they appear in translations of Shakespeare's plays, only approximate to the conception of the English poet, always leaving something that is essential unexpressed. The actors from Continental Europe who, in their professional tours of America, have presented themselves as *Hamlet* have invariably failed to show anything more than a faint, shimmering semblance of Shakespeare's conception of that character. Each has presented an ideal of it, and each, in doing so, has exemplified, more or less efficiently, the resources of trained executive art; but in every instance, however meritorious in execution, the ideal has been conspicuously wrong. The predominant, pervasive characteristic of the Continental method of acting is "realism." *Hamlet* has been assumed on the American Stage by many Continental actors; chief among them being Daniel Edward Bandmann, Bogumil Dawison, Charles Fechter, Tommaso Salvini, Ernesto Rossi, Ludwig Barney, Friedrich Haase, Adolph von Sonnenthal, Jean Mounet-Sully, Sarah Bernhardt, and Ermete Novelli. The performances given by the German actors, although generally tedious, are remembered as more nearly consonant with Shakespeare than those given by actors from Italy and France. The presentments of *Hamlet* by Fechter, Mounet-Sully, and Sarah Bernhardt, considered as attempts to portray the character delineated by the English poet, were fantastic and sometimes ludicrous.

DANIEL EDWARD BANDMANN.

One of the most talented actors of foreign origin and style who have appeared in America was Daniel Edward Bandmann (1840-1905), a performer whose youth promised much but whose maturity achieved little. He acted in both German and English. His first appearance in America, as an English-speaking *Hamlet,* was made at Niblo's Garden, New York, on September 29, 1863, and his performance awakened interest and caused discussion. Bandmann was a stalwart, muscular person, having an Hebraic, aquiline face, sanguine complexion, small, dark eyes, and abundant long, dark hair, curled and brushed back from the brow. His manner was animated, eager, ostentatious, ebullient, and he possessed much vitality and enthusiasm,—that wild emotional fervor which, tinged with sentimentality, is often characteristic of the race from which he sprang. His voice was strong, but neither deep nor sympathetic. In nature he was selfish, crafty, and insincere. As an actor, whether in youth or manhood, he lacked repose, self-command, and mental concentration. His presentment of *Hamlet,*—both at the first, and later when given at the Standard Theatre in New York, on October 2, 1879,—was disfigured by a strenuous striving to be " original " by means of capricious innovation. He spoke all the hysterical words of *Hamlet,* after the disappearance of the *Ghost,* in the final Platform Scene, and he restored the passage, usually omitted, in which *Fortinbras* appears. The former of those restorations was commendable, because in those fevered apostrophes of the *Prince* to the phantom,—grief and horror culminating in delirium,—the keynote is struck of *Hamlet's* dazed, wavering, distracted condition. Bandmann, however, while expressing a certain bitter pathos, fell far short of indicating *Hamlet's* agony and mental shock. Then, and thereafter, like most actors in the part, he was merely executive, evoking no response of sympathy. His *Hamlet* was a young man arrayed in elegant mourning attire, sorrowful for the demise of his father, ashamed of his mother's indecency of hasty nuptial contract with his uncle, and embittered by immediate circumstances; but the foundations of his mind were unshaken; no spectre haunted his thought; no tinge of madness colored his melancholy; no sense was imparted by him of the isolation and remediless misery of a great soul overwhelmed and bewildered by the awful mystery of life and death. In short, he did not possess either the mind or the temperament of *Hamlet,* and his performance stopped short at professional utility. One piece of his stage business well indicated its general character: when the *Ghost* appeared, in the Closet Scene, he started backward and fell, speaking thereafter in a recumbent position.

BOGUMIL DAWISON.

Bogumil Dawison came to New York in 1866, and on December 10, that year, at the Thalia Theatre (which had been known as the Bowery, and later was again so designated), he acted *Hamlet,* for the first time in America. Dawison was a tall, slender man, having a leonine head, somewhat suggestive of that of Daniel Webster; clear, penetrating, expressive dark eyes, regular features, a demonstrative, commanding carriage of the body, and an unusually sweet though not a strong voice. There was no fire of inspiration in his performance of *Hamlet,* but there was a clear ideal, however questionable, combined with felicity of executive art. His presentment was both robust and sentimental, full of animation, and continuously diversified by stage business, but it was devoid of the introspection and the desolate grief which, consistently sustained and continuously obvious, are intrinsic attributes to the character and inseparable from a right performance of it. *Hamlet,* as acted by Dawison, was an absolutely sane, self-contained person, occasionally simulating insanity. The more sympathetic, effective parts of his performance were the level speaking,—as in *Hamlet's* colloquies with *Horatio,* before the Play Scene and in the church-yard,—the aspect, infrequent but right whenever assumed, of meditation, the denotement of the *Prince's* sad, forlorn humor,—as in the descant on "Yorick's skull,"—and the depth of filial feeling and mortal anguish, in the Closet Scene, wherein the actor's assumption of *Hamlet* reached its highest eminence of truth and of effect. In pathos Dawison was exceptionally strong, yet that element of his temperament was only fitfully elicited by the part of *Hamlet.* The actor was foremost, not the per-

sonation. When *Hamlet* was told of the apparition
he at once became wildly excited, flurried, gesticu-
latory, neither dazed nor appalled, and during *Hamlet's* scenes with the *Ghost* he busied himself in
maintaining a continuous trembling of the body and
in making pantomimic responses to the words of the
spectre, so that the attention of his auditors was
diverted equally from the phantom and the *Prince*
and concentrated on the industrious devices of the
expertly agitated performer. Once, when the *Ghost*
was describing the murder committed by *Claudius,*
Dawison's *Hamlet* wrapped his cloak around his
head, as though to shut the horrible spectacle from
his sight,—an obstructive and therefore hurtful device.
Discreet ingenuity of business is sometimes exceedingly effective, but the obvious expedient for the
actor of *Hamlet,* at that point, is a state of horror-
stricken absorption, intense rigidity, motionless attention, tremendous, concentrated feeling,—such as would
be denoted by the ghastly face, the fixed, entranced
gaze,—and involuntary, almost breathless exclamation.
Dawison, however, was an exceptionally interesting
actor,—the most interesting German tragedian,
indeed, who has visited America in our time. The
version of "Hamlet" in which he appeared was
mutilated in the Fourth and Fifth Acts,—a fault
unusual with the Germans, who, as a rule, give too

much of Shakespeare's text, in their stage versions, rather than too little.

CHARLES FECHTER.

Charles Fechter, who mostly turned "Hamlet" into prose, told my friend Lester Wallack, by whom the fact was mentioned to me, that, in his opinion, the *Prince's* soliloquy on life and death ought to be omitted in the representation, because an impediment to the action. He spoke it, but he spoke it rapidly and unimpressively, as though "making a few remarks," not at all as though an overburdened soul were uttering itself in an involuntary, irrepressible strain of thought. Fechter was an actor of rare ability in romantic drama, such as is typified by "Ruy Blas," "Monte Cristo," "The Corsican Brothers," "Obenreizer," and "The Lady of Lyons." He was an artist of the French school, the original representative of *Armand Duval,* in "La Dame aux Camélias," and on the Paris stage he gained brilliant distinction, following in the track of Frédéric Lemaître. He spoke English, but his speaking of it was broken and much marred by a singsong cadence, and his delivery of English blank verse, accordingly, was abominable. At the time of his advent on the American Stage he was a stout

person, of gross aspect, and incapable of looking like
Hamlet, even had he been capable of speaking English
verse,—which he was not. His acting of the *Prince,*
as of all other parts in which he appeared, was
authoritative and expert. As *Hamlet* he presented
an impetuous, lachrymose, highly explosive French-
man. He wore a suit of solemn black, with a heavy
gold chain about his neck, to which was attached a
miniature of the *Prince's* deceased father. He made
the face fair and somewhat florid, disfiguring it with
a finical moustache and a very small, two-pointed
beard. His purpose was said to be imitation of the
appearance of the conventional portrait of the Christ.
His eyelids were reddened, as though from excessive
weeping. On his head was a wig of flaxen hair, to
signify that *Hamlet* was a Dane, it being incorrectly
assumed that all ancient Danes were of the blond
type. His "business" throughout the performance
was expositive of a purpose to be "natural" and
to illustrate the behavior of every-day life. His
delivery of the text was colloquial. In the Ghost
Scenes he was manifestly familiar with spectres,
as is customary with Continental actors, indicating
neither awe, terror, nor pathos, and in the churchyard colloquy with the *Grave-digger* he seated himself on a convenient flat tombstone and nursed one
of his knees, with the nonchalance of a *Rip Van*

Winkle. Fechter's performance, nevertheless, was much commended, admirers of it not hesitating to declare that the audience had now seen the part for the first time correctly represented. Fanny Kemble, in her "Recollections," mentions a conversation which occurred at a London dinner-table, at the height of the Fechter fever in that city. One of the diners, a gentleman, asked a lady whether she had seen Fechter as *Hamlet.* "No," she replied, "I have not; and I do not think that I should care to hear the English blank verse spoken by a foreigner." The inquirer gazed thoughtfully upon his plate for a moment, and then he said, "But *Hamlet was* a foreigner, wasn't he?" That silly question illustrates the ignorant and extravagant commentary that was elicited by the acting of Fechter, an ebullient and ridiculous enthusiasm caused almost solely by the fact that he was a man of foreign extraction and an actor habituated to a foreign method. Neither the energy, the vitality, nor the professional skill of the performance could be questioned, but, in view of its generally fantastic details and the turbulent, repellent nature which it disclosed, the claim that was widely and arrogantly made for Fechter, of colossal genius and supereminent excellence as a Shakespearean actor, and, particularly, as an expositor of *Hamlet,* certainly was unwarranted. Essential constituents of the part are spiritualized intellect, haunted, overwrought imagination, exquisite sensibility, sombre dignity, a wavering mentality, piteous isolation, and bitter scorn, commingled with a forlorn, fitful, moody humor: not one of those attributes could be discerned in Fechter's performance. He interested the observer, but it was not by presentment of the personality of Shakespeare's *Hamlet;* it was by his tumultuous fervor and his professional expertness. He was animated; he was picturesque; he created and sustained plentiful turmoil; and his representation was embellished with peculiarities of stage business—so numerous and often so eccentric that they monopolized attention. He was continually in motion, and he delighted in stage tricks and innovations. In his arrangement of the play *Horatio* and *Marcellus,* in the second Platform Scene, Act I., Sc. 4, were made to enter from one side of the stage, and *Hamlet* to enter, alone, from the other side,—for the reason that the *Prince* had said to them, in a precedent colloquy, "Upon the platform, 'twixt eleven and twelve, I'll *visit* you"; and that device was deemed commendably ingenious. The stage direction in the First Folio is: "Enter *Hamlet, Horatio,* and *Marcellus.*" Common sense would prescribe that they should enter together, as there is no form of greeting exchanged between them, such as would naturally be incident to a meeting of

the Prince of Denmark with a courtier and a soldier
of the guard. In the course of *Hamlet's* colloquy with
Rosencrantz and *Guildenstern*, after the Play Scene,
Act III., Sc. 2, several musicians, who had been sitting in a gallery during the performance of "the
Mouse Trap," came upon the main stage, filing out,
in order that the *Prince* might,—exclaiming, "Oh,
the recorders,"—take from one of them the pipe
with which he proceeds to tantalize his treacherous
"friends." When he entered to speak the solemn and
beautiful speech on life, death, and after death, he
appeared with a drawn sword in his hand,—the most
preposterous of all expedients that possibly could be
adopted in that situation, unless, indeed, an actor
should make *Hamlet* enter, like Harlequin, jumping
through a hoop. In *Hamlet's* touching scene with
Ophelia, on the other hand, he wisely and commendably omitted the old business of making the distracted, agonized *Prince* aware of the espial of the
King and *Polonius.* In the Closet Scene with the
Queen he threw away his sword, after stabbing
the hidden *Polonius,* by way of intimating to the
affrighted lady that no physical harm to her was
intended, and when the remorseful woman would
have expressed maternal affection by embracing him
he sternly held out before her his dead father's picture,
pendent on his breast: his theory was that the *Queen*

should be regarded as an accomplice with *Claudius* in her husband's murder. In his arrangement of the last scene there was an elevated gallery, accessible by two flights of stairs, one at each end, and, at the climax of the duel, *King Claudius,* endeavoring to escape, fled up one flight, while *Hamlet* rushed up the other, meeting the fugitive monarch in the centre of the gallery and there slaying him. All such matters, while very well in their way, are, after all, inconsiderable, and only "limbs and outward flourishes," beside the central question: whether an actor does or does not get inside of the character and impersonate it. Every actor of experience invents or adopts devices of expression, and such means are sometimes illuminative and sometimes admirable, but much more is essential in a presentment of Shakespeare's *Hamlet* than dexterity of business and proficiency of treatment. Form is one thing: substance is another. Both Montgomery and Milton wrote verse on sacred subjects, and the verse of the one is as correctly constructed as is the verse of the other: but Montgomery is very far from being Milton. Fechter, in his treatment of *Hamlet,* was as enterprising and expeditious as Julius Cæsar in his conquest of Gaul, and therein he completely misrepresented the part; yet his acting of it was extolled as perfection, even by writers of such massive literary authority as Charles Dickens

and Wilkie Collins. "From the first appearance
of the broken glass of fashion and mould of form,"
said Dickens, "pale and worn with weeping for his
father's death, and remotely suspicious of its cause,
to his final struggle with Horatio for the fatal cup,
there were cohesion and coherence in Mr. Fechter's
view of the character . . . Its great and satisfying
originality was in its possessing the merit of a distinctly conceived and executed idea." "Cohesion and
coherence" no doubt there were, and there was an
"idea," but the idea was radically wrong, and therefore the "cohesion and coherence" signified nothing.
Quite as much "cohesion and coherence," furthermore,
had been manifested in many performances of *Hamlet*
given on the British Stage prior to that of Fechter,
and, finally, Dickens's certificate of excellence was
somewhat damaged by the fact that Fechter omitted,
deeming it an impediment to the action, *Horatio's*
attempt to drink the poison, and cut out *Hamlet's*
"final struggle with him for the fatal cup." "From
Macready downward," said Wilkie Collins, "I have, I
think, seen every *Hamlet* of any note and mark during the last five and thirty years. The true *Hamlet*
I first saw when Fechter stepped on the stage. These
words, if they merely expressed my own opinion, it
is needless to say, would never have been written;
but they express the opinion of every unprejudiced

person under fifty years with whom I have met."
Collins, unfortunately, did not define "the true *Hamlet*" and there were contemporaneous presentments
of *Hamlet* which he had not seen,—notably those of
Edward L. Davenport and Edwin Booth. I remember Collins as a dear friend, and I remember that he
was possessed of at least one unprejudiced and directly
opposite opinion relative to Fechter's performance of
Hamlet—namely, mine. It is significant that the
greatest admiration for that performance was elicited
from persons themselves remarkable for inclination
and ability to produce, in art, effects of intense
sensation, and from impressionable women. The
accomplished Kate Field, another enthusiast of
Fechter's acting, wrote a particular record of his
performance and stage business in the part, which
is a valuable contribution to the chronicles of the
acted drama, but her writings about *Hamlet* exhibit
only a superficial knowledge of the subject, and her
remarks on Fechter show far more enthusiasm than
judgment. "The world has seen *Hamlets*," wrote
George Henry Lewes, "in which the execution was
masterly, while the conception was so weak as to be
dishonoring to Shakespeare. Such was, in some
respects, the *Hamlet* of Fechter."

From a photograph.   Courtesy of Evert Jansen Wendell

TOMMASO SALVINI AS *HAMLET*

From a photograph by Brady

EDWIN FORREST AS *HAMLET*

Tommaso Salvini, the greatest of the Italian actors,
appearing as *Hamlet,* presented a stalwart, puissant,
dominant, capable man, who would have disposed of
uncle *Claudius,* without the least hesitation or difficulty, in the twinkling of an eye. His massive frame,
his leonine demeanor, his iron firmness, and his aspect
of resolute, overwhelming executive faculty combined
to make him the literal opposite of everything that
Hamlet is or means. He wore the customary black
garments and did much of the conventional stage
business, but he was invariably physical, never
spiritual,—a man of action, "four-square to opposition," formidable, robust, somewhat treacherous, competent to every trial, master of every situation, and
pursuant, with needless, tedious indirectness, of a
direct purpose of revenge. He was not princely in
bearing, he was not dejected in the 'havior of his
visage, he was not weighed down by the sorrow of
a broken heart and a despairing mind, and there was
nothing in his soul o'er which his melancholy sat on
brood. He manifested a lively antipathy toward his
uncle and a stern disapproval of his mother's conduct, making both feelings too obvious. His mind
had received no wrench, suffered no abiding shock.
He simulated insanity, and he did so with a degree of

histrionic skill entirely worthy of *Hamlet's* interest
in the acted drama and impeccable authority as a
stage manager, but why such a giant of will, resource,
and faculty should have felt constrained to simulate
any condition, or have hesitated to clear the Castle
of Elsinore and the domain of Denmark of all impediment to his inheritance, his marriage, and his imperial
sovereignty he intimated no reason. His sinuous course
of conduct appeared to result not from incertitude,
but from a natural propensity to deceit. His delivery
of the profound soliloquy on life, death, and the something after death was finely rhetorical in utterance,
and was accompanied by impressive gesture, but it
seemed no more relevant to the state of his mind than
a discourse might have been on the binomial theorem
or the differential calculus. We met, in his dressing-
room at the old Academy of Music, New York,
immediately after he had given his first performance in
America of *Hamlet* (October 2, 1873). The late
Maurice Grau, then his manager, made us acquainted
with each other, and we exchanged greetings. The man
whom I saw (he had not yet laid aside the black-
velvet stage-dress of the melancholy *Dane*) looked like
a gladiator. His performance, although mechanically
efficient and worthy of a thoroughly practised actor,
had been a complete failure, as it continued to be.
In parts that he comprehended, such as *King Saul*,

Conrad, and *Niger,* Salvini was a great actor, but he could not, and never did, act Shakespeare's *Hamlet.* His published remarks on the part,—if his performance had been insufficient,—show that he did not even comprehend it; for he designates the *Prince* as "the *adipose, lymphatic,* and *asthmatic* thinker of Shakespeare," a notion derived from words spoken by *Queen Gertrude* in the fencing scene: "He's *fat* and scant of breath." The right reading of that remark, as long ago suggested, is, probably, "He's *faint* and scant of breath." All that is said in the play, descriptive of *Hamlet,* aside from that single observation, indicates a man of exceptional personal beauty, marred, indeed, to attenuation by the ravages of sorrow, but essentially retentive of nobility, symmetry, and involuntary elegance. In the Fencing Scene, notwithstanding that he has "been in continual practice," the *Prince* becomes momentarily heated and wearied by exertion in combat with a superior swordsman whom he feels to be playing with him. Nothing could be gained dramatically by suddenly describing "the glass of fashion and *the mould of form*" as a "*fat*" man. At the moment the obvious purpose is merely to effect a pause for the introduction of stage business as to the "drink." The silly conjecture long current that the line was provided to make the situation comportable with a fat actor is too trivial for

serious consideration.   Whatever else *Hamlet* may be,
he is—of all things!—neither adipose, lymphatic, nor
asthmatic!   It may be true, as readers are frequently
informed, although no evidence to prove it has been
presented, that the Latin races, dramatically, excel
the Anglo-Saxon in artistic feeling and capability,
but, meanwhile, it would be rational to remember, in
considering the character of Shakespeare's *Hamlet,*
that, such as it is, it was drawn by an Englishman and
that, like all his characters, it is essentially English.
Also it would be wise to observe the decisive fact that
Hamlet is a poetical figure in a poem.

It is singular, but it is true, that Salvini evinced a
deeper insight into the subject of "Hamlet," and a
more definite grasp of it, in the awful solemnity of
his assumption of the *Ghost* than in his laborious performance of the *Prince*.   He acted the *Ghost* only
once (April 30, 1886), at the old Academy of Music,
in association with Edwin Booth as *Hamlet,* by way of
returning a compliment to Booth, who had acted *Iago*
to his *Othello*.   In his personation of the *Dane*
Salvini merely embodied a man named *Hamlet* whose
domestic affairs were sadly disordered, who suffered under the distemper of love and disappointment, who saw a ghost with much the same self-
possession that would have attended his meeting
with an expected acquaintance, and who died a

violent death, after undergoing much vicissitude of
fortune, assuming many and various attitudes and
conditions, and causing much disturbance. His pantomime was invariably expressive of his ideal, but his
ideal was irrelevant to Shakespeare's *Hamlet,* and
was never impressive, except as the clever assumption
of the central part in a prolix and awkwardly constructed drama of situation. In that personation,
however, as in every other performance that he gave,
he manifested, to the delight of all competent
observers, his thorough knowledge and absolute command of the technicalities of his art and of the means
of creating stage effect. Rapid transition was one
of his favorite expedients, employed in sudden assumptions of posture, quick turns of the head, abruptly
suspended movements, and swift, piercing glances, as
well as in business. He did not, as so many Continental actors have done when trying to act *Hamlet,* place particular stress on innovations. He had
seen Irving as *Hamlet* before he ever played that
part in England or America, and he had observed
the business used in Irving's production of the
tragedy, and to some extent he copied what he had
seen. One piece of business which I believe was
invented by him was the making of the *Prince,* a
moment before his death, endeavor to draw *Horatio's*
head close, so as to kiss him, and, being blinded by

the mists of death, to search, feebly, with a tremulous hand, for the face of that dear comrade, his only friend in all the world. According to the custom of Continental actors who have appeared as *Hamlet* he turned his back upon the *Ghost,* when freeing himself from *Horatio* and *Marcellus,* as they endeavor to restrain him from following that apparition. His finest action, though it was not original, was shown in the Play Scene, at the tremendous climax of which, as the affrighted *Claudius* flies from the throne, he sprang wildly up from the floor, where he had been lying, tore asunder the leaves of the manuscript which he had been feverishly gnawing while the play was in progress, scattered them in the air, and with a voluble outburst of frenzied, exultant rage fell into *Horatio's* arms. That manuscript business was invented and first used by Kemble, and was copied by later actors, among them Fechter. The chief element that Salvini contributed to the situation was that of prompt and tremendous energy. He did not make *Hamlet* lovable, nor, except in the moment of his death, pathetic. His parting scene with *Ophelia* was full of grimace; his Closet Scene with the *Queen* was full of sound and fury. A man more competent than Salvini's *Hamlet* to conduct all his affairs to a successful conclusion has never been shown upon our stage.

ERNESTO ROSSI.

Ernesto Rossi, who on the Italian Stage had long been distinguished for his acting of *Hamlet,* played that part for the first time in America, at Booth's Theatre, New York, November 1, 1881. He was welcomed with enthusiasm and he gained troops of admirers. He was a robust man, heavy and muscular; he did not and could not look like *Hamlet,* and, considered according to the English-speaking or -reading standard relative to Shakespeare's tragedy, he did not and could not act *Hamlet.* The person whom he presented under that designation was massive and portly. The *Queen's* statement that her son is "fat" has been a solace to many obese performers. The royal lady, it has been alleged, was caused to interject that remark in the Duel Scene because a corpulent actor,—Burbage, as is most frequently declared,—chanced to be playing *Hamlet,* and because the fact of his fatness, which must have been visible throughout the first four acts of the play, had not, until the last scene of the Fifth Act, been observed. That assumption is, manifestly, nonsensical. The condition of fatness is at variance with all the characteristics of *Hamlet,* physical and mental. No reasonable person wants blubber with the Melancholy Dane. No evidence has been furnished that Burbage was fat. Davies says that he was a thin, dark man. "An infinite deal of nothing" has been uttered relative to the physique of *Hamlet,* and it seems as though a period ought to be put to it. He was a blond, hirsute, blue-eyed Berserker; he was a slender Gaul; he was middle-agèd; he was a youth of eighteen; he was a paragon of muscular strength; he was asthmatic and lymphatic. The fact is that he is not any of those things as drawn in Shakespeare's play. *Queen Gertrude* intimates that he was short in the wind, a characteristic that protracted observation has failed to discover in stage representation of him. Rossi presented him in a state of bulk and endowed him with such prodigious impetuosity of conduct as must have enabled him to terminate the royal career of *King Claudius* in much less time than is required to act the play. There was not the slightest indication of the essential spirit of *Hamlet* in any part of his performance, except in the delivery of the soliloquy on suicide, and remembrance of it recovers no concrete image but only particulars of the execution. Rossi's *Hamlet* was as much and as wildly agitated on hearing of the apparition as he was on seeing it. At first sight of the *Ghost* he fell backward with a wild cry. Later his bearing evinced reverence, and he seemed especially impressed by the monition of the spectre not to contrive any punishment of the *Queen.* He did not indicate any conclusion as to *Hamlet's* mental state,—whether that of perfect sanity or of incipient derangement. His management of his eyes was particularly fine, as part of the mechanism of acting. He caused an effect of pathos, touching the feelings of his audience, by showing grief through an air of sarcastic humor in the scenes with the courtiers. He incorrectly caused the words of *Polonius,* "Look, whether he has not changed color and has tears in 's eyes," to be spoken as a reference not to the *Player,* but to *Hamlet.* His method was full of those quick transitions which are always effective and sometimes surprisingly illuminative. In the scene of *Hamlet's* parting from *Ophelia* he caused the *Prince's* discovery of *Polonius* and the *King* to occur near the middle, not near the beginning: *Hamlet's* paroxysm of madness can be regarded as actual, and as caused by *Ophelia's* repulse of him, signified by her precedent refusal to see him and her present return of his gifts, or as fictitious, assumed on his perception that he is being furtively watched. Rossi's acting in that scene was expressive of *Hamlet* as a lover,—despairing, indeed (and elderly), but ardent. In the Play Scene he caused the *Prince* to indulge in profuse antics: he was insolent to the *King,* offensive to *Polonius,* harsh and violent toward *Ophelia,* generally obnoxious. When, at the climax of the play, the *King* fled from the throne *Hamlet* intercepted him with remarkable celerity, and they screamed in each other's face. In the Closet Scene the killing of *Polonius* was so badly done as to be entirely ineffective; *Hamlet,* after much bluster toward his mother, threw away his sword, to signify that no harm to her person was intended, and crowned his melodramatic proceedings by tearing the miniature of *Claudius* from the *Queen's* bosom and grinding it beneath his heel, in a spasm of picturesque stage fury. The killing of the *King* was effected with bowl as well as dagger,—*Hamlet* forcing him to quaff the poisoned liquor,—and with such fury it was felt to be a signal mercy that the enraged *Prince* did not close the proceedings by dancing on the royal stomach and taking the anointed scalp. Rossi, in a word, applied what is called "realism" to poetry; and realism, applied to "Hamlet," is desecration.

SONNENTHAL AND BARNAY.

Adolf von Sonnenthal made his first appearance in America on March 9, 1885, at the Thalia Theatre, New York, as *Uriel Acosta,* and on March 20 he appeared as *Hamlet,* giving one of the most insignificant performances of that part ever presented by an actor of proved ability and distinguished rank. His *Hamlet* was a stout, heavy, lymphatic young man,

dressed in black and crowned with a wig of yellow
hair. He was called a *Prince* but his demeanor was
never princely. At times he was splenetic, as in *Hamlet's* colloquy with *Polonius;* at other times violent, as
in the colloquies of the *Prince* with the courtiers; not
at any time noble, or introspective, or haunted, or pathetic, or even interesting. The motive of all *Hamlet's*
proceedings, as indicated by him, seemed to be merely
animal, not intellectual. In level speaking, though
fluent, he was dull; in soliloquy, monotonous. His
Hamlet displayed no "antic disposition," no insanity,
whether actual or assumed, but complacently dominated alike himself and his circumstances. In the
Ghost Scenes he manifested fright and consternation,
but was neither awed nor able to communicate anything like a thrill to the imagination; yet the terror
which is inherent in those Ghost Scenes is potent
enough to make *Hamlet* himself almost a spirit
entranced. In the delivery of the speech ending
"Foul deeds will rise, though all the earth o'erwhelm
them," he displayed not only a foreboding of the
horrible truth that his father had been murdered but
a complete conviction of it, yet on being apprised of
that circumstance by the *Ghost* his amazement knew
no bounds. There was lack of articulation in the
whole anatomy of the performance, and nothing about
it caught pleased attention except adroitness in the

use of stage business. Sonnenthal was a careful, good actor, but completely out of place in *Hamlet.* His production of the tragedy was, in a way, unique. The scenery ranged from the garish opulence of an Eighth Avenue barber-shop to the tawdry luxury of a railway-station lunch-room, with an occasional suggestion of a country church. The *Ghost* was a brightly caparisoned phantom that gleamed in the attendant limelight like a burnished warming-pan and told its doleful tale from the middle of a burning bush. The throneroom, when arranged for the "Mouse Trap" play, disclosed a miniature stage, with the *Player-King* airily perched on a modern stepladder, so that *Hamlet,* when delivering his instructions to the *Players,* could, and did, sit on a step of that useful piece of furniture, at the feet of the mock monarch. The actor of *Polonius* suggested a typical German professor,—possibly of chemistry. *King Claudius,* much resembling Holbein's King Henry the Eighth, changed his raiment after the Play Scene, and tried to pray in the semblance of the Wandering Jew. *Queen Gertrude's* apartment was provided with two full-length and very hideous portraits of her two spouses, and when the *Ghost* penetrated into that bower of nuptial bliss he abruptly took the place of his "counterfeit presentment" and remained within the picture frame. The

Closet Scene was much prolonged, and the corpse of *Father Polonius,* visible beneath the arras, becoming weary of the protracted proceedings, presently conveyed itself away in a manner more expeditious than impressive. At the end of each scene a red curtain was lowered over the stage.

Herr Barnay was an actor of fine presence and exceptional executive ability, but his field was that of the heroic drama. He gave a noble performance of *Marc Antony,* in a German version of "Julius Cæsar." In *Hamlet,* acting that part for the first time in America on April 5, 1888, at the Thalia Theatre, New York, he was distinctly a failure. On the occasion named his distinguished compatriot Ernst von Possart coöperated with him, appearing as *Polonius.* It is not worth while to follow in detail the course of his misdirected ingenuity as *Hamlet.* When he came upon the stage to speak the speech on suicide Fechter carried a drawn sword: when Barnay came on he carried a dagger—the "bare bodkin,"—as though he were then debating the expediency of puncturing himself. At the end of the Closet Scene he embraced the *Queen.* One incident of the representation alone sufficed to indicate Barnay's natural incongruity with *Hamlet* and to illustrate the artificiality of his method: between the *Prince's* first meeting with the *Ghost* and the colloquy which presently ensues between them a tableau curtain was lowered, and the actor appeared before it, to acknowledge the plaudits of his admirers, before resuming the awful interview by following the spectre to "a more removèd ground."

JEAN MOUNET-SULLY.

The representation given by Jean Mounet-Sully, under the name of *Hamlet,* was an interesting manifestation of that actor's personality and of his dramatic skill. Though "Hamlet" as it exists in English does not exist in French, adaptations of it exist in that language and one of them was performed by the French actor and his company, at Abbey's Theatre, New York, on April 9, 1894. *Hamlet,* as interpreted by Mounet-Sully, was an amiable young man who loved his father, grieved for his father's death, saw his father's ghost, and thereafter pretended to be a grinning, skipping lunatic. A study of the profound spiritual misery of *Hamlet,* the misery of a mind that is overwhelmed and distraught, would, no doubt, have been attempted by the eminent French actor had that theme been existent in the French language, and probably the result of his study would have been well expressed, within the limitations of his nature and his artistic method. The substance of the character could not reasonably be expected in a performance that aimed only to present those elements of it which can be made melodramatic. Mounet-Sully showed himself to be proficient in the art of effective expression, but in mind and spirit he evinced slender calibre, and the *Hamlet* of Shakespeare was seen to be beyond his perception. He was the graceful personification of an affectionate son and a melancholy lover. His expression of awe and terror was sometimes picturesque, notwithstanding a peculiar obliquity in his eyes. He illumined the Play Scene with sufficiently illustrative business. His killing of *Polonius* was accomplished with alacrity and vociferation,—the inquiry, "Is it the king?" (*"Serait-ce pas le Roi?"*), being incidentally added, as of no special import. During much of the performance he was lachrymose, not afflicted; and in no part of it did he manifest the princely personality of *Hamlet,* or his preordination to the desolate eminence of haunted delirium, or his corrosive grief. The pleasure imparted by his personation was that of gazing upon fine attitudes, supple movements, flexible gesticulation, diversified and sometimes felicitous facial expression, abundant stage business, and a deft management of well chosen pictorial drapery. In nothing was Mounet-Sully as fine as in chivalrous delicacy and romantic grace. His manner, accordingly, was sympathetic and charming, however inappropriate, at moments in *Hamlet's* colloquies with *Ophelia.* The *Hamlet* of Shakespeare has ceased to love *Ophelia* and has passed beyond love of woman, but that is not the French view of the subject,—a view in which without *amour* there can be no *vie.* The actor was impressive in his expression of reverence for the ideal of the father and of grieved, tortured affection for the desecrated holiness of the mother. Filial feeling was, in fact, the keynote of Mounet-Sully's performance of *Hamlet.* The radical defect of it was deficiency of high and right ideal,—a presentment of *Hamlet* not in the relation of finite man dazed by an environment of infinite mystery, but only as a character circumscribed within the limits of a play. The less material, though disillusionizing, blemishes of it were a dapper, frisky demeanor, an artificial elocution,—ranging through many varieties of growl, shriek, whine, and patter,— melodramatic action, a general shallowness, a finical pettiness, more characteristic of an elegant French dandy, a fluttering exquisite, than of a haunted, heartbroken, miserable man, tired of life yet hesitant to die. His *Hamlet* turned his back upon the spectre, and likewise personally officiated in the mechanical work of moving chairs and platforms, when making ready for the Play Scene and giving instructions to the *Players.* After the Ghost Scene he fainted and fell. At the climax of the Closet Scene he followed the *Ghost* off the stage, out of the *Queen's* room, and screamed, with hysterical terror, unseen, in the passage. The performance was a singular exhibition and is memorable only for singularity.

FEMALE *HAMLETS*.

Many women have appeared as *Hamlet,* incited to that adventurous endeavor by the romantic allurement of the part, and encouraged in it by the critical assurance, which has been mistakenly urged, that the character is more feminine than masculine. It is difficult to understand why *Hamlet* should be considered feminine, seeing that he is supereminently distinguished by a characteristic rarely if ever discerned in women: namely, that of considering consequences, "of thinking too precisely on the event." The propensity to love, to depend upon another heart for affection, sympathy, and happiness, is no more characteristic of woman than it is of man. It can be doubted, furthermore, whether woman is nearly as capable as man has often shown himself to be, and as *Hamlet* shows himself to have been, of forming and cherishing and adoring, even to idolatry, an ideal of celestial loveliness and excellence in a human being of the opposite sex. *Hamlet* is a man of originally sweet, gentle, affectionate nature, and in no way feminine, unless it be feminine to be of an exquisitely sensitive temperament.

Mrs. Siddons acted *Hamlet,* and to some extent was approved in the part by audiences in Edinburgh and in Dublin, but she never acted it in London and no particular account of her performance has been found. Among the female *Hamlets* who have been conspicuous on the American Stage were Mrs. Bartley, Mrs. Battersby, Eliza Marian Trewar (first Mrs. Shaw, afterward Mrs. T. S. Hamblin), Ellen Bateman, Fanny Wallack (Mrs. Charles Moorhouse), Charlotte Cushman, Charlotte Crampton, Charlotte Barnes (Mrs. E. S. Connor), Clara Fisher (Mrs. James G. Maeder), Alice Marriott (Mrs. Robert Edgar), Emma Waller (Mrs. Daniel Wilmarth Waller), Susan Denin, Mrs. Frederick B. Conway, Julia Seaman, Marie Seebach, Winnetta Montague, Adele Belgarde, Louise Pomeroy, Anna Dickinson, Nellie Holbrook, and Sarah Bernhardt. Miss Cushman played *Hamlet* only a few times, and with no striking effect. For abnegation of sex her *Cardinal Wolsey,* not her *Hamlet,* was the more important performance. On one occasion, in Boston, she wore the *Hamlet* costume of Edwin Booth (it must have been a tight fit), and her close friend and fervent admirer, Lawrence Barrett, who was in the

cast that night, as *Laertes,* wrote that "she gave a
novel color to that complex character." Eliza Shaw
was better in it, and by some observers was highly
commended, but she gained her authentic fame as a
woman, not as a man, and in high comedy, not in
tragedy. Charlotte Barnes, with her frail physique
and mournful, wandering eyes, languished through it,
wearing a Vandyke garb, speaking the words, doing
the business, and conveying an impression of refinement and poetic sensibility. Miss Seaman's endeavor
was a jack-knife affair, and so was that of Miss
Belgarde. Miss Marriott, whom I saw in the part,
at Wood's Museum, New York, March 29, 1869,
was earnest in endeavor but rather gloomily comic in
effect. In person Miss Marriott distantly resembled
Charlotte Cushman: her figure was massive and her
demeanor somewhat masculine. Her face was broad
and square, and her features could well express cogent
emotion. Her voice, although it had then been
worn by hard use, was sympathetic and strong. She
evinced, in all her acting, a cultivated mind and a sensitive temperament. Her assumption of *Hamlet*
manifested careful study, intention of sensational
effect, and pleasing skill. Her delivery of the text
was fluent and at times it was fraught with deep
feeling. Her action occasionally became excessively
violent, as when, in the Play Scene, she crept toward

the *King's* throne, and later when she dashed "his picture in little" to the floor. Her method was invariably conventional. In the Ghost Scenes she created no sense of the atmosphere of mystery and dread that should accompany such a portrayal of human contact with preternatural environment. *Hamlet's* intrinsic misery was not suggested. The performance was an ordinary theatrical effort by an experienced old hand, typical of scores of other such performances, which, stopping short at mechanical proficiency, do not transcend the intelligence of a careless multitude, are irrelevant to the poet's conception, and possess no intrinsic importance. Miss Anna Dickinson, emerging as the Melancholy Dane, appeared at the Fifth Avenue Theatre, New York, March 20, 1882, attired not in "customary suits of solemn black," but in purple raiment, and presented an obvious female, somewhat resembling a boyish male. Her demeanor was neither semblable for a man nor graceful for a woman, and it was devoid of dignity. Her countenance expressed force of character and earnest purpose. Her voice, while unsympathetic, proved adequate in level speaking, but in passages requiring fervor it was feeble, and at all times it was monotonous. Her reading of the text was intelligent, but her delivery was oratorical, and there was, in her elocution, the twang of the conventicle. Many words were clipped and slurred. There was little or no impersonation, the performer, instead of the character, being conspicuous, and only a slight sense was signified of *Hamlet's* supernatural environment. The expression of the mingled emotions of *Hamlet* relative to *Ophelia* was constricted by a metallic, inflexible manner. The killing of *Polonius* was done in a perfunctory way, *Hamlet* seeming to be afraid of his own sword. In brief, Miss Dickinson's attempt, while ambitious, conscientious, and earnest, proved a mournful failure. She had been trained to lecture, not to act, and she had not liberated herself from the trammels of forensic education.

SARAH BERNHARDT—"ALAS, POOR *HAMLET!*"

The several female *Hamlets* whom I have seen were either affectedly and unpleasingly mannish or they were experimental, confused, indefinite, and insignificant. It was a bad day for "the glass of fashion" when some misguided essayists began to call him "feminine" and the ladies heard of it. The most recent and the most pretentious female endeavor to act *Hamlet* which it has been my misfortune to see was that of the great French actress Sarah Bernhardt.

Mme. Bernhardt appeared in the part for the first

time, on May 20, 1899, at the Théâtre des Nations, Paris, and she presented herself in it for the first time in America, on December 25, 1900, at the Garden Theatre, New York, and gave a performance well calculated to commend itself to persons interested in the study of freaks. *Hamlet* has been roughly handled on the stage, but a long remembrance of his sufferings does not recall a time when he was more effectively crucified than he is in the French play and was by the French actress. The translation of "Hamlet" that was presented by Mme. Bernhardt and her associates is in prose. It was made by Eugène Morand and Marcel Schwob, and it has been published, with a preface and notes, in a volume of 254 pages. The French prose is level, smooth, and respectable, and it imparts about as clear a perception of Shakespeare's poetry as might be derived from listening to the whistle of the wind through a bung-hole. It is not quite such a desecration as the Italian "Hamlet" (fabricator unknown) that was inflicted on the community by Signor Salvini, but as remarked by *Mercutio* " 'T will serve." It consorts well with Abraham Hayward's English prose translation of "Faust," and in that congenial category of sinful things it can be left.

In Mme. Bernhardt's presentment of *Hamlet* there were peculiarities of apparel and likewise several

paltry novelties of business. The dress consisted of
a black silk tunic, embroidered with fur; black-silk
tights; a white ruffle, around the neck; a jewelled belt;
a black cloak, so arranged as to depend from the
left shoulder; a rapier, steel-hilted, in a black scabbard,
with an ornamental chain; a flaxen-haired wig
(adopted in accordance with the usage conspicuously
introduced by Fechter, but an unwarranted, objec-
tionable device, because *Hamlet* ought, for every
reason, to be dark), and velvet footgear. The face
was made up beardless and pale. The figure was
padded, so as to make it look as much as possible
like that of a man, but in this respect no illusion
was created,—the actress looking exactly like what
she was, a thin, elderly woman, somewhat disguised.
Novelties of business were *Hamlet's* knocking
together of the heads of *Rosencrantz* and *Guildenstern,* in the course of his first talk with them;
his kicking of the shins of *Polonius,* and his catching
of a fly on the nose of that statesman; together with
the transformation of the dead *King's* portrait into
a ghost, in the Closet Scene,—first done on the American Stage by James Henry Hackett,—and the
Prince's obtainment of the play-book of "The Murder of Gonzago" from the *First Actor,*—who con-
veniently carried his whole repertory in his belt.
An electric light was used in the *King's* oratory,

and a silly intention was indicated, on the part of *Hamlet,* to use the long golden hair of *Ophelia* as a screen, through which, in the scene of "the Mouse Trap" play, to observe the face of the *King.* At the climax of that scene *Hamlet* was made to thrust a lighted torch before the monarch's face,—but that wonderful exploit had long been stale. In the presence of the *Ghost* Mme. Bernhardt's *Hamlet* was as valiant as a gander; the business, indeed, involved a kneeling posture, some time after the spirit had vanished, but Mme. Bernhardt's *Hamlet* was a man who had seen whole regiments of spectres, and to whom the haunted rampart of Elsinore was about as impressive as the Traitor's Gate was to Artemus Ward,—who thought as he gazed on it "that as many as twenty traitors might go in abreast." The counsel to the *Players* was spoken on a little stage set for the presentment of the interlude. That business was also stale, having been done by the German trage- dian Sonnenthal. The method of exchange of weapons by *Hamlet* and *Laertes* might have seemed tolerably fresh, if Mr. Sothern, having seen or heard of the device, had not previously introduced it in his presentment of the tragedy. At the climax of the duel *Hamlet's* sword-hand was made to show a trace of blood, and the *Prince's* face and person were made to reveal pathological symptoms of the

approach of death by poison. Mme. Bernhardt's
Hamlet died standing, and his reeling body was caught
by *Horatio;* and subsequently it was borne away,—to
the general relief,—upon huge shields. Much of the
business was tedious and all of it was laboriously
capricious. The English Stage learns nothing from
such treatment of *Hamlet* as that to which the part
was subjected by Mme. Bernhardt. To use one of
Shakespeare's similes, there was no more poetry in
her *Hamlet* than there is milk in a male tiger.
Technical knowledge and executive efficiency were
apparent; but actors who appear as *Hamlet* are
expected,—not unreasonably,—to reveal something
more than the usual resources of histrionic experience
and skill.

With reference to the character of *Hamlet* a fact
most essential to be continuously considered,—for the
reason that it indicates all the other facts,—is that
this prince, when first encountered, is found to have
been contemplating suicide, out of temperamental
propensity. His "prophetic soul" has warned him to
beware of *Claudius;* but his "prophetic soul" has
not revealed to him either his father's murder, his
uncle's guilt, his "seeming virtuous" mother's sin,
or the ominous contiguity of the dead *King's* ghost.
He is the born victim of melancholia, the preordained
genius of sorrow. He typifies misery, and his misery

is congenital and inherent. No circumstances are conceivable under which such a man could be happy. Whatever the conditions might be, he would react upon them and make them either gloomy or tragical. His very smile casts a shadow: his laughter is sadder than tears. A preternatural visitation, divulgent to him of the afflicting secret of a horrible and loathsome crime, shocks his already dejected and drifting mind, and thereafter his will is shattered, and anything like steadfast, continuous action,—notwithstanding his feverish and incessant mental activity,—becomes impossible. It might, indeed, be contended that *Hamlet,* in the last analysis of him, defies question; that no skill of vivisection avails to define and designate him: but, on the other hand, it certainly is true that *Hamlet* is a man not of action but of thought; a man overwhelmed and dazed with the immensity and perplexity of his spiritual surroundings; ravaged with grief, self-disgust, and disgust at humanity; who has survived love and become completely isolated; who continually resolves and as continually reasons away every opportunity of executing his resolution; a man around whom, and somewhat because of whom, all things crumble into ruin, and who ends in total failure; and yet a man to be viewed with profound sympathy by all persons who are capable of thought.

In the tragedy of "Hamlet," obviously, the dramatic values are secondary to the meaning of the central character and to the solemn purport of the poet's commentary upon life, death, and the something after death. It should, accordingly, always be treated not simply as drama but as poetry, philosophy, and spiritual truth. The emergence of a female as *Hamlet* has always had the effect of futile experiment; semi-masculine women, such as Charlotte Cushman, Miss Marriott, and Mrs. Waller, could, and did, measurably, impart at least an impression of sincerity and weight; but they were never consistently impressive as *Hamlet;* and, indeed, of the women who have played the part in America no one has really succeeded in it. The female *Hamlet* must, of necessity, always suggest either an epicene hybrid or a paltry frivolity. Women sometimes succeed in creating an actual, if fleeting, illusion of masculinity in presentments of dashing young cavaliers, or of roguish girls masquerading as such; the tradition of Peg Woffington as *Sir Henry Wildair* still survives, and old play-goers still remember with delight the admirable grace and charming swagger of Mrs. John Wood as *Donna Hippolyta;* but the great, serious male incarnations of dramatic poetry have never been, and they never can be, adequately impersonated by females. Women as *Hamlet* are as absurd and out of place as they would be as *Macbeth,* or as men would be as *Ophelia* or *Queen Katharine.* Here, as elsewhere in drama, "Nature's above art" in that respect.

Hamlet means great intellect, the wildness of genius, a glowing imagination, a deep heart, exquisite sensibility, and, over all, and permeating all, an essentially poetic temperament—grace, nobility, and grandeur in ruins. Mme. Bernhardt, an eccentric, volatile, ardent, capricious Frenchwoman, not possessed of those attributes, and speaking a language into which it is absolutely impossible that Shakespeare's essential poetry and wonderful lingual felicity should be conveyed, no more resembled *Hamlet* than a wax figure resembles a living being. She was recognized as an expert actress, even a genius, but some things are beyond the reach of the most expert and the most inspired of the female sex. *Hamlet,* without the sex, the temperament, the poetry, the meaning, is not *Hamlet* at all—and that was the image presented by Mme. Bernhardt: dapper, shrill-voiced, anæmic, vapid, and yet full of fussy, shrewish energy; a splenetic, loquacious stripling, now gloomily glowering, now chattering like a parrot, at all points whimsical and at no moment impressive. The killing of *Polonius* was completely insipid,—whereas, suitably done, it is one of the most tremendously tragic points in the whole wide range of drama. There was no delirium, nor even a hint of mental shock, after the

Ghost Scene. The madness was mere mimicry; and, like all other Continental players who have acted *Hamlet,* Mme. Bernhardt's *Prince* was easily able to turn his back upon the *Ghost* and to pass through the most awful of all conceivable ordeals of mortal experience with airy nonchalance and a fantastic laugh.

Mme. Bernhardt not only presented the person whom she supposed to be *Hamlet* but printed her views of the character; and, if her superficial and expeditious performance had left any doubt as to her total inability to grasp the Shakespearean conception, her published statement would have sufficed to remove it. *Hamlet,* according to Mme. Bernhardt's deliverance, is "manly and resolute," and, being "manly and resolute," the character is one eminently fit to be assumed by a woman. *Hamlet* should not be overwhelmed upon meeting with his father's ghost, because he has come "expressly to see it": that is to say, an experience completely outside of anything known as possible, an experience so awful that it unsettles the brain, an experience so incredible that the recipient's mind involuntarily rejects it, almost as soon as it has passed ("That undiscovered country from whose bourn *no traveller returns"),* is to be encountered with equanimity and dominated by energetic resolution, merely because the *Prince* has said that he will accost the phantom if it assumes his father's person. *Hamlet* wildly declares that he will speak to the apparition, though hell itself should bid him to be silent: therefore, says Mme. Bernhardt, he is "not a weak or languid person." *Hamlet* hysterically threatens his restraining friends, in his first Ghost Scene, and insists on being permitted to follow the spectre: therefore he is "not a feeble man." *Hamlet*, in the scene of the *King's* prayer, refrains from killing that monarch, "not because he is vacillating and weak, but because he is firm and logical," desiring to kill his enemy "in a state of sin, not of repentance; to send him to hell, not to heaven." That is to say, *Hamlet* is "manly and resolute," "a young, strong, determined character," who "thinks before he acts," and who possesses "great strength and great power of mind," because, at certain moments, he shows an evanescent capability of vehement speech and of delirious action, and because, in his obvious condition of partial derangement, he puts aside an opportunity of righteous vengeance, with the avowed purpose of presently committing the most horrible of imaginable crimes,—the infernal crime (infernal to a Catholic or any other Christian believer) of sending a soul into eternal hell. In other words, *Hamlet* is a sane, potent, expeditious individual, to whom a ghost is as incidental as an omelette, because he makes brave speeches and pur-

poses to act like a moral monster. Nothing could be
further from the truth. "Shakespeare, by his colossal
genius," said Mme. Bernhardt, "belongs to the universe, and a French, a German, or a Russian brain
has the right to admire and to understand him."
Assuredly! But the *right* to understand does not
always include the *capacity*. Mme. Bernhardt's ideal
of *Hamlet* was radically and absolutely wrong, and
her performance served only to illustrate her error.

When that eminent French actress first tried to
play *Hamlet,* in Paris, a prodigious mental illumina-
tion befell the French capital. The performance lasted
six hours. Many spectators were so delighted that
they left the theatre before it was over, in order
to read the play. The survivors of those who remained
to the last went home to breakfast completely
enthralled and practically exhausted. M. Rostand,—
much interested in the Bard of Avon, from whose
works he had "conveyed" the Balcony Scene, for
"Cyrano de Bergerac," and the Mirror and Spectre
Scenes, for "L'Aiglon,"—declared that he was now
"able, for the first time, to comprehend Shakespeare's masterpiece." That tremendous person Mr.
Walter, proprietor of "The London Times," since
deceased (a writer who had never manifested even
the slightest capability of dramatic criticism, but
merely had inherited a position that enabled him to

make himself conspicuously public), had a spasm, in the course of which he ejaculated the information that, "having seen all the great tragedians for thirty years he had only now seen *Hamlet* acted to perfection." Two Parisian citizens,—one of them a local bard, the other a silvergilt dandy,—went into the lobby of the theatre to dispute about Shakespeare, and presently smote each other upon their respective noses, even unto the spilling of gore. All "fashionable Paris,"—which, of course, had given its days and nights to the study of "Hamlet" and learned all about it,—made to the obliging newspaper press the novel announcement that Mme. Bernhardt's portrayal of him was "a revelation." Well—it was! In particular it was noted that the French actress had kindly removed from *Hamlet's* character all predisposition to dream and drift, all lassitude of the will, and every trace of melancholy; and likewise that,— "with one auspicious and one dropping eye," beholding feminine prettiness at one angle and romantic youth at the other,—she had reduced his age from thirty to twenty-one. Altogether it was a great night for Gaul, and thereupon the victorious Mme. Bernhardt, much encouraged, invaded England with her popinjay *Hamlet,* and actually exhibited him in the Shakespeare Memorial Theatre at Stratford-upon-Avon.

VI.

MACBETH.

"Lo! the mystic volumes rise
Wherein are lapt from mortal eyes
Horrid deeds as yet unthought,
Bloody battles yet unfought,
The sudden fall and deadly wound
Of the tyrant yet uncrown'd
And his line of many dyes
Who yet within the cradle lies."
　　　　　　　　—Joanna Baillie.

HISTORICAL COMMENT.

In some of the editions of the works of Shakespeare the tragedy of "Macbeth" is included among those of his plays which are called "Histories," but as there is no authentic historical basis for it, any more than there is for "Cymbeline" or "King Lear," that classification is incorrect. The plot was ingeniously deduced from Raphael Holinshed's "Chronicle History of Scotland," 1577, and it is recorded that the old Scotch poet and historian George Buchanan (1506-1582), more than fifty years before Shakespeare wrote the play, "had remarked how well

the legend of Macbeth was fitted for the stage."
There are passages in the writings of those old
chroniclers Holinshed and Hall,—writings which
Shakespeare's plays show that he had read,—such
as no impressionable person can read without a sense
of weirdness and a thrill of dread, and undoubtedly
they fired the imagination of the poet. The legend
of Macbeth, however, as related in the "Chronicle,"
while strongly suggestive of dramatic situations, could
have been made practicable for the stage only by
a complete rearrangement of details, radically regardless of historic fact. That was the method pursued
by Shakespeare. The early history of Scotland is
an appalling record of promiscuous, savage slaughter.
The "Chronicle" teems with narratives of frightful
barbarity and hideous crime. The chief incidents
that the dramatist selected from it for use in his play
are the meeting of Macbeth and Banquo with witches,
Macbeth's accession to the throne, the murder of
Banquo and escape of Fleance, and the defeat and
death of Macbeth. In the play *King Duncan's* army,
commanded by *Macbeth* and *Banquo,* has vanquished,
in quick succession, two forces of insurgents, the first
led by a rebel chieftain, *Macdonwald,* the second led
by another rebel, the *Thane of Cawdor,* leagued with
Sweno, King of Norway. In fact, a part of northern
Scotland was, in King Duncan's time (1034-1039),

overrun by the Norwegians, with whom and with the Danes he was continually at war, and it was after a battle in which he had been defeated by Danish invaders that Macbeth,—by birth Thane of Ross and by marriage Thane of Moray, and until then a loyal chieftain,—conspired with Banquo against their sovereign; confederated with his foes; attacked and defeated him in battle; and, coming upon him in the shop of a blacksmith near Elgin, inflicted on him a mortal wound. The place was called "Bothgowanan," meaning "the smith's bothy." Duncan expired at Elgin and was buried at Iona. The story of the murder of *King Duncan,* as told in Shakespeare's play, is an artistically embellished variant of the "Chronicle" narrative of the assassination of King Duf (961-965), by command of Donwald, one of his chieftains, incited to that treacherous and dastardly deed by Lady Donwald, his wife. King Duf met his cruel fate, in a castle near Forres, about sixty-five years before the murder of King Duncan and many years before Macbeth was born. Holinshed's account of the murder is circumstantial and peculiarly suggestive.

"The King got him into his privy chamber, only with two of his chamberlains, who, having brought him to bed, came forth again, and then fell to banqueting with Donwald and his wife, who had prepared divers delicate dishes and sundry sorts of drinks for their rear supper or collation, whereat they sat up so long, till they had charged their stomachs with such full gorges, that their heads were no sooner got to the pillow but asleep they were so fast that a man might have removed the chamber over them sooner than to have awaked them out of their drunken sleep.

"Then Donwald, though he abhorred the act greatly in heart, yet, through instigation of his wife, he called four of his servants unto him (whom he had made privy to his wicked intent before, and framed to his purpose with large gifts), and now, declaring unto them after what sort they should work the feat, they gladly obeyed his instructions, and, speedily going about the murder, they entered the chamber (in which the King lay) a little before cock's-crow, where they secretly cut his throat, as he lay sleeping, without any bustling at all; and immediately, by a postern gate, they carried forth the dead body into the fields. . . . Donwald, about the time that the murder was in doing, got him amongst them that kept the watch, and so continued in company with them all the residue of the night. But in the morning, when the noise was raised in the King's chamber how the King was slain, his body conveyed away, and the bed all beraid with blood, he, with the watch, ran thither, as though he had known nothing of the matter, and, breaking into the chamber, and finding cakes of blood in the bed and on the floor about the sides of it, he forthwith slew the chamberlains as guilty of that heinous murder. . . . For the space of six months together, after this heinous murder thus committed, there appeared no sun by day, nor moon by night, in any part of the realm; but still was the sky covered with continual clouds, and sometimes such outrageous winds arose, with lightnings, and tempests, that the people were in great fear of present destruction."

King Duf had incurred the enmity of Donwald
and his wife by slaying several of their relatives. He
was the great-grandfather of Lady Macbeth, who had
been Lady Gruoch, wife of Gilcomgain, Thane of
Moray, and who was a widow when she became Macbeth's wife. That lady's experience of sanguinary
proceedings appears to have been intimate. Her
first husband, Gilcomgain; her grandfather, King
Kenneth the Fourth; and her only brother were killed
by Malcolm—grandfather of King Duncan—who
afterward reigned as King Malcolm the Second (1003-
1033). She had a son, by Gilcomgain, named
Lulach. After the death of Duncan Macbeth
ascended the Scottish throne, reigning from 1039
till 1056, and exhibiting as a sovereign both vigorous
authority and fervid piety: in 1050 he made a pil-
grimage to Rome. In 1054 his realm was invaded
by Siward, Earl of Northumberland, who encountered
him in battle and defeated him, with great slaughter
of his forces. Macbeth escaped and he succeeded
in partially retrieving his position and retaining
the crown, but two years later he was defeated
in another desperate battle, by Malcom Ceanmore
("Malcolm of the great head"), eldest son of King
Duncan, and while flying from the field was overtaken
and slain, at Lumphanan, in Aberdeenshire, where
a cairn is still existent which is, conjecturally, said

to mark his grave. His corpse, it is probable, was conveyed to Iona and there buried in the sepulchre of the Scottish kings. His adherents placed his step-son, Lulach, on the throne, but the resolute Malcolm, steadily continuing the war, overpowered and killed that prince,—whose reign had lasted only four months and a half,—at Essie, in Strahbogie, on April 3, 1057, and immediately assumed the crown, as King Malcolm the Third (1057-1093).

A wild and dreary plain, called the Harmuir, sit-uated on the borders of Elgin and Nairn, is, tradi-tionally, declared to be the place where Macbeth and Banquo, returning victorious from the field of battle, met the Witches, who are, in Shakespeare's play, so significantly denominated the *Weird Sisters*. That moorland is,—or was, when I saw it,—a desolate expanse, seeming to be partly fens and partly swamps, variegated with white stones and bushes of furze. At all times bleak and lonesome, it was unspeakably gloomy when swept by storm, or when the streamers of fog, so frequent in Scotland, trailed over it, or when night was coming down. Such places power-fully affect the imagination and it is not wonderful that the inhabitants of Scotland, particularly in the Highlands, should have been, or should be, peculiarly amenable to romantic fancies and superstitious beliefs. Fancies, however, should not be permitted to authen-

ticate misrepresentations of fact. The traveller in
Scotland can, if he pleases, imbibe much traditionary
lore which is also visionary. At opulent and picturesque Inverness he will hear that Macbeth's
Castle "stood on an eminence to the southwest"
of the stately town, and, if he has my experience,
he will be told of the actual room in which King
Duncan was murdered, in a modern castle which
stands there now. In the neighborhood of Glamis
Castle, situated about four miles from Forfar, within
view of Birnam Hill, and in that of Cawdor Castle,
about six miles from Nairn, he is likely to learn that
both those edifices were once inhabited by Macbeth,
that deeds of darkness were done in them and that
haunted chambers are not the least of their charms.
Not long ago it was announced that a popular
American actor intended to act *Macbeth* in both
Glamis and Cawdor castles, because of their direct
personal association with him, and it has been mentioned, as a denotement of fidelity to the actual time
and surroundings of the ancient Scottish monarch,
that in the production of Shakespeare's tragedy
recently effected in London by Herbert Beerbohm-
Tree the interior walls of *Macbeth's* castle were hung
with tapestry, as they are at Glamis. The fact is
that castles in Scotland, in the tenth century, were
made of timber and sod, that they have disappeared,

and that probably not a vestige remains of any building that Macbeth ever entered or ever saw.

The tragedy of "Macbeth" is a poetic fabric, a work of the imagination, and it should be read and treated as such. The student of Shakespeare, whether reader or actor, ought to be acquainted with whatever historical basis exists for any of Shakespeare's plays, because such knowledge, interesting in itself, is an aid to comprehension of the poet's art and of the workings of his wonderful mind; but the student is not aided by encumbrance of those plays with fictitious trappings or by the reading into them of references and significations unwarranted by their text. Shakespeare is, of all poetical writers, the simplest. His plays, primarily, were written for representation on the stage. No one of them, it is perfectly obvious, was designed to illustrate any specific philosophical proposition or to expound and enforce any specific moral. But their author, great as he was as a dramatist, was greater as a poet; and the great poet saw human life not as a fragment, but as a whole; not as circumscribed to an individual, but as comprehensive of the human race; not as a transcript of the past, a reflection of the present, or a forecast of the future, but as a combination and spectacle of all of these, and so it happens that his plays not only satisfy the needs of the stage but often far transcend its requirements, providing such "a wide and universal" depiction of human nature and experience—the infinite longings of the mind and the strange, wayward impulses of the heart—as no expedients of stage art, employed by the genius and skill of its most efficient representatives, have done more than to suggest. Clarity of poetic vision necessarily induces unity of design. Each of the great tragedies of Shakespeare is pervaded by a dominant quality. In "Othello," the supreme exposition of the terrible passion of jealousy, that quality is Action. In "Hamlet," the perfect portrayal of the spiritualized intellect, dazed and baffled by the unfathomable mystery of life and death, it is Thought. In "King Lear," the most stupendous creation with which genius has enriched the literature of the world,—the representative drama of the human heart,—it is Misery. In "Macbeth," the final epitome of preternatural forces, terrific crimes, and haunting horror, it is Imagination.

The play of "Macbeth" has been on the stage for more than three hundred years. Trustworthy authority names 1606 as the date of its composition. In 1610 that subtle knave Dr. Simon Forman, the nefarious astrologer, saw a performance of it at the London Globe and recorded the fact in his diary; but that record is only a meagre synopsis of the story and it provides no account of the acting. One remark in it, however, to the effect that *Macbeth* and *Banquo,* when they met the *Witches,* were *riding* through a wood, possesses a certain significance, seeming to indicate that those chieftains made their first appearance on the stage on horseback. The first publication of the tragedy occurred in the Folio of 1623. It had remained in manuscript, in the possession of the managers who owned it, for about seventeen years, and the text, there is reason to believe, was freely altered and seriously marred in the interval. This fact— that the play survives in a mangled form—must necessarily be considered by every student, actor or reader, who endeavors to comprehend the scheme of it and to form a correct ideal of the poet's conception of the character of *Macbeth.* The Witch element, expressive of the occult power that impels *Macbeth,* is of primary importance, and the evidence is conclusive that the Witch Scenes of Shakespeare were changed and expanded by another hand.

THE PLAY AND THE CHARACTER.

Tragedians of authority have designated *Macbeth* as, among all Shakespeare's characters, the most difficult of adequate representation. Indeed, a great embodiment of that part has seldom been seen. No performance of it is impressive that does not inspire sympathy, and an actor must possess peculiar and exceptional magnetism in order to inspire sympathy with a man who receives into his home a friend and benefactor, steals to his bedside in the depth of night and murders him in his sleep. *Macbeth* should be embodied and displayed as a person who is intrinsically noble, but in whose nature, nevertheless, there are seeds of evil, and who is *compelled* into crime by preternatural, infernal agency which he is absolutely powerless to resist. Thus embodied, he is shown as a massive type of agonizing, colossal conflict between good and evil. He arouses the imagination; through the imagination he thrills the mind and, at some points, touches the heart. No situation has been devised in English tragedy which is at once as awful, terrible, and pathetic as that in which *Macbeth* and his *Queen* are placed at the close of the Banquet Scene in this play, when they are left alone at the summit of their ambition, their guilty triumph, and their immedicable misery.

EARLY PRODUCTIONS.—THOMAS BETTERTON.

As Richard Burbage was the first representative of *King Richard the Third* it has been assumed that he was also the first representative of *Macbeth,* but the manner of his acting that part, if he did act it, is

unknown, nor is informing testimony extant as to
the appearance of any of his contemporaries in it, or
as to his and their successors in it down to the time of
Queen Anne. Betterton, in the course of his third
season at Lincoln's Inn Fields Theatre, acted *Macbeth,* November 5, 1664, on which occasion the tragedy
was produced according to the original text (Genest)
as given in the First Folio; but later, in 1672, at Dorset Garden, he presented it as a melodrama, using a
version made by Sir William Davenant. Many *Sing-
ing Witches* were employed in that representation,—
pretty women, arrayed in fantastic, comic attire, such
as Burns indicates in his devils' dance in "Tam o' Shanter," with music, undeniably effective, composed by
Matthew Locke, which is still in use and well known.
That music has been attributed to Henry Purcell, but
Purcell was only fourteen years old in 1672. It has
also been attributed to Richard Leveridge, who was
only two years old at that time. One authority states
that the music in question was written by Purcell for a
production of "Macbeth" in 1689, and long afterward
was erroneously ascribed to Locke by the musical
composer Dr. William Boyce. It is certain, however,
that music was used by Davenant in the presentment
(1672) of the tragedy at Dorset Garden.

It has been customary to state that Betterton gave
a grand performance of *Macbeth.* Colley Cibber,

writing in 1739, twenty-nine years after Betterton's
death, declared, "All the *Hamlets, Hotspurs, Mac-
beths,* and *Brutuses* whom you have seen since his
time have been far short of him." Cibber was a good
observer; his statement may be true; the nature of
Betterton's great superiority in *Macbeth,* however,
is not indicated. There is no account of the business
which he used, nor is there specification of the garments that he wore when acting the Scottish warrior.
The custom seems to have been to wear a military uniform of the actor's period, and probably Betterton
conformed to that custom.

DAVID GARRICK AND HANNAH PRITCHARD.

Davenant's mutilation of Shakespeare's play, which
had already been mutilated, probably by Thomas Mid-
dleton, continued to be used until the time of David
Garrick. In 1744 that expeditious innovator produced " 'Macbeth,' as written by Shakespeare," adver-
tising it in those words, and if contemporary testimony can be trusted he gave a performance of the
fiend-driven, haunted, agonized, desperate, almost
maniacal murderer which was marvellously imaginative
and effective. A particularly instructive comment on
Garrick's performance, made by one who saw it, testifies that "Every sentiment rose in his mind and

showed itself in his countenance before he uttered a word." Mrs. Pritchard played *Lady Macbeth* and overwhelmed beholders by the horrible force of implacable cruelty, the grandeur of imperial manner, and the poignant pathos of ultimate, withering desolation; yet it is alleged on credible authority that she had never read the play, her only knowledge of the subject having been derived from "the part," as delivered to her by the prompter, and from rehearsals and performances in which she participated. Dr. Johnson unjustly called her "a vulgar idiot." She was a woman of fine character and exemplary life, and there is abundant testimony to her rare professional talents. The business ever since used by *Lady Macbeth* in the Banquet Scene was invented by her. The colloquy immediately after the murder was spoken by Garrick and Mrs. Pritchard in deep, hollow, fearful whispers, a method which also has been used ever since. Garrick, holding the gory daggers, seemed absolutely frantic; "his face grew whiter and whiter" as he spoke,—a phenomenon of nervous sensibility possibly observable in a time when "make-up" was often neglected,—and the expression of horror when he saw and held up his bloody hands was tremendous. His delivery of the speech beginning "Canst thou not minister to a mind diseased?" was accounted exceptionally beautiful.

In presenting " 'Macbeth,' as written by Shakespeare," Garrick did not closely adhere to the original,
because he not only allowed the use of abundant musical embellishment but added a long "dying speech,"
of his own composition, for *Macbeth* to deliver after
the combat, so that he could keep the stage till the
last; but his treatment of Shakespeare's play was
more respectful than that of Davenant, who, among
many other liberties, added, in Act IV., an insipid
colloquy between *Macbeth* and his *Queen,* in the
course of which the *Ghost of Banquo* appeared and
was seen by both of them, to the special consternation
of the lady. That Garrick knew and highly valued
the expressive art of his acting of *Macbeth* is specifically denoted by the circumstance that when he
was in Italy, in 1763, having been asked by a local
prince to show his skill in the art of expression, he
immediately assumed the position and demeanor of
Macbeth when seeing the dagger in the air, and
repeated the accompanying speech, with, it is related,
astounding and convincing effect. His dress for *Macbeth* was the uniform of a British army officer of his
day, a scarlet or a sky-blue coat ornamented with gold
lace, snug white breeches, top-boots, and a powdered
wig. He seldom gave attention to propriety of costume. When acting *Hotspur,* for example, he wore
a ramillies and a laced frock-coat. All the male

actors of the Garrick period (except, in a few instances, Macklin) were equally heedless, and every
character, irrespective of era or nationality, was
dressed with a huge periwig, large sums of money
being expended for the decoration.   Once in a while
a monarch,—*Richard the Third* or *Henry the Eighth,*
—would be more or less properly attired, but he
would be singular in his suitability.   English kings
customarily glittered in scarlet and gold; French
kings gleamed in white and silver.   The ruffians who
are employed by *Macbeth* to murder *Banquo* were
invariably provided with swarthy complexions and
plenty of dark hair.   "What is the meaning," asked
King Charles the Second, when present at a performance of "Macbeth," "that we never see a rogue
in a play but, oddsfish! they always clap him on a
black periwig, when it is well known one of the
greatest rogues in England [meaning the Earl of
Shaftesbury] wears a fair one?"   In Garrick's production of "Macbeth" the *Witches* wore plaited caps,
laced aprons, red stomachers, ruffs, and mittens.

GARRICK'S CONTEMPORARIES.

Among the actors contemporary with Garrick no
one seems to have made an impression of supreme
merit in *Macbeth*.   The part was played by James

Quin, Spranger Barry, Henry Mossop, Barton Booth,
Robert Wilks, John Henderson, and Charles Macklin.
Quin possessed a formidable person, consonant with
the ideal of "Bellona's bridegroom," but in poetic
parts he was an inflexible and monotonous actor, the
exponent of "dignity and declamation," and he did
not act it in a manner to touch the imagination.
Horace Walpole wrote that his *Macbeth* was better
than Garrick's—an opinion of dubious value. Barry,
the *Romeo* of his time, showed himself to be tem-
peramentally unsuited to it, being of a soft, silvery,
insinuating order of character. Mossop, the originator
of the "tea-pot" attitude (the right arm a spout, the
left a handle), although he evinced comprehension of
it and was correct in purpose, lacked variety of
action. Barton Booth, a person of medium height,
having a round, ruddy face and tense muscles, was
deemed better fitted for such parts as *Othello* and
Jaffier—"emotional parts," as they are now called—
than for imaginative, weird, ghastly characters, like
Macbeth. Wilks, essentially a comedian, failed in it.
Mills, a ponderous, conscientious performer, was
heavy in it, though he spoke some of the lines with
discretion, feeling, and good effect. Henderson seems
to have given a performance much more than respectable, and as he is known to have been a diligent
reader of every narrative of horror that he could

obtain he probably felt and expressed an acute sympathy with the spirit of the poet's weird conception.

Macklin's assumption of *Macbeth* was remarkable because of his investiture of it with a more appropriate dress than had ever before been worn. That original actor played it for the first in 1772, when he was eighty-two years old, and the audience, which had been accustomed to see *Macbeth* arrayed in scarlet and gold and surmounted by a bag wig, then first saw him suitably attired. The garments and appurtenances used by Macklin were Scotch, and the example thus set has ever since been followed; and of course the instruction has been bettered. Macklin's acting of *Macbeth,* while fine at some points, appears to have been more informing than impressive. In the Dagger Scene and the Banquet Scene he was inefficient, but in the colloquy with the ruffians employed to assassinate *Banquo* he was exceedingly effective, and he delivered the speech beginning "If thou speak'st false" in a manner that "almost petrified the audience."

JOHN PHILIP KEMBLE.

John Philip Kemble acted *Macbeth,* apparently for the first time, in 1782, at York, and thereafter retained the part in his repertory; and though his crowning achievements were *Penruddock* and *Coriolanus* (he

played 172 parts of record) he was thought to have
greatly excelled in it. In 1788, when manager of
Drury Lane, he brought out "Macbeth" in what was
deemed sumptuous style, and his presentment of it
both then and later, in 1794, exhibited some commendable innovations. Davenant's version was used, and
the Witch Scenes were freely embellished. Creatures
supposed to be incarnations of the four elements
participated with the *Witches* in the incantations, and
the beautiful Mrs. Anna Crouch led the diabolical
revels, arrayed in fine linen, point-lace, and a conical
hat, her face rouged and her hair powdered. Kemble
habitually gave close attention to detail. The sound
of a clock striking two, instead of the sound as of
a single stroke, or a tinkle, on a bell made by *Lady
Macbeth,* was heard at a point during *Macbeth's*
delivery of the dagger speech ("The bell invites
me"), agreeably to an intimation of the time of the
murder of *Duncan* ("One, two"), in the Sleep-
walking Scene. The replies to the questions of
Macduff and *Lenox,* just before the discovery of the
murder of *Duncan,* were finely uttered, with an air
of intense preoccupation. Kemble was the first actor
to dispense (1794) with the actual apparition of
Banquo. From Shakespeare's time the custom had
been for *Banquo* to walk on, his head gory and his
throat gashed and bleeding, seat himself at the table,

gaze at *Macbeth,* and indicate by a gesture his blood-stained neck.   Kemble, at "Here is a place reserved, sir," saw the spectre in the empty chair, and his action is represented as having been thrilling in its effect. "You look but on a stool" says the *Queen.*   The omission of the actual, visible representative of the spectre had been advised by critics of the period, notably, in verse, by that miniature Churchill, Robert Lloyd.   The precedent thus provided was followed by Macready, by Edwin Booth, and, though not at first, by Irving.   Edwin Forrest, on the other hand, adhered to the ancient practice in this respect, as also did Edmund Kean, Robert William Elliston, George Frederick Cooke, Lewis Hallam, John Hodgkinson, Charles Mayne Young, Thomas Abthorpe Cooper, Edward L. Davenport, Gustavus Vaughan Brooke, Barry Sullivan, and George Vandenhoff.   The view that Kemble took of *Macbeth* was the view afterward stated by his biographer, James Boaden: "*Macbeth* is a fatalist and conceives that certain beings may be the organs of *destiny.*   Fate will always bring its decrees to their completion.   It is useless to question what has been pronounced by the spirits, to whom 'all mortal consequences' are known."   If an actual *Ghost* is to be introduced, an effect both dramatic and appalling could be caused by showing the *Ghost of King Duncan* as the second apparition

in the Banquet Scene. That expedient has not, as
far as I can ascertain, ever been used, though it has
been contended that *Macbeth* sees and apostrophizes
the *Ghost* of the murdered *King* when he says "Take
any shape but *that!*" The better way, no doubt,
always provided that the actor is able to create the
requisite illusion and maintain in that terribly exacting
situation his hold upon his audience, is to leave the
spectres to the imagination.

Kemble's costume for *Macbeth* was composed mostly
of a short woollen coat, a belted plaid over ring-mail,
and a cap with tall, heavy, nodding plumes in it. One
night when he was to act the part he was visited
in his dressing-room at the theatre by Sir Walter
Scott, who took the plumes out of the cap and inserted
an eagle's feather, which he had brought, in place
of them,—a fitting ornament, which afterward Kemble
always wore when playing *Macbeth.* Charles Kemble,
John's brother, who also played *Macbeth,* gave a
respectable performance. The best praise of it which
I have found refers to the excellent effect of his
look and attitude while listening at the door of *King
Duncan's* chamber before entering to do the murder.
One recorder, the caustic "Joe" Cowell, a shrewd
observer, considered Charles a better actor than John,
and it is not impossible that Charles's merit was
overshadowed by John's earlier acquired reputation.

SUPERNATURAL ATMOSPHERE.—EDMUND KEAN.

In a representation of "Macbeth" the obtainment
of decisively right poetic and tragic effect depends
almost exclusively on an artistic maintenance, throughout the representation, of an atmosphere of preternatural agency. *Macbeth's* phrase for it is singularly
suggestive—"This supernatural soliciting." The
Witches embody the malignant power of hell. In
Shakespeare's day, and for a long time after his day,
the belief was widely prevalent that demons, embodied
spirits of wickedness, intent to accomplish evil, are
permitted to infest the earth. The poet possibly participated in that belief; several of his eminent intellectual contemporaries did. The *Witches* of Shakespeare, as acutely remarked by Lamb, "originate deeds
of blood and begin bad impulses to men." Davenant's
treatment of them in his scheme of melodrama,
although it served to popularize the play, perverted
them from their author's design, degrading them from
the attitude of potent, compulsory demons to the
position of mere theatrical expedients. The practical
restoration of them as "the weird women" to the place
that Shakespeare obviously intended they should
occupy and to the function they should exercise
in his tragedy is due to the example of Edmund
Kean, who, in 1814, at Drury Lane, acted *Macbeth,*

and, according to the best testimony obtainable,
gave a magnificent performance of it, presenting
the play in its original form. "I'll have the *Witches*
played properly," he said. "The rubbish shall be
cleared away; I'll have none of it." He also in some
particulars improved the style of dressing the play—
a style inherited from Kemble, who had followed the
lead of Macklin; but the literal apparition of *Banquo*
was retained. In the exposition of *Macbeth's* mental
conflict before the murder of *Duncan*, the delivery of
the dagger speech, and the frenzied agony of conscious guilt, abject terror, and shuddering remorse,
expressed in word and action, after the assassination,
he was astounding. "The manner in which his voice
clung to his throat and choked his utterance," said
Hazlitt, describing Kean's acting in that Murder
Scene, "the force of nature overcome by passion, beg-
gared description." His searching glance at *Banquo*
and the assumed carelessness of tone with which he
said *"Your* children shall be kings" were noted as
delicately artistic points in his performance. In the
combat, at the close, he caused a startling effect when
pausing to vaunt his invulnerability to any mortal
hand—"I bear a charmèd life"—and by the terrific
and deadly glare with which, after standing for a
moment as though petrified on hearing *Macduff's*
answer, "Despair thy charm," he rallied to meet the

final catastrophe. In falling he pitched forward at full length, and dropped face downward.

In memoirs of Edmund Kean it is alleged that when a child of seven he was employed at Drury Lane and assigned to represent one of many goblins in a new Caldron Scene which John Philip Kemble had devised for the embellishment of a revival of "Macbeth." The date is variously given, but as the performance is mentioned as the one in which a lake of actual water was used it must have been April 21, 1794. Mrs. Siddons played *Lady Macbeth*. Charles Kemble, making his first appearance at Drury Lane, played *Malcolm*. That was the occasion on which the *Ghost of Banquo* was for the first time treated as a phantom visible only to *Macbeth*. Little Kean, then bearing the name of Carey, was wearing irons on his legs, to rectify their shape, which had been injured by the pantomimic contortions he had been trained to make. The goblins were placed in a row at the mouth of a cave, with Kean at their head, the direction being that, as *Macbeth* entered, they should encircle the caldron. When *Macbeth* came on Kean made an awkward step and, being unable to right himself because of his irons, reeled against another goblin; that one fell against a third, and so on, the whole line of imps being toppled over and sprawled in confusion, to the disgust of Kemble and the merriment of the

audience. "I tripped the goblins up," Kean is reported
to have said, relating the incident in after years,
"and they fell like a pack of cards." It is stated
also that when censured for the mishap, which was
surmised to have been a mischievous prank on the
part of the boy, he proffered to the angry manager
the demure excuse that it was "the first time I have
performed in tragedy."

It was said of Edmund Kean's *Macbeth* that it was
like his *Richard the Third*—that he did not completely discriminate between the two characters. The
same comment might have been made relative to the
acting, in those parts, of any actor, the most judicious
that ever appeared. *Macbeth* and *Richard* possess
certain conspicuous attributes in common, and
although, as a whole, each character is sharply distinct from the other, there are points of similarity
between the two, which acting serves only to emphasize
and enforce. Both are inspired and swayed by ambition; both seek a royal crown; both commit murder
to obtain it; both succeed temporarily by dissimulation and by deeds of blood; both are haunted by men-
acing phantoms from the spiritual world; both become
frenzied and desperate; and both perish on the battle-
field, each slain by his particular foe. The radical
difference between the two, nevertheless, is very great.
In the character of *Macbeth,* notwithstanding his valor,

intrepidity, and fortitude, there is a certain weakness—
the weakness incident to infirmity of will, remorseful
consciousness of guilt, and dread of ultimate disaster.
In the character of *Richard* there is consistent and
terrible strength,—which only once is shaken by
terror of inexorable Fate. *Macbeth* is an instrument
in the hands of a demon: "The angel whom thou still
hast served." *Richard* is incarnate, infernal power,
sufficient unto itself. *Macbeth* is compact of tremulous
imagination; *Richard* of fiery, malign intellect. *Macbeth*
loves and suffers. To *Richard* love is impossible
and suffering is a transient spasm. *Macbeth* depends
on his wife for aid and comfort, and the condition
of that dependence is so pathetic that it excites sympathy. *Richard* depends entirely on himself, causes
the murder of his *Queen,* the innocent, trusting,
unfortunate *Lady Anne;* ordains and accomplishes
the slaughter of his close associates *Hastings* and
Buckingham; and in his frenzy, desperation, and
violent death is consistently terrific, exciting mingled
abhorrence and admiration.

In every performance of *Macbeth* that has been
given by an actor of fine ability the intention has been
manifest to denote the haunted condition of his mind—
the susceptibility of it to "supernatural solicitings"—by
a specially illuminative treatment of the soliloquies,
and, in particular, of the soliloquy relative to "the air-

drawn dagger." Macready, esteemed in his day the
greatest *Macbeth* that had ever appeared, gave exceptional attention to the Dagger Scene, gazing fixedly
for a moment into space, and presently throwing himself, in a delirium of horror, upon the illusion. In all
those passages of the play which involve the element
of the preternatural Macready particularly excelled.
Such is the almost unanimous testimony; yet even that
scrupulously scholarlike and highly imaginative actor
could, and did, mar the appearance of *Macbeth*, in
the scene immediately sequent to the murder of *King
Duncan*, by assuming a flowered chintz dressing-gown!
Davenport and the younger James W. Wallack, who
had seen and studied Macready's performance of
Macbeth and had become imbued with the influence of
his style, copied him in the Dagger Scene and at some
other points, as in dropping the truncheon from the
extended right hand, at "The queen, my lord, is
dead." Wallack, a superb actor when he chose to be,
even copied Macready's grunts, gasps, and long, por-
tentous pauses. As *Macbeth* Wallack's exit into the
King's chamber, at "Hear it not, Duncan," was prolonged to such an extent that his left leg remained in
view of the audience for a considerable time after the
rest of his person had disappeared. Davenport was
a noble and impressive figure as *Macbeth* and his
acting evinced a greatly excited imagination, an

acutely sympathetic sense of the mystery and terror of preternatural agencies of evil controlling the actions and determining the destiny of a human being, absolute authority, and complete competence in the artistic expression of a distinct and right ideal. His elocution in this part was exceptionally fine. He used, in the Banquet Scene, the effective stage business which had been invented by Macready,—not striving to repel the horrible spectre, but shrinking from it, hiding his face, and then, on fearfully recovering and observing that the phantom had vanished, evincing delirious exultation: "Why, so, being gone I am a *man* again!" He elicited the great pathos that is in the part, and he laid much stress on the frightful energy of desperation by which, toward the last of his wretched life, the will of *Macbeth* is reanimated. There was not in his performance any attempt at eccentricity of embellishment: it was simple, and it exactly exemplified the good designation of the character conveyed in a few words by that deep thinker and extraordinary writer Bulwer-Lytton:

"*Macbeth* was the kind of character which is most liable to be influenced by a belief in supernatural agencies, a man who is acutely sensitive to all impressions, who has a restless imagination more powerful than his will, . . . who has moral weakness and physical courage, and who alternates perpetually between terror and daring,—a trembler when opposed by his conscience and a warrior when defied by his foe.''

The simplicity so commendable in Davenport's treatment of "Macbeth" afforded a grateful relief from the custom, long prevalent, of overloading that marvellous play with artificial trappings inconsistent with its spirit and detrimental to its rightful dramatic effect. No one of Shakespeare's plays has been subjected to so much of misdirected experiment. The stage history of the play mentions many devices that one or another experimentalist has applied in the strenuous endeavor to exhibit novelty in the illustration of it, particularly where there is employment of phantoms. In Davenant's version, while *Banquo* was personated by one actor (Smith), whose countenance was engaging, the *Ghost of Banquo* was personated by another actor (Sandford), whose face was ugly. On one occasion Kemble, as already noted, introduced gnomes and a lake, on the principle of the "real tubs" of *Mr. Crummles*. Fluctuation between the text of Shakespeare and that of Davenant has been frequent. Samuel Phelps, one of the greatest of English actors, when he assumed management of Sadler's Wells Theatre,—where so much was accomplished for the art of acting and the benefit of the public,—began,

May 27, 1844, with a production of "Macbeth," but although a staunch contender for the original text of the poet he presented a variant of Davenant's version. Afterward, on September 27, 1847, he effected another revival of the tragedy, on that occasion reverting to Shakespeare and scrupulously following the stage directions given in the original,—directions which cast an instructive light on the coarse manner in which plays were presented in the poet's time. *Macbeth* was killed "off the scene" and his head was brought in on a pole, as ordered in the First Folio. The embodiment of *Macbeth* by Phelps was declared, by some contemporary writers, to surpass that given by Macready, then famous in the part and generally accepted as incomparable. The London "Athenæum" stated, of Phelps's *Macbeth,* that "since Edmund Kean we have seen nothing better for vigor and vivid effect." Earnest commendation was bestowed on his impartment of imaginative influence and poetic feeling in the acting of *Macbeth* and on his restoration of the original text, but his bringing in of the gory head of the slaughtered tyrant was condemned as "a mistaken literality." In Phelps's first presentment of "Macbeth" *Lady Macbeth* was acted by Mrs. Warner, whose performance was declared to be admirable in every particular. The practice of juggling with Shakespearean spectres still continues. *Hecate's* numerous vocal spirits still warble and Pepper's Ghost invention has been utilized.

Many representatives of *Macbeth* have appeared on the American Stage; few are extolled in authentic dramatic biography and few are remembered. Cooper's fame in it has not perished. John Bernard (1832), a sagacious judge of acting, deemed Cooper's performance of *Macbeth* "only inferior to Garrick's"; S. C. Carpenter (1810), a competent critic, declared it "preferable, in many parts, to those of Kemble and Cooke"; and Joseph T. Buckingham, a much respected authority, sixty years ago and more, characterized it as "terribly sublime" and "certainly Cooper's masterpiece." According to Buckingham "he played the Dagger Scene in a style altogether his own" and made it "one of the sublimest efforts of human genius. The terrible agonies of his mind, proclaiming their existence with 'most miraculous organ,' were too powerful to be long the object of attention. In the latter part of the play, after *Macbeth* has 'supped full with horrors,' the moral reflections were given with such exquisite beauty and feeling that we almost forget the crimes of the murderer and pity the wretched victim writhing with the tortures of his own conscience."

EDWIN FORREST.

Forrest's ideal of *Macbeth* was that of the robust warrior. At his first entrance he was simply a victorious military chieftain returning home from the wars, cheerful and with nothing in his appearance indicative of sinister prepossession. The burly figure lacked distinction. The manner of speech was commonplace. *Macbeth* comments on the state of the weather, but he is already brooding over an ambitious, treacherous, evil thought. Forrest's misfortune in that character and in kindred characters was lack of imagination. His realm was that of fact and obvious, human feeling—the realm of *Othello* and *Virginius*. His embodiment of *Macbeth* was unwieldy, lumbering, prosaic; effective at some points by reason of violent action and sonorous vocalism, but completely deficient of mystical atmosphere—the sense of being haunted and of being impelled by preternatural powers of evil. He did not particularly like the part, and he decidedly disliked to share with any other performer the chief honors of a representation. After his experience in London, where he played for a short season in 1845 with Charlotte Cushman, who, as *Lady Macbeth,* obscured his popularity, he seldom appeared in the tragedy and his appearance in it did not enhance his professional reputation. He

customarily dressed *Macbeth* in short breeches and a
cloth tunic, belted at the waist and extending from
neck to knees. Flat rings of metal sewed on the tunic
gave that garment a resemblance to chain-mail. The
sleeves reached to the wrists, which were provided
with cuffs. Over-sleeves extended from the shoulders
half-way to the elbows. At the neck the tunic was
edged with white linen. Over the right thigh was suspended a long dirk; over the left thigh a sword.
Across the left shoulder a cord was passed, sustaining
a horn. The actor's large, hirsute legs were bare
from knees to ankles, and his feet were furnished with
thonged sandals. At his first and second entrances
and also in the scenes of battle he carried on his
left arm a metal-covered "target," having a long,
massive spike in the centre of it. His head was
covered by a wig of short, dark hair, and usually his
face presented embellishments of a mustache, a "lip-
tuft," and small side-whiskers. On the head was a
large cloth cap somewhat resembling a tam o' shanter,
about which was twined a wide band ornamented with
steel spangles, and in the front of which, fastened
by a clasp in the shape of a thistle, were two long
feathers.

In one of Forrest's productions of "Macbeth" (he
did not invariably employ the same business) he
employed a device which I believe was original

with him,—certainly I never saw or heard of any one else who used it,—and it is worthy of record as being more imaginative than most of his technical expedients were. After *Macbeth* had entered the *King's* chamber to do the murder, the scene being a courtyard within the Castle of Inverness open to the sky, the three *Witches* appeared above the fretted battlements at the back, slowly and steathily rising, as if they were floating in the air and had come to preside and exult over the atrocious crime which they had stimulated their victim to commit. There are several ways in which that idea, with the aid of modern mechanical devices, could weirdly and well be employed, though perhaps it is questionable whether the expedient does not detract from the awful suspense of a supreme moment; whether preference should not be given to a vacant, dim scene and a momentary deathlike stillness before *Lady Macbeth* enters, saying "That which hath made them drunk hath made me bold"; but it is remembered as having caused a thrill.

John McCullough and Lawrence Barrett, both of whom were ardent admirers of Forrest, followed his example to a slight extent in the dressing and acting of *Macbeth,* but each of them, possessing more gentleness of temperament and naturally more refinement of style, almost insensibly modified their respective embodiments of the character, Barrett in particular,—who acted the part when associated with Charlotte Cushman,—conveying in a large measure the imagery and the desolate pathos of it. Neither McCullough nor Barrett, however, stood boldly out from the general rank of actors in that character.

EDWIN BOOTH.

In Edwin Booth's embodiment of *Macbeth* the predominant qualities were imagination and poetic sensibility. In the early part of his professional life his ideal was wrong and his expression of it indefinite and crude, but both his ideal and his performance underwent much change, from year to year, and, at last, ceasing to be melodramatic and violent became clear and smooth, presenting a distinct study of fiend-inspired, compulsory criminality. Like Macready, whom he never saw, Booth, ultimately, insisted on inherent majesty and martial heroism as the basis of the character. He had seen his famous father in the part, and he derived his ideal from that instructive example as well as from devoted study of Shakespeare's text. He told me that, on an occasion when he was to act *Macbeth* in association with Charlotte Cushman and was rehearsing with her she expressed interest in his treatment of the part, but good-naturedly dissented from it, saying "*Macbeth* is the great-grandfather of all the Bowery ruffians." That estimate of the character would be warranted if the fact were ignored that *Macbeth* (though, indeed, before meeting the *Witches* he appears to have thought of removing *Duncan* from his path to the throne, and to have communicated his thought to his wife) is irresistibly impelled and violently precipitated into perpetration of crime by an overwhelming demoniacal power. Upon any other theory, meantime, *Macbeth* is a mere monster, a sort of mediæval, romantically glossed, blank-verse *Bill Sikes,* and utterly abhorrent. It should be observed, as illuminative on this point, that *Macbeth* is never shown as exultant in crime, but always, before and after, as tortured on the borders of it, and ultimately as in a delirium of desperation. Edwin Booth took a high, poetic view of the character, and, as his genius was tragic, his appearance romantic, his action superb, and his elocution perfect, he gave a magnificent performance. His acute comprehension of *Macbeth's* nature and of the spirit of the tragedy was particularly exhibited in his thrilling utterance of those expressive speeches which abound with weird, imaginative figures and phrases,—night's yawning peal, the blanket of the dark, the dunnest smoke of hell, the rooky wood, the shard-borne beetle, the sentinel wolf, the silent horror,

Courtesy of Evert Jansen Wendell

EDWIN BOOTH AS *MACBETH*

FROM A DRAWING BY W. J. HENNESSEY

the walking shadow, the winds that fight against the churches,—figures and phrases that denote an atmosphere of baleful omen and shuddering dread, enveloping and permeating the whole play and making it inexpressibly awful. The passages beginning "Had I but died an hour before this chance" and "She should have died hereafter" can never have been spoken with deeper feeling or more exquisite beauty of elocution, conveying their message of grief and despair straight to the heart, than were evinced in his delivery of them. When he said "Now o'er the one half world Nature seems dead" he appeared the authentic image of demoniac obsession. His tremulous absorption and electrical frenzy when gazing on the vacant chair in which *Macbeth* sees the *Ghost of Banquo* were so terrific that it made the phantom a reality to the spectator. His conflict with *Macduff* at the close was frightful in its maniacal vitality, expressive to the utmost possible extent of the recklessness of defiant valor and the fury of desperation. When he was beaten down and bereft of his sword he wildly fought on, stabbing the air with his hand, and on receiving the death-blow reared himself for a moment in agony, and then plunged forward, dead, at the feet of his antagonist. That also was the elder Booth's way of closing the performance of *Macbeth*—to die as a man predestined to perish, knowing his doom, but fiercely fighting to the last.   The *power* of art, said Goethe, consists in *conveying* your impressions.   Edwin Booth possessed that power in a superlative degree, and his embodiment of *Macbeth,* fulfilling every mental and spiritual condition of the part, was the most poetic that has been seen in our time.   It did not, however, please everybody.   Forrest, who disliked Booth,— not perhaps unnaturally, as Booth surpassed him as an actor and succeeded him in leadership of the stage,— was emphatic in disapproval of it.   At a theatre in Philadelphia that veteran attended a performance of the tragedy in which Booth and Charlotte Cushman played the two great parts.   With him was John McCullough, who told me of the incident.   At *Macbeth's* first entrance Forrest snorted with disgust. Booth, preoccupied and moody, was gazing toward the ground.   "What's the damn' fool doing?" Forrest asked: "He looks like a super hunting for a sixpence."   When Miss Cushman, in the Sleep-walking Scene, referred to her "little hand," his patience became completely exhausted.   *"Little* hand!" he exclaimed.   "Why, it's as big as a codfish!"

HENRY IRVING.

All things considered, the most impressive production of "Macbeth" that has been effected was

made by Henry Irving in 1888. Scrupulous attention was given by him to every detail of scenery
and costume, and he acted *Macbeth* in such a way
as to flutter the critical Volscians on both sides of
the ocean. His theory, which he set forth in writing, and caused to be published and widely circulated, was ingeniously devised to create controversy.
"Macbeth" (so wrote Irving) "was a poet with his
brain and a villain with his heart. . . . Hypocrite,
traitor, and regicide, he threw over his crimes the
glamour of his own poetic, self-torturing thought":
that is, the suffering of *Macbeth* was to be attributed
not to pangs of conscience, but to pangs of imagination, regardless that without conscience the imagination can not and does not cause suffering through
torture of the moral sense. The man was to be found
exclusively in his deeds, not at all in the cause of them,
and not at all in his words—which are the reflex of
his mind and character when he speaks in soliloquy,
and which plainly express the utter anguish of his
condition:

> "Better be with the dead,
> Whom we, to gain our place, have sent to peace,
> Than on the *torture of the mind* to lie
> In *restless ecstasy.*"

In further support of his contention that *Macbeth*
is an out-and-out villain Irving wrote: "How any

student, whether he be of the stage or not, can take those lines, 'Strange things I have in head, that will to hand; Which must be acted ere they may be scanned,' and, reading them in any light he may, can torture out a meaning of *Macbeth's* native nobility or honor, I am truly at a loss to conceive." No student could wish to "torture out" or in any other way educe any meaning from the text of the tragedy that the text does not contain. The words, "Strange things I have in head," etc., are spoken by *Macbeth* late in his career of crime (they occur at the end of Act III., Sc. 4), and after he has specified, in a terribly significant sentence, the desperate condition into which he has been driven and from which he cannot escape:

> "I am in blood
> Stepp'd in so far, that, should I wade no more,
> Returning were as tedious as go o'er."

The native nobility of the man is, by implication, premised, and unless that premise be admitted the whole structure topples. In every human nature, however good, there is existent a capability of evil, but unless it be developed it does not militate against the goodness. *Macbeth* is not drawn as exempt from human weakness or as invulnerable to temptation. He can be tempted and he will yield. The powers of hell,—the evil "spirits that tend on mortal thought,"—incarnate in the *Witches,* encounter him at precisely the moment when he is most likely to succumb, and they subdue him to their purpose. For what other possible reason did the poet introduce them into the fabric of his tragedy? It is sometimes fortunate that the performances of actors do not exemplify their theories. Irving's theory did not virtually influence either the spirit or the effect of his performance. There is an illuminative and true remark by Fanny Kemble which that performance precisely illustrated: "From the first scene of the play to the last, the wounded soul of *Macbeth* writhes and cries and groans over its own deterioration; from the beginning to the end of his career the several stages of his progress in guilt are marked by his own bitter consciousness of it." That realm of consciousness,—the haunted mind, the agonized spirit, the tremulous human will nerving itself to oppose phantoms of terror and beating against the adamantine force of eternal law,—is the particular realm in which Henry Irving preëminently reigned, and accordingly, in the weird scenes of "Macbeth," the meeting with the *Witches,* the doing of the murder, the vision of "the blood-boltered Banquo," the awful desolation at the close of the Banquet Scene, and the visit to "the weird sisters,"—"You secret, black, and midnight hags, what is't you do?"—he was entirely great. His struggle against collapse after the disappearance of the spectral *Banquo* and his appalled demeanor, affrighted turn and lingering look of horror upon the empty chair caused a chill shudder in those who saw him. Although a tall, wiry man, Irving did not possess the massive physique of the warrior who cleaves his adversary "from the nave to the chaps," and on the physical side his *Macbeth* was not robust; but he has not in our time, and probably not in any time, been surpassed in that part of the interpretation of *Macbeth* which particularly exhibits the remorse of a mortal creature of good and evil environed by immortal spirits of wickedness, the shuddering, combative, tortured, afflicted servant of an angel of hell. Irving, in his dressing, considered poetic effect rather than historic accuracy, which, indeed, would attire old Gaelic warriors in skins, chiefly their own: he wore tawny red hair and a long, drooping mustache of the same color, and he made much use of picturesque, draped cloaks—garments which he wore with more grace than any other actor has shown whom I ever saw. In the Combat Scene with which it is customary to close the performance he wore complete armor that made the doomed *King* gleam afar like a tower of gold. When he first acted *Macbeth,* in 1875, and when he repeated the performance, in 1888, he introduced the visible *Ghost of Banquo,* in the Banquet Scene, in accordance with the old stage custom, but ultimately he discarded that expedient and left the spectre to the perceptive imagination. His earlier practice, in closing that scene, was to take a blazing torch from a sconce on one of the pillars of the "room of state" and then, turning away, to become suddenly again frenzied with fear and horror, dash the torch to the ground, muffle his face in his robe and reel against the pillar,—*Lady Macbeth,* meanwhile, kneeling at his feet and gazing up at him in sympathetic agony. That extravagant business he did not retain. His final treatment of the situation was to move toward the back of the scene, where there were several wide, shallow steps,—the *Queen* walking at his right and assisting him to move. When the steps were reached the *Queen* ascended, so as to be a little above him, and he paused, his extended right arm resting in her grasp, and after a moment, as though by horrible, irresistible compulsion, he slowly turned till his gaze could settle on the empty stool, at which he looked with an awful glare of terror, his eyes growing wide and wild, and, through contraction of the facial muscles, his long mustache fairly bristling with fright. The picture, over which the curtain descended, was afflicting and terrible. "Macbeth" was acted, on the occasion of the revival in 1888, 151 times—a much longer run than has been obtained for that tragedy at any other time or in any other place. It was during that season that the accomplished Herman Vezin acted *Macbeth,* in Irving's place, the latter being ill, from January 17 to 26, 1889.

TOMMASO SALVINI.

In Acting there are two basic elements,—the thing that is done and the method that is employed in doing it. In Salvini's acting the method, generally, was unimpeachable, but in his representations of Shakespearean character the thing done was almost invariably wrong. His *Macbeth* was less false to Shakespeare than his *Othello;* there was some fidelity in his ideal; but his assumption of the *Thane* was neither as coherent, as massive, nor as potent and overwhelming as his assumption of the *Moor.* He appeared as *Macbeth,* for the first time in America, on February 10, 1881, at Booth's Theatre. The figure that he presented was that of a huge, hirsute, heavily armed warrior. His hair was red and very long, his beard thick and tangled, obscuring his face. He was arrayed in skins and woollens and he wore a large, spiked helmet, provided with towering wings. There was no denotement in either his aspect or demeanor of the haunted condition of *Macbeth's* mind. He

represented him, substantially, as a barbaric chieftain, living and fighting in a barbaric age. His
histrionic skill was effectively shown in *Macbeth's*
peculiar contemplation of *King Duncan,* at their first
meeting, his manner of listening to *Banquo's* words
about "allegiance," his expression of *Macbeth's*
remorse after the commission of the murder, and
his abrupt transition from delirium to courtesy, in
the Banquet Scene. The chief merit of his performance was his fine delivery of the speech beginning
"Methought I heard a voice cry 'Sleep no more!'"
His behavior after the murder of the *King* was in
purpose both terrific and piteous, yet it was so
obviously mechanical that no effect of pathos resulted
from it. The despairing cry "Wake Duncan with
thy knocking!" was given in a quick, sharp tone,
indicative of nothing but impatience. No effect of
intent, ominous preoccupation was produced by his
manner of reply to the question (usually asked twice)
"Goes the king hence to-day?" at the awful moment
when the murderer is awaiting the discovery of the
murder. The manner of Salvini's *Macbeth* toward
his wife was merely domestic, commonplace, such as
might befit a *John Mildmay,* and his speech was
colloquial,—a kind of manner and speech that is
distinctly inharmonious with poetical tragedy. The
treatment of the Dagger Scene was conventional and

ineffective. *Macbeth* is a haunted man, from the first, and the actor of him should convey that impression. Salvini did not, at any moment in the performance, convey it. No sense was imparted by him of the influence of "supernatural soliciting." The intention to indicate an ambitious mind fatally tempted and a vacillant will propelled into crime might have existed, but it was not decisively shown. The spectator, never enthralled by the performance, was left free to observe with cool attention the professional mechanism of it. At the close of *Macbeth's* colloquy with the villains whom he employs to murder *Banquo* those wretches tried, with fawning servility, to seize the hem of his regal robe, and thereupon he repulsed them with a deportment of imperial disdain and a momentary shudder. The *Ghost of Banquo,* gory and besmirched, was, in the Banquet Scene, produced in the *King's* chair and likewise brought up through a trap-door, and *Macbeth* raved and ranted and gesticulated, in the spectral presence, after a conventional manner. For one fleeting moment, though, the actor imparted a thrill of terror when he swiftly hid his head in his robe. At the end of the Caldron Scene he became insensible and fell, headlong, and *Hecate* and the *Three Witches* reappeared and hovered over him, with mysterious, grewsome gestures. That unwarranted expedient,—which is directly at variance with the text and also interruptive of the action,—together with the introduction of the *Third Murderer,* usually omitted in Act III., Sc. 3, and the slaughter of *Banquo* in the presence of the audience, were the chief novelties of stage business in Salvini's singularly unimaginative, even prosaic, representation of the tragedy.

VARIOUS MENTION.

Descant on individual performances of *Macbeth* might be prolonged till "the crack of doom" to which he refers. The line of them, seemingly, is endless, and so is the critical discussion of them. Mention here of a few names which have been associated with the part will usefully augment a record which cannot be made absolutely complete. George Bennett, Junius Brutus Booth, Edmon S. Conner, Frederick B. Conway, Charles W. Couldock, Charles Dillon, Barton Hill, George W. Jamieson, Charles John Kean, Charles R. Pope, James Booth Roberts, William E. Sheridan, George Vandenhoff, Daniel Wilmarth Waller, James William Wallack, Charles F. Coghlan, and Joseph Haworth acted *Macbeth,* and all those performers, except Bennett, were seen on the American Stage. Bennett was an actor of the Kemble school, and his repertory included not only *Macbeth* but

Hamlet, Shylock, Othello, Iago, and *Richard the Third.* His performances were described by the old critic James A. Heraud as of a "rough and vigorous character, with a tinge of poetic extravagance in them." Junius Brutus Booth, as *Macbeth,* was highly commended for much and various excellence and especially for his skill in speaking false sentiments with pretended sincerity. George Frederick Cooke, as *Macbeth,* according to Leigh Hunt, "exhibited nothing but a desperate craftiness."

Many years have passed since William Creswick was seen on our stage, and the memory of his acting has gradually faded. He was a man of gentle temperament, a ripe scholar, and in his profession exceptionally able, amply experienced, and highly distinguished. His acting was uninspired, but it was impressive by reason of fine intelligence and winning sincerity. Characters which are intellectual and contemplative rather than those which are passionate seemed to be the more influential in arousing his sympathy and eliciting his best art. In 1871 he acted at Booth's Theatre as *Macbeth,* in association with Charlotte Cushman, giving a performance which, while somewhat inert, was replete with finely suggestive touches, indicating a right comprehension of the character and an expert method of expression. *Macbeth's* delirium of remorse and horror, after the commission of the

murder, was effectively exhibited, and in the pathetic
moments at the close of the Banquet Scene, when the
guilty wretch collapses under the strain of fear and
horror, the humanity which suffuses Shakespeare's
conception of the part and which is essential to a
right representation of it was strongly emphasized
and touchingly conveyed.

George Vandenhoff, son of the more renowned
English actor John Vandenhoff (1790-1861), was a
popular representative of Shakespearean characters
sixty years ago, and his performance of *Macbeth,*
which was seen as late as the time when Charlotte
Cushman finally left the stage, was much admired
in its day. He was an accomplished artist, presenting
every part that he played in a symmetrical form and
enhancing the symmetry of his artistic fabrics by the
melody and grace of his elocution. His manifestation
of *Macbeth's* mental strife,—the last effort of his better nature to withstand evil impulse, immediately before the murder of *Duncan,*—was in the highest degree
affecting, and at the moment of the knocking at the
gate he expressed affrighted consciousness of guilt
and terror of discovery in a way to thrill the heart.
He created an overwhelming effect of pathos, also,
in showing the agony of a remorse which yet cannot
impede the deadly purpose of "slaughterous thoughts,"
in the scene, Act III., Sc. 2, precedent to that of

the Banquet, when he is found by *Lady Macbeth,* alone and brooding over crimes that have been committed and crimes that must follow. The touching lines "Duncan is in his grave," etc., as spoken by him, were made to impart an infinitude of desolation. A sense of completeness of artistic finish rather than of emphatic points lingers in recollection of Vandenhoff's *Macbeth.* Around the whole personation there was a poetic atmosphere of mingled splendor and gloom, as when the fading sunset light is slowly obscured by the clouds of impending storm.

Charles Coghlan applied to *Macbeth* a "natural" method, in itself pleasing but not appropriate. His evolution of the power and pathos of the part was sluggish and indefinite. His reading of the text was often beautiful. He expressed the weak will of the haunted murderer but not his misery, yet his voice and action at "Wake Duncan with thy knocking" and at "Protest me the baby of a girl" indicated a sense of suffering and delirium. He proved unequal to the ordeal of the scene of the murder of *Duncan,* but he was exceptionally expressive in the colloquy with the *Murderers* employed to kill *Banquo.* The pathetic passage which follows the disruption of the Banquet was omitted, and an astonishing funeral service, in which a considerable number of surpliced

clergymen participated, was instantaneously introduced, upon the discovery that *Duncan* had been murdered. Mrs. Langtry, as *Lady Macbeth,* was Coghlan's associate in the presentation of the tragedy, which
occurred at the Fifth Avenue Theatre, New York,
on January 21, 1889.

Joseph Haworth, an actor of uncommon ability,
whose style had been formed under the excellent
influence of John McCullough and in whose death
the stage suffered a serious loss, attempted the part
of *Macbeth,* in association with Mme. Modjeska, in
1898, but proved unequal to its exacting requirements.
In March, 1899, when Mme. Modjeska again presented the tragedy in New York, *Macbeth* was undertaken by Mr. John E. Kellerd, an admirable, conscientious, ambitious actor, but unsuited both by temperament and style to that part.

ROBERT BRUCE MANTELL.

Robert Mantell's impersonation of *Macbeth* when,
November 13, 1905, at the Garden Theatre, New
York, he first assumed that part in America (he had,
many years before, acted it, at short notice, in the
British provinces), was undecided in ideal and melodramatic in expression, but by study and practice it
was gradually matured, until it became what now it is,

a work of perceptive imagination, cumulative power, and evenly sustained and vigorous display. Among all the characters drawn by Shakespeare there is no one whose speech is as amply replete as that of *Macbeth* is with poetic imagery, and it would seem impossible for an actor of sensibility long to continue repeating his words without becoming imbued with the weird spirit of the character. Mantell, finally, embodied *Macbeth* as a man originally noble and of a kind disposition who, at a moment when insatiate ambition has made him peculiarly susceptible to wicked enticement, is enmeshed by those dark and deadly forces of evil which steadfastly contend with good, throughout universal life, and thus becomes a remorseful, tortured, suffering victim. The spectator of his performance saw, upon the first entrance of *Macbeth,* an unmistakable warrior, a man of large, powerful, panoplied frame, outwardly calm but inwardly stirred and shaken by conflicting emotions, his face pale, his features bold, his hair and mustache dark and long,—enhancing in his aspect the element of the picturesque,— and his demeanor communicative of a sense of mystery and dread. The implied theory,—entirely tenable,— was that *Macbeth* has been brooding over the idea of making himself King, and unawares has already been approached by those ministers of sin who eventually meet him on the "blasted heath" and by "prophetic

ROBERT MANTELL AS *MACBETH*

greeting" confirm in his mind the purpose of murder, to make clear his path to a throne. In Mantell's treatment of the Heath Scene and the scene of the meeting with *Duncan* and the *Princes* the furtive side glances of the chieftain's luminous blue eyes, which, it can be assumed, have been clear and frank but which have become suspiciously apprehensive, anxiously watchful, and stern because of the secret workings of sinister thought, were wonderfully expressive of a soul at war with itself, and his continuous denotement of that conflict,—which grows more and more intense until the hour of the assassination and thereafter is made agonized by accession of remorse,— was alike true in spirit and fine in method, giving effect to the pathos of the tragedy and thus fulfilling the chief requirement of the part. His speaking of "Had I but died an hour before this chance" and, later, of "She should have died hereafter" was not only eloquent of profound feeling but decisively significant of a right comprehension of *Macbeth,* not as a melodramatic miscreant but as a suffering man. It was authoritatively said of Edmund Kean's *Macbeth* that he did not look like a man who had met the *Weird Sisters.* Mantell's *Macbeth* was seen to have been haunted from the first moment, and throughout the whole awful experience of temptation, crime and remorse, impelled against his will, and in ever increasing agony. The sensibility of the performance was acute, the feeling intense, the passion volubly uttered, the action, especially at the climax of the Banquet Scene, instinct with fiery vitality. As the performance proceeded the effect of suffering upon the physical condition was indicated by the haggard visage, the deepening tones of the voice, the fevered manner, and the graying of the hair. The actual *Ghost* was introduced in the Banquet Scene, and the effect was exceptionally bad, because of bad management of lights and the insignificance of the player assigned to act *Banquo*. The fight was one of desperate ferocity. Throughout the latter part of the play Mantell's *Macbeth* was a man oppressed alike in mind and body, but defiant and terrible. One of his principal costumes comprised a woollen jerkin, reaching nearly to the knees, leathern sandal-shoes, thongs twined over tights on the legs, a breastplate of leather studded with metal squares, chain mail about the neck, a long cloak ornamented with fret-work around its edge, a helmet, surmounted by a single feather of the eagle, as a plume, and having metal wings on either side. He carried, by turns as occasion required, a battle-ax, a truncheon, and a sword.

It is by the voice more decisively than by any other means that the soul reveals itself. Mantell's voice has been injured by hard usage during many years of acting in "one-night stands,"—by the strain put upon it through effort to carry all the weight of performances and to satisfy an injudicious public taste as to acting,—but it retains much of its original quality, character, and power, and it is one of the most sympathetic voices now to be heard in our Theatre. Though he is often a careless reader those affecting speeches of *Macbeth* which have been mentioned were spoken by Mantell as they have not been spoken by any actor since the days of Edwin Booth,—in tones so melancholy, solemn, and afflicting, so fraught with the desolation of a seared, hopeless mind and a broken heart, that memory will long treasure them as among the most expressive and touching achievements of elocutionary art that have been known in recent years. Mantell's only serious competitor in the great parts of the legitimate drama on our stage is Edward Hugh Sothern, an actor who, in every part which both players customarily represent, except *Hamlet,* is distinctly inferior to him. Sothern appears to be the more ambitious, for he has wrought himself out of his natural channel: Mantell is, by nature, better equipped for the great tragic drama. The purpose Sothern has manifested,—to present the best plays in the best manner,—is in the highest degree honorable to him: it is a splendid evidence of his sincerity, inflexible determination, and indefatigable labor that, being, as he is, distinctively a comedian, he has so wrought upon himself that, while it is not a great performance, his *Hamlet* is the best given by any actor now on the American Stage: and that achievement seems the more remarkable and is the more significant when it is remembered that Sothern is also the best *Malvolio* of our day. But Sothern's low stature is a serious disadvantage to him, while his unsympathetic voice and often deplorably defective elocution, his sometimes finical method, and his lack of distinction are still more obstructive. Mantell will never accomplish what once he might have done: life's evening is not the time for beginning a long journey: but he possesses more natural affinity with romantic condition than his rival does, he retains much of the fiery spirit, the vibrant nervous intensity, and the personal charm which gained victory for him long ago, and, though it is not the amplest in degree nor always manifested, he does possess true tragic power and, in general, a direct and simple style. Aside from all consideration of newspaper publicity and of material prosperity Robert Mantell, by right of what he is and what he does, is the legitimate leader of the Stage in America to-day.

LADY MACBETH.

Many women have appeared on the American Stage as *Lady Macbeth*. Among them, in the earlier days of our Theatre, were Mrs. Whitlock, Mrs. Merry, Mrs. Snelling Powell, Mrs. Charles Gilfert, Mrs. Warner, and Mrs. Duff. Mrs. Whitlock was Elizabeth Kemble, sister of Mrs. Siddons. Mrs. Merry was Anne Brunton; after the death of her husband, Robert Merry, the "Della Crusca" rhymester, she married Thomas Wignell, and after his death she married William Warren. Mrs. Powell was Miss Harrison. Mrs. Gilfert was Miss Holman, daughter of the excellent actor Joseph George Holman. Mrs. Warner was Miss Huddart. Mrs. Duff was Mary Anne Dyke, the first love of the poet Thomas Moore, who married her sister Elizabeth. Mrs. Duff (1795-1857) was declared by many of the most thoroughly experienced and capable contemporary judges of acting, both in and out of her profession, and likewise by the general public voice, to be perfection as a tragic actress. She acted all the great tragic heroines in Shakespeare. In later days *Lady Macbeth* has been performed by Mrs. Mason, Isabella Glyn (Mrs. Dallas), Mrs. Coleman Pope, Mrs. Farren, Julia Dean, Mrs. Barry, Mrs. Bowers, Mme. Ponisi, Matilda Heron, Fanny Janauschek, Clara Morris, Helena Modjeska, and Julia Marlowe.

CHARLOTTE CUSHMAN.

The most imperial representative of *Lady Macbeth* seen in our time was Charlotte Cushman. It was as *Lady Macbeth* that she made her first appearance on the dramatic stage in 1835, at New Orleans, and her personation of that part was, for many years, a theme of ardent popular and critical admiration. In her artistic method there was no defect. She embodied the character; she seemed to live it; she made her audience oblivious that her exhibition of wickedness and misery was mere simulation. Her ideal, on the other hand, was almost savage. The beauty and the pathos of the tragedy are not fully expressed unless the hero and heroine of it are suitably invested with attributes of humanity. The wife of *Macbeth* is an instrument in the hands of the powers of darkness to effect his ruin. He is not a brutal ruffian: she is not a cruel virago. Shakespeare's conception of the characters will bear the highest estimate that, rationally, can be put upon them. Miss Cushman did not make *Lady Macbeth* a virago, but she did make her,—customarily, not always,—essentially masculine, and seeing her performance as usually given the enthusiast of Shakespeare craved for it

some infusion of that feminine charm by which woman
captivates and subdues the sterner nature of man.
Miss Cushman's *Lady Macbeth,* until the murder of
King Duncan had been accomplished, occupied toward
her consort the attitude of a hard, potent, relentless
spirit, repressing an almost contemptuous impatience
of vacillation and weakness. Her affinity with
him seemed to be of the mind more than of the
affections, and the words "From this time, such I
account thy *love*" fell from her lips without material
effect. She did not clearly enough indicate the
humanity and moral sense which must, in nature, be
supposed to underlie the misery of a human being
who is continuously and inexorably agonized by
remorse, and who, for that reason, ends life by suicide.
There was, consequently, felt to be a certain lack of
rational sequence between the murderess of the beginning and the doomed, tortured, horror-stricken
somnambulist of the end. I have seen Miss Cushman
act *Lady Macbeth* when she relaxed her iron rigor
and imparted to the performance a mournful gentleness,—especially in the scene of *Banquo's* dismissal;
the scene of *Macbeth's* gloomy and afflicted isolation
when his wife tries to comfort him; and in those
moments of agony and desolation which ensue upon
the broken feast: but usually Miss Cushman's embodiment, massive, regal, and darkly tragic, exhibited a

woman of great physical power and of still greater will, and of a fierce, implacable, terrible spirit. A lurid light of horror was spread over the whole performance. The massive identity, breadth and freedom of gesture, blood-curdling atmosphere, wondrous facial mobility, magnetic force, intellectual and emotional life,—flowing into every point of action and every tone of utterance,—made up a personation which, in grandeur, intensity, and magnificent grace, had no parallel on the stage of her time and has had no equal since. Her figure, towering above *Macbeth* and pointing beyond him to the coming *Duncan* who "must be provided for," or crouching against the door-post of the chamber in which the midnight murder is afoot, was indescribably awful, and it has not passed from the memory, of persons who saw it, nor will it pass from the most glowing page of the annals of our Theatre. She was nobly authoritative in the Banquet Scene, and she harrowed the heart in depicting the anguish of the sleep-walker, whom guilty conscience is hounding into death and hell. All her points were made with superb spontaneity and precision.

It was Miss Cushman's opinion—an opinion based in part on the frequency of reference to wine, drink, and carousal, which occurs in the text—that throughout the play *Macbeth* and his wife are more or

less intoxicated. It was also her opinion that
they should be stalwart persons, and that the representation of the tragedy should be swathed in a
sanguinary, semi-barbaric atmosphere. Speaking to
me about actors of *Macbeth,* she commented in a
half-impatient, half-playful tone on the fact that
they often were *"little* men," and I had no doubt
she was thinking of Edwin Booth and Lawrence
Barrett, with both of whom she had acted, and both
of whom were slender and of medium height. I
sometimes wonder, considering the peculiar views of
Miss Cushman as to this subject, that her performance
of *Lady Macbeth* should have been essentially poetic;
yet essentially poetic it was, in spite of its ferocity.
Art could do no more toward making actual the
"sightless substances" that "wait on Nature's mischief"
than it did in her wonderful demeanor, gesture, and
tones of voice when invoking "the murdering ministers"; when whispering to herself at the door of
Duncan's chamber "The sleeping and the dead are
but as pictures"; and, in the awful episode of somnam-
bulism, moaning, with a long, dreadful, heartbreaking
sigh, "All the perfumes of Arabia will not sweeten
this little hand." The agonized voice in which she said
"What's done, cannot be undone" fell upon the
heart as a voice of doom, signifying eternal misery.
Old records mention "the horrid sigh" of Mrs. Pritch-

ard: it could not have been more heartrending than the abject, desolate suspiration of Charlotte Cushman in that overwhelming portrayal of hopeless anguish. The performance, as a whole, was traditional; that is to say, it was in line with the tradition of Mrs. Pritchard, Anna Maria Yates, and Sarah Siddons, her great predecessors. The achievement of Miss Cushman was the infusion of her own great personality into the character,—the regal mind, the indomitable will, the burning passion, the colossal courage,—and therewithal she blended the precision and smoothness of perfect executive art. The element of femininity which it usually lacked has been infused into later personations of *Lady Macbeth,* notably, by Ellen Terry. Mrs. Siddons, who never acted according to her declared theory of the character, but made a terrific personality predominant, was the first to suggest that *Lady Macbeth* should be represented as a slight, delicate, alluring, blond woman, full of fire, but exquisitely feminine, the literal opposite of the formidable, tremendous woman whom she embodied. Miss Cushman did not invent any new business for *Lady Macbeth,* except that, after reading the letter, she put it into her bosom. One great foreign actress, Adelaide Ristori, whom I have seen in this part, after reading that letter, walked to the side of the scene and tossed it away,

MRS. SIDDONS AS *LADY MACBETH*

AFTER THE PAINTING BY G. H. HARLOW

as if she were throwing it out of the window! Miss Cushman's business of queenlike welcome to *King Duncan* and of a diversified and quieting courtesy toward the guests at the banquet was superb in execution, but it was not new: Mrs. Pritchard set the example. To what extent, if at all, Mrs. Pritchard was indebted to stage traditions as to *Lady Macbeth* which had been established by her predecessors in that character the investigator finds no means of definite ascertainment. Among those predecessors of superior ability and merited renown were Mrs. Betterton, Elizabeth Barry, Mrs. Yates, and the actress who successively was Mrs. Dancer, Mrs. Spranger Barry, and Mrs. Crawford. Mrs. Pritchard was not a student. She appears to have been a person of original mind and to have acted from intuition and inspiration. The chronicles of the stage afford abundant evidence that the faculty of acting can exist apart from scholarship and, indeed, apart from a high order of mind. Mrs. Siddons told Dr. Johnson that she had never seen Mrs. Pritchard. She was thirteen years old when Mrs. Pritchard died and at that time was employed on the stage in her father's dramatic company, performing in English provincial theatres. Her first performance of *Lady Macbeth* was given in 1779, at the age of twenty-four. She was acquainted with the tradition of Mrs. Pritchard's acting of that part, and to some extent she appears to have followed it. She has recorded that on the occasion of her first London performance of *Lady Macbeth* (1785, at Drury Lane) she approached it with diffidence and terror and "with the additional fear of Mrs. Pritchard's reputation in it." Unlike Mrs. Pritchard, however, she was highly intellectual and a diligent student who thought much and reasoned well. No doubt she was willing to follow good precedents, but she could lead as well as follow. Mrs. Pritchard, in *Lady Macbeth's* somnambulation, had invariably kept the taper in her hand. Mrs. Siddons, contrary to the urgent request of Sheridan, set it down, in order that she might act in accordance with the text:

"*Doctor.*   What is it she does now?
"*Gentlewoman.*   It is an accustomed action with her to seem thus washing her hands; I have known her continue in this a quarter of an hour."

VARIOUS PERFORMERS.

Charlotte Cushman took her final farewell of the stage in 1874, at or about which time the urgent necessity of supplying her place seemed suddenly and forcibly to impress itself upon the minds of many female performers of that period, and representations of the part of *Lady Macbeth* became almost ludi-

crously frequent, in various American cities. No
aspirant for the laurel of Miss Cushman succeeded
in grasping it, and as one by one the younger dramatic sisters of the retired veteran attempted the feat
and failed, a voice of impatient remonstrance seemed
to make itself heard, all round the theatrical welkin,
exclaiming "Infirm of purpose, give ME the daggers!"
Among the actresses who successively appeared as
Lady Macbeth were Clara Morris, Carlotta Leclercq,
Bella Pateman, Mary Prescott (who performed in
association with Salvini), and Matilda Heron. There
were others, less known to fame, but of that group
the most important were Miss Heron and Miss
Morris.

Matilda Heron, emerging from retirement, appeared
in the part on Christmas night, 1874, at Booth's
Theatre, playing it then for the first time. That
actress had gained popularity throughout the country
by acting *Camille,* in an English version of "La
Dame aux Camélias." In early life she was a beauty
and throughout her life she displayed both the magnetic power and the eccentricity of genius. Her
vitality was prodigious and so was her capability of
expressing emotion, but of dramatic art she possessed
slight equipment. She had, in her day, appeared in
widely contrasted parts,—such as *Parthenia* and
Juliet, Mrs. Haller and *Medea,*—but the part in

which, at all times, she was best was that of Matilda Heron. Her favorite theme for dramatic illustration was ruined virtue at war with its miserable fate. Seen in any image of that conflict, when her spirit became fully aroused, she was seen to be an extraordinary woman. She suggested a wild and awful tumult, like that of the storm-swept ocean, tossing and raging under a midnight sky. Such characters have not frequently appeared in stage history, but whenever they have appeared their acting has been hailed as magnificent for precisely the quality that makes it defective, that of disorder. The part of *Lady Macbeth* involves terrible emotions, but it cannot be rightly exhibited by use of the method which is called "natural." Miss Heron when at her meridian could not have acted it: in her decadence her attempt was painfully abortive. The ideal was that of a fierce termagant; the execution lawless. The performance was characterized by cadent elocution, redundant gesture, contortions of the face, gyrations of the body, sudden assumptions of threatening pose, and general extravagance: nevertheless through all its incapability and turbulence there was a gleam of the strange genius of the woman,—always original, and, in herself, interesting to the last.

Clara Morris essayed *Lady Macbeth* for the first

CHARLOTTE CÚSHMAN AS *LADY MACBETH*

time in New York on May 17, 1875, at Booth's
Theatre, the English actor George Rignold then,
for the first time, acting *Macbeth*. Miss Morris wore
a blond wig, but otherwise dressed the part in a
conventional manner. She appeared to have apprehended it as that of a fascinating young woman who
sways her husband by personal charm. She moved
with a willowy motion, evinced intensity of feeling
by distention of the nostrils, employed tigerish little
smiles, and was a charming modern person assisting
at a murder in a mediæval castle. In the Sleep-
walking Scene her simulation of suffering was
expert and effective. The traditional business, as
made authoritative by Charlotte Cushman, was copied
in the Banquet Scene and, indeed, throughout the
representation. Clara Morris, who long ago retired
from the stage, was, in her best time, an admirable
exponent,—as Matilda Heron had been,—of emotional
conflict in the woman whom passion or circumstance
has caused to be untrue to herself or has entangled
in a web of amorous complication or domestic adversity. She was capable of great ground-swells of
emotion and could powerfully affect the feelings of
her audience, but her art was wild, except at rare
moments when she chose to control herself, and she was
hopelessly out of place in poetic drama. She turned

verse into prose and was literal in everything. Her representation of *Lady Macbeth* was neither imaginative nor powerful.

Fanny Janauschek's performance was stalwart and predominant, exhibiting all the harsh and fierce properties of the character. Her person was massive, her countenance severe, her style remarkable for authority, distinction, and exactitude of finish, and for splendid breadth of gesture.

Fanny Morant, the best *Mrs. Candor* of her time, made *Lady Macbeth,* which part she performed in association with Edwin Booth, a violent shrew who might have driven her husband to the ale-house,— had there been such resorts in his period,—but would never have been instrumental in making him a regicide.

Helena Modjeska, who adopted the part into her repertory in 1888, acting with Edwin Booth, retained it till the last. Her ideal was the one set forth in print by Mrs. Siddons but never set forth by her on the stage. That ideal would make of *Lady Macbeth* an enchanting woman whose power over her husband springs from allurement, and who impels him to crime because she loves him and passionately desires his advancement to a throne. Mme. Modjeska possessed little or no aptitude for tempestuous tragedy, and alike in temperament and style she was unsuited to *Lady Macbeth,* her performance giving no manifestation of the power and the terrible intensity of wicked purpose that are in the character. Her puny sarcasm and petty taunts, in prompting *Macbeth* to murder *Duncan,* exemplified nothing of that "valor of the tongue" with which, like an inexorable angel of evil fate, the terrible woman had determined to "chastise" all the weak scruples of her irresolute "partner of greatness." Her exit, carrying the imbrued daggers, was singularly ineffective, for that proceeding, which, by itself, usually compels absorbing interest, became, in her treatment of it, merely incidental. One piece of her stage business was new and also it was infelicitous: she produced one of *Macbeth's* letters and showed it to him, as documentary evidence that he had sworn to kill the *King* and was therefore inexorably bound to do so. In the Sleepwalking Scene she was, however, entirely great,—an image of wonderful, woful beauty, pallid, haggard, spectral, profoundly pathetic. Like Helena Faucit and Ellen Terry, she failed to unify, in a credible character, an inflexible purpose of murder, treacherous and cruel, with a condition of intrinsic feminine loveliness. There is, indeed, formidable difficulty in the way of investing with sweet attributes and human propensity a woman who has invoked the demons of hell, saying

"Unsex me here
And fill me, from the crown to the toe, top-full
Of *direst cruelty.* . . .
Come to my woman's breasts
And take my milk for gall, you murdering ministers,
Wherever in your sightless substances
You wait on Nature's mischief!"

Yet human attributes she must possess, for through them she suffers and is driven to death. The foreign lingual cadence of Mme. Modjeska's enunciation of the English verse served to weaken her tragic effort, by infusion of prettiness.

Ellen Terry, in her embodiment of *Lady Macbeth,* placed strong emphasis on the feminine fascination that the wife exercises over the husband, and in that respect she supplied the element that was wanting in the performances given by Charlotte Cushman and her imitators. On the other hand, she greatly lessened *Lady Macbeth's* attributes of power and will, imparting no considerable sense of the deadliness of her bloody-minded resolution, the iniquity of her conduct, and the grisly horror that enshrouds her life. The predominant note in her performance was that of pathos. This was inevitable, because of the temperament of Ellen Terry, clearly displayed in her great characteristic performances, such as Shakespeare's *Ophelia* and Goethe's *Margaret.* Her portrayal of

Lady Macbeth's poignant remorse was profoundly truthful and irresistibly affecting. She excelled in the expression of bleak, hopeless misery in the closing moments of the Banquet Scene and in the agony of the Sleep-walking Scene. Her appearance, in rich raiment befitting a Queen, was stately and exceedingly beautiful. She wore a close-fitting green robe, encircled by a jewelled girdle, and a voluminous blue mantle, with long, wide-flowing sleeves. Her hair was golden red, abundant, and worn in two very long, heavy braids depending on either side of her face.

Helena Faucit (Lady Martin), who in performance of *Lady Macbeth* preceded Ellen Terry by forty-two years but survived to witness the triumphs of her distinguished successor, set the example of presenting the character as essentially feminine,—her theory being that *Lady Macbeth,* in urging *Macbeth* to the act of murder and participating with him in "the guilt of our great quell," is impelled by the wife's absorbing love for the husband and her passionate desire that his ambition to wear the crown shall be gratified. Miss Faucit measurably disliked the part and dreaded being, at any time, constrained to play it, but when she did she exhibited a gentle spirit urged into crime by the violent impulse of passionate love, and divested it of all ferocity and placed the emphasis on the pathos of its suffering. Her excellence was, it would seem, shown only in the Banquet Scene and the Sleep-walking Scene. Macready, in association with whom she first played the part, particularly commended her acting in those passages, saying that in the latter her walk was "heavy and unelastic," and that she marked "the distinction between the muffled voice and seeming mechanical motion of the somnambulist and the wandering mind and quick fitful gestures of a maniac, whose very violence would waken her from the deepest sleep." Her embodiment of *Lady Macbeth* has been designated as "fascinating and persuasive." That of Ellen Terry might be fitly described in the same words. Neither, it is obvious, was more than half right.

THE SPIRITUAL ELEMENT.

As observation investigates the past and thought ranges the long avenues of memory, reviewing the numerous and zealous efforts that have been made to interpret the wonderful tragedy of "Macbeth," the mind realizes a profound impression of genius, intellect, study, passionate devotion, and noble endeavor, ardently employed on that terrible subject. Next to "Hamlet" among the plays of Shakespeare "Macbeth" has awakened the deepest interest and caused the most extensive controversy, the reason being that,

From a photograph by *Window and Grove. Copyright*

ELLEN TERRY AS *LADY MACBETH*

like "Hamlet," it opens the vast, mysterious realm of spiritual life, the boundless environment of the unknown, the abyss of the universe, into which all thinking persons sooner or later peer with anxious eyes, awestricken and perplexed. Whence did we come and whither are we going? Does death end all, or is it only the portal to life? Do angels of light and angels of darkness hover over us, to make or mar? Is the individual human being a waif of chance, or a creature of the fixed decree of Fate? Those considerations and others like to them are in the depths of all analysis of the vast subject of "Macbeth." Imagination has not in any work of literature taken a higher flight than it takes in that tragedy. The theories and the technical expedients of the great actors who have attempted illustration of it possess an intrinsic interest for the student of dramatic art, but the greater value of their testimony is the help which it provides toward clarification of our thought on the conditions of human life and the destiny of Man.

VII.

KING HENRY VIII.

"A little rule, a little sway,
A sunbeam in a winter's day,
Is all the proud and mighty have
Between the cradle and the grave."
—JOHN DYER.

HISTORICAL COMMENT.

THE play of "King Henry VIII.," neither symmetrical in construction nor uniform in style, commingles the constituents of spectacle with those of drama, but while it is not a rounded work of art it depicts with affecting fidelity the ruin of greatness and illustrates with deep admonitory significance the mutability of fortune and the transitory lot of man. The expedient employed by Shakespeare to precipitate the downfall of *Wolsey,*—that of causing the *Cardinal,* through haste and inadvertence, to inclose to *King Henry* a private letter, respecting the divorce of *Queen Katharine,* which he had intended to send to the Pope of Rome, together with an inventory of his wealth,—was drawn from Holinshed's "Chronicle." (That admirable com-

mentator Dyce remarks that in "King Henry VIII.,"
"Frequently we have all but the very words of
Holinshed.") No such mistake was ever made by
Wolsey, but such a mistake actually was made by
Thomas Ruthall, who held the office of Bishop of
Durham from 1509 till 1522. That ecclesiastic had
been ordered to prepare a record of the estates of
the kingdom, to be delivered to Wolsey. He told
his servant to bring from his study a book bound
in white vellum. The servant obeyed, bringing, by mis-
chance, another book, bound in white vellum, which
contained an account of Ruthall's private possessions,
and that volume was despatched to the Cardinal.
It appears to have shown that some of the Bishop's
gains had been ill-gotten. Ruthall, dismayed by
that unlucky exposure of his secret affairs, soon
afterward died, of humiliation and shame. Expert
use of that mishap is made in the drama (Act III.,
Sc. 2), providing one of the best pieces of the action,
and, for the actor of *Wolsey,* one of the most telling
passages—the soliloquy which ends

> " I shall fall
> Like a bright exhalation in the evening,
> And no man see me more."

There is in this play a considerable disregard of
the actual sequence of historic events. In the first

scene there is intimation that war between England
and France is then current, and one incident of the
scene is the arrest of the *Duke of Buckingham,* on a
charge of high treason.   The Duke was arrested
April 15, 1521, but war with France had not then
been declared by England, and, in fact, was not
declared till May, 1522.   In the play *King Henry
the Eighth* and *Anne Bullen* meet, Act II., Sc. 4,
prior to the execution of Buckingham,—which occurred
on May 17, 1521,—whereas, in fact, they did not meet
till some time in 1527.   In the play the marriage of
Anne. Bullen to the *King* is made to occur prior to
Wolsey's disgrace and death: in fact, *Wolsey* had been
dead nearly three years when that marriage was
solemnized: the great Cardinal died on November
29, 1530.   *King Henry* and *Anne Bullen* were
privately married in January, 1533.   In the play
Wolsey's death is immediately followed by that of
Queen Katharine: in fact, she survived him nearly six
years, dying on January 8, 1536.   The play represents
that *Queen Katharine* had died prior to the birth of
Queen Anne's daughter, the *Princess Elizabeth,*
whereas, in fact, the death of *Queen Katharine* did
not occur till more than two years after that birth,—
the *Princess Elizabeth* having been born on September
7, 1533.   In the play *Cranmer* appears before the
hostile Council, Act V., Sc. 2, and subsequently

assists at the christening of the *Princess:* in fact, it was not till eleven years after that christening that the Council summoned him and endeavored to effect his disgrace. Discrepancy, however, is not unnatural between Drama and History. The supposed time of this play is about one year; the events to which it relates were strewn over a period of many years,—at least from 1520-21 till 1544. The ages of the principal characters at the beginning can be determined, approximately if not exactly, by reference to the veritable dates of their birth and death. The *Norfolk* of this play was the second duke bearing that title, who, as Lord Surrey, commanded at the battle of Flodden Field, September 9, 1513. He died May 21, 1524. The *Surrey* of the play was Thomas, eldest son of the second Duke of Norfolk. He, as Lord Howard, was in "command of the main body of the first line" at Flodden (Hume). He was created Earl of Surrey in 1514, at the same time that his father was made Duke of Norfolk. This Surrey was, in life, the father of that Henry Howard, statesman, soldier, and poet, who, as Earl of Surrey, was decapitated, January 21, 1547, by order of King Henry the Eighth. He had, at that time, succeeded to the title of Duke of Norfolk and he escaped the fate of his son Henry only through the fortunate death of the King. It is, in several instances, desirable for the sake of dramatic effect that the ages of persons implicated in this play should be shown on the stage as greater than, in fact, they were at the time of its beginning. The date of the birth of Anne Bullen is given as 1501 and also as 1507. If the latter be correct—as there is reason to believe— she would not have been of marriagable age in 1520. Queen Katharine was eight years older than King Henry. Assuming that the play begins in 1520, the following table shows the actual ages, at that time, of some of the characters in it:

	Born	Died	Age in 1520
King Henry the Eighth	1491	1547	29
Queen Katharine	1483	1536	37
Thomas Wolsey	1471	1530	49
Thomas Cromwell	1490(?)	1540	30
Campeius (Campeggio)	1474	1549(?)	46
Gardiner	1483	1555	37
Norfolk	14—	1524	(?)
Surrey	1473	1554	47
Anne Bullen	1501	1536	19

COSTUME.

The play of "King Henry VIII." is especially suitable for representation as a spectacle. Holbein's portraits of King Henry, of several of his wives, and of Cardinal Wolsey and Thomas Cromwell, engrav-

ings of which are accessible, provide authority as to
costume. The learned and instructive scholar Charles
Knight gleaned from old writers,—largely from Hall
and Cavendish,—much information as to dress, and the
following brief citations, condensed, from the product
of his devoted industry are usefully illustrative of
custom in King Henry's time:

"Sumptuary laws regulated dress. The use of the fur of
the black jennet was reserved to the royal family and only
noblemen above the rank of a viscount could wear sables. Crimson or blue velvet, embroidered apparel, or garments bordered
with 'gold sunken work,' were restricted from all persons
beneath the quality of a baron's or knight's son or heir. Persons who possessed as much as two hundred marks per annum,
and those only, were allowed to wear velvet dresses of any
color, furs of martens, and chains, bracelets, and collars of
gold. The sons and heirs of such persons were permitted to
wear black velvet or damask, and tawny-colored russet or
camlet. Satin and damask gowns were allowed only to persons
who possessed at least one hundred marks a year. Knights could
wear plaited skirts, garnished with gold, silver, or silk, but these
garments were forbidden to all persons of lower rank. The hair
was, by peremptory order of the King, cut close to the head.
Beards and mustaches were worn, at pleasure. Cavendish describes Wolsey as issuing forth in his Cardinal's habit of fine
scarlet or crimson satin, his cap being of black velvet. The
gentlemen in his train wore black velvet livery coats, and large
chains of gold around their necks, while his yeomen, who followed his gentlemen retainers, were clad in French tawny livery
coats, embroidered on the backs and breasts with the letters

T and C, under the Cardinal's hat. Feathers were worn in profusion."

The attire of Queen Anne when she went in procession from the Tower to Westminster on the day before her coronation is thus described:

"She wore a surcoat of white cloth of tissue, and a mantle of the same, furred with ermine, her hair hanging down from under a coif, with a circlet about it, full of rich stones." On the next day, when she went to the Abbey to be crowned, she wore "a surcoat and robe of purple velvet, furred with ermine, the coif and circlet as before. The Barons of the Cinque Ports, who carried the canopy over her, were in crimson, with points of blue and red hanging on their sleeves." The ladies, "being lords' wives," that followed her, "had surcoats of scarlet with narrow sleeves, the breast all lettice [fur], with bars of borders [i.e., rows of ermine], according to their degrees, and over that they had mantles of scarlet furred, and every mantle had lettice about the neck, like a neckercher, likewise powdered [with ermine], so that by the powderings their degree was known. Then followed ladies, being knights' wives, in gowns of scarlet with narrow sleeves, without trains, only edged with lettice." The Queen's gentlemen were similarly attired with the last. The Lord Chancellor wore a robe of scarlet, open before, and bordered with lettice. The dukes were in crimson velvet, furred with ermine, and powdered according to their degrees. The Duke of Suffolk's doublet and jacket were set with Orient pearl; his gown of crimson velvet, richly embroidered; and he carried a white rod in his hand, being that day high steward of England. The Knights of the Bath wore "violet gowns with hoods purfled with miniver, like doctors."

THE PLAY.

Conjecture has long been busy with the play of "King Henry VIII.," which was first published in the 1623 Folio. The date of its composition is not known, neither is the date of its first presentment on the stage. Some Shakespeare editors, among them Theobald, Malone, and Dr. Johnson, maintain that it was produced before the death (1603) of Queen Elizabeth; other Shakespeare editors, among them Collier, Dyce, and Knight, contend that it was not produced until after the accession of King James the First. A favorite belief is that it was performed, under the title of "All is True," on June 29, 1613, at the Globe Theatre, London, on which occasion the discharge of small cannon,—perhaps in the Coronation Scene, Act IV., Sc. 1, or, more probably, in the scene of *King Henry's* entrance, as a masker, at a festival in the palace of *Cardinal Wolsey,* Act I., Sc. 4,—set fire to the theatre and caused its destruction. Controversy on this subject hinges mainly on the Prologue to the play and the speech delivered by *Cranmer* at the christening of the royal infant.

Two plays relative to the story of Cardinal Wolsey,—one of them being ascribed to Henry Chettle, a printer, publisher, and dramatist of Shakespeare's

time, of whose biography little is known, but with
whom, according to Collier, three other dramatists,
Michael Drayton, Anthony Munday, and Went-
worth Smith, coöperated in making a drama about
the illustrious Cardinal,—were acted in London
in 1601, and the usually careful editor Malone
assigns Shakespeare's "King Henry VIII." to that
year. The play is one that would have pleased
Queen Elizabeth more than it could be supposed
likely to please her successor, King James the First.
That Queen delighted in servile adulation, and she
exacted abject deference to her authority, but her
sense of delicacy was not such as is easily shocked.
There is no reason to suppose that Queen Elizabeth
would have resented *Queen Katharine's* eminently
queenlike statement of her position or been displeased
by a representation of the gallant behavior of King
Henry the Eighth, her father, on the occasion of
his meeting with the fair Anne Bullen. She knew the
reason why he had desired and procured the annul-
ment of his marriage to Katharine of Arragon,
and though the demeanor of *King Henry* toward
Anne Bullen, in the Masque Scene, is that of a bold
and expeditious wooer, it is not such as Queen Elizabeth's coarse taste would have regarded as unseemly.

On the other hand, King James had no reason
to revere the memory of Queen Elizabeth, who is

specifically honored in Shakespeare's play, that sovereign having kept his mother, Queen Mary of Scotland, for eighteen years incarcerated in prison, subjected her to indignity, and finally sent her to death, on the block; and it is known that, in fact, he abhorred her memory. The speech which is delivered by the *Archbishop of Canterbury* in the scene of the christening was well calculated to please Queen Elizabeth, but it does not contain anything, aside from the lines of homage to her successor, likely to have gratified King James. Those lines,—seventeen in number, beginning "Nor shall this peace sleep with her," and ending "Thou speakest wonders,"—break the continuity of the address, but they serve the purpose of adulation of a vain monarch, notoriously susceptible to flattery. As suggested by Theobald, they probably were interpolated into *Cranmer's* encomium some time after the first presentment of the play, when Queen Elizabeth had died and King James had ascended the English throne. Shakespeare himself might have inserted them, or they might have been inserted by another hand, possibly that of Ben Jonson.

It has been surmised that the offering of the play in the summer of 1613 was prompted by a wish to profit by contributing to the general public rejoicing incident to the marriage of the Princess Elizabeth, daughter of King James, to Frederick V., the Elector Palatine. That marriage occurred about the middle of the previous February, and it is hardly reasonable to suppose that the production of an "historical masque or show play" (Coleridge) intended as a spectacle apposite to that occasion would be deferred till the end of June, a period of more than four months. In the absence of definite, decisive information it seems probable that Shakespeare's "King Henry VIII." was first presented toward the end of the reign of Queen Elizabeth, and that the play called "All is True," acted in 1613, with disaster to the Globe Theatre, was Shakespeare's play, revived for an occasion, and altered in such a way as to make it acceptable to the time of King James. The compliment to that monarch, supposing it to have been then first inserted in the text, miscarried, because the theatre caught fire before the performance had reached the Christening Scene, and *Cranmer's* honeyed words, occurring in the last act, were not spoken. No record has been discovered of the cast of "All is True," but among the Harleian Manuscripts there is a letter, addressed by the Rev. Thomas Lorkin to Sir Thomas Puckering, dated "this last of June, 1613," in which a reference is made to the burning of the Globe Theatre: "No longer since than yesterday, while Bourbage his company were acting at the Globe the play of Henry VIII and there shooting of certain chambers in way of triumph, the fire catch'd." The implication would seem to be that Burbage participated in the representation. If so he would have played one of the principal parts,—either *King Henry* or *Cardinal Wolsey*,—for he was then in the prime of his renown. Contemporary reference to "All is True" sometimes calls it by that name and sometimes by the name of "Henry VIII."

No mention has been found of any presentment of this drama in the interval between 1613 and 1663, the interval, roughly speaking, between the period of Burbage and that of Betterton. Shakespeare's manuscript remained in the possession, and at the mercy, of Heminge and Condell, the managers, who owned it, from the time when the play was first performed (whatever time that may have been) till the time of its first publication. To what extent or by what hand (if at all) it may have been altered after the death of Shakespeare, 1616, and before it was published, 1623, investigation has failed to discover. Modern scholarship has assumed that, because of certain peculiarities of the versification, notably the use of "double endings," much of the play must have been written by some hand other than that of Shakespeare, and John Fletcher has been named as possibly or probably the dramatist who thus contributed to it, because the use of double endings was, with him, habitual. That theory, like other theories, which, resting on surmise and not on evidence, would discredit Shakespeare's authorship of his writings, is merely conjectural. It was suggested (1850) by the accomplished scholar James Spedding (the J. S. of Tennyson's beautiful elegiac verses), whose conclusion was that, in writing the play of "King Henry VIII.," Shakespeare had proceeded "as far, perhaps, as the third act, when, finding that his fellows of the Globe were in distress for a new play with which to honor the marriage of the Lady Elizabeth, he handed them his manuscript," and that they intrusted it to Fletcher, "already a popular and expeditious playwright," to be completed. The surmise was ingenious and it has been widely accepted. It is, however, visionary and groundless. If a practice of writing blank verse with a new kind of line,—a line containing more than the usual ten syllables, or with frequent "double endings,"—chanced to become prevalent, it is not unlikely, as remarked by the great Shakespeare scholar J. O. Halliwell-Phillipps, that Shakespeare might have been influenced by it, and might have adopted it. "Expeditious" Fletcher may have been, but there is abundant reason to believe that Shakespeare was at least quite as much so, and that he could himself have finished his play with equal despatch. It would be amusing, if it were not painful, to observe the assurance with which theories about Shakespeare are adopted and proclaimed as established facts, sometimes by thoughtful commentators from whom a larger measure of discretion might reasonably have been expected. In reference to the general practice of idle conjecture relative to Shakespeare and his writings the late Albert Henry Smyth,—the ablest literary critic who has appeared in our country since the golden day of Edwin P. Whipple and that marvel of intellectual faculty Henry Giles, and one of the most accomplished of Shakespeare scholars,—wrote this refreshing protest against the evil of such commentary:

"There has been a great throwing about of brains over the determination of the chronology of Shakespeare's plays. In some vain hope of approaching nearer to the personal life of Shakespeare, the scholars of the Shakespearean Guild have occupied their wit and ingenuity in dividing the poet's career into definitely marked periods, and seeking for a parallel between the works of each period and the events, ascertained or imaginary, of Shakespeare's life. The old Shakespeare Society, represented by Halliwell, Thom, Dyce, Collier, and Peter Cunningham, scrutinized Elizabethan documents for every rag and remnant of external evidence bearing upon dramatic history. When in 1874 the New Shakespeare Society was founded, an original method of inquiry into questions of chronology and authorship was instituted. Mr. Hales, in two lectures upon the occasion of the founding of the society by Mr. F. J. Furnivall, that indefatigable king of clubs, defined seven tests for determining the growth of Shakespeare's mind and art from the witness of the plays themselves: (1) external evidence, (2) historical allusions, (3) changes of metre, (4) changes of language and style, (5) power of characterization, (6) dramatic unity, (7) knowledge of life. Metrical tests soon overshadowed everything else in the society's works, Shakespeare was turned into a calculation table for the enumeration of feminine endings, stopt lines, middle cæsura, weak endings, middle extra syllables, and for the experiment of the initial trochee test, pause test, prevalent word test, and choric reflection test. Out of these researches and the development in the so-called æsthetic criticism is of such uncouth terminology as 'first reconciliation period,' 'second recognition period,' etc., etc., there was constructed an ideal biography of Shakespeare. And without being actually advanced a single step in our knowledge and enjoyment of the Shakespearean drama, we were told to recognize in the order of the plays as fancifully set forth by the commentators the whole of Shakespeare's spiritual experience. We were to see him 'in the workshop, in the world, out of the depths, and on the heights.' Moreover, the New Shakespeare Society made much of the discovery of strange hands in Shakespeare's text. This reference of dubious or dolorous lines to anonymous or conjectural aliens is as old as Coleridge, who, like Simpson, of Edinburgh, who was unalterably convinced of the infallibility of Euclid, fancied it impossible for Shakespeare to drowse, and so pronounced all his faults to be the intrusion of some unknown playwright. Our better informed critics identify the perpetrator of the outrage and brand upon him his mischievous meddling."

The first positively recorded representative of *King Henry the Eighth* was John Lowin, one of the best actors of Shakespeare's time, and in contemporary favor second only to Richard Burbage. Authentic assurance is furnished by Downes that Lowin was instructed by Shakespeare himself as to the performance of this part. Lowin, born in 1576, lived to be eighty-two years old, became very poor in his latter days, kept an inn, called The Three Pigeons, at Brentford, and died there, in 1658. Sir William Davenant (1605-1668), was acquainted with the acting of Lowin, and when, in 1663, he cast the part of *King Henry the Eighth* to Thomas Betterton, he instructed that actor relative to the method of his admired predecessor. Betterton's performance was accounted essentially royal, and the example of stalwart predominance, regal dignity, and bluff humor thus set has ever since been followed. Barton Booth imitated Betterton, and when Quin assumed *King Henry* he avowedly, but not successfully, imitated Booth. In this part Quin is described as having been ungraceful in manner, deficient of the requisite facial expression, and vocally weak. Booth, on the contrary, satisfied every requirement of it. There was grandeur in his personality, vigor in his action, and at times a menace in his look which inspired terror. In life King Henry, as the reader of the excellent memoir of Wolsey by George Cavendish clearly perceives, was essentially selfish, despotic, tyrannical, capricious, and capable of cruelty. In Shakespeare's delineation of him the rigor of his character and the harshness of his temper have been much softened, and while he is shown as egotistical, haughty, arbitrary, impetuous and self-willed, he is credited with a certain amiability, a sense of justice, good humor, and even geniality of disposition. It appears that he was thus represented, with admirable fidelity and effect, by Booth. That actor's enunciation of "Go thy ways, Kate," after the *Queen's* majestic exit from the Trial Scene, was considered exceptionally expressive of the *King's* character and humor.

Specific information as to details of the dressing of *King Henry the Eighth* by the early English actors cannot be obtained. Kings, on the stage, in the seventeenth and eighteenth centuries, wore scarlet cloth ornamented with gold lace. Sometimes an opulent nobleman, patron of the drama, would give to a favorite actor the costume that he had worn at the coronation of the reigning monarch, and that was considered and used as an appropriate garb for theatrical majesty. Burbage, if he acted *King Henry,* wore robes of red and gold. Betterton and his followers continued the custom, but as it was well known that *King Henry* wore his hair short they discarded the usual ramillies when playing that part. Davies declares that *King Richard the Third* and *King Henry the Eighth* were garbed in something like appropriate costume, while suitability of attire, in presentment of the coöperative characters, was, for the most part, disregarded. As late as the beginning of the nineteenth century the actors who personated the ecclesiastics in "King Henry VIII." wore such garments as had been worn by the Protestant Episcopal clergy of the time of King Charles the Second, while some other participants in the performance wore accoutrements of the time of King George the Third. The chronicle of notable performers of *King Henry the Eighth,* in England, includes the names of Matthew Clarke, John Palmer, Joseph George Holman, Alexander Pope, Francis Aicken, Thomas Abthorpe Cooper, George Frederick Cooke, George Barrett, John Ryder, Walter Lacy, William Terriss, and Arthur Bourchier. The list is not complete.

BRITISH STAGE.—*CARDINAL WOLSEY.*

On the occasion (1663) when for the first time Betterton acted *King Henry the Eighth* his asso-

ciate and competitor Henry Harris acted *Cardinal
Wolsey,* "doing it," says Downes, "with such just
state, port, and mien that I dare affirm none hitherto
has equalled him." The word "hitherto" refers to
the period of about sixty years immediately
prior to 1663, as to which period theatrical
history affords comparatively little exact and particular information. Harris was a painter and a
singer as well as an actor. He was a profligate
person, but he was possessed of dramatic talent of
a high order, and it is certain that his ability was
versatile, for he excelled as *Romeo* and also as
Sir Andrew Aguecheek. He was one of the intimate
friends of Samuel Pepys, the quaint diarist, and a
portrait of him as *Wolsey* is in the Pepys Library
at Cambridge, England. Detailed description of
his performance of the *Cardinal* has not been
found. He was prominently succeeded on the old
London stage by John Verbruggen, 1706; Colley
Cibber, 1723; Anthony Boheme, 1725; Lacy Ryan,
1743; West Digges, 1772; Robert Bensley, 1772;
John Henderson, 1780; Alexander Pope, 1786; John
Philip Kemble, 1805; William Charles Macready,
1823; Charles Mayne Young, 1844; and Samuel
Phelps, 1844. On the Irish Stage *Wolsey* was acted
by Henry Mossop, in 1751.

Opinion as to the diversified representations of

Wolsey that were given by those actors, long passed away, must necessarily, now, be somewhat vague. Such records of them as exist are in almost every case meagre. Authorities are often misleading. Adjectives, sometimes laudatory sometimes condemnatory, are freely employed, but at best they seldom do more than convey general impressions. Few details are furnished showing precisely what the actor did and how he did it. Verbruggen is commended as fine in *Cassius* but is scarcely more than mentioned as *Wolsey*. He was a pleasing actor, apparently exuberant, lawless, and defective in art. Cibber is credited with a suave demeanor and a clever assumption of crafty deference in the Trial Scene, but he lacked dignity and he was incapable of a convincing show of serious feeling. One recorder mentions that when, in *Wolsey's* soliloquy on the *King's* marriage, he said "This candle burns not clear, 'tis I must snuff it," he made a gesture with his fingers as though he were using a candle-snuffer. Another and more propitious recorder, Charles Macklin, stated that he did ample justice to *Wolsey*. Boheme had been a sailor, and he walked with a straddle, but he was tall and of good presence, and he excelled in pathetic passages, so that his delivery of *Wolsey's* Farewell may have been touching. Ryan was a judicious actor, of respectable abilities, and his per-

formance of *Wolsey* was creditable. Digges is said
to have marred by extravagance of gesture a performance which otherwise would have been perfect.
Mossop could express the pomp and severity of the
part, and he is praised for energetic delivery of the
text, but his demeanor was awkward. Bensley, who
had been an officer in the British army (he served in
America at one time), was a formal, correct, conscientious actor,—a good *Malvolio,*—but he did not
make a special mark as *Wolsey.* Henderson, superb
as *Shylock, Iago,* and *Falstaff,* was notable in *Wolsey*
only for his correct elocution. Pope possessed a
fine voice but an inexpressive face; he excelled, nevertheless, in moments and passages of pathos, and his
Wolsey was effective in the scene of the great minister's fall. Kemble, Macready, and Young must each
have been magnificent as the *Cardinal,* for each
possessed intellectual character, dignity, scholarship,
stately presence, and facile command of the resources
of expressive art. Phelps gave an intellectual, noble,
austere, touching performance of *Wolsey,* invariable
in its dignity, singularly expositive of a politic character, and in the parting scene with *Cromwell* profoundly affecting. A superb portrait of Phelps as
Wolsey, painted by Johnston Forbes-Robertson, adorns
a wall in the Garrick Club, London, and will preserve
to a distant posterity the expressive lineaments of an

SAMUEL PHELPS AS *CARDINAL WOLSEY*

AFTER THE PAINTING BY JOHNSTON FORBES-ROBERTSON

authentic image of passionate grief commingled with desolate submission.

Later representatives of *Wolsey,* on the British Stage, were Charles John Kean and Henry Irving, each of whom acted the part in America as well as in England. Herbert Beerbohm-Tree also has acted it in England, but his performance has not (1911) been seen in America. Kean made a fine production of "King Henry VIII.," at the Princess's Theatre, London, in 1855. Irving produced it, at the London Lyceum, January 5, 1892. When Kean made his fourth and last professional visit to America (his previous visits had been made in 1830, 1839, and 1845), he began his engagement at the theatre which had been Wallack's (situated in Broadway, near Broome Street, then called the Broadway, long ago demolished) with "King Henry VIII.," appearing as *Wolsey,* with Mrs. Kean (Ellen Tree) as *Queen Katharine.* Colman's comedy of "The Jealous Wife" was acted as an afterpiece. Irving presented "King Henry VIII." at Abbey's, now the Knickerbocker, Theatre, New York, on December 4, 1893.

AMERICAN STAGE.

On the American Stage the play of "King Henry VIII." has not been, at any time, especially popular.

The first performance of it in America occurred at
the old Park Theatre, New York, May 13, 1799, on
which occasion it was acted for the benefit of Mrs.
Barrett, who played *Queen Katharine.* That actress
had come from England about two years earlier, and
her acting in tragic parts had gained esteem. In
England she had been known as Mrs. Rivers, and
stage chronicles mention her as having been instructed
by Macklin, with whom, at the beginning of her
professional career, she acted *Portia.* No description
has been found of her acting of *Queen Katharine,*
but as she was tall, of a noble aspect, and possessed
of ability and experience, it can reasonably be assumed
that she gave a good performance. On the occasion
named, *Cardinal Wolsey* was acted by her husband,
Giles Leonard Barrett, while *Cromwell* was assumed
by Cooper. Other presentments of "King Henry
VIII." in the early American Theatre were few, but
in every instance they are associated with distinguished names. On October 2, 1811, the play was
acted at the old Park, with George Frederick Cooke as
King Henry, Mrs. Stanley (Mrs. Twistleton,—Stanley
being an assumed name) as *Queen Katharine,* Cooper
as *Wolsey,* and Edmund Simpson as *Cromwell.* On
April 29, 1834, at the same theatre, when Fanny
Kemble and her father, Charles Kemble, were fulfilling an engagement there, it was represented for her

benefit, that beautiful and brilliant woman, then only twenty-three years of age, acting *Queen Katharine,* and her father acting *Wolsey.* On that occasion the effect of the appearance of celestial phantoms, in the Vision Scene, was heightened by the vocalism of Emma Wheatley, who sang the solemn song, by Handel, "Angels Ever Bright and Fair," then for the first time thus introduced. Four years later, at the National Theatre, in Church Street, New York, Emma Wheatley (1822-1854) herself appeared as *Queen Katharine,* John Vandenhoff being the *Wolsey* and Henry Wallack the *King.* Miss Wheatley, only sixteen years old when thus she ventured to assume one of the most majestic characters in Shakespeare,—a character that no mere girl ever did or ever could really impersonate,—was regarded as a prodigy of genius and beauty: in 1837 she became the wife of Mr. James Mason and soon afterward retired from the stage. In 1847 "King Henry VIII." was produced at the old Bowery Theatre, New York, with Eliza Marian Trewar (Mrs. Shaw, afterward Mrs. T. S. Hamblin), a remarkably beautiful woman and a fine actress, as the *Queen.*

The part of *King Henry the Eighth* has been acted in America by Lewis Hallam, H. B. Harrison, Henry Wallack, Thomas Sowerby Hamblin, Daniel Wilmarth Waller, John Gilbert, William Rufus

Blake, John Jack, William Terriss, and Otis Skinner.
The *King's* age, in the play, is 29. Otis Skinner
presented him as a young man,—therein wisely and
for the first time in American theatrical history (preceded only by William Terriss, in England), departing from the stage custom, which has been to present
him as an elderly, portly person,—according to Holbein's portrait.

Cardinal Wolsey has been acted in America not
only by Kean and Irving, but, among others, by
Macready, 1827; Charles Walter Couldock, 1849;
Charlotte Cushman, 1857; Edward Loomis Davenport,
1858; John Gilbert; William Creswick, 1871; Milnes
Levick, 1874; George Vandenhoff, 1874; Lawrence
Barrett; Edwin Booth; John McCullough, and John
A. Lane, 1892. Gustavus Vaughan Brooke's embodiment of *Wolsey* was shown in Australia, and enthusiastic encomium of it is cited from the Melbourne
press by his judicious biographer, W. J. Lawrence,
of Comber, Ireland.

KEAN.—CRESWICK.—VANDENHOFF.—BOOTH.

Kean's *Wolsey*, which it was my privilege several
times to see, was remarkable for intellectual character, grim power, and an austere refinement which,
more than ecclesiastical, was spiritual. His aspect

was noble, his demeanor majestic. His pale face,
dark, bright eyes, massive brow, and iron-gray hair
suited the part. He wore robes of scarlet cloth
adorned with lace. His manner, at first, was that
of repose, but it was lofty and predominant. The
glance that he directed toward the defiant *Buckingham* as he paused, after partly crossing the scene,
on his first entrance, seemed literally to pierce his
enemy. In *King Henry's* presence his bearing was
that of obsequious but not servile deference. His
handling of the ruinous papers that the *King* returns
to *Wolsey,* combined with changes of facial expression, a ruminative pause, and then an utterance of
hopeless surrender, was supremely eloquent. In speaking the lines which incorporate the reference to the fall
of Lucifer he stretched his arms upward and forward,
conveying a grand image of the poet's thought, and
then, upon the sad cadence of the verse, completely
collapsed, uttering the abject desolation of a broken
spirit in the four simple words, *"never* to rise again."
Kean's delivery was often marred by a nasality of
speech, and his acting was not illumined by those
flashes of lightning which are said to have characterized that of his renowned father; but he was a noble
actor, and his performance of *Wolsey* made actual
on the stage an ideal that rose to the full height of
the poet's conception.

Creswick's performance of *Wolsey* was notable for intense mental concentration, symmetry of method,— the gradual exhibition of the character as wrought upon by changing circumstances,—momentary flashes of wrath, as of an old lion turned at bay,—and ample effusion of feeling at the pathetic close. The last words that *Wolsey* utters were spoken by Creswick in a way which affected the listener to tears and impressively pointed that moral, the vanity of worldly greatness, which Shakespeare's portrayal of the great *Cardinal* is so well designed to convey. Perhaps the most telling moment of Creswick's performance was that of fiery, tumultuous anger, suddenly curbed into contempt, at the vulgar insult given to *Wolsey* by *Surrey* (Act III., Sc. 2), when the *Cardinal,* restraining himself by great effort, exclaims:

" How much, methinks, I might despise this man,
But that I'm bound in charity against it."

George Vandenhoff's acting of *Wolsey,* especially indicative of intellectual character, was marked by exquisite refinement and it gave simple expression to a clear ideal. He was tall and slender and his fine countenance, somewhat suggestive of the picture of Addison, commingled in its expression austerity and kindness. His manner was formal. He had been educated (at Stonyhurst) for the Bar. "I practised law" (so wrote Vandenhoff in 1878), "in Liverpool, for three years, but in an evil hour quitted wig and gown to don sock and buskin, and so it happens that to-day I play Henry the Eighth's Lord Chancellor, having forever cut myself off from the possibility of being Queen Victoria's." By temperament he was well fitted to the part of the *Cardinal*. He acted it in association with Charlotte Cushman, and his performance skilfully combined the outward calm and inward disquietude of the ambitious, crafty, resolute, potent schemer. His elocution was superb,— his finely modulated tones giving every shade of meaning to the poet's text. During the scenes that precede the downfall of *Wolsey* he maintained a perfect poise, holding deep feeling in careful restraint, but through an artfully curbed demeanor he allowed the observer to perceive, in the worn face, the fiery eyes, and the air of vigilant self-control, a passionate heart and a towering mind, so that when the collapse came and the conflict of a storm-tossed soul was laid bare the spectator was less surprised than touched by the sad fulfilment of all which had been indicated of latent power and passionate emotion. There were no violent outbursts in the performance: it was fluent and even.

Edwin Booth acted *Wolsey* for the first time on December 13, 1876, at the Arch Street Theatre, Philadelphia, and on January 19, 1878, he played the

part for the first time in New York, at Booth's Theatre. His stage version of the play compressed it
into four acts, the third of which contained only 126
lines. Later, when editing his "Prompt Book," I
induced him to add an abridged Fifth Act, which
appears in the printed copy. Scrupulous attention was
given to the dressing of the play. Booth's embodiment
of *Wolsey* was interesting and impressive but the
part did not deeply stir his feelings and he did not
greatly care for it. He was essentially a tragedian
and his genius required tragedy as a vehicle. The
pervasive quality of his performance was poetic condition. He presented a noble image of authority
tempered by exquisite grace, and he denoted austere
intellect and the capability of subtle craft. No actor
has appeared in our time who could better present the
aspect of ecclesiastical majesty. The points usually
made by actors of this part,—in the soliloquy about
Anne Bullen and *King Henry,* at "How much,
methinks, I might despise this man!" and at *Wolsey's*
exit with *Campeius,*—were admirably made by him,
and, as always, his elocution was superb,—especially
in the parting scene with *Cromwell* and when he spoke
those solemn words:

> " Had I but served my God with half the zeal
> I serv'd my king, he would not, in mine age,
> Have left me naked to mine enemies."

Courtesy of Evert Jansen Wendell

HENRY IRVING AS *CARDINAL WOLSEY*

AFTER THE DRAWING BY J. BERNARD PARTRIDGE

HENRY IRVING.

Henry Irving's *Wolsey* commingled in one symmetrical identity the stately ecclesiastic, the suave diplomatist, the commanding statesman, and the polished, elegant, highly intellectual man of the world. He wore chimere, rochet, mantle, and red hat, and his tall figure, ascetic face, piercing eyes, authoritative bearing, incisive speech and incessant earnestness of personification combined to make the performance impressively life-like and deeply sympathetic. He employed, as Kean had done, the traditional business relative to *Buckingham,* in the opening scene,—a scene in which the *Cardinal,* sure of his ground, is perfectly composed. In the Trial Scene his manner toward the *King* was profoundly respectful and toward the *Queen* bland, almost humble, ingratiating, and speciously ingenuous. *Wolsey,* until the moment of the catastrophe, is continuously dissimulating, and Irving's impersonation was remarkably indicative of that condition—alert, vigilant, full of transitions from assumed candor to subtle artifice, this being revealed to the audience by a deft use of the expedient of transparency. Touches of mordant sarcasm,—as when, replying to *Campeius,* he said, in a dry tone, "We live not to be grip'd by meaner persons," and when, in the moody soliloquy on the *King's* marriage, he murmured "I'll no Anne Bullens for him,"—here and there lit the performance with a biting gleam of humor. There was, in the scene of defeat and ruin and in the delivery of the Farewell, a touching simplicity of grief and resignation, together with an impressive impartment of profound knowledge of human suffering.

When Irving effected his first production of "King Henry VIII." (January 5, 1892, at the London Lyceum), the play was acted 172 times. That Shakespearean revival was the most costly one made by Irving and one of the most costly ever made. The large sum of $60,000 was expended on it. The public is often told that great amounts of money have been spent in setting plays, but, in fact, such expenditure seldom occurs. The gross receipts during the run of "King Henry VIII." at the Lyceum were nearly $300,000, but the cost of the production combined with that of keeping the play on the stage considerably exceeded that income. The pageant, practically unchanged, was brought to America. An example of Irving's scrupulous fidelity as an actor is quoted by his biographer, Austin Brereton. "A friend of mine," said Irving, "possessed an old cardinal robe of just the color that Wolsey wore, and I sent my robe to Rome to be dyed like that; but the old tint was no longer used there and I had it *reproduced* in London.

If I am told that this was a prodigal caprice, I reply that it was quite in keeping with Wolsey's taste. When you are getting into the skin of a character, you need not neglect his wardrobe." Irving got more completely "into the skin" of *Wolsey* than any other actor of the part has done, in our time, or, apparently, in any time, for he not only made the poetic ideal an actuality but garnished it with many peculiarities of the man. In further justification of his lavish expenditure on the play Irving said "If you look into the Italian archives of the period you will find that the ambassadors were astonished at his [Wolsey's] magnificence." It is not necessary to search "the Italian archives" for testimony to the prodigal opulence with which the Cardinal invested his proceedings, whether abroad or at home. The account of his splendor that is given by Cavendish would amply substantiate any showing of gorgeousness, however resplendent, that might be made. *Norfolk's* glowing account of The Field of the Cloth of Gold,—where "every man that stood showed like a mine," all "order'd by the good discretion of the right reverend Cardinal of York,"—is not exaggerated. One striking felicity of Irving's performance of *Wolsey* was its intimation, from the first, of an element of goodness in the character, operative notwithstanding pride, arrogance, and craft: the revulsion of feeling in the

Cardinal's farewell to greatness was consequent on this, and therefore natural and credible. Another felicity, one of stage business, was seen at the close of the colloquy between *Queen Katharine* and the two *Cardinals.* Irving caused the *Queen,* when they were leaving the room, at "Come, reverend fathers," to reject the proffered arm of *Wolsey* and accept the assistance of *Campeius,* and as those two went out he made *Wolsey* pause and gaze after them with an expression of mingled compassion and contempt, as though pitiful of the *Queen's* broken state, resentful of her obvious antipathy toward him, ruminant as to the best way in which to make her sensitive feeling and her pride useful in managing the *King,* and contentedly perceptive that her health was gone and her influence no longer considerable.

BUCKINGHAM AND GARDINER.

The character of the *Duke of Buckingham,*—proud, self-assertive, and of an imperious temper in his prosperous day, but simple, manly, patient, and pathetic in his ultimate state of ruin and in the hour of death,—can be made exceedingly effective on the stage. Robert Wilks acted the part, in 1723, and by his fine discrimination between impetuosity at the beginning and nobility of resignation at the close invested it with superlative dramatic importance. Johnston Forbes-Robertson, acting at the London Lyceum Theatre, in 1892, in Irving's production of "King Henry VIII.," gave a memorably dignified, gentle, and touching performance of the unfortunate nobleman, presenting an image of innate aristocracy, and doing especial justice to the moving eloquence of the *Duke's* farewell speech. Impressive performances of *Buckingham* have been given on the American Stage by Charles Wheatleigh, Milnes Levick, Beaumont Smith, and Frank Cooper.

Stephen Gardiner, Bishop of Winchester (1485-1555), was a bigoted, austere, and cruel person, and in the play he is represented as arrogant and vindictive. The part, nevertheless, in the eighteenth century, was thought to be susceptible of facetious treatment and was customarily allotted to an eccentric or low comedian. Thus, Ben Johnson acted it, in 1723; John Hippesley, in 1743; William Parsons, in 1777; and Richard Suett, in 1788. Mention is made of a player named Taswell, prompter at Drury Lane, who, performing *Gardiner,* carried a crutch and in following the *Archbishop of Canterbury,* when making the exit at the close of the scene of the *Primate's* discomfiture of the hostile Council, shook that implement, derisively, over *Cranmer's* head! Parsons also used a crutch when playing *Gardiner.*

It is a fact of common knowledge that before 1660 all characters in plays performed in England, whether male or female, were presented by men or boys. Some one of the twenty-six male persons named in the list prefixed to the First Shakespeare Folio as "the principal actors in all these plays" was, presumably, the first performer of *Queen Katharine.* The first woman who ever acted the part was Mary Betterton, wife of Thomas, she having coöperated with her husband in the representation of "King Henry VIII." which was given at Lincoln's Inn Fields in 1663. No description of her acting in it is extant, but she was highly esteemed as an actress and it can be reasonably assumed that she gave a competent performance. The Vision Scene (Act IV., Sc. 2), in which the death-stricken *Queen* asks for music and presently lapses into slumber, and then, on the stage, into death, was elaborately treated as a spectacle, in the time of Mrs. Betterton, and that method, required by ample and explicit stage direction in the Folio, was followed in the time of her distinguished successors, Elizabeth Barry, 1706; Mary Porter, 1721; and Hannah Pritchard, 1743. Mrs. Porter, tall, fair, not handsome, but impressive by reason of great dignity and winning by reason of acute sensibility, is said to have acted to perfection such parts as Shakespeare's *Hermione,* in "The Winter's Tale," Otway's *Belvidera,* in "Venice Preserved," *Queen Elizabeth,* in John Banks's "The Unhappy Favorite" (a play based on the story of the Earl of Essex, that ill-starred lover of Queen Elizabeth), and *Leonora,* in Dr. Young's "The Revenge." Her embodiment of *Queen Katharine* was admired by her contemporaries, and the dramatic chronicles of her day commend it for royalty of demeanor, depth of feeling, and grace of sympathetic expression. Her voice was tremulous. She specially excelled in her delivery of the *Queen's* adjuration to the *King,* in the Trial Scene. In early life she had attended on the fascinating Elizabeth Barry, and it is probable that she formed her style on the model of that great actress. Mrs. Pritchard, who succeeded her in this character, was accounted majestic in deportment and natural in method of speech, but less effective upon the feelings of the audience. Mrs. Porter and Mrs. Pritchard dressed *Queen Katharine* in imitation of the attire worn by royal persons of their period. There is no specific, detailed account of the stage business used in this part by those eminent performers. Mrs. Porter, in accordance with the stage direction,—often disregarded by modern players, —knelt before the *King,* when speaking the *Queen's* appeal to him,—"Sir, I desire you do me right and justice,"—and she pathetically suppressed her tears, when uttering the *Queen's* retort upon the *Cardinal,*—a treatment of the situation which was much admired.

SARAH SIDDONS.

It is not until Mrs. Siddons comes upon the scene that the investigator of this subject finds particular mention of striking expedients that were employed in the acting of *Queen Katharine,* and even then the specifications of stage business are not numerous. In 1788-89 John Philip Kemble, at Drury Lane, revived "King Henry VIII.," making a new stage version of it,—which was published in 1804,—and giving special attention to scenery, costumes, and processions. All was done that his sound scholarship could warrant and his liberality of expenditure compass to make the production splendid. Mrs. Siddons acted *Queen Katharine.* Robert Bensley appeared as *Wolsey.* Kemble "doubled" in the characters of *Cromwell* and *Griffith* (reserving his essay in *Wolsey* till a later time, when he acted that part with distinguished success). That was the occasion when Mrs. Siddons made her first appearance as the *Queen.* The peculiar, expressive business,—haughty, imperious, and openly and grandly hostile,—of pointing at *Wolsey* and addressing him without looking at him, in the Trial Scene, when *Queen Katharine* delivers the trenchant speech beginning, "Lord Cardinal,—to *you* I speak," was invented by her, and her pause after the word "Cardinal," and the marked emphasis, incisive and scornful, that she placed on the word "you" were accounted wonderfully expressive. That point in the performance was chosen for representation by George Henry Harlowe, when he painted the spirited picture of the Trial Scene in which John Philip, Charles, and Stephen Kemble and their inspired sister are well portrayed. To Mrs. Siddons also is due the excellent, because natural, informing, effective business of restless movement in the preliminary part of the Vision Scene, that of a person in persistent physical pain, who vainly tries to find ease in change of position and to maintain composure under acute suffering. Some of the business devised by Mrs. Siddons became traditional, and later was employed by Mrs. Warner, Isabella Glyn, Charlotte Cushman, Emma Waller, Genevieve Ward, Fanny Janauschek, Ellen Terry, and Helena Modjeska. The beautiful, pathetic Eliza O'Neill played the part, but she was not suited to it and she did not consider herself to be so. Mrs. Warner acted *Queen Katharine* when Phelps produced "King Henry VIII.," April 10, 1844, at Sadler's Wells Theatre, and her performance was accounted majestic and tender,—a noble image of royal womanhood, gracious in her eminence and patient in her distress. That fine actress (she was Mary Amelia Huddart,—born 1797, died 1854), it is interesting to remember, visited America, appearing at Burton's Theatre, New York, September 22, 1851, as *Hermione,* in "The Winter's Tale," but she was not seen on our stage as *Queen Katharine.*

AMERICAN STAGE.—*QUEEN KATHARINE.*—CHARLOTTE CUSHMAN.

Charlotte Cushman as *Queen Katharine* was the consummate image of sovereignty and noble womanhood, austere and yet sweetly patient, in circumstances of cruel injustice and bitter affliction. Her identification with the essential nature of the injured *Queen* was so complete that it made the spectators of her performance forget the stage and feel that they were looking upon a pathetic experience of actual life. Her portrayal of this character was the impressive revealment of a great soul. Only a woman of the loftiest spirit could thus have interpreted and made actual Shakespeare's beautiful conception. It was innate grandeur of character that made Charlotte Cushman so great in this part. There was in her artistic treatment of it a wonderful felicity of

TRIAL OF QUEEN KATHARINE

MRS. SIDDONS AS KATHARINE, WITH JOHN PHILIP, CHARLES, AND STEPHEN, KEMBLE

FROM THE PAINTING BY G. H. HARLOW

smoothness,—the blending of womanly tenderness with stately manner, the union of dignity with grace, the deft conjunction of intellectual power with spiritual humility: she spontaneously exhibited the natural fluctuations of emotion, and she spoke the magnificent language with a perfect sense of its meaning and with splendid effect: her performance was a heart-breaking image of oppressed virtue, dethroned majesty, and a soul of inflexible goodness that no adversity could shake: but aside from all that she did as an actress there was a singular magnetism in what she was as a woman—a strange, wild charm, such as sometimes seems to hallow the lonely ocean, in the gloaming and on the eve of tempest—a magic of genius which, while it separated her from the race of usual women, made her the interpreter of all women, the symbol of all their sorrows, the voice of all their longing and aspiration. That charm flashed from her luminous eyes and trembled in her sympathetic voice. It was at once power and weakness, gladness and grief, revelation and prophecy. She understood woman's nature and she could express it, and of woman's nature *Queen Katharine* is an exceptionally comprehensive type.

There is supreme satisfaction in seeing on the stage a person who possesses imperial mind, stalwart character, the faculty to form a great ideal and the artistic

ability to embody it; a person of deep feeling but
also of commanding intellect, whose touches, in the
art of acting, are as firm and as precisely regulated
as those of the trip-hammer,—light or heavy as the
occasion requires and the will ordains; a person who
makes and sustains the impression of inevitable truth.
Such was Charlotte Cushman, and such peculiarly
she showed herself to be when she acted *Queen
Katharine.* Her rebuke to the *Surveyor,* "Take good
heed you charge not in your spleen a noble person,"
was spoken with an awful solemnity of tone and
manner, and in the Trial Scene her delivery of the
apostrophe to the *King,* "Sir, I desire you do me
right and justice," was at once stately and humble,
patient and sweet, and in its simplicity deeply pathetic.
Later, when the indignation of the *Queen* is struggling to repress her tears, there was a thrilling, bell-
like ring in her voice as she said "Lord Cardinal!—"
and then, after a momentary pause, a withering
scorn in the tone in which she added "To *you* I speak."
All that is superb in the contempt of lofty womanhood
for duplicity and meanness was expressed by her at the
moment when the *Queen* finally repudiates the juris-
diction of the court and makes her appeal to the Pope.
The majesty with which she moved across the scene,
leaving the tribunal of the two *Cardinals,* cannot be
described. When the *Crier* called "Katharine, Queen

of England, come into court," and *Griffith,* who had
been walking backward before her, paused and told
her of the summons, her massive figure fairly towered
and her large, lurid eyes,—gray-blue, but darkened
then by emotion,—burned and glowed with anger, as
she answered, in deep, vibrant tones:

> "What need *you* note it?   Pray you keep your way:
> When YOU are called *return.*—Now the Lord help!—
> They vex me past my patience.   Pray you, pass on.
> I will not tarry: no, nor evermore,
> Upon this business my appearance make
> In *any* of their courts."

And so speaking she passed from the Presence, with
perfect dignity.   In the *Queen's* subsequent scene
with the two *Cardinals* the lovely refinement of
a pure, sweet nature colored and made at once
beautiful and pathetic a bitter struggle of virtue
and innocence against potent malice disguised as
friendship.

In the Vision Scene Miss Cushman, following the
lead of Fanny Kemble, made use of the song "Angels
Ever Bright and Fair," with Handel's music: it was
sung off the scene, and it served to deepen the pathos
of a deeply affecting situation.   She highly valued
that accessory, and Lawrence Barrett, who, as *Wolsey,*
had acted with her, told me that when he was leaving

her company at the end of his engagement she earnestly besought him, if at any time he should ever present the play of "King Henry VIII.," not to introduce that song, as she was desirous that the public recollection of it and of the impressive effect it produced should remain undisturbed in association with her embodiment of the suffering *Queen*. Charlotte Cushman's greatest performances were those of *Queen Katharine, Lady Macbeth,* and *Meg Merrilies,* but of the three she chiefly valued the first. The part of *Lady Macbeth* she did not like.

VARIOUS PERFORMERS.

Mary Duff left the stage about 1836 and it can perhaps safely be assumed that no person now living possesses definite remembrance of her performances. I have not met with any detailed account of her acting of *Queen Katharine,* but since all the printed testimony which has descended from her time declares that she was pre-eminently and surpassingly great in characters that involve pathos, and at the same time could splendidly express the workings of fierce passion, it seems reasonable to infer that she gave a performance which was both noble and tender. An actress who was deemed perfection by Edmund Kean, J. B. Booth, Cooper, Forrest,

and John Gilbert must have been a dramatic
genius of the highest order. Mrs. Duff acted the
Queen on November 30, 1826, at the Bowery Theatre,
or "the New York Theatre, Bowery," as it was then
called,—*Cardinal Wolsey* being personated by William
Augustus Conway. That faithful chronicler John
Norton Ireland, who saw the performance, has
recorded that Mrs. Duff's *Queen Katharine* was
"exquisite"—an interesting but not illuminative
designation.

Fanny Janauschek (1830-1904), equally remarkable
as a woman and as an actress, adopted *Queen
Katharine* into her repertory in 1874. In that personation, which I observed with care and recorded
with admiration, a stronger emphasis was laid on the
inherent potency and predominant royalty of the
character than on its womanlike elements of sensibility and gentleness. There was, however, an involuntary spontaneity of feeling in Mme. Janauschek's
acting,—a native warmth of temperament,—which,
aided by intense earnestness and scrupulous fidelity
of executive method, made her deeply interesting.
She had gained distinction on the stage of Germany
before she came to America. On October 9, 1869,
she appeared in New York, at the old Academy of
Music, acting in German, as *Medea*. Later, she
learned English and for many years she traversed the

United States, acting, in English, tragedy, comedy, and domestic drama. She was a woman of commanding presence, a rich brunette beauty, having regular and uncommonly expressive features, dark eyes that seemed to glow with interior light, and there was in her aspect a singular, lurid repose, as of concentrated calm over slumbering fire. Her expression of the *Queen's* resentment toward *Wolsey,* in the Trial Scene, was fiercely passionate, without sacrifice of dignity, and in her exit from the court she was a magnificent image of stately sovereignty and offended womanhood.

The most resplendent scenic presentment of "King Henry VIII." made in America prior to that effected by Henry Irving in 1893 was the one made at Booth's Theatre, New York, on September 23, 1878, under the management of Henry C. Jarrett and Henry David Palmer. The opulence of the scenery on that occasion somewhat dwarfed the effect of the acting, which nevertheless was exhibitive of much and various ability. In the scenic pictures accuracy of detail was combined with a charming mellowness of color, and old historic places, if not literally copied, were faithfully suggested. Two tableaus were introduced,—one showing the death of *Wolsey,* as described by *Griffith* in narration to the *Queen,* the other showing the *Queen's* vision of "angelic spirits of peace." The scenes of the Coronation and the Christening—then first shown on the American Stage—were made tributary to rich display and the spectacle was rounded and closed by Telbin's panorama of Old London. Genevieve Ward appeared as *Queen Katharine,* George Vandenhoff as *Cardinal Wolsey,* J. H. Taylor as *King Henry,* and Milnes Levick as *Buckingham.* Miss Ward, one of the finest minds among women of the stage, greatly excelled in exposition of the resolute spirit, the authority, and the fortitude of the persecuted *Queen,* not much softening the sterner attributes of the character by any infusion of pathos. That actress was remarkable for brilliancy, not tenderness, and she was a consummate artist, but it was in executive rather than injured and suffering characters that her excellence was chiefly shown.

HELENA MODJESKA.—ELLEN TERRY.

Helena Modjeska, an actress who possessed a magic power to charm the fancy and touch the heart, acted *Queen Katharine* for the first time on October 10, 1892, at the Garden Theatre, New York, and thereafter retained the part in her repertory till almost the end of her career. A dominant beauty of her acting, in general, was its blending of intellectual character with tenderness and grace. She somewhat lacked the sustained force required in tragedy, but in romantic or domestic drama she excelled. Few players have evinced a personality as alluring, a style as flexible, an artistic instinct as true, and a capability as ample and decisive of identification with romantic character and of the dramatic utterance of deep feeling. The beautiful personal characteristics of the actress,—the delicate features, the dark, dreamlike eyes, the soft, gentle voice, and the high bred, distinguished manner,—were closely indicative of her delicate organization; and the intellect that animated her beauty and her art was singularly powerful. Modjeska was peculiarly sympathetic with the part of *Queen Katharine*. There was, indeed, some indication of effort in her presentment of its imperial aspect: her personality was more harmonious with winning loveliness than with regal authority and passionate resentment, and therefore she was less effective in the Trial Scene than in the scenes that follow the *Queen's* dethronement. In the Vision Scene, while essentially noble, she was supremely pathetic,—the veritable image of fine womanhood, uttering, in a melting strain of spontaneous sorrow, a piteous protest against the cruelty not only of man but of fate. Her pathos was profoundly true and in that element her performance ranked with the best which have been recorded.

The *loveliest* embodiments of *Queen Katharine* that have been seen on the American Stage in our time were those of Helena Modjeska and Ellen Terry,— the one making actual a perfect ideal of a patient sufferer subjected to cruel wrong; the other expressing, with afflicting simplicity, the grief of a heartbroken woman. Neither of those accomplished performers followed the Siddons tradition in all respects, and neither of them could vie with Charlotte Cushman in passionate intensity and resolute will. Ellen Terry, in her assumption of *Queen Katharine,* discriminated with unerring intuition between the grief which is noble and that which is merely forlorn, and the fortitude which is sublimely patient and that which is merely lachrymose or bitter. There was no deficiency of the imperial element: her *Queen* was felt to be a person born to queenly station: but the supreme beauty of the performance was its intrinsic loveliness of womanhood. In the Trial Scene, while her eyes shot forth no lightnings upon her enemy, *Queen Katharine* was made the victor over the great *Cardinal,* because shown to be the superior individual in nature and stronger in the armament of a just cause. Thus the actress enforced the principle that is conveyed by the play,—that although in the strife of the world it is the hard, selfish, cruel, material force which conquers at the moment, the ultimate triumph comes to integrity of character, honesty of purpose, nobility of mind, and purity of life. The wily ecclesiastic may prevail for a time, but he has built upon craft, and his craft is a sand that will crumble beneath his feet. The fickle, sensual, arbitrary monarch may divorce his true wife and take a younger and comelier mate, but his day of retribution is appointed and it will surely come. The *Queen,* dethroned and exiled, may die of a broken heart, but she has lived nobly, and her name will be cherished by the love of mankind and her bright example will animate many a suffering soul to meet all trials with fortitude and endure with patience to the end.